LIFE'S TRIUMPH

by Bill R. Moore

Book I:
Reflections in Broken Glass

Book II:
Self-Conscious Schizophrenia

Book III:
The Best Medicine: Light Verse

Edited by
David M. Fitzpatrick

Epic Saga Publishing
Brewer, Maine, USA
www.EpicSagaPub.com

LIFE'S TRIUMPH:
A LIFETIME OF POETRY

ISBN: 978-0-9833346-3-7

Foreword

Volume I:

Reflections in Broken Glass

Volume II:

Self-Conscious Schizophrenia

Volume III:

The Best Medicine: Light Verse

About the Author

Foreword

by David M. Fitzpatrick

I first met Bill R. Moore when… well, technically speaking, I never met Bill. We knew each other only in email, never even having chatted on the phone.

Bill first emailed me in October 2009 when he submitted a story for consideration for an anthology I was editing. We hit it off right from the start, even though I rejected his story… and the next one… and the next one. They were well written—just not what I was looking for. I did end up accepting a story from him, but along the way he tried to sell me poems for that anthology.

It's not that I don't appreciate poetry. It's just not my thing, and not something I feel I'm qualified to edit. I don't have my finger on the pulse of the poetry world, I guess you could say.

That didn't stop Bill from trying to wow me with his poetry, and I had to admit I enjoyed every piece he sent me. This led to discussions about publishing, with Bill asking my advice on how to shop his books of poetry around. I don't think I was much help, but tried to offer what help I could.

I remember that he was excited when he tentatively sold a book of poetry to a publisher, but his hopes were dashed when the publisher— apparently a fly-by-night outfit that wasn't terribly interested in actually making the project happen—wasn't responding much, or at all, to his emails. He was frustrated, but didn't let it get him down.

In the meantime, we talked about possibly collaborating on a poetry collection—one that he would edit and I would publish. My interest is primarily speculative fiction, so poetry tended to catch my attention when it was "science-fiction poetry" of "fantasy verse" or "supernatural-horror rhyming." Bill was also a great spec-fic writer; so, with someone like him, who knew a whole lot more about poetry than I ever would, and our combined sense of good spec-fic writing, we'd probably put together a decent book.

However, it wouldn't happen. For Bill's creative works, there was little time left for any of it to happen. Bill didn't know that, of course.

A lot was happening in Bill's life through 2010. Most notably, he relocated from Oklahoma to New York state, as his wife, Jade, had received a scholarship to attend Cornell University for her graduate studies. Jade Woods Moore, named Susan at birth and changing her name at age 19, was from Colorado. Born premature and with a heart problem, she dropped out of high school in the ninth grade and schooled herself. She and Bill met online and visited back and forth for a while before she moved to Oklahoma, earned her GED, and started college with Bill. Both of them graduated summa cum laude from Southeastern Oklahoma State University, Jade with a degree in political science, and Bill with a degree in English.

Jade's dream was to go to law school, and eventually to be a lobbyist for the March of Dimes in Washington. Her goal was to help disadvantaged people, and going to Cornell had been her dream. The scholarship was for the Cornell Institute of Public Affairs, a two-year program through which Jade would earn a Master of Public Affairs.

The last time I traded emails with Bill was in June 2010, when he and Jade were preparing for the big move to New York. We made tentative plans to get together for lunch the following spring or summer; I live in Maine, so we figured we'd meet somewhere in Massachusetts, finally shake hands, and spend some real-life time together. I guess it's safe to say I was never so excited at the prospect to meet someone I'd talked with so much in email.

On October 16, I finally finished editing the stories for the anthology Bill's story would appear in and sent edits out to their respective authors for approval. I didn't hear from Bill right away, which should have seemed odd, because he was usually very quick to respond. I didn't think much of it, but I had no way of knowing what had happened just eleven days before.

On Tuesday, October 5, 2010, at about 3:15 p.m., Bill and Jade were traveling along Mineah Road, Route 13, in Dryden, New York. Jade was driving their 2005 Honda, and there was a terrible accident at an intersection. A tractor trailer smashed into the driver's side of the car. Both vehicles ended up in the ditch. Jade was pronounced dead at Cayuga Medical Center a short time later. Bill suffered massive head trauma; he was transported to Robert Packer Medical Center in Sayre, Pennsylvania, where he died the next day. She was 24; he was 25.

I only knew because Bill's mother had gotten his computer and was going through the difficult task of cleaning up all the loose ends of her son's life. His contribution to my anthology was one of those loose ends, and she really wanted to make sure his story could still get published.

I was so crushed and devastated—I couldn't imagine what Bill's loved ones were feeling. When my uncle died a few months later, I was at first stunned to realize that Bill's death had hit me far harder. I cried a lot over Bill, but barely shed a tear over my uncle. I didn't really know my uncle that well, and didn't have any relationship with him. But Bill—we had a connection, one forged out of a love of writing and a few other things, all through email.

I spoke with his mother about the two writing projects I knew were dearest to him. One was a critical review of the works of Bob Dylan, which was way out of my league. The other, of course, was Bill's poetry. She and Bill's family wanted to see his work published, and I offered my assistance with the poetry. I could advise her on how to go about publishing it, or I could publish it for her. They opted for the latter. It was the very least I could do for a grieving family and to honor Bill's memory.

This has been a long task—over three years since Bill's death. Luckily, Bill made it easy for me. The thing about poetry is that, unlike prose, it doesn't have to adhere to strict rules of grammar, and Bill was a competent writer anyway. And with much of Bill's work being freeform poetry, it wasn't like there were problems with rhythm and meter... not that I really understood all the technical aspects of poetry, mind you.

The first task was to get the poetry from Bill's family. There were three books, and a lot of poems. His style varied so much that the first two books purported to showcase the poetry of different people, who were all fictitious personae Bill created to serve as mouthpieces for his various voices. As I read, I learned more about the kind of person that Bill was, and about the complex mind that saw so many things in so many different ways. I got insights into Bill that I had never gotten before.

Occasionally, I had questions, concerns, issues, and requests for edits and minor changes. But the one person who could answer those questions, address my concerns, deal with those issues, and approve any edits was no longer alive. Technically, his mother owned the copyrights, but I knew she'd agree with me that Bill was the final authority on his work. As such, with precious few changes beyond fixing typos, and a few minor corrections in prefaces and non-poem text, the three books of poetry you hold in your hands is everything Bill intended them to be.

This process was difficult—maybe the hardest project I've ever undertaken. I couldn't work on it for a dozen hours at a stretch, because the emotions ran so high. When Bill's poetry would touch me, the feelings were overpowering. Whenever I looked at the photos his family sent, I'd have to cry. Just considering that I was working to publish the life's work of someone I knew, respected, admired, and considered a friend... it was overwhelming. I had to do it piecemeal—an hour here, two hours there. And since there are hundreds of hours of work into this, you can see why this went on for three years.

Now, considering the effect Bill Moore had on someone who only knew him in email and never even spoke to him on the phone, much less met him in person, can you just imagine how he touched the lives of the people who *really* knew him?

But there's something that stuck with me all through the process— through the probably dozen times I've read every poem in this collection as I read, proofed, edited, laid out, edited again, read again, and so forth—that made it possible to deal with the emotions: Bill was a writer, and this was probably the most important writing project of his life.

As a writer, I very much understood this. A writer often has that one project that absolutely defines him—the thing that, to him at least, is his masterwork. People may read other works by that writer and prefer this one or that one, and might even read the purported masterwork and wonder why this, of all things, was the most important. Sometimes the reasons are only for the writer to understand.

It might be a short story he's been fiddling with for years, the one that everyone else might think should long have been completed but that has such deeper meaning that he takes years to tinker with it. Or maybe it's the novel he's been tweaking since high school, with it always evolving as he evolves as a writer. It could be a collection of stories he carefully assembles throughout his career—a lineup that he feels is the best of his work, a collection of the things he's put his heart and soul into. It's the passionate project that he's worked on for years—maybe all his life. It's what matters most to him.

It's his magnum opus. It's built with all his skills and experience, all his hopes and dreams, all of the many deep facets that make him who he is. And it's a tour de force — the culmination of the endless hours of work and effort, the writing and editing, the proofing and rewriting, the reworking and rewriting again, and so on, and so on. It's the sort of process that writers truly understand, and others think us mad for embracing.

It's the project that, when he's gone, he hopes will represent who he was forever — that thing that will outlive him, and show others what he felt, what he believed, what he could do... that thing that will tell others that he was here, and who he was. It's what he knows is his crowning achievement.

What follows is Bill's masterwork, his magnum opus, his tour de force, his crowning achievement. It's what meant so much to him — three books of poems that represent so much of what was important to him. He's gone now, but this collection lives — the poet immortalized. There's no doubt in my mind that if Bill lived for another hundred years, there would be a lot more to come, and perhaps the poetry here wouldn't be in his final collection of what he wanted to represent him. But Bill didn't live another hundred years; he died at 25, and we must acknowledge and celebrate what he has left us.

As well as I felt I knew Bill in the year we knew each other, after I read his poetry, it was clear there was so much more to the man he was. And as you read it, you'll begin to see a picture in your head of the kind of person Bill was. It won't be the Bill that really was, but it will be a good start.

The title of this book comes from the title of a poem in the first book in this collection: "Life's Triumph." When considering potential titles, every time I read that poem it jumped out at me. Nothing is more fitting than to publish this book with that name, because although Bill was taken from us far too early, his work shows us, fiercely and unapologetically, that in his 25 short years on Earth, he used every minute he had.

"Life triumphs over us all," Bill wrote to close that poem, "whether or not we triumph in it."

He did indeed triumph in it. It's woefully regrettable that he didn't have more time to continue triumphing.

-David M. Fitzpatrick
December 2013

LIFE'S TRIUMPH

by Bill R. Moore

Old at 25

With those my age I've nothing in common,
They think life is flippant, careless, and free.
Why such mixture of age under the sun?
What have I to do with them, they with me?
Why are we thrown together rather than put beside those of
    the same temperament?
If not random chance, but some kind of plan,
We must wonder at the creator's bent;
Some still say that it will be resolved,
This sad farce put to rights but history
Shows us that's not how the world is revolved.
O sad, sad fate! O bitter mystery!
How will I feel when old, if sadly still alive,
If I already feel like this at twenty-five?

– Bill R. Moore
August 2010
Two months before his death

Book I:
Reflections in Broken Glass

by Bill R. Moore

Preface

A Reflection on the Artistic Legacy and Some Notes toward a Contemporary Poetry

Like all artists ready to send their work into a world likely indifferent at best and hostile at worst, I feel compelled to justify my creation. Perhaps it says much about our society that art must be justified; though noble and admirable, the nineteenth century idea that society should value "art for art's sake" long ago faded like the vain conceit it was. This, of course, does not mean the ancient debate over whether art itself is inherently valuable has finally been definitively decided. It is certainly true, as George Orwell noted, that all writers are "driven by some demon whom one can neither resist nor understand."[1] All writers—all other artists, no doubt—readily admit it. Still, there is more to the writing motivation; if there were nothing else, only the most masochistic would ever carry their tasks through, and the world's stock of books would be accordingly decreased. All artists—at least those not just out for money, which I sincerely hope is the great majority—deeply believe their art has inherent value. The feeling may well be ill-defined, or even indescribable, but nonetheless real. If not, few works would be completed, as artistic creation is a largely thankless task, and there are far better ways of putting food on the proverbial table. The demon motive is certainly a factor, perhaps even primary, but not alone. After all, who can deny all humans are almost constantly haunted by mysterious demons urging them to do all manner of illogical, unnecessary, and even harmful things? A quick glance at the morning's headlines shows not all are able to resist, but I assume it is safe to testify nearly all are usually able to successfully ignore them. If artists did not deeply believe their work has inherent value, their finished creations, both failures and masterpieces, would never have even been started. The first thought would have simply been ignored like any other crazy, half-formed idea the demons constantly throw at us all. Yes, all artists believe their work has inherent worth; it is the only thing that keeps them going when praise and—more vulgarly, but surely not unimportant—compensation cease to come, if indeed they ever existed. It is true few, if any, artists know their work's exact value; indeed, if anything, most, including this humble author, know it is infinitesimal in art and life's grand schemes. Still, the knowledge itself, however mysterious or insignificant, is something—and that, after all, should not be taken for granted. Artists are generally quite easy to please; this is often the only bone they must have thrown. The proverbial "starving artist" is after all not a myth; neither is the sad but true platitude that most artists don't become famous and esteemed until dead. They know their chances of being appreciated, much less praised or esteemed, in life are almost nil; just being tolerated is good enough for most. Perhaps, after all, this is more than they have any right to expect, as few other professions can boast as much. The eternal conviction of inherent worth, however vague or miniscule, is thus what keeps them going. Indeed, at times, it may be the only thing.

This is of course not particularly noteworthy. Everyone from janitors—who are after all of more practical value to society than any artist, many argue—to heads of state may be similarly driven. Even so, we know all human societies have art; indeed, as even a cursory glance at Lascaux's caves shows, so-called "civilized" humanity does not even have a monopoly. Every culture likes to flatter itself by calling others "barbaric," "uncivilized," or "savage," yet every culture, however backward others may see it, has some kind of art. It may not be held in very high regard by other cultures, or even its own, but its existence cannot be denied. Thus, for all practical intents and purposes, artists have always existed, even if not always in vogue. Indeed, they have survived all the aforementioned indifference and hostility—not to mention the best efforts of both the powers that be and regular citizens to eradicate them. At the same time, untold thousands, perhaps even millions, of professions have disappeared, usually for one of two reasons: society no longer has use for them, or their very presence is distasteful to the powerful. It has already been shown—nay, this book's very existence shows—art has survived the latter; it may have been nearly eradicated, or at least forced underground, for long periods in certain eras but has never died. If so inclined, one could attribute this to artists' steely determination, but anyone looking for an answer along such lines will find a dead end. Despite some notable exceptions, most artists, the world agrees, are quite meek, and we must assume their continuing existence is due to something else. As they have somehow managed to survive even the most determined annihilation attempts, the rational observer is forced to conclude, against common sense and contrary evidence, that it is because society, however belatedly or begrudgingly, recognizes their worth. As Sherlock Holmes, that most splendid artistic creation, says, "When you have eliminated the impossible, whatever remains, *however improbable*, must be the truth."[2]

This worth, such as it is, may be divided into three main categories. Examining it essentially attempts to answer the question "Why do we read?" and, more broadly, "Why do we admire and patronize art?" In today's world, of course, the most obvious—and possibly most accurate—answer is simply "We don't." There is much truth in this, as even casting a quick eye at the latest functional illiteracy rates or reading surveys makes clear. Still, for all this precipitous, twenty-first-century decline back into Cro-Magnonism, there remain those—the chosen few, or the meek?—who actually still read. More broadly, there are those who still, despite society's disincentives and punishments, continue to admire and patronize art. Some choose to call us "the educated elite"; others prefer "snobs," "pretentious," "stuck-up," or the latest dismissive sobriquet. Whatever the case, the fact is, against all odds, we exist. Now that this strange phenomenon has been established, we must look to causes.

The first is the simplest, and perhaps most foundational, but so obvious it is easily-overlooked. I refer, of course, to the fact that good art is *enjoyable*. Few, if pressed, would deny this basic truth, but many are, for a variety of reasons, reluctant to admit it. First, in today's anti-intellectual culture, where ignorance is prized and anything even remotely approaching intelligence is seen with suspicion and distrust at best and open hostility at worst, many are reluctant to admit they enjoy any kind of art, even the most vulgar. It has connoisseurs and champions to be sure, and it is probably true that artists do not value them enough; such patronage is after all the only reason we are suffered to exist, as it is surely more than obvious that the rest of the world cares little enough. Among these noble souls are not only those who purchase art (an essential condition for its existence, after all), but also critics who, often through negative inspiration as much as positive, give us the fuel to keep going. However much artists may love or hate critiques, their central importance cannot be denied; after all, as Oscar Wilde said long ago, "Diversity of opinion about a work of art shows that the work is new, complex and vital. When critics disagree the artist is in accord with himself."[3] As we unfortunately all know, pseudo-intellectuals also patronize it in their way, or at least pretend to—but the less said of them, the better.

Excepting these last two, who make up an infinitely small amount of the population in any case, there remains the mass of mankind—and the masses, as Voltaire subtly put it, are asses. That, at least, is one point on which all artists are agreed, yet who could deny these very asses play an important—if, indeed, not paramount—role in art's perpetuation? Seeing this requires realizing all artists aim for commercial success; this is not to say it is their only or chief aim, but it is nonetheless present. Many artists like to claim otherwise, but few, if pressed, would deny they would rather make a living from their art alone than be required to supplement it. After all, being obliged to hold another job and write only on the side cuts into writing time—and, besides, as Robert A. Heinlein slyly put it, "it would be very inconvenient to have to go back to working for a living."[4] However much we would like to deny it, the asses indisputably *do* patronize art, at least occasionally—otherwise bestsellers could not exist, as a handful of critics, who usually get copies free of charge anyway, and a motley crew of pseudo-intellectuals do not a bestseller make. The biggest asses of all are of course reluctant to admit they patronize, or even admire, any type of art, as society does not see such an action—which, after all, could possibly be construed as vaguely "intellectual"—positively. Still, even the most vulgar of the vulgar enjoy films, if nothing else—and films, at least at their best, are undeniably art. If one were to ask the average ass why he or she patronizes or admires his or her favored art, one would undoubtedly be told, "Because I *like* it!" It is as true for books and paintings as for music and films. Artists and critics may tend to condescendingly see it as unsophisticated or ignorant, and therefore harmful, yet even they must admit, if they search deep-down for foundational motives, that they also love art for the same reason. They may have others, including those they view, however accurately, as vastly more important, but it is certainly one. People admire and patronize art because they enjoy it—a proposition so simple one can easily overlook it, yet its basic truth is inarguable. This simple, yet undeniable, truth brings all people together, from highbrow artists and critics to bubble gum-smacking teenagers crowding movie theaters. Enjoying art is perhaps a primary human characteristic. The so-called "lower" animals, we assume, do not, and here we are better; greater intellectual standing lets us enjoy art. We should not be ashamed; indeed, if anything, we should cherish and cultivate it, as few rallying points are more common in today's divided world. Anything we can agree on should not be ignored, as there are seemingly fewer such things each day; we may not agree on what is good art, but there is a consensus that it exists. Even aside from such practical considerations, there are many other reasons to embrace artistic enjoyment. After all, at its best, art is a refuge when the world and everything in it steadfastly refuses to throw one a crumb; it can heal wounded souls, ease tortured pains, and even mend tragically broken hearts, as little else can. Of course, it is not perfect—but then, neither is anything else, and it is far closer than most. As Leonard Cohen truly says, "There is a crack in everything/That's how the light gets in."[5] One could, of course, argue this is mere escapism. Perhaps; yet that does not diminish art's therapeutic value or erase the fact that, if nothing else, it is one of the few things in life one can truly *enjoy*. To my mind, this, and this alone, is enough to forego having to justify enjoyment. However, even if it needed to be justified, we could all say of art generally what I have said for years about stories featuring the aforementioned Holmes—it may be escapism, but it's damn good escapism. Besides, as C. S. Lewis accurately puts it, "The only people who think there's something wrong with escapism are jailers."[6] Few things are unqualifiedly enjoyable; art is one, which is reason enough to justify it. I hope to add to the enjoyment quota, however slightly; if I add but one iota, I will have done the world a good service. I do not expect it to thank me, but knowing I did it is at least something.

The second reason for art's continuing existence is that it can change the world—or, at any rate, artists continue to believe it can. If they did not, they would cease to attempt changing it through art, as even a quick glance at new releases in any medium convincingly shows they most certainly have not. All art with political overtones is created—at least partly, and often fully—to change the world. No one would deny it almost always fails, yet the few successful examples inspire a perpetual string of new attempts. In his usual optimistic way, Kurt Vonnegut once "proposed that we adopt a basic unit of 'conscience measurement' called the 'Stowe,' after Harriet Beecher Stowe, 'the only writer in history who had an effect on the course of world affairs.'"[7] The great man's point about the paucity of books that have ever succeeded in changing the world, despite so many attempts, is well taken, but he is surely at least somewhat hyperbolic. The number is undoubtedly very small, but there is surely more than one—at least if one reasonably defines "changing the world," certain areas being outside influence for the foreseeable future because of physical and/or cultural distance from the developed world. A short list that springs quickly to my mind includes these: Plato and Aristotle's collected works; Confucius' *Analects*; Niccolò Machiavelli's *The Prince*; Isaac Newton's *Principia Mathematica*; Adam Smith's *The Wealth of Nations*; Sir Walter Scott's historical novels, of which Mark Twain said, "Sir Walter had so large a hand in making Southern character, as it existed before the war, that he is in great measure responsible for the war"[8]; Karl Marx's *Communist Manifesto/Das Kapital*; Henry David Thoreau's "Resistance to Civil Government"; Helen Hunt Jackson's *A Century of*

Dishonor/Ramona; selected Freud; Upton Sinclair's *The Jungle*; Rachel Carson's *Silent Spring*; and Betty Friedan's *The Feminine Mystique*. Perhaps one need look no further than the inclusion of several women to see the reason many, in today's still heavily-patriarchal society, insist art is unable to change the world. As for those dismayed about the lack of fictional or poetic works, there are actually several very strong possibilities; for example, Homer's *Iliad/Odyssey* and Virgil's *Aeneid* have strong claims, as they were a prominent culture's mythical foundation. As for fiction, to cite but one instance, many astronauts, engineers, and others in astronautics were inspired by science fiction to take up their careers; this is highly significant, as the space age's opening is one of our era's defining characteristics. Indeed, one could convincingly argue Vonnegut himself, along with the other artists — Heinlein, Bob Dylan, Joseph Heller, Norman Mailer, etc. — who helped create the 1960s consciousness themselves changed the world. As a writer, I am inclined to cite literary examples, but the truth is not limited to one medium; for example, who would deny Elvis Presley, The Beatles, and Dylan changed the world with music — perhaps not least by ending, as some seriously suggest, the Soviet Union and all it symbolized? I have of course deliberately left unmentioned the most obvious examples of all — religious texts. Examples from other fields also abound.

All artists who have tried to change the world via art, and that may well be all of them, know their chances are microscopically slim but also know they still have to try. The demons compel them — as do their consciences, if they have any. It is tempting to view art that tries to change the world but does not as a failure, but it is not necessarily so. It fails in its intentions but may well succeed otherwise. For example, it may inspire someone else to do something, artistically or otherwise, that actually does change the world — thereby making it eventually successful, however belatedly and indirectly. If nothing else, it may at least give joy. John Dryden indisputably failed to change the world as he hoped with "Absalom and Achitophel," yet the admirable poem has undoubtedly given substantial enjoyment to many. This is nothing to scoff at; after all, few works can claim as much. Of course, as Vonnegut continues, enjoyment can be a proverbial double-edged sword: all artists who try to change the world fear "people, having read *Uncle Tom's Cabin* and cried, or having read *Nat Turner* and cried, feel that they have somehow dealt with the problem."[9] Constant fear of misinterpretation is another artistic dilemma; as Dylan wryly advised, "do Not create anything, it will be/misinterpreted."[10] Yet even this does not negate the effort. This is good for the artistic conscience — which the muse surely already tortures enough. All artists who try to change the world are aware of this possibility, but their consciences, and those ever-present demons, just will not let them give up. After all, if completed, their work just may make a difference—if not change the world, at least make some small but tangible change. Odds are against it, but the possibility keeps them going, and they cannot let such concerns dissuade them. What have they to lose?

The world may be no better off with their work, but at least it will be no worse—or so they think, which brings up another double-edged sword. We have established that art can change the world, so far assuming it is always positive, but it can just as easily be negative. The number of occurrences is debatable, but I take it few are willing to defend the paradigm shift Adolf Hitler's *Mein Kampf* brought. I end the list here, as it is already depressing enough, but one could add at least several more items—including, depending on one's views, Marx's aforementioned work, of which Heinlein said, "Remember Karl Marx and note how close that unscientific piece of nonsense called *Das Kapital* has come to smothering out all freedom of thought on half a planet without—mind you—the emotional advantage of calling it a religion."[11] The power of art to affect the world negatively cannot and should not be denied, but I feel safe in assuming all artists trying to change the world believe they are doing so for our general good. It of course does not mean they are right, as some unfortunate examples clearly show. If so inclined, one can condemn creators of such art as at least partly responsible for the havoc it wreaks; the debate resembles the question of scientists' responsibility for their discoveries. Many, especially non-artists, are understandably quick to blame, while artists may be inclined to defend themselves with Wilde's maxim: "There is no such thing as a moral or immoral book. Books are well written, or badly written. That is all."[12] I do not propose to answer this, assuming it is even answerable; I propose to show that art's continuing ability to dramatically alter world events is one of the key reasons for its continual existence. Thus, whatever the answer, demons and conscience drive artists on regardless, and the fact that art is able to change the world at all shows its considerable potential power and therefore deems it worthy of respect, even in some of the most unwilling eyes. Artists know they wield this awesome, enormous possibility—and so have the powers that be, from Jesus-like reformers to blood-stained dictators, throughout history, and only the most ignorant of them have failed to use it for their own ends. "The pen is mightier than the sword" is after all more than just a cliché; it has been a guiding principle for many forces, both good and evil, throughout history and will undoubtedly continue to be for the foreseeable future. Thus, as Percy Shelley noted, "Poets are the unacknowledged legislators of the World."[13] Some, including many artists themselves, scoff at the very idea of art having utilitarian value and continue to insist it should be valued in and of itself. It is hardly surprising that I am inclined to agree. Still, I firmly believe art's world-changing potential is inestimably valuable; if for no other reason, any method of positively altering the world peacefully is immensely important. It seems few such methods are left; we should value them while available and—hopefully—utilize them before it is too late. The potential of art to affect the world in profoundly meaningful and tangible ways is thus the second reason it continues to exist.

The third reason is that it speaks to something deep inside us; indeed, it may very well be our highest and most noteworthy achievement. It speaks straight to the heart of what it means to be human; at its best, it makes our heartstrings throb, our brain buzz, our blood chill, our spines tingle. Few things, aside from the stark reality of everyday life itself, can so move us. Surely, then, it must speak to something important in us; it touches deep nerves and emotions, strikes both buried and prominent chords that bring out the best and worst in us. It has both intellectual and emotional components. As for the former, great art is more thought-provoking than nearly anything else, inspiring us to think outside the narrow confines in which we were raised and move beyond ourselves into the unknown and—perhaps—into greatness. It pries open eyes long-accustomed to being shut—eyes that, perhaps, would have been forever shut. The many—including this humble, Bible Belt-raised writer—who thank Heinlein's *Stranger in a Strange Land* for taking their intellectual virginity prove this. It thus makes heretofore undreamt of horizons and possibilities tangible—and there is no going back once the eyes have been opened. Art is thus a window to the universe in its many aspects—from good to evil, love to hate, joy to depression, and everything between them. This is its intellectual component, which is widely-acknowledged, though possibly undervalued.

Less well-known, but possibly even more important, is its emotional aspect. Of course, some forms of art, such as music, have well-recognized emotional capabilities that cannot be overemphasized, but it is important to realize all forms have it to a greater or lesser extent. Anyone who has cried over a book or film will agree—and, after all, those unable to say such a thing have simply not read and seen the right ones. I have already shown how art is enjoyable, which itself testifies to its emotional value. Indeed, this may be present in the most mediocre—or even the worst—art, as it is a field where, at least in enjoyment terms, subjectivity is supreme. However, great art brings out far more than simple enjoyment; it can arouse feelings of love, hate, jealousy, scorn, greed, pity, and hope to name just a few. It can shift a mood between any set of extremes—and back again. It can bring out latent philanthropic impulses and even change one's very way of think-ing—can even inspire others to change the world. Few things are able to do this so consistently and thoroughly, and art's capacity should not be under-estimated or undervalued. Its ability to affect us so powerfully is the third reason we keep it around; whether only escapist or monumentally world-changing, its powers are clearly manifest, and we long ago realized dis-pensing with something of such epic proportions is neither practical nor desirable.

Related to this is something mentioned before—art constitutes mankind's greatest achievement. I say this seriously. Many would deny—if not simply laugh—at this, especially coming from an artist, but I rest my case on these questions: What else inspires us to reach higher and go farther? To continue after everything else has led us to quit? To strive for the best in ourselves and others and push beyond self-imposed limits? To reach for the admira-ble and lofty, the apex, and even the seemingly impossible? Indeed, what else drives us to keep going at all, to surpass outside barriers, records, and supposed limits? I would argue art does so at least as thoroughly and con-sistently as anything else, if not more so. Many would deny it, but I need only point to its abilities to change the world and inspire people to do great things as proof. It brings out our best; it is that rare thing actually capable of showing our few truly noble and admirable qualities. This is of course in addition to the many and substantial reasons numerous artists, critics, and some others believe it should be valued per se. Needless to say, chief among these is beauty—the value of which, and its prominence in art, are long acknowledged. Wilde thus writes, "The artist is the creator of beautiful things"[14]; Keats famously intones, "Beauty is truth, truth beauty."[15] Those who look for a utilitarian value in everything, including art, may scoff at such metaphysical niceties, yet who loves not beauty? We clearly disagree on what is beautiful, but we all love beauty; even the most vulgar asses have something they find beautiful and treasure accordingly. It cannot, af-ter all, be treasured too much, as the world has little beauty; all beauty still in existence should be guarded as priceless treasure that can disappear at any moment. As Ralph Waldo Emerson describes, beauty's redemptive power is beyond expression:

> Some thoughts always find us young, and keep us so. Such a thought is
> the love of the universal and eternal beauty. Every man parts from that
> contemplation with the feeling that it rather belongs to the ages than to
> mortal life. The least activity of the intellectual powers redeems us in a
> degree from the conditions of time. In sickness, in languor, give us a
> strain of poetry, or a profound sentence, and we are refreshed; or pro-

duce a volume of Plato, or Shakespeare, or remind us of their names, and instantly we come into a feeling of longevity. See how the deep, divine thought reduces centuries, and millenniums, and makes itself present through all ages.[16]

Great art is beautiful; that we know—and that, I hope I need not argue, is enough to justify its continuing existence. In sum, art is extremely valuable in both its practical, utilitarian aspect and its metaphysical beauty. I thus declare it our highest achievement; after all, what else has such a strong claim to both poles of greatness? Many other things can claim one, but few, if any, can claim both—and surely none as thoroughly and consistently. Art speaks to the very root of what it means to be human and contains all humanity, showing the best we have been and suggesting the further greatness toward which we can strive. It is thus our highest achievement.

If one asked the average person, at least among those who think about such things at all, what our highest achievement is—or, alternately, what we have over so-called "lower" animals, which may be much the same—the answer would undoubtedly be "science." To be sure, our scientific achievements are impressive and often have high utilitarian value; some may even see beauty in them. Such can at least be said of science today. But what of yesterday? For example, science once held that we are dominated by humours that largely determine personality and health; we laugh at such an idea, but it dominated Western medicine for nearly a millennium. To cite but a single random example, it also once said Earth was the center of the universe and/or solar system. In fact, it has held over the centuries countless things we now believe incorrect—often laughably so. Indeed, one could take any period and find many beliefs held by mainstream scientists that anyone would be ridiculed for now. One may of course dismiss my examples as hopelessly antiquated and of no relevance to modern science; yes, scientists believed them, but it was long ago. Fair enough; however, I would also draw attention to the fact that scientists have openly advocated equally absurd ideas far more recently. Phrenology and eugenics are but two examples; I could name far more but will refrain, as I trust my point is proven. Indeed, if pressed, even all but the most impertinently stubborn scientists will agree.[17] I am not trying to discredit science; on the contrary, I fully believe it is eminently valuable, useful, and admirable—perhaps our second-greatest achievement. My point is that, while science has taken thousands of years to reach its present level of maturity and usefulness, art's great qualities have virtually always existed. As influential scientist Thomas S. Kuhn puts it (italics mine),

> Every civilization of which we have records has possessed a technology, *an art*, a religion, a political system, laws, and so on. In many cases those facets of civilization have been as developed as our own. But only the civilizations that descend from Hellenic Greece have possessed more than the most rudimentary science. The bulk of scientific knowledge is a product of Europe in the last four centuries.[18]

It is indeed no exaggeration to say comparing art and science from any era but the most recent shows the following: numerous mainstream scientific views would be laughed at by even today's most ignorant, while it is nearly certain the same era's most prominent art has beauty and truth that can still be recognized and valued. To cite but one instance, let us look at the Western world roughly a millennium ago. What did it have for science? Pliny the Elder, who talked of spontaneous sex changes and countless other patent absurdities that now make even the most willfully ignorant laugh. Despite this, his observations—many of which, admittedly, are still quite valuable—and "facts" were accepted as unquestioned truth in the Western world for fifteen hundred years. So much for science. What art then existed? Virgil, whose works are loved and admired worldwide two thousand years later. They were of course not exact contemporaries, but the principle holds. I could indeed cite numerous other examples from virtually any era, but I trust my point is made.

However, for an additional illustration, let us compare Pliny, the Western World's *de facto* science authority for a thousand and a half years, to Shakespeare, currently the Western World's preeminent artist. Pliny discourses on pregnancy:

> Whatever the sex of the child, the mother is sensible of the greatest languor at the time when the hair of the fœtus first begins to grow, and at the full moon; at which latter time it is that children newly born are exposed to the greatest danger. In addition to this, the mode of walking, and indeed everything that can be mentioned, is of consequence in the case of a woman who is pregnant. Thus, for instance, women who have used too much salted meat will bring forth children without nails: parturition, too, is more difficult, if they do not hold their breath. It is fatal, too, to yawn during labour; and abortion ensues, if the female should happen to sneeze just after the sexual congress. It is a subject for pity, and even for a feeling of shame, when one reflects that the origin of the most vain of all animated beings is thus frail: so much so, indeed, that very often the smell even of a lamp just extinguished is a cause of abortion.[19]

Again, though we now laugh, this was accepted almost without question century after century as legitimate science—an eye-opening, perhaps startling realization. There is far more where it came from; the book is quite long and covers nearly every conceivable subject. It is indeed quite a magnificent achievement; we no longer believe in most of it but can still admire its intellectual breadth and breathtaking ambition. It may well be a failure from modern science's perspective but was at least a grand one. Again, I am not trying to discredit science, or even disparage it in any way; my point is simply that its relevance varies considerably over time. Despite being the leading authority for so many years, no one now considers Pliny a legitimate scientist; furthermore, barring catastrophic scientific regression, no one will in the future. One even feels safe in assuming prior cultures would not have seen him favorably. His usefulness window was thus relatively short-lived, even in terms of civilized history—and this for a scientific text with a longer lifespan than nearly any other.

What, then, of art? Let us view a Shakespeare passage that just happens to be both one of my favorites and one of his most famous then compare it to Pliny. Here is Shakespeare at perhaps his apex:

> To-morrow, and to-morrow, and to-morrow,
> Creeps in this petty pace from day to day
> To the last syllable of recorded time,
> And all our yesterdays have lighted fools
> The way to dusty death. Out, out, brief candle!
> Life's but a walking shadow, a poor player
> That struts and frets his hour upon the stage
> And then is heard no more: it is a tale
> Told by an idiot, full of sound and fury,
> Signifying nothing.[20]

If ever art spoke for itself, surely it is here. Art at its best cannot be paraphrased; any attempts to summarize, or even explain why it is beautiful or meaningful, inevitably fall short. Comparing such an exquisite passage to Pliny seems unnecessary or even an insult to its brilliance, but I will make my poor attempt for the most pigheaded of vulgar asses. Surely we can all see that, while Pliny's passage held, at best, dubious temporal significance, Shakespeare's transcends time, place—and, indeed, everything. We will surely never stop responding to it. It is surely not hyperbolic to say that, if translated into the local vernacular, it would powerfully affect anyone from any time and place. It evoked passionate responses four hundred years ago and continues to do so; its relevance will also project far into the future, just as it would have been viable nearly any time in the past. I used this particular example because of Shakespeare's status but could just as easily have used one from thousands of years ago—or fifty, as art has consistently given them throughout human civilization's relatively short existence. However, as shown above, the same cannot be said of science. Upon this, I rest my case—or, in reference to this book, as Jesus said to Peter, "upon this rock I will build my church."[21] I will let Shelley, who said all this and more far more eloquently than I could ever hope to in his brilliant "Defence of Poetry," have the last word:

> It is admitted that the exercise of the imagination is most delightful, but it is alleged that that of reason is more useful....But it exceeds all imagination to conceive what would have been the moral condition of the world if neither Dante, Petrarch, Boccaccio, Chaucer, Shakespeare, Calderon, Lord Bacon, nor Milton, had ever existed; if Raphael and Michael Angelo had never been born; if the Hebrew poetry had never been translated; if a revival of the study of Greek literature had never taken place; if no monument of ancient sculpture had been handed down to us; and if the poetry of the religion of the ancient world had been had been extinguished together with its belief. The human mind could never, except by the intervention of these excitements, have been awakened to the invention of the grosser sciences, and that application of analytical reasoning to the aberrations of society, which it is now attempted to exalt over the direct expression of the inventive and creative faculty itself.[22]

Convinced or not, the observant will have noticed that, though I may have established a justification for the existence of art per se, I have done very little to justify my own little book. Why, then, do I usher it into a world that neither asked for it nor, in all likelihood, will care much for it or be in any way affected by it? Like all artists, I know its chances of being little more than a proverbial blip on the literary radar—hardly very active in any case—are next to nil. It will almost certainly fade into obscurity like countless other works—most of them rubbish, some good, perhaps a few even great—before and since. I know this, of course—yet, as you surely also know if you have made it this far, those demons, not to mention that damned conscience, force me to go through with the ordeal. As Orwell implied, all artists are somewhat masochistic, and I am certainly no exception. I fully expect the world to ignore me at best and, at worst, punish me for my arrogance in even harboring the thought that it could possibly care about me at all.

Then why go through with it? Let me speak plainly, as subtlety is not my intention; simply put, I am engaging in the difficult and perhaps hopelessly vain attempt to put poetry—and, on a larger and even more ambitious scale, art itself—back where it rightly belongs: near mainstream culture's center. This is not because I believe poetry is art's highest form, as even Wilde admits it is clearly music: "The type of all the arts is the art of the musician."[23] But I am no musician and must do what I can. As an artist, of course, I would prefer poetry and other arts to be at the very center, but that is undoubtedly too much to expect in today's decidedly anti-intellectual and generally non-artistic age, so I will settle for this. I have little doubt that the vast majority oppose giving it such a prominent spot. Perhaps they prefer the razor-thin, anti-intellectual, celebrity-worshipping pop culture currently reigning; I would not know. However, that is exactly where art has been throughout most of civilized existence. Such people undoubtedly find this hard to believe, but who can imagine ancient Greeks without Homer? Romans without Virgil? Elizabethans without Shakespeare? English Puritans without Milton? Eighteenth century Europe without Voltaire, Rousseau, and their illustrious contemporaries? Victorian England without Dickens? Early nineteenth-century America without Emerson and the transcendentalists? The Gilded Age without Twain? The Jazz Age without Fitzgerald and the expatriates? Post-World War II, pre-1960's America without Kerouac, Ginsberg, and the other Beats? The 1960s without Dylan and The Beatles? I thought not. I could give far more examples, but I trust these will suffice. Their work defined their eras; indeed, it is nearly impossible to think of their eras without thinking of them. They are synonymous for all practical purposes. Even those unaware such artists ever existed see their respective periods through their lenses, whether or not they know it. Art has thus long had a predominant social role; whether or not one considers it important, one must at least grant this.

It thus must surely mean something, perhaps even something important, that art is conspicuously absent from its traditional pedestal. I do not propose to say precisely what this means, but surely the reader need make no great leap to realize I consider it an aesthetic, intellectual, and (perhaps) even moral travesty. However, this is for philosophers to debate. I propose to zero in on its undeniable absence. After all, who can name a contemporary poet—even one? At best, those who follow contemporary literature closely can probably name a handful, while virtually everyone else would be lucky to come up with even one. Those inclined to condemn may attribute this to collective ignorance of literature or art or even to the general idolization of ignorance in today's culture, but this would be unfair. In fact, ignorance is beside the point. The important thing to realize is simply that poetry—nay, all art except films, the vast majority of which are utter, contemptible garbage that does not even belong in the same sentence as the word "art"—is simply not prominent. It makes no headlines, is not talked about by movers and shakers; indeed, its pulse is hardly even detectable. The (very) few who care echo Vonnegut's lament in his last speech: "James Whitcomb Riley, 'The Hoosier Poet,' was the highest-paid American writer of his time, 1849 to 1916, because he recited his poetry for money in theaters and lecture halls. That was how delighted by poetry ordinary Americans used to be. Can you imagine?"[24] No one of my generation, or perhaps even the prior one or two, can possibly imagine something so unbelievably outlandish; the moon turning blue is comparably passé. Anyone proposing to charge for reading would be laughed at; it is hard enough to find an audience at all. Far from ordinary Americans paying (yes, *paying*!) to hear poetry—a poet now nearly forgotten even by connoisseurs, no less—, one can hardly pay *them* to sit through it. Even my high school English teacher, presumably an oasis of poetry promotion in today's poetic desert, gave us not a single poem to read, saying she was being magnanimous in saving us from "the drudgery of poetry." Not surprisingly, in great contrast to Riley, poets now struggle to get paid at all. As anyone who has tried the almost impossible task of getting poetry published anywhere that it is even remotely likely to be read knows, few such places exist, and virtually none pay. This is not because small publishers are greedy—I say nothing of big ones or agents, virtually neither of whom now touch poetry at all—but simply because they also are nearly always on shoestring budgets, often working with little or no pay themselves. The infinitesimal world of poetry publishing is a labor of love to the few who still participate—or even notice its existence. Yet I have gone to great lengths to show art is any society's lifeblood; one without it can thus only be ailing. Indeed, what concerned, rational observer can deny it is ailing—that, in fact, it may well have suffered a mortal blow? When I look at society and see the utterly contemptible bile—"reality" shows, glorified karaoke, and 99.9+% of everything else on television; a film industry almost devoid of anything even approaching mediocrity; an unaccountable, indefensible worship of vain, vapid celebrities; and the foul, festering stench of a culture that generally worships ignorance and apathy while endlessly ridiculing anything that could even come remotely close to approaching something that might be termed "intellectual" or "artistic"—I feel utterly dejected, dispirited, and depressed. It leaves me with virtually no hope that we, barring some unforeseeable miracle, can ever raise society above a vast, empty, and seemingly endless wasteland. Contemplating its sorry state even briefly fills my disenchanted mind with

William Wordsworth's thoughts from more than two hundred years ago:

> A multitude of causes, unknown to former times, are now acting with a combined force to blunt the discriminating powers of the mind, and, unfitting it for all voluntary exertion, to reduce it to a state of almost savage torpor. The most effective of these causes are the great national events which are daily taking place…To this tendency of life and manners the literature and theatrical exhibitions of the country have conformed themselves. The invaluable works of our elder writers, I had almost said Shakespeare and Milton, are driven into neglect…When I think upon this degrading thirst after outrageous stimulation, I am almost ashamed to have spoken of the feeble effort with which I have endeavoured to counteract it; and, reflecting upon the magnitude of the general evil, I should be oppressed with no dishonorable melancholy, had I not a deep impression of certain inherent and indestructible qualities of the human mind, and likewise of certain powers in the great and permanent objects that act upon it which are equally inherent and indestructible; and did I not further add to this impression a belief, that the time is approaching when the evil will be systematically opposed, by men of greater powers, and with far more distinguished success.[25]

I could not have said it better. It would be hard to articulate my thoughts on today's society more aptly—yet the early nineteenth century culture Wordsworth so reviled, "sickly and stupid German tragedies"[26] and all, now looks very vibrant. When one reflects that the great poet's lament was written long before anyone had ever heard of Hollywood, television, and the multitude of other banes currently keeping culture in the gutter, one sees we are in a very sad state indeed.

At this point, the practical and realistic will likely object that social degradation and malaise stem from far deeper and more troubling causes than the mere absence of art. I do not deny it; I acknowledge the unfortunate reality as readily as the next pessimist. I am not crazy or vain enough to believe I can stem the evil tide single-handedly; even if I thought so, I have neither the stomach nor the patience for such a long, involved, and thankless task. As an artist, I can do little more than make an honest effort to inject art back into society and hope "men of far greater powers" will take it from there "with far more distinguished success." I indeed know I have little hope of even making a noticeable artistic impact, as I am under no illusions that the present work can even come close to rivaling the epoch-forming productions of the great authors chronicled earlier. Even so, I also know the artists who preceded me in this noble and possibly hopeless endeavor in the last several decades have failed. I mentioned that contemporary poetry is well-nigh invisible but went not into causes. The less charitable will undoubtedly say it is because these artists' work is subpar, perhaps even execrable. This is of course debatable, but the fact that contemporary poetry fails to even make a dent in the national consciousness means the claim cannot just be dismissed out of hand. Certainly no contemporary poet has achieved anything even remotely approaching fame, and few, if any, have garnered any measure of critical or popular renown — which is not to say they are non-existent. Poetry is a lowly enough profession in most eyes, but a substantial number still engage in it — perhaps even as many, percentage-wise, as in any other comparable era. One would hardly know it, though, as their profiles are so incredibly low — a fact that presumably does not derive from their desires. To be sure, at least a handful have amassed a modicum of praise and even some fairly brisk sales — for poets. Some are actually read; a few even occasionally make it into popular literary anthologies. That they make enough from their works to live as professional writers (or do they? most seem to double as university instructors), and even continue to win Nobel Prizes, proves their existence. After all, *someone* has to win the Nobel Prize, just as *someone* has to be poet laureate. The list of contemporary poetic candidates for both may well be quite slim, and certainly far from prestigious, but it is all we have, and we must somehow find a way to make do. However, one would be hard-pressed to find anyone willing to go out on a proverbial limb and say any of these poets will ultimately enter the canon. No one seems to think they will still be read centuries, or even half a century, from now — and with good reason. Many concerned observers honestly believe America has not produced a truly great poet since Ginsberg; I, along with an emerging critical consensus, move this up to Dylan — but no further. Far from lamenting, perhaps we should celebrate; most other countries are probably jealous that we can claim someone so recent. The days of having multiple great poets working simultaneously have long since disappeared — seemingly forever. Many current literary anthologies cover little or no poetry published after the 1950s — presumably because it is not good enough. One could of course object that it often takes a long time — decades, even centuries — for works to become canonical, and perhaps we should not judge those from the second half of the twentieth century forward too hastily. This is valid and may even contain some truth but is little more than cold comfort at best. It does not account for the apparent dearth of quality poetry and does not make the sad situation any less depressing to the few who still care. Also, it may well be that masterpieces are unfortunately lounging in obscurity because of the general lack of interest. Maybe—but even the most hopeful and optimistic are not holding their breath. At any rate, it seems safe to say there are no Walt Whitmans or T. S. Eliots in either limelight or shadow. The situation is indeed so dire that those who truly love and admire poetry—and practically any other art, as the problem hardly affects only one medium—are undoubtedly teetering on the edge of hopelessness, the same precarious position in which I now find myself.

And now, after all that depressing drivel, we again find ourselves at the seemingly perennial question: what, pray tell, can my poor, little book do to rectify this? Perhaps nothing; indeed, in all likelihood, exactly nothing. Yet, like all lone soldiers before me, I know I still must try. I am suffering from no illusions about its greatness; I have no hope—indeed, real no reason to believe—it will some day join the canon, as the last several decades' poetry has so conspicuously failed to do. Still, I will not allow any false modesty to imply anything other than the fact that I sincerely believe it towers above the vast majority of contemporary poetry—which after all is not saying much. I say this in all humility; being crowned king of contemporary poetry, laurels and all, is akin to being the world's tallest midget. Despite this, I know full well far better works have recently failed, and I am not optimistic enough to think fate will be any kinder to me. I am nevertheless determined to try, no matter what the outcome; besides, it is far too late to back out. I have staked out my ground, drawn my line in the sand…and the clichés continue. I have little else to add. I sincerely hope the work henceforth speaks for itself, as all recent predecessors, both superior and inferior, have unfortunately failed to do.

Footnotes to the Preface

1 "Why I Write." 1947.
2 *The Sign of Four*. 1890. *The Complete Sherlock Holmes* (Pages 89-158). Preface. Christopher Morley. New York: Doubleday-Bantam Doubleday Dell. Page 111.
3 Preface. *The Picture of Dorian Gray*. 1891. New York: Dover, 1993. Page viii.
4 "Concerning Stories Never Written: Postscript." 1952. *Revolt in 2100 & Methuselah's Children*. Riverdale, NY: Baen, 1999. Page 266.
5 "Anthem." *The Future*. Columbia, 1992.
6 Quoted by Arthur C. Clarke in McAleer, Neil. *Arthur C. Clarke: The Authorized Biography*. Chicago: Contemporary, 1992. Page 251.
7 "The Conscience of the Writer." *Publisher's Weekly* 199 (1971): Pages 26-27. Rpt. in Allen, William Rodney, ed. *Conversations with Kurt Vonnegut*. Literary Conversations Series. Jackson: UP of Mississippi, 1988. Page 43.
8 *Life on the Mississippi: Authorized Edition*. 1883. New York: Bantam-Bantam Doubleday Dell, 1988. Page 220, chapter 46.
9 See note 7.
10 "Advice for Geraldine on Her Miscellaneous Birthday." 1964. *Lyrics, 1962-1985*. New York: Knopf, 1985. 124-125.
11 See note 3.
12 Wilde, page vii; see note 2.
13 "A Defence of Poetry." 1821. Bruce Woodcock, ed. *The Selected Poetry and Prose of Shelley*. The Wordsworth Poetry Library. Ware, UK: Wordsworth, 2002. Page 660.
14 Wilde, page vii; see note 2.
15 "Ode on a Grecian Urn." 1819. *Complete Poems*. New York: Book-Of-The-Month Club, 1993. Line 49, pages 134-135.
16 "The Over-soul." 1841. *Self-Reliance and Other Essays*. New York: Dover, 1993. Page 54.
17 For a scientist's perspective on this very issue, see Thomas S. Kuhn's influential *The Structure of Scientific Revolutions* (1962. 3rd ed. Chicago: U of Chicago P, 1996.)
18 Kuhn, pages 167-168; see prior note.
19 *The Natural History*. Circa 77-79 C.E. Bostock, John and H. T. Riley, eds. and trans. *The Perseus Digital Library*. Accessed 07 Feb. 2007 via www.perseus.tufts.edu
20 *Macbeth*. Circa 1603. New York: Dover, 1993. 5.5.21-30.
21 Matthew 16:18.
22 Shelley, pages 653-655; see note 13.
23 Wilde, page vii; see note 2.
24 At Clowes Hall, Indianapolis. 27 Apr. 2007. *Armageddon in Retrospect*. New York: Putnam, 2008. Page 28.
25 "Preface to *Lyrical Ballads, with Pastoral and Other Poems*." 1802. Abrams, M. H. and Stephen Greenblatt, eds. *The Norton Anthology of English Literature*. 2 vols. 7th ed. New York: Norton, 2000. Pages 243-244.
26 Ibid.

Hard Times in These Times:
Reflections on the Contemporary Scene
By John Feldman

"I'm sentimental, if you know what I mean
I love the country but I can't stand the scene"
–Leonard Cohen, "Democracy"

John is a young, idealistic, and optimistic Midwestern boy on his own for the first time. His exact age is unknown, but he is widely-believed to be in his late teens or early twenties. Unsubstantiated rumors that he ran away from home persist. He genuinely believes he can change the world via art, or at least inspire others to—and is determined to try at any rate. He cares little about critics; his goal is to move the masses. A working-class populist, he makes an honest effort to put himself in the position of other members of his generation and describe the cold, post-post-modern world as he truly believes they see it. He knows this is not without a certain presumption, even arrogance, but wishes to be his generation's voice and cannot be overly burdened with such concerns. His fantasy is to be a folk singer. Only two minor stumbling blocks stand between him and his dream: he cannot play a note and cannot sing. (Oh, *he* thinks he can sing, all right—but no one else does.) Faced with this unfortunate and convenient situation, he has taken the path of numerous other lyricists like him—issuing his words as poetry. He thinks it a poor substitute but also sees that, after all, it is better than nothing. I include few of his poems not because there is insufficient news for a protest artist. After all, perhaps no era has had more since the 1960s; he sings the pain of a generation whose defining moment is 9/11 and is accordingly prolific. It is because, like all artists trying to make works relevant to the masses, he ever walks the thin, thin line between being matter-of-factly didactic, thus losing art, and too artistic, thus losing relevance and mass appeal. These poems are his best attempts at bridging the proverbial gap. If even they fail, it testifies to the challenge's great difficulty. He nonetheless hopes to make a name for himself and just may do it. The discerning critic will do well to keep an eye on him, as he just may succeed. If not, he will still be able to comfort himself with the fact that he truly tried his best—a noble failure if ever there were one.

This Thing of Darkness I Acknowledge Mine

"We have done with Hope and Honour, we are lost to Love and Truth,
We are dropping down the ladder rung by rung,
And the measure of our torment is the measure of our youth.
God help us, for we knew the worst too young!"
–Rudyard Kipling, "Gentlemen-Rankers"

My generation inherited pain
 Like each before
We had "Little to lose and much to gain" —
 Good advice we never even got to ignore
Future generations can have their happiness and joy,
 Their hope and optimism so sublime,
But we saw everything we had suddenly destroyed —
 This thing of darkness I acknowledge mine

When I saw the plane hit the building,
 Our future hopes were suddenly cut short
We were shocked and disgusted at the senseless killing,
 Amazed and angered at the unbelievable report
We lost our innocence right there and then,
 Along with that ignorance that is bliss so divine
Our youth and idealism were smothered out by sin —
 This thing of darkness I acknowledge mine

We knew not what to think of such unfathomable evil —
 What to tell our future children, or even ourselves at the time
"Why," we wondered, "would anyone so ruthlessly kill?"
 To cut off innocent lives so early is such a crime
Like Cain banished from paradise,
 We never knew our lives could so suddenly turn on a dime
Our goals and ambitions vanished before we could even think twice —
 This thing of darkness I acknowledge mine

We knew not what to say or how to think,
 Everything had changed so suddenly
Our lives flashed before us every time we stopped to blink,
 Wondering if we, too, would end so tragically

The looks of horror on each other's faces were a nightmare to behold,
 We struggled to find some kind of hopeful sign
No one ever said it would be like this! Why weren't we ever told?
 This thing of darkness I acknowledge mine

No generation should ever have all its hopes and dreams
 Taken so suddenly and tragically from it
Life is so simple, it initially seems,
 And then something leaves you wondering how come it
All disappeared so thoroughly and so fast
 I hope future generations get their carefree youth back; I'm
Still lost in the depths of this tragedy so vast—
 This thing of darkness I acknowledge mine

Sometimes I wonder if things will ever be the same,
 If we'll ever return to normality
I still wake up in the middle of the night half insane
 From the same old nightmares of the tragedy
I struggle to find an answer to it all,
 But peace and understanding are so hard to find
The existence that once seemed so vast now feels so very small—
 This thing of darkness I acknowledge mine

I try to think back to my youth before it,
 But it all seems so far away
Could it be that I've ignored it,
 Or has the whole world gone astray?
I once hoped and strived for a bright future,
 But now I wish only for the ordinary kind
I have my lost fantasies, as you have yours—
 This thing of darkness I acknowledge mine

The whole damn world seems to have fallen apart,
 Its swan song seemingly sung
So long to everything I once held so close to my heart—
 God help us, for we knew the worst too young!
I admit those both before and after have had ups and downs,
 I don't want to pitifully whine—
But where others have been able to turn things around,
 This thing of darkness I acknowledge mine

I feel for all the dead and their families,
 I feel for all the lives needlessly lost
I hear their cries, and I hear their pleas,
 I count the bodies, and I count the cost—
But I just can't help thinking something was stolen from us,
 I guess it just calls for yet another sorrowful shrine
Here's the epitaph for our generation and the future we can no longer trust:
 This thing of darkness I acknowledge mine

2006

I Became a Soldier

I'm young, Lord, and afraid to die
I'm looking up at the ominous, dusty sky
I'm beginning to wonder how I ever bought into this lie
I miss my home and family; I feel like I could cry
Lord, I'm starting to wonder why
   I ever became a soldier

I signed up to fight for my country
Just like my father and his father before me
I thought I could help show others the path to liberty,
To help spread freedom and democracy —
But, God, I don't think I've ever been truly free
   Since I became a soldier

Just like you, I saw what they did on 9/11,
It shattered my world, shattered my heaven
I wanted to fight back, wanted to get even,
So I signed up and told my wife and kids I was leavin'
Lord, I knew it was the right thing to do, but I hated to see 'em grievin'
   When I became a soldier

I saw what they did to our country — Lord, it made me mad,
Forced me to sit down and take a long, hard look at all I had,
At all I held sacred and all that made me glad
It was a war between right and wrong, good and bad
I felt I owed it to my country, but I never felt so bad
   As when I became a soldier

I thought I was fighting for freedom, fighting for love,
For those who died before me, and for God above,
For my family back home, and, when push came to shove,
For all the good things this country's done and all the others it should've —
But now, Lord, when I look back on my regrets, the one thing I think of
   Is when I became a soldier

'Cause now I'm out in the desert, and I don't know who to trust
I still do what I'm told, but it's about to make me bust

'Cause the more I see, the more it seems to me, the enemy's just like us
They're fighting for their country, for their freedom, for what they must
They pray to the same God, and some of 'em probably feel just
  Like me when I became a soldier

I get sick when I see innocents killed
They ain't the ones fightin'; their blood shouldn't be spilled
Hell, I know we're all under pressure, but no one should be willed
Into doin' somethin' against their conscience, even out here in the field
What happened in that prison just ain't right, and I wish it had been re-
    vealed
  Before I became a soldier

Before I bought into their promises of fame, fortune, and glory,
Before I cried when I saw that tragic news story,
Before I was out here where it's hot and dangerous and gory,
Before I let my old man's war stories bore me
Yes, and before I charged out with the stars and stripes flyin' o'er me
  When I became a soldier

Hell, I was an ordinary guy, just like you,
I wanted to fight for what I felt was right and for my country, too
I thought it was the just and right thing to do—
But now I'm stuck in this hellhole, and I'm starting to think things through,
And I can no longer believe in what I thought was true
  When I became a soldier

'Cause what I see out here every day has nothing to do with that jive,
With those half-baked truths they tell our kids and wives
I just ain't got time no more for bullshit and lies
Out here, it's hard enough just to survive—
And, tell me, who gives a good goddamn if we ever get out of here alive?
  I wish I never became a soldier

Circa 2005

Hoist That Rag (Ballad for New Orleans)

"We hold these truths to be self-evident, that all men are created equal, that they are endowed by their Creator with certain unalienable Rights, that among these are Life, Liberty and the pursuit of Happiness. — That to secure these rights, Governments are instituted among Men, deriving their just powers from the consent of the governed, — That whenever any Form of Government becomes destructive of these ends, it is the Right of the People to alter or to abolish it, and to institute new Government, laying its foundation on such principles and organizing its powers in such form, as to them shall seem most likely to effect their Safety and Happiness."
–The Declaration of Independence

"The ultimate weapon was invented in pre-history. It is a kitchen knife in the hands of a determined man — who is fed up."
–Robert A. Heinlein, "The Future Revisited"

Seems times are hard everywhere these days,
From the urban ghettoes to the rural backways,
Yet all our hard times seem to get lost in the world's smoky haze
    It seems all we can do is hoist that rag

I've always tried hard to live my life the right way,
I get up every morning and go to work each day,
But now my home is gone, and I have nowhere to stay
    All I can do is hoist that rag

I've always believed in working hard, never tried to get off easily,
And things usually worked out fine when it was just me,
But now I'm struggling just to be able to feed my family
    It isn't enough anymore to just hoist that rag

I always figured I was doomed to my lot,
To work hard for every lousy dime I got
I always assumed I'd be forever stuck in the same old spot
    Condemned to forever hoist that rag

But I never thought I'd be abandoned like this,
That I'd live to see my own country cross me off its list—
But now I've seen it, Lord, and it's making me pissed
  I'm getting tired of having to hoist that rag

It sickens me what I'm seeing now—
People like me struggling to live by the sweat of their brow,
While all the rich folk live better anyhow
  Makes you wonder why you bother to hoist that rag

My president's turned his back on me,
He wouldn't give a damn if my whole town drowned in the sea
I overlooked his mistakes for years, but now I finally
  Am beginnin' to ask why I have to hoist that rag

I'm beginnin' to wonder how much longer I can survive,
I've lost my zest for life an' my ol' inner drive
Nobody gives a good goddamn if we ever get out of here alive!
  How much longer will we have to hoist that rag?

The people supposed to be representing us don't speak for me,
They don't have the slightest idea what it's like to be in poverty
Those power hungry bastards are livin' it up while we drown in misery
  And I don't know how much longer I can stand to hoist that rag

I was always told charity begins at home,
But they overlook us to spend money in some god-forsaken foreign zone
How much longer can they leave us here all alone
  All broken down and beaten, forcing us to hoist that rag?

I laugh now at all the lies I used to believe
About how if I worked hard, I'd have no reason to grieve
It frightens me to think how recently I was naïve
  And how long I've had to hoist that rag

I don't know when others are gonna wake up and see the light
That we can't let these motherfuckers keep taking away our rights
It's now up to us to take up the fight
  Otherwise we'll have to forever hoist that rag

I'm sick of our government ignoring our demands
And tired of putting up with their outrageous commands
We just can't trust freedom if it's not in our hands
   It just condemns us to hoist that rag

I've put up with it all for years without saying a word,
But now I think the situation's become absurd,
So now, Lord God, let my poor voice be heard
   I'm fed up with having to hoist that rag

I don't think I have to remind anyone of those horrible days
Or of how the man showed up at last, snapped a few pictures, and went
  away
We have to show these people that ignoring us doesn't pay
   And that we will no longer be content to hoist that rag

They talk of a war somewhere far from here,
But the real war is right here at home, it's clear
It's time for us to rise up; we have nothing to fear
   We must refuse to hoist that rag!

We live in a country that's been stripped of its constitution,
That's full of corrupt politicians and broken institutions
I think it's time for a new revolution
   We no longer have to hoist that rag

You may say you're too weak or that you're satisfied,
But how much longer can we let them keep stepping on our pride?
Come on out into the light; we have nothing to hide
   We must refuse to hoist that rag

You may say you don't have the courage or what it takes inside
Or that there won't be enough flesh and blood to fight by your side,
But tell me, brother, can you swallow all those tears you've cried?
   How much longer will you be content to hoist that rag?

I'm giving voice to the voiceless, and we're getting stronger,
The "silent minority" is silent no longer
It's time to take back our country from those who wrong her
   It's time to give up having to hoist that rag

LIFE'S TRIUMPH by Bill R. Moore

I'm sick of waiting around for others to hear the call,
The time has come for a hard rain to fall
We're getting closer now; I can hear the rattling walls...
  Oh, the time's coming when we'll no longer have to hoist that rag!

Our oppressors had better be ready 'cause we're poised for attack,
The time has come for us to take our country back
We will no longer live forever on the other side of the tracks
  We will no longer hoist that rag!

They may say we lack the numbers, say we lack the might,
That our hopes are few and our chances slight—
But that's okay; we won't go down without a fight
  Anything's better than having to hoist that rag!

These tyrants shall fall just like Goliath and Macbeth—
Oh, I can still hear the words coming from our forefather's breath:
"Give me liberty or give me death!"
  We, too, must refuse to hoist that rag!

Ever since the day those levees burst
We've been looking forward to the day when the last shall be first,
When the final oppressor will be carried off in a hearse
  We're out for blood and will no longer hoist that rag!

But we can't wait around any longer for help from on high,
The time has come to either do or die
We've been looking long enough for a reason why
  We have to hoist that rag

We can't wait around any longer for our hopes to be fulfilled,
I've seen too many of my family and friends killed
Yes, my friend, there is blood to be spilled
  Unless we want to forever hoist that rag

They say we deserve to stay poor while the rich get rich,
But we can't pull ourselves up by the bootstraps when we're stuck in the
  ditch
Still, I think it's time we did more than just sit around and bitch
  It's time we refused to hoist that rag

Can you really just sit there and let them deprive your kids and your wife?
There's no more fooling around, brother; this is your life
If you don't have a gun, go and grab a knife
　　　This is the last time we will ever hoist that rag

The time has come for a decisive split,
To put an end once and for all to their oppressive shit
It's either that or let them get away with it
　　　And go on hoisting that rag…

2005

Life's Triumph

How do we fall into this trap called Life,
Forever condemned to fruitless toil and strife?
How do we fall under work's heavy spell,
Eternally damned to worry and living hell?
How do we fool ourselves into thinking it's right
When we force ourselves through all day and curse it all night?
How do we allow ourselves to believe,
To deceive others, and to gratefully receive?
How do we go on day after day,
Forever justifying because we can't wish away?
How do we sell ourselves short and give positive report
To the one thing we're always ready to retort?
How long will it go on? How did it come to this day?
Does it really have to be this way?

It begins as soon as we're born,
Throwing us into Life as from the womb we're torn
Soon as we're alive we rush toward death,
Cursing our Maker with every other breath
We're born to trouble as the sparks fly,
Inheriting it soon as we open our eyes
Soon as we can talk we start asking why,
And the wise soon see they're already living a lie
Our parents load us with lies as they're taught to do
'Till we can't see straight or think things through
They teach us what's righteous and true and holy and legal,
Fully equipping us to fight the world's evil —
"Just work hard, do what's right, and believe in God" —
But just to be sure, they don't spare the rod

When we're old enough they send us to school,
Where we're taught to play by the rules
They make us machines to be society's slaves
And tell of a rainy day we must work hard for and save
The nail that sticks up gets hammered down,

Conformity's reality when authority's around
 "Stand in line, raise your hand, do what you're told" —
 They reward the meek and punish the bold
They try to square the circle, force us into their little peg,
You can't cut in line, but you damn sure can't beg
 We learn to be from others' society,
 Quickly learning to avoid notoriety
We form hopes and fears from peers,
Locking ourselves in a pattern we'll follow the rest of our years

They leave us alone when they've stuffed us full of knowledge,
And we're supposed to choose work or college
 The poorest take the former, the rest the latter,
 Unless we must do both to get ahead or flatter
We put nose to grindstone, wasting our days
In menial chores and spiritual malaise
 We're bored to tears but so full of fears
 We put off plans for years and years
Until one day we see half our Life is gone,
We've done nothing, but the world's gone on
 It would've done just as well without us, and we'll never move,
 Too tired to prove what we always felt we had to prove
Our best years are behind us 'cause to the ugly truth they blind us
Until it's too late to remind us

How the hell are we supposed to figure this out?
It seems only yesterday we were learning to be a good Boy Scout
 Now there are jobs to find, bills to pay, errands to run—
 Never time to have even a little fun
The change is just too sudden and drastic,
We'll bust before we adjust, though they molded us like plastic
 All the people and places we used to turn to are closed to us now,
 They tell us self-reliance is a solemn vow
We agree and want to be a success just as much as they
But drown in doubt trying to figure out how to make it our own way
 Everything comes crashing down on us at once,
 It seems we went from kid to adult in just a couple of months
It seems only yesterday we would play; now we're heading for the tomb—

How the hell did it get here so soon?

We want off Maggie's Farm but can't bring ourselves to harm
The Life everyone swears is a charm
 We hate our jobs, our bosses, our destinies,
 Speak jealously of the free
We'd do anything to escape,
But there's too much red tape—
 Sometimes we just wanna give it all up and shout,
 But everyone pretends not to know what we're talking about
We're held back by self-doubt
But try to make the most of our little clout
 And convince ourselves we make the world a better place—
 But we're not even important in our own little space
We lie and sigh, say our lives have meaning,
But deep down inside, we just feel like screaming

They try to keep us in the system, on that you can bet,
We can't stop working 'cause we're so full of debt
 We work to pay it off even if we hurt or cough
 'Cause any minute they might lay us off,
Fire us 'cause we couldn't hack it or for nothing at all—
In the end, it just makes us feel small
 'Cause we try our best to be a success
 But just can't ever seem to pass the test
Our best is never good enough, or so it seems,
We never seem to live up to anyone's dreams
 One day we lift our heads up and see
 We're not even half what we thought we'd be
Even worse, we've disappointed those we look up to—
But it seems there's nothing left to do

The undeniable desire for acquisition
Makes us ever strive for a better position
 We have to have a classic American Life—
 The house, the car, the kids, the wife—
After all, there's no other way

Haven't we seen it from our very first days?
 We have to have more than our neighbors
 And don't wanna take favors—
No handouts if eyes are about,
We want it known we got all by our own clout
 The relentless drive to get more and more
 Has driven us perilously near bankruptcy's door—
But we'll work it all off some sunny day,
Figure it out, find a way…

So we tell ourselves until even we can't believe it,
And there's no one on the other end to receive it
 We have to do at least as well as our folks
 And must far outdo the blokes
Who always said we'd amount to nothing—
But sometimes even we think we're bluffing
 When we sit up alone at night
 Unable to sleep from sheer fright
Of what will happen if the next check doesn't come—
We just can't leave our whole family numb
 Even if it's too much for us to take,
 We have to put up with heartache
'Cause we brought them into the mess—
It's our responsibility, our loneliness

Oh, if only we'd known what we were getting into!
There'd be nothing we wouldn't undo—
 But it's too late now that we've brought them into it,
 Too late to change, too late to quit
We could quit on ourselves but not on them,
They're too young to know it's sink or swim
 We have to hide reality until they're old enough to swallow it,
 Just as others did for us; we hate it but will follow it
After all, we see no other choice
What right have we to complain or rejoice?
 Our ancestors got by on less,
 Who are we if we can't pass their test?
The unending drive to move ever forward

LIFE'S TRIUMPH by Bill R. Moore

Won't let us go in the reverse we drift ever toward

So diplomas hang on the wall
But never really helped at all,
 Never gave one bitter taste of real Life—
 The relentless struggle, the endless strife—
Never taught us what was real,
What to think or how to feel,
 How to go on when we want to shrivel up and die,
 How to conform when we know the norm is a lie
Our resumes are full but have gotten us nowhere,
We're always held back by unforeseen cares
 We've worked our way up the ladder
 But just keep getting sadder
The more we make the less we keep—
Just like all the other sheep

They keep us doped with sex, religion, and TV,
Trying to make us believe we're classless and free
 Walls of denial come tumbling down
 When we see the empty future to which we're bound
It's hard to stay motivated to climb
When they keep moving what we've worked for the whole time
 Sometimes we get lowdown and think the whole thing's a sham,
 Wonder why the hell we ever gave a damn,
Why we worked so hard, gave so very much
When of the things we want we haven't even gotten a touch
 Sometimes we can't help but wonder if it's all worthwhile,
 If we should really go on with fake hellos and phony smiles—
But always fall back on the central fact
That we're in the red, and others are in the black

So we swallow pride, push dreams deep down inside,
Find a bearable job in which to hide—
 But just can't shake the feeling we're better than all this,
 It makes us cry, gets us pissed
It seems everything's against us, we can't catch a break,

We've paid more than was earned by mistakes
 Others get ahead despite less cred,
 Can't understand why it's not us instead
We cross our fingers every time someone's selected,
But it's always someone better, younger, or more well-connected
 Sometimes we get so goddamn mad we just wanna say, "Fuck it all!"
 But that little voice inside always makes us heed its call
We just can't bring ourselves to give up
Every dream we've tried to live up

A day eventually comes when we look around
And see we're still stuck in the same dead end town
 Dreams have been crushed, ambition turned to mush,
 Yet we head every day into the same old rush
Sometimes we just get so fed up and disgusted,
Wonder why we ever believed the things we always trusted —
 Just wanna take it out on whoever holds us back
 Or whatever unlucky bastard happens to cross our track;
And sometimes we just wanna end it all,
Kill ourselves and let the whole damn thing fall
 But are held back by an inner need, a family to feed —
 Something always forces us to bleed
Most of the time we don't even feel able
But still have to find a way to put food on the table

There are so many things we're dying to get off our chests,
But we tell others we feel nothing but blessed
 It seems unfair to admit the awful truth,
 To take away the innocence of youth,
 Burst the bubble of trouble we're all living in —
We're forced into silence by lack of a real friend
 We keep telling ourselves some day it'll be better
 But know deep down we're in the same rut forever
So many troubles and doubts we force ourselves to ignore,
But we go back the next day just like the one before
 Every diary entry looks just like the prior page —
 Same old rat race, Life in the same old cage
We know without doubt we'll never get out

But still don't know what it's all about

How did it ever get this way?
Why did they tell us hard work always pays?
 We've played fair, tried hard to get there,
 But can't ever seem to stay on top of our cares
Now the job's closing just as all the bills are due,
We just don't know how we're gonna pull through
 There's no one left to borrow from,
 The thought of ruin leaves us numb
We've always gotten one step closer, been put two steps back,
But now it seems it's really gonna crack
 We can't deny it's desperation we're feeling —
 Hell, there isn't even anything worth stealing —
But see no end to it for the rest of our days...
How will we ever find our way out of this maze?

We've mortgaged our future, sold our past,
Given up the present to a lie so vast
 We've lived for years from paycheck to paycheck,
 And now we can't even afford to fix the wreck
We wasted the years that should have been our best,
Never even stopping to take a rest
 There's nothing left now, nothing to steal or loan,
 We've worked too hard to call our lives our own
All those years of slaving as anonymous drones,
Working our fingers to the bone,
 Have gotten us nowhere —
 We can't help but think it isn't fair;
But what else can we do? Where else can we go?
Does anyone care? Does anybody know?

We wasted so much time making others rich,
They sit in their mansion while we dig their ditch
 They'd be nowhere without us
 But don't care about us,
Would spit on us if they'd so much as notice we exist —

It's enough to make a calm man pissed
 All that force-fed bullshit about man and god and country
 Has ever done for you and me is mediocrity
We spent our whole lives worshipping that stuff,
But I believe at long last we've suffered enough
 We should do something about it, me and you,
 Our kind are so many, theirs so few
Surely there's nothing we couldn't do
If we all pulled together and to each other were true…

They took a part of us we're really starting to miss,
We keep wondering how long it can go on like this
 How long must we put up with the strife
 Of a worthless existence in a meaningless Life?
Is it right that the heaven of so few should come
From the hell of so many? The sum
 Is on our side but the power on theirs,
 We inflict the curse of work on our heirs,
But their posterity can be wanton and carefree—
How can this be in the land of the free?
 They talk of upward mobility, but to nobility it's synthetic,
 They have no respect for the Protestant work ethic
Surely there's got to be a better way…
I know one thing—some day someone's gonna have to pay…

But we're tired, so goddamn tired,
Our hearts are racing, our brains are wired
 Too tired to take over the town, vote out the clown,
 Take somebody down
We're fragile shells in a cold, hard world
That doesn't have mercy or give a damn what it's hurled
 At us and our miserable little lives,
 We're just replaceable workers in short-lived hives
We're doing our best just to live from day to day
But have debts no honest people can pay
 We sweat the same filthy jobs from morn to morn,
 Go home down the same dirty streets where we were born
Surely we can be forgiven if we find it all obscene,

LIFE'S TRIUMPH by Bill R. Moore

Curse our fates, beg to know what it all means

Why do we sweat it out from day to day
When others have no price to pay
 And work our whole lives for a prize some get in the cradle?
 Why do we buy into the fable?
We could retire on the interest off the change
In some people's couch cushions; isn't it strange
 That we wear the yoke against our own will?
 Why do we agree to be slowly killed?
Our hands are raw, our backs bent,
But we can't even save enough to pay our rent
 We've never gambled or smoked, drank or bought
 Anything but what we ought—
Not from morality, but to make ends meet—
Yet others get such things thrown at their feet

Why must we work all our lives to do
What some are born to?
 Why must we earn by the sweat of our brow
 What some enjoy even now?
Why must we go without while those with clout
Don't even give a damn about
 Us as long as they have enough for themselves?
 We make them rich by making their sales
We waste our lives toiling in vain,
Pushing down doubt, ignoring pain,
 To be nothing more than something they invest in
 Making capital out of people is the gravest sin
Why go on with it all? What's the use?
It's getting harder and harder to come up with an excuse

Working class heroes don't amount to zero,
We stopped believing in them a long time ago
 They go up a little 'til they fall to the bottom and die a broken death,
 Working for every last dime to their dying breath
The rich and well-born jeer at them just as they jeer at us

When they even deign to so much as leer at us
 They act like we're lepers they're too caste-high to touch —
 But tell me, do you think what we're asking's too much?
Hell, we're not asking to thrive,
We're just trying to stay alive,
 Wanting only enough to keep body and soul together —
 We just wanna make it through this stormy weather
Hell, some of us never even thought we'd have to borrow,
But now we don't even know if we'll be eating tomorrow

We want only clothes to wear and something to be fed —
Little enough for working every day 'til we drop dead
 Surely there's more to Life than this wretched fate,
 Working for every penny, saving, and struggling against hate? —
But no; we will forever sow what others reap,
Forever make what others keep
 Work ourselves to death for just enough pay
 To live from day to day,
Go on working long past our prime, in sickness and health,
Never learning to stop chasing ever-elusive wealth,
 Go to our graves with heads low and bodies nearly broken,
 Success' door never having opened
Ever striving, always failing — a vicious cycle with no exit;
Life triumphs over us all, whether or not we triumph in it

2009

An Epitaph for American Exceptionalism
Part I

Some day, perhaps not too far down the road,
 When the fruited plain's a barren wasteland
And the amber grain's long ceased to corrode,
 A new short-lived race of conquering man
Will happen on a torn and fragile sheet,
 With a few small words blurry and faded,
At the end of some long abandoned street,
 And they'll stop, scorn the bare place they raided,
And read, in some old, long-forgotten hand,
 Vain words that will cause temporary mirth
But which they will not really understand
 And soon put aside for thoughts of more worth —
"And I'm proud to be an American" —
And they'll laugh at the vanity of man.

2009

An Epitaph for American Exceptionalism
Part II (The Last Laugh)

Long after our brief time on the stage has ended,
 A new race of mortals will find an ancient scroll
Buried in a vault long ceased to be defended,
 And they'll laugh with vain humor conceited and droll
At the words printed in an antiquated script,
 Secure in their own superiority and
Eternal fame, scarcely knowing they will be clipped
 Nearly as soon by Fate's ever-unsparing hand.
"God bless America" the tiny words will say,
 And they'll wonder what America was and tell
How poor and barren it must have been in that day
 And laugh to think God would bless any but themselves.
And the stars will shine on this empire new and vast,
Those that shone on the first and will shine on the last.

2009

Philosophical Pessimism: Constructive Misanthropy Exercises

By Mark Wong

"The life of man, solitary, poor, nasty, brutish, and short."
–Thomas Hobbes (1588-1679), Leviathan

"It is hard for thee to kick against the pricks"
–Acts 9:5, 26:14

Mark is an eighty-year-old Chinese immigrant in San Francisco. He is bitter, misanthropic, pessimistic, world-weary, hopeless, and cynical and does not suffer fools gladly. Like most misanthropes and pessimists, he is a disappointed idealist—not least because his life has been an unbroken series of disappointments, failures, catastrophes, mistakes, and regrets. Many have come from his own numerous and varied faults, but many, perhaps even most, simply stem from the utter harshness of life and man's inhumanity to man—or so he thinks. He is wise, has lived long and learned much. Long retired, he has more than enough time to think and tends to use it as he believes best—by philosophizing, which usually takes a dark turn in his blackened mind. He takes himself seriously, of course, but the first poem below shows he is not above self-mockery. He has no friends; true, he had a few in youth, but they long ago drifted away, scared by what they saw as his callousness. He certainly has a tough outer shell but prefers to think he is just being honest and forthright, unlike nearly everyone else; needless to say, he sees the mass of man as compulsive bullshitters. He is generally inclined to forgive, as he half believes their vile, savage nature prevents them from rising above their worst impulses, but their constant cruelty, inhumanity, and simple stupidity destroy his charitable nature. He lives alone; his wife, who never truly returned his love in any case, died years ago, and no one else could possibly stand to live with him—not even a dog. He writes alone in his room, late at night, in dim light. He keeps his ever-trusty drugs and alcohol—now his only friends—always within reach; they whet his melancholy muse. He also keeps glass shards and a shotgun—which he bought decades ago in disgust but has never been able to actually use—on hand in case he ever decides to end his miserable life. He has considered it many times but is always unable to muster the will, even though no one would miss him, and the world would probably not even notice. He knows this, and it makes him feel even more bitter. He prominently put his favorite quote, plus his favorite from his least favorite book, as an epigraph to his volume, which is presented in full under the assumption that anything worth doing is worth overdoing.

Dear You

Dear You:

Hi there, how are ya? I feel like shit. I tried to stop doing this — but, hell, we both know I can't quit. Life can be so mysterious, sometimes — hairs to split, pieces that won't fit. But right now I'm lonely, as lonely as can be — and I have nothing to do, other than write this song for you 'cause you're just as fucked up as me. Admit it, you're just as fucked up as me.

They say we all have a purpose — what's mine? To peddle this strife. I know it don't make any sense, but it wasn't my vote. I hope you'll buy into these words I wrote.

Now, I can write a love song like the way it's meant to be. And I can write a confession that'll set this restless soul free. I can use this piece of paper as a pulpit to relieve my misery. I deal in easy, deal in melancholy, deal in free — and maybe I'm not that good anymore, but, baby, that's just me.

Now, I know how to steal the best lines from someone else — or, if I really feel like it, I can write them myself. But don't let any of 'em tell ya they're doing it for you; it isn't true. We only do it for ourselves — to ease our guilty consciences, to ease the pain where our trouble ails. We do this when all else fails, you see — which is usually.

Most never liked me, and now some of the few who did don't like me as much. They say I've changed my ways, lost my touch. But, hell, all I've ever done is what I'm doing now — trying to relieve my boredom somehow.

I once believed in you, maybe you once believed in me, but I don't seem as profound now as you always made me out to be. I'm really just a bullshitter, as you can now so plainly see.

I'm probably a lot more like you than you care to admit. After all, how common is a pile of shit? But no, they say there's people out there who're just as fucked up as me — but, come on, I don't even have a TV.

Now, you could go and trivialize this mess. You could say I'm in distress, could say a lot of other things, too — but you're wrong about this particular piece of shit. It's gonna be a hit, goddamn you. They say there's such a thing as justice, and all my other masterpieces now lie in rot. So why the hell not?

I hate to admit it, but I'm lonely, as lonely as a solitary sailor on the sea. And I ain't got nobody in the whole world to care for me.

I'd tell all my friends, but they wouldn't believe me. They'd think I'd finally lost it completely. I'm supposed to be so tough and solitary and hard to crack. It'd break their poor little hearts to know I was a quack.

So, when you're out on your own, being beaten down by the wind, you're all alone, and you don't have a friend, remember — I don't, either. We're in the same boat, brother.

Actually, you're all I have left. You can take this from me, and it won't be considered theft. So, as a way to show my gratitude, I sat down and tried to write you this song. The words came out all wrong — but I guess it'll have to do.

So, goodbye, see ya later. Maybe by then I'll be feeling better, and we can resume our normal routine. If not — well, we'll make do, as you have just seen. I trust you'll forgive me, if I lay it on the line. That's good; I always thought you were a friend of mine.

Sincerely,

Your "favorite mistake"

2001

Young But Daily Growing

I woke up in the middle of the night
 Aroused from my dreams
In the midst of a terrible fright—
 Everything was exactly as it seems
Nothing's changed; nothing's moved
 In at least a million years
The truth was distorted, the fiction proved,
 I'm lubricating my love life with tears
If you kill one man, you're a murderer—
You know, that's what happened to her;
 And, if you kill a nation of men, you're a king—
 For you people will do anything;
But, if you kill them all, if you really break out the rod,
Then, oh, oh, oh—you're a God
 Always guessing, never knowing—
 Young but daily growing

They say Jesus walked on water—
 Well, I tried but got cold feet
I just can't live up to his standards,
 I'm more lamb than sheep;
But I've tired of this life
 And its price—so steep
I don't even have the courage now
 To venture out into the street
You know, it's been a long time
 Since I've gone to the swap meet
It was always so crowded,
 Never could find a decent seat
Now, I've done my fair share
 Of cunning and cheat,
But it's four on the floor,
 And I just lost my sheet
I don't even know where I'm going—
Young but daily growing

It's something about life,

Something about love
Something about a glimpse of greatness
Seen from above
I lost my sanity
When push came to shove
I told myself I'd never fall for
The same tricks everyone else is always scared of,
But just look what happened —
I clipped the non-existent dove
Your charms have broken many hearts,
Now you can add mine to the list
The problem with me and all the rest
Is we're blind to all but your best
We never see the flaws until after we've been kissed,
And by then it's too late; you're already pissed,
And then the blood starts flowing —
Young but daily growing

I searched in the holy books,
Searched in my Nanny
I searched in heroes and crooks,
Searched every nook and cranny —
Do you know what I found?
That everything's been written down,
It just hasn't been read
You can follow your nose straight to the holy town,
But we'd rather be spoon-fed
I found out a long time ago that wasn't for me,
I'd rather be dead;
And yet something just won't keep
These goddamn demons outta my head
Was it love, or the idea of being in love,
That seemed better than any blessing from above?
Was it a crawl, or was it a shove,
That led you to her that night?
Whatever it was, it didn't work,
I still feel the same old frights
Maybe there's no cure, just temporary spotlights glowing —
Young but daily growing

And I swore I'd never feel that way again—
What was it about you that made me act so true
  Yet wind up on the wrong end?
I thought I'd finally found something
  That made time and pain suspend,
But all the while you were dropping subtle hints
  That it was all about to splinter
I'm sorry; I just can't repent
  And admit it was nuclear winter
I still think of you, sometimes, when I lie awake at night—
  Where the hell is the tolling bell
That's supposed to rid me of your sight?
  The process is ongoing—
  Young but daily growing

I know fortune
  Is waiting to be kind,
But I can't just keep waiting
  For time out of mind
It's what's on the inside that counts—
  After all, that's where pain is
I'm sure I look all right on the outside,
  But that's not where the game is
I could never push you out of my mind,
  And now it's way too late
The last remaining embers of our love
  Have been burned at the stake by fate
Will you ever stop being so controlling?—
  Young but daily growing

You should stop this childish charade
  Of acting so shy
You know I can't even hold myself together
  When I see you walk by
How can you look without shame
  At all the men who've been in my shoes?
  I guess to you it's just a game,
  But they've been sentenced to death by the blues
There's never enough time in the day
  To say what I need to say

LIFE'S TRIUMPH by Bill R. Moore

Why don't you just get out of the way?
I have a few games of my own to play,
This is where it all comes back your way
 I always said you'd be sorry,
And today could be the day
 Open the floodgates,
This is when the tears start flowing —
Young but daily growing

I don't love you anymore,
 Maybe I never did it right;
But I'm slipping out the backdoor,
 I'm stealing away to you in the night
I know it's the same old thing all over again,
 The lion lies down with the lamb;
And I'm sure I could have killed you,
Or at least maybe thrilled you,
 But that's just the way I am
Yeah, I know it's wrong —
 In truth, I'd rather die,
But let's sing another song, boys,
 Sometimes you just can't tell the truth from a lie;
And I didn't mean to hurt you,
 I'm just a jealous guy
So let's be truthful
 Before they start squirming under the covers
 Let's tell these star-crossed, psychopathic lovers
 Why they can never have each other
Now the futile horn can start blowing —
Young but daily growing

Please don't be offended
 If I say I wish I could store you away on a shelf
You should know better than anyone
 How good you are for my health
As for her — Well, it's true
 I sometimes still think of the times we kissed;
But damn if her manic depression
 Isn't so hit and miss
You're what I've always wanted —

Why don't you come here?
You're the only one in the world
Who can ease this pain, so severe
You make it so concise and clear,
You alleviate all the fear
When I'm with you, I can set my course and steer
And forget she was ever near
I bared my wounds, and you started sewing—
Young but daily growing

You always complained you had no one
And that you couldn't let anyone near
Well, here's a toast to your problems—
Here, have another beer
There's still dark clouds and shadows that hang down,
The gloom is such we'll never completely see through
There are just so many mistakes we never can undo
Here's my advice to you—start anew
I know you're sorry, darlin'; I'm sorry, too
Well, it's cold out now, and it's snowing
Oh, my love, I must be going
I bid you adieu
So long, farewell—see you in hell
Where we'll still be young but daily growing

2001

Working on a Dream
(A Lament for My Inadequacies);
or, The Failure of Idealism

Like many young men I have
 A passionate desire for reforming the world
I thought little was right
 When into it I was hurled
And have grown ever less satisfied
 As my life has unfurled

Working on a dream,
 Right from the start
Working on a dream,
 Trying to bring the world closer to the heart

So many wrongs to right,
So many evils to fight,
So many real and perceived slights —
 How to fight it all?
 How to make injustice fall?
 I try so hard, but it just makes me feel so small

Working on a dream,
 My conscience won't let me quit
Working on a dream,
 Gotta get on with it

I'm drowning in insecurity,
Can't get over my impurity
All my concern for futurity
Can't shake this feeling of inadequacy
 I'm beginning to fear I can't pass the test,
 I'm drowning in hopelessness

Working on a dream,
 But it's falling apart

Working on a dream,
 Losing touch with what's so dear to my heart

So I bitched just like all the rest,
 Carried out duties mechanically
Seemingly stuck forever between
 Fretful apathy and complacent mediocrity
Oh, but I still can't quench
 The great longing for change that burns in me

Still working on a dream —
 Oh, to be satisfied like all the rest who don't try!
Can't stop working on a dream,
 Or have the courage of my convictions and stop living this miserable lie

All the people I admire
Whose ideas are sung by the human spirit's lofty choir —
I've always had the desire
 To add my star to your illustrious list
Oh, but greatness must be baptized in fire,
 And I can't face the tempest

Working on a dream,
 Always thought I'd make it real some day
Working on a dream,
 But it's slipping away

So now I think it's time to
 Face exactly what I am —
I'm no Redeemer or Reformer,
 I'm just the lamb
Sometimes it's hard to convince myself
 I ever even gave a damn

No longer working on a dream,
 I'm weak-willed to the core
Stopped working on a dream,
 Can't even recognize it anymore

No, I'm not really the kind

To lend a helping hand
Don't really have the courage
To stand where I should stand
O woe to he who sees what he wants to be
But can't live up to his plan!

No longer working on a dream,
Don't even have the will to do it over again
Stopped working on a dream —
Oh, what a vast gap between "is" and "might have been"!

2009

Evil Is Alive and Well

"There are many here among us who feel that life is but a joke"
–Bob Dylan, "All Along the Watchtower"

"As the hierarchy of the universe is disclosed to us, we may have to recognize this
chilling truth: if there are any gods whose chief concern is man, they cannot be very
important gods."
–Arthur C. Clarke, "Space and the Spirit of Man"

No one needs to say
Evil is alive and well today —
 It on TV, it's outside the door,
 It's too powerful for you to ignore
It's in the headlines, it's on the news,
It eats at you each time you lose,
 Leaving your soul to rot and decay —
 Evil's alive and well today

Every moment seems like a dirty trick,
Happiness comes and leaves just as quick
 When you can't see reality for all the blinding smoke
 And all your hard-won wisdom turns out to be a joke,
When you can no longer reconcile yourself to a world that isn't fair,
And the stench of human sin is more than you can bear,
 There's really nothing else to say —
 Evil's alive and well today

The pistol and Bible you dutifully keep
And the drinks and pills that help you sleep
 Won't chase away the phantoms that haunt your mind,
 Eat at your soul, and hit you from behind
All philosophy adds up to nothing,
And every inkling of human kindness reveals itself as bluffing,
 Leaving nowhere for your head to lay —
 Evil's alive and well today

Don't come to me with your problems, buddy; I got enough of my own,

LIFE'S TRIUMPH by Bill R. Moore

Life reduces every single one of us to skin and bone
 I know your trail of woe will follow you into tomorrow,
 But I'm too busy nursin' my own sorrow
Nothing I can say will bring you back from the brink,
Don't ask me what I feel or what I think
 There's only one thing anyone can say —
 Evil's alive and well today

You can live your whole life without seeing one single act of kindness,
We're cut off from each other by narcissistic blindness
 There's no use lookin' for someone's who's kind,
 We all have only one thing on our mind
Your message of mercy, pity, peace, and love
Is trampled underfoot when push comes to shove
 It looks like this is the way things are gonna stay —
 Evil's alive and well today

There are those with no trace of kindness or love,
To whom nothing is sacred on earth or above
 They'll betray you and waylay you when you think they're your friend,
 There's really no one on whom you can depend
Even those closest to you run and hide when pain comes pourin' down,
You can't even scrounge for decency at the Lost and Found
 It always turns out the same way —
 Evil's alive and well today

Science and religion both decay and rot
When you realize someone else has something you haven't got
 You can walk through your whole life ignoring your blues,
 Seeing only the good through the holes in your shoes —
But, deep down inside, you know you're livin' a lie
When you tell yourself it'll all be okay when you die
 Sooner or later, we all get lost in the gray —
 Evil's alive and well today

You can ask hard questions, but you never get an answer,
Doubt just keeps gnawing at you like cancer
 Until it hurts so much you just want to explode
 And start wond'rin' why you ever went down this road
There's no forgiveness in a world without pity,

We're all stranded in the same heartbroken city,
 And it'll always be that way —
 Evil's alive and well today

Lookin' through the papers makes you wanna cry,
 I swear no one cares if people live or die
 We're all alone on this road, drivin' blind,
 I won't destroy your illusions if you don't destroy mine
 The most we can hope for is mutual self-interest, my friend
 'Cause sometimes the only thing keepin' you alive will kill you in the end
 No one's above the fray —
 Evil's alive and well today

You say some are worse than others, but I say it's all moot,
 We're all burned out from happiness' pursuit
 We go 'round and 'round in circles 'till we burn out and die,
 Secure in the knowledge we did it all for a lie
 Bitterness hits hardest when we realize we were right all along,
 Death undoes life's dividing of weak from strong
 Sooner or later, we all gotta pay —
 Evil's alive and well today

You'll never see truth reflected in the human eye,
 We're stuck in a meaningless universe and don't know why
 You always pick yourself up when you're about to give up and die,
 But other times you wonder why you even try
 There's just something repulsive about failure that makes us hope against
      hope,
 But we eventually all hang ourselves on the same tangled rope
 It's the only way —
 Evil's alive and well today

You can curse the non-existent God every time you look up at the sky
 When you realize we all go the same place when we die
 There's nothin' to be thankful for and little reason to hope,
 But we all find a lie we can believe in and cope
 We're drownin' at the bottom of a well full of lies,
 Long past the point of lookin' for truth in each other's eyes
 And what else can I say? —
 Evil's alive and well today

"Forgive and forget," a wise man once said,
But I just can't get these Romantic dreams outta my head
 We shouldn't be too hard on each other; we all wear the same yoke,
 We're all victims of the same cosmic joke
One day we all wake up to find
We're the playthings of gods malicious or blind,
 And that's all anyone can say —
 Evil's alive and well today

2008

The Kindness of Strangers

"Whoever you are – I have always depended on the kindness of strangers."
–Tennessee Williams, A Streetcar Named Desire

"Who knows what evil lurks in the hearts of men?"
–Walter B. Gibson, The Shadow

The kindness of strangers is one of the great American myths –
 You may think you can trust others,
But you can't trust anyone you can't bring down with your fists –
 No friend or acquaintance, stranger or brother

Evil lurks in the hearts of us all,
 There's no denying this basic truth
For private reasons great and small
 We sometimes let it loose

Some of us can keep it buried forever,
 Keep that lid on tight –
But others can hardly hold together,
 They're just itching for a fight

We've all had times where it's hard to hold back,
 Where we could just barely keep it inside –
The slightest thing could've caused us to crack,
 But somehow the evil impulses were denied

Who can deny they've had a hard time holding it down,
 That they've had to force it to stay put –
Anything could've set it off; the slightest movement or sound,
 And our opponents would have been crushed underfoot

Others have a harder time keeping it in check,
 It slips out from time to time –
They might break some poor fool's neck,
 Or let loose with a confrontational line

It just comes out of them, despite their best intentions,

LIFE'S TRIUMPH by Bill R. Moore

There doesn't seem to be much they can do about it—
None of our peaceful efforts and pacifistic inventions
Can keep them from the need to shout it

Others don't try to hold back at all
But let their evil intentions loose on the world,
Causing great empires to fall
Once their tragic actions have been unfurled

You can't trust them for one second,
They'll kill their own mother if it benefits them
They might rape you if they find you decadent
Or just kill you on a whim

Some people are just plain evil,
We all agree on this —
Yet who has not felt the impulse to lie or kill
With either sword or kiss?

I'm telling you, buddy, we're all living on the brink,
Any little thing could set us off
People are generally peaceful, we like to think,
But no one is really quite so soft

Well, I look like someone you can just push around,
Like so many others in this life —
But I'm not nearly as nice or forgiving as I sound,
I've seen enough heartache and strife

If you fuck with me, you'd better be prepared,
Because I'm gonna fuck you back —
No doubt about it, you're gonna be scared
When I mount my counterattack

This is nothing unique in me,
I'm the same as everyone else
Before you test the limits of others' decency,
You should take a good, hard look at yourself

I don't expect you to trust me

'Cause I sure as hell don't trust you
There's no security,
  You'll never be in the clear 'til you make it through

There's no hiding out, no crossing fingers,
  No getting off easily
No matter where you go, evil always lingers
  As long as you're within reach of humanity

There are many reasons someone might want to do you in —
  Hell, deep down, people just ain't kind —
You might piss them off unknowingly, even a friend,
  Or just be in the wrong place at the wrong time

Each day could be your last,
  You just can't take anything for granted
If you look carefully at your own past,
  You'll see the seeds of evil are those from which we're planted

Young and old, rich and poor —
  We're all alike in this
There's just no denying the truth anymore,
  Each human promise is a potential Judas kiss

When that anger comes bubbling up to the surface, man,
  You better get out of the way —
I wouldn't wanna be alone with anyone in this land
  Who lets self-control slip away

How many potential killers lie in hiding
  Among us right now as we speak?
How many have sins they aren't confiding?
  How many are truly meek?

We all know the truth
  But do our best to deny it
If you still need proof,
  Just look at the headlines for those who defy it

I don't trust my fellow humans for one minute,

LIFE'S TRIUMPH by Bill R. Moore

Not even as far as I can throw them
Anyone will crack, if you push them to their limit,
It doesn't matter how well you know them

I don't open my door to anyone,
 Don't let anyone intrude
You may think letting others in is no harm done,
 But it could be Alex and his droogs

It's hard to abandon belief in basic human decency,
 But it just isn't borne out by facts
I watch the news and my own street every day and only see
 Still more reasons to watch my back

It's time for us to face the truth
 That people just ain't no good
In the wisdom of old age and the innocence of youth,
 We all struggle to keep evil under the hood

Maybe you can ignore some of the signs that tell you so,
 Maybe you can push your doubts back to a distance place —
But it's hard to ignore the rock thrown through your window
 Or the fist in your face

Maybe you can overlook some of the wars being fought
 And convince yourself reality is otherwise draped —
But who can overlook their son being shot
 Or daughter being raped?

Man is the lowest animal,
 Even the most despicable insect has us beat
We alone kill only to be cruel,
 So why should I trust that man in the street?

We torture and murder, rape and steal,
 Sometimes we try to justify but often just shrug our shoulders
Every street's a potential killing field,
 And it doesn't get any safer as you get older

Solitude is lonely and hard,

But we can't deny these realities exist
It's never safe to let others in our yard,
 Why even take the risk?

Sure, we all think we know at least a few
 Who can take decency's test and easily pass —
Hell, though, I don't know about you,
 But I'd rather cover my own ass

Self-control is volatile, easy to corrode,
 No one lives forever in peace's lofty loft
Each of us is a ticking time bomb just waiting to explode,
 Better not set it off...

2007

Is It Really Any Wonder, Baby?

Well, I'm half-crazy most of the time,
 An' all crazy the rest
I got a hundred heavy sorrows, mama,
 Weighin' down my breast
I got a thousand people pullin' me different ways
 An' a million things I can't get off my chest
Is it really any wonder, baby,
 That I ain't at my best?

I know I lose,
 Yes, an' I know I win—
Yet I know I didn't call for
 The shape I'm in
You can chase all your sorrows away, man,
 But they'll just keep comin' back again
Is it really any wonder, baby,
 That I ain't got no friend?

Wakin' up in the middle of the day
 An' goin' to bed at 8:00 a.m.,
Readin' Hugo an' Dostoyevsky an' knowin'
 You'll never be as great as them,
Thinkin' 'bout how great Jesus was an' knowin'
 You can never be like him
Is it really any wonder, baby,
 That my lightbulb's gettin' dim?

Listenin' to the crickets chirpin'
 An' the cold wind knockin' 'gainst my windowpane,
Searchin' for inspiration an' realizin'
 I got love for you, an' it's all in vain
There ain't no other passengers, honey,
 I'm the lone rider on this lonesome train
Is it really any wonder, baby,
 That I can't break free of this chain?

Yes, I know I can't understand you—

Hell, I can't even understand myself
Every time I look over somethin' I've written,
I feel like it was written by someone else
There just ain't much I can say anymore,
I think it's startin' to affect my health
Is it really any wonder, baby,
That nothin' I write ever sells?

Well, I know it must've been me this time,
That I couldn't have been in the right
I guess that's what happens when you starve yourself
An' then stay up all night
Cursin' your insomnia an' sleepin' pills
An' readin' The Bible by a forty-watt light
Is it really any wonder, baby,
That I'm not up for the fight?

Well, I'm talkin' to myself an' cursin' my fate,
Rollin' up dope in a paper bag
Searchin' for the origins of my love an' hate,
Lightin' up an' takin' a drag
They just found my father in the swimmin' pool,
An' now my mom's an old hag
Is it really any wonder, baby,
That I'm sufferin' perpetual lag?

My sense of self has gone down the drain,
My love of humanity's walked out the door
I just can't go back where I used to be,
Lord, I just don't feel that way anymore
They say there's always somethin' to fall back on,
But you can't fall back where you fell before
Is it really any wonder, baby,
That even breathin' is gettin' to be a chore?

Well, sometimes I feel I'm near the end,
I swear I could almost kill myself sometimes
I been livin' vicariously on a steady diet
Of weed, cocaine, an' wine
Everything that used to be precious to me

No longer even seems to be mine
Is it really any wonder, baby,
 That I tell everyone I'm doin' fine?

Well, I know I've made some bad decisions,
 But, hell, I couldn't please 'em all
No matter what I did, everyone hated me,
 An', off-balance, I found love the only place to fall;
But I know you can't come to rescue me
 Every time you hear me call
Is it really any wonder, baby,
 That I've built up a wall?

Well, I had just about convinced myself
 That I no longer gave a damn
I kept tellin' myself I hadn't been this happy
 Since the end of Vietnam —
But I swear I left a piece of myself back there,
 That what I was is no longer what I am
Is it really any wonder, baby,
 That I identify with the Lamb?

Well, I guess I'll be leavin' now,
 I figure it's about time I gave up
My creativity's gone to hell,
 An' the whole damn world's gone corrupt
I lost the best thing I ever had,
 An', damn it, I don't even give a fuck
An' is it really any wonder, baby,
 That I've had enough?

2006

Me or Him (An Apology for Capitalism)

Well, I've never had any illusions about human nature,
 People will turn on you the moment it benefits them
Issues that once enjoyed community stature
 Have a way of becoming your own problem —
And sometimes I have to fight against it, you know,
 In this world of sink or swim
I'm sorry, but he just had to go,
 It was either me or him

Sure I've cheated, sure I've lied —
 And I'd expect the same from you
We do what we must to get by,
 Everyone else does it, too
I've said what I've had to say,
 Sometimes you have to go out on a limb
I regret all the foolish games we play,
 But it was either me or him

All these lies people sell,
 We swallow them whole
We buy them up so well,
 And it eats away at our soul —
But I'm not goin' down without a fight,
 No, I won't be pushed off the rim
In this world might makes right,
 And it's either me or him

You can't complain about the fist in your face,
 Or the other blows that have been hurled
You'll lose the race if you stay in your place
 In this dog-eat-dog world
In this land of conditions, I'm not above suspicion,
 Buddy, the prospects look pretty grim
You can hire the best, or use your own intuition,
 But it's either me or him

Well, we trip over each other on the way to paradise,

There ain't no stoppin' on this road
If you so much as look me in the eyes,
 You'll be breakin' the sacred code
"Depersonalization" and "alienation" are the latest buzz words,
 I'd say the future looks pretty dim
Hell, man, haven't you heard?
 It's either me or him

We bite the bullet
 And hope the other guy trips along the way
This isn't the place for your sentimental bullshit,
 You must've gone the wrong way
I know you don't trust me; you know I don't trust you,
 This is the real world, not some fuckin' sim
I hope my god can forgive me for what I have to do
 'Cause it's either me or him

There are only two kinds of people in life —
 The quick and the dead
So what if we cause each other strife,
 We do what we must to stay ahead;
'Cause it's either black or white,
 There's no fat to trim
There is no wrong or right,
 It's either me or him

We push each other out of the way, cut in line,
 Trample others beneath our feet
If you don't, you get left behind,
 Won't be able to make ends meet
You say you got troubles, buddy — well,
 That ain't my problem
Show me someone who don't, hell —
 Besides, it's either me or him

They say nice guys finish last,
 And there ain't no shortcuts in this rat race
Don't ask for help; you can kiss my ass
 If you slip up, you might lose your place
There ain't no handouts, man,

This is capitalism
You grab up all you can and keep it in hand
'Cause it's either me or him

They say you get what you pay for,
 And success don't come easily
They ain't gonna open you any doors,
 You won't get anything for free
You can look for your reflection in the broken glass,
 There ain't no rainbow prism—
'Cause, when things come to pass,
 It's either me or him

If you fall along the way
 And need some help or assistance,
If you can't make it another day,
 'Can't stand all the resistance—
Well, I'm sorry, buddy; that's just how it is,
 It's either sink or swim
You can fold your cards or get pissed,
 But it's either me or him

Don't even bother askin' anyone for help,
 They'll just leave ya feelin' numb
If you can't make it all by yourself,
 You shouldn't have even come
They might sell ya a house, sell ya a new car,
 But the odds of getting help are slim
Sorry, buddy—that's just how things are
 'Cause it's either me or him

Better not close your eyes; better not even blink,
 You might slip a little off your pace
Things can change quicker than you think,
 Better not give up your place
I know it makes you mad; just go ahead and shout it,
 But no one gives a damn about your whim
What the hell do you expect me to do about it?
 It's either me or him

If you wanna change things, rearrange things,
 You'll have to cause a revolution
'Cause we're livin' under the freedom that freedom brings,
 And there ain't no easy solution
Change has to come from the bottom,
 The top ain't gonna let ya get at them
You'll have to get them right where you want 'em
 'Cause it's either me or him

You know, I really like you, buddy — I really, really do,
 But I just ain't willin' to accept second-best
Who knows, maybe you even like me, too,
 But I hafta treat ya just like all the rest
There's no friendship in this world; love's mighty hard to get,
 Your hopes are pretty fuckin' slim
You think you've seen it all, but you ain't seen nothin' yet
 'Cause it's either me or him

Don't even bother lookin' out for me,
 I ain't lookin' out for you
Don't hold your breath for harmony,
 Just keep on doin' what you do
You watch your back; I'm watchin' mine,
 The situation looks pretty grim
We're all walkin' on a razor-thin line
 'Cause it's either me or him

You know, I'd really like to help you —
 I really, really would —
But all my bills are due;
 Sorry, buddy, I'd help ya if I could
There ain't no easy way outta this game,
 All roots lead back to the same old stem
You can die in obscurity or win your way to fame,
 But it's either me or him

Why are you starin' at me, buddy —
 Don't you know this is war?
There ain't nothin' cute or funny,
 Just the same old shit we've dealt with before

Sorry, buddy, "love thy neighbor" is out of fashion,
 Now it's either sink or swim
Don't look for understanding or compassion,
 It's either me or him

So long, buddy, I've got to go —
 What the future holds for us no one can tell;
But I'm tired of you steppin' on my toes,
 I'll see you in either heaven or hell
There's nothin' you can do for me; I can't do nothin' for you,
 We're all working on our own problem
Maybe some day there'll be something new,
 But right now it's either me or him

2007

Something to Believe In Part II

I've searched all my life for answers,
 Now I feel like I'm done
I don't care that I haven't answered any of 'em,
 I'm almost glad the race is run
Well, I'm half in love with easeful death,
 Life's just not any fun
I've given up hope that someone will ever come and save me,
 I keep finding myself staring longer and longer at that gun...

Now I turn to you, who are so much better at searching —
 Oh, tell me where the answer lies!
Could it be that I might find it
 Swimming in the depths of your eyes?
Or perhaps you have buried it
 Somewhere deep between your thighs?
I just don't know what to say or do anymore,
 It seems faith and hope are wearing a disguise

I need something to believe in,
 Some kind of god above
Give me something to believe in,
 Some kind of hope or love

I've watched everything I ever believed in
 Fall apart one by one,
And all the friends I ever had are gone
 Now that the day is done
I just can't stand the pain anymore,
 I think I'm gonna turn and run
I've wasted half my life fighting
 Wars that can't be won

I might open up to you, but I probably won't,
 I just don't feel like talking anymore
There are things I could say, but I don't,
 On everyone else I've shut the door
I quit trying to figure things out a long time ago,

Quit trying to figure out what this life is for
If you ask me what I'm living for, I'll say, "I don't know" —
It doesn't tell you much, but honesty cuts to the core

I need something to believe in,
 Some kind of god above
Give me something to believe in,
 Some kind of hope or love

I used to have hope and ambition,
 But keeping up such pretences is just too tough
I've given up trying to convince myself I'm still happy,
 The world's just much too rough
I'm choking on the bitter fruit of happiness' pursuit,
 I think it's about time I called my own bluff
'Cause nothing much excites me anymore,
 And all the things I used to believe in are no longer quite enough

I regret the past, I've given up on today,
 And have little hope for tomorrow
You say you ain't made many mistakes, babe —
 Well, I have extra, so you can borrow
I'm not trying to justify or defend decisions
 That have led to other people's sorrow —
But, hell, babe, I think we can both agree playing this blame game
 Doesn't get anyone very far, no?

I need something to believe in,
 Some kind of god above
Give me something to believe in,
 Some kind of hope or love

Well, I think I'll just give up now,
 I'm folding my cards
I just can't be bothered to give a shit anymore,
 This vain pursuit of happiness is just too hard
I ain't keeping no secrets anymore,
 I have nothing more to guard
You say you don't need me but continue to bleed me,
 I wish you'd just end the farce

LIFE'S TRIUMPH by Bill R. Moore

I can't give you no easy answers, babe,
 No matter how long you continue to prod
You know, deep down, I've always thought
 Your behavior was a little odd
You can believe in your heroes and your miracles,
 Your religion and your god —
But don't tell me about it; I can live without it,
 I've had enough of the whole façade

I need something to believe in,
 Some kind of god above
Give me something to believe in,
 Some kind of hope or love

I long ago gave up trying to decide
 What's wrong and what's right
It doesn't matter very much, babe,
 We're all in the same fight
There's no glee, but you're with me,
 And I guess that'll have to do for tonight
I no longer doubt that I'll never figure it out,
 But my conscience makes me keep trying out of spite

I apologize to everyone I've hurt,
 I'm sorry I let you down
You were fools to trust me
 As I'm sure you've finally found —
But I trusted you, and you let me down, too,
 I guess what goes around really does come around
It's the same old hard luck story, nothing new,
 We all wear the same thorny crown

And there's nothing I can believe in,
 No kind of god above
I apologize to all those I've been deceivin'
 With vain fantasies of hope and love

2007

The Complicated Futility of Ignorance

There's some people I like,
 But they're few and far between
Most are too stupid,
 Some are too mean
Many are hopeless cases,
 But some are just green
Ignorance is excusable,
 It can be cured and dispersed
Stupidity is another degree,
 But apathy is worse

 What good lurks in the hearts of men?
 None, to the power of ten
Just when you think they're getting better,
 They disappoint you again
Right when they start to surprise you,
 They recede into sin
Worldly pleasures are just too much,
They can't resist the temptation of a touch
 Materialism is a vice—
 You get what you want, but you pay the price
Starving yourself is a noble stealth,
But hedonism just turns out to be too much

Fate can seem unfair sometimes
 When you're taking a beating
Nature deals her cards so oddly,
 She must surely be cheating
I tried to hold out some hope
 But just ended up conceding
When every ray of light
 Turned out to be defeating
I thought I'd found an answer,
 Thought I'd found a cure—
Yeah, I thought I could cure cancer,
 But now I'm not so sure
When every single morsel of truth I dangle

Just wastes away on the lure

And now I don't know what to think,
I had it all, but someone robbed the bank
I gave you everything I had —
It wasn't much, just a little human touch —,
But was it askin' too much to expect thanks?
I don't know what to do now,
Not even the Well of Knowledge is drier than my tank
Not that I ever had much,
But that was before my fortune shrank
There's not even enough left now
For scavengers to take
I could go jump in the lake,
But I don't even have a bone left to break;
And I wish I could help you
As you edge ever closer to the brink,
But there is no missing link;
And all I can do is watch helplessly
As you slowly sink

Tottering on the edge of madness,
You're on a permanent binge
All I am is overcome by sadness,
Just another night on the lunatic fringe;
And you might say you want to kill me,
But, darlin', there ain't no revenge;
And they won't let a woman kill you here —
No, not as long as I can still singe
Now, you might mount an attack,
You might challenge and thrill me;
But you can't break my back,
The most you can do is kill me

For I will still be standing here —
Alone yet enlightened —
While you and all your friends are dying in hordes,
Dropping like flies, and frightened
Now, I'm not so inclined as to believe
There is no hope for us yet —

Why, if not for suicide obsession,
 We might yet repent;
But, when they said that awful word "quit,"
I wondered what they meant,
I wondered what they meant

It's not that we don't have the tools to save ourselves,
 It's just that our resources are spent
All the money in the world, my friend,
 Ain't gonna help us one cent
For, when all is lost,
 We will pay the price,
But we will not count the cost
I believed you when you said you loved me,
 I believed you still more when you said the love had died—
But all the lies in the world, darlin',
 Couldn't equal the river of tears I've cried
Since you've been gone,
And there's just no point in goin' on

Love, like death, will happen in the end,
No one can get by with just a friend
 You'll find out soon enough; it won't be long
Lots of people like to believe they can perceive,
 But no one in the world is that strong
So you better figure it out now
 Or be left all alone,
Because there is no help—merely a yelp
 When you're sinking like a stone

I've tried to love these idiots,
 Tried so hard—but no dice
I managed to overlook their faults and everything,
 But you just can't be nice
I tried staying together,
 Tried being alone
 I tried it all—but no bones;
I guess that's what happens
 When you should have known

LIFE'S TRIUMPH by Bill R. Moore

Don't just call me a pessimist,
 Try an' read between the lines
If you do, I guarantee you,
 You'll see more than you expect to find;
So take these words to heart—
Let them be your start,
 Though there is no solid rock to touch
Let it stand as a shining beacon of integrity,
 Though we all know there really is no such
What are my crimes against humanity?
Despite their insanity,
 I think I love them too much

2001

After Us, the Deluge

I've seen a lot of things by now,
 I've been living this life, after all
I've seen a million faces,
 I've heard a million calls
I've seen many rise up,
 And I've seen many stumble and fall
I'm in the middle ground,
 Sometimes I hit the wall
I often wonder about the meaning of life,
 Other times I think it doesn't matter at all
We have all our options,
 They take them away
They give us no choices,
 Just one shade of gray
Well, I don't dare stutter,
 And I don't dare blink
Maybe in the next life, motherfucker,
 I'll be able to hear myself think,
But I'm more than just an object you can use—
After us, the deluge

It's hard to think for yourself sometimes,
 You must obey authority
You try to be an individual,
 But they just get in your head so easily
Sometimes I look in the mirror
 And swear it's someone else, not me
Although I search myself,
 It's always someone else I see
Well, masters make rules
For the wise and for fools—
 But in the end it doesn't matter
As long as you're considered cool;
But you and I, my friend, are out of luck,
 We're swimming in the drowning pool;
And I know what you mean
 When you say you can't take the heat

LIFE'S TRIUMPH by Bill R. Moore

Sometimes it's hard to convince yourself
 You're more than just a piece of meat
For someone else to abuse —
After us, the deluge

 And life, it just gets so hard to swallow —
It's hard to swim in a sea
 Where lies wallow
I say, "You lead the way,
 And I'll follow"
I just can't find the truth by myself,
Sometimes you have to rely on someone else
Yes, the sea is terrible,
 I'm in a jerkin' boat
I just don't know what to do anymore,
 Don't know how to vote
 No, I still haven't read the letter you wrote,
 I'm tryin' to read that other person's note
You seem half-right, and she seems half-right,
 Together, you've gotten my goat
Well, on the sea it gets hard
 To keep your head above the moat
Some people sink or swim,
 Others just float
None of us are excused —
After us, the deluge

And soon change will come,
 Things won't be like they was
I keep on thinkin' somethin's comin',
 But it never does
Where in the hell are all the answers,
 Where are all the reasons why?
I've been lookin' to the wind,
 Lookin' to the sky —
But nothin' grabs my attention
 Or catches my eye
I went and asked an old man
 'Cause experience makes you wise,
But he couldn't tell me anything

I hadn't already stopped believing in—
 I got no use for those kind of guys
Trials and tribulations don't
 Make it any easier to get through hell,
All they do is teach you
 Another million ways to fail;
 And they got nothin' more to sell
Except the blues—
After us, the deluge

Somewhere out there, there's a man
 Who truly does need you—
Far past the frozen corridors of lust
 Where all the Romeos bleed for you
All of them will say
 They agreed with you,
 Any of them could seed you—
But how many do you think
 Would really heed you?
Well, maybe all of 'em,
 Maybe all of 'em through the years—
But who else but me comes to you
 With a garden of freshly-cut tears?
Surely you would appreciate them more
 Than a joint and a couple a-beers…
But who knows? This isn't Easy Street
There are no small feats,
 Only huge—
After us, the deluge

Well, look at all the men sitting there—
 They see only the good through the holes in their shoes
Even though they have nothing
 Left to live up to,
 They've been sentenced to death by the blues
Well, there's a palace with five thousand dirty windows
 Where the plaster on the walls is beginning to crack
There's a desolate place where loneliness goes
 When she needs to take a few steps back
I don't want to go either place,

They both scare me to death
That wind you sucked from my lungs, baby,
 It was my dyin' breath;
And I have nowhere to go now,
 They're selling tickets to my refuge —
 After us, the deluge

I once had a rosy-cheeked girl,
 They called her the Goddess of Gloom
They say she could take the most optimistic man
 And send him off to his doom
I don't know if it's true —
 I was always lyin' up in her room,
Hopin' against all hope
 That she'd come and join me soon;
But they're gonna have mass suppers when I die,
 They're gonna burn all the holy books
And let the fire rise to the sky
People are gonna cry,
 There'll be truckloads of apathetic and decadent fans
Suddenly motivated to try
 Well, I tried to impress you,
But I told a lie —
 It's really just the norm
I'm just like you — and him, too;
And so the tired undertaker,
 He blows a futile horn
He's got nothing left to lose —
After us, the deluge

2001

Stop Me If You Think You've Heard This One Before (A Cosmic Joke in Three Parts)

"As flies to wanton boys are we to th' gods;
They kill us for their sport"
–*William Shakespeare,* King Lear

Part I: History's Vicious Cycle

We live in uncertain times
 Just like all before us—
There's a yearning undefined,
 And the powers that be ignore us
We don't know where the future lies
 Or what we're living for,
We wonder if they'll ever listen to our cries—
 Stop me if you think you've heard this one before

Thoreau cried out against materialism,
 Socrates lamented the demise of youth
Many have thought they'd seen the greatest schism
 And had convincing evidence as proof
Emerson lashed out against the demise of religion,
 The Puritans thought they were overrun with whores;
Each generation comes to the same conclusions—
 Stop me if you think you've heard this one before

They say history repeats itself,
 That past catastrophes are bound to reoccur
You and I and everyone else
 Are caught in the midst of this blinding blur
Every era has the masterpiece of literature
 And the war to end all wars,
Of these things they are sure—
 Stop me if you think you've heard this one before

We all think we're experiencing something new,
 But it's really just the same old shit

All the clichés you've heard are true,
 And there's nothing you can do about it
Put aside all your delusions of grandeur,
 The past has already opened the door
We all like to think we have something newer —
 Stop me if you think you've heard this one before

Part II: A Human Dialogue

We can try to rise above it all we want,
 But we're still stuck in the same old trap
The same old ghosts continue to haunt,
 And we're guided by the same old maps
We can try to break out of it and push ahead,
 Try to find out what the whole thing's for,
But all attempts at progress are long dead —
 Stop me if you think you've heard this one before

Though we continue to struggle and scrape,
 Our tenuous connection to success long ago broke
It's a vicious cycle from which we cannot escape,
 Sometimes it all seems like some kind of colossal joke —
But there's nothing we can do about it,
 No way we can score
I know you disagree; just go ahead and shout it —
 Stop me if you think you've heard this one before

I know you think you can rise above it,
 But you're no better than me —
Much less all the others who've tried to shove it
 Throughout all the centuries
I'm sorry, man, the gods just don't care,
 Our pleas they routinely ignore
No one told us life was fair —
 Stop me if you think you've heard this one before

In this life, the masters make the rules,
 We all must follow their lead
The wise and the fools,

They're all given the same creed
Do you think anything makes you stand out
 Above all those who failed in days of yore?
Some day, you'll see what it's all about—
 Stop me if you think you've heard this one before

You can try to scale majestic heights,
 But fate will just smack you back down again
I know it just doesn't seem right,
 But no one is allowed to win
I'm carrying the same burden as you,
 The same one we all deplore
You may not want to believe me, but it's true—
 Stop me if you think you've heard this one before

You can curse the cosmos
 And rage against the machine
Others choose to doze,
 Satisfied with what they've seen
It doesn't matter which path you choose in the end,
 Doesn't matter which road or door
We're all trapped in Time that has chosen to suspend—
 Stop me if you think you've heard this one before

You can take your wrath out on the gods
 Or the powers that be
Either way, there's no beating the odds,
 None of us are free
I've tried and failed, man,
 Now it's time for you to add to the score
Go ahead and play your hopeless hand—
 Stop me if you think you've heard this one before

All your efforts are futile,
 Time and Fate grind us all down in the end
All your intelligence and skill
 Will never serve to mend
We're all going down, friend,
 You and I are but two more
It's a process that will never end—

Stop me if you think you've heard this one before

It doesn't matter if you're a king or a dog,
 We're all dealt the same losing hand
You're just one microscopic cog
 In the catastrophic plan
Don't come to me looking for a reason—
 What would you do that for?
Although giving up is surely treason—
 Stop me if you think you've heard this one before

I ain't here to give you no easy answers—
 Who are you that I should have to lie?
All these forces that eat at us like cancers
 Are enough to make our hearts shrivel up and die
The cause is hopeless; the game is fixed,
 They've already shut the door
You say you're tired of their dirty tricks—
 Stop me if you think you've heard this one before

Part III: A Divine Dialogue

Stop me if you think you've heard this one before—
 Humanity has been fucked over
They're tied down by hate, religion, and war,
 And now they're looking for some kind of closure
They look to the sky; they look to the gods—
 They're always looking to someone else
I've always thought their behavior was odd,
 For they have no one to blame but themselves

2007

Intro (Soliloquy)/A Better Failure

Bartenders lying in a pool of blood
Your feet are heavy, caked in mud
There's no use giving up now; it's time to admit defeat
Oh, God damn! you just did it right here in the street
And no one speaks English, and everything is broken
And the Fat Lady's sung, and the Devil hath spoken
And it's falling apart, and you gotta go back to the start
And you just pierced a goddamn arrow through my motherfucking heart
And no one brings anything small into a bar around here
They're all too busy smoking Kashmir and drinking beer
But there's nothing left to look at, nothing left to fear
The hand of God is drawing near
Well, by God, I just shed a tear
I am the Prophet, and you are the Seer
I'm gonna take you, babe; get over here!
And I just took your heart in my hand
And crushed the son of a bitch like a snapped rubber band
And, by God, if the damn thing wasn't a heavy load
My heart just keeps on poundin'; I don't know why it don't explode
And I just can't stand this shit anymore; I've seen that movie, too
It's the greatest cure for insomnia since the moon turned blue
And now I just don't know what I'm gonna do
Our days are through; let's move on to something new
This is the end of the road, babe; everything's become clear
I'm gonna take you, babe; get over here!

You're mad at the world,
Sick of the dirty tricks it's hurled
 You've been suffering so long under the shadow of doubt
That you're just dying to get out and let happiness be unfurled
You're tired of the darkness,
 You're dying to see the light
No one can ever tell the difference anymore
 Between wrong and right
Things I could once distinguish so easily
 Are no longer black and white;

And you say you have all the answers,
 But you're keeping them for your own stash —
 Well, you can kiss my ass
We need a better failure
 'Cause this one's running out of gas

Oh, I've loved you ever since the moment
 I laid eyes on your beautiful face
I lost myself and everything else
 In the depths of our first sweet, warm embrace
Ah, but things change, don't they?
Times'll get strange, won't they?
Well, I'm still holding your hand,
 Walking down the road
My heart just keeps on pounding,
 I don't know why it don't explode
Well, they crucified Jesus,
 Put him up on a cross
Hope began to corrode,
 And it's our loss
The blow struck us straight to the heart;
 And we need a better failure
'Cause this one's falling apart

Oh, babe, it ain't no lie —
 I didn't attempt to save you,
I didn't even try
 I think about it sometimes; I regret —
 I shuffle around and fret,
 I worry and sweat
I try so hard, but I just can't quit —
 Still, I always just begin to break down and cry,
Happiness can turn to torture
 In the blink of an eye;
But we need a better failure
 'Cause this one's left us high and dry

Let me question authority,
 I carry a big stick
You may be up now, buddy,

But you can be down just as quick
Confusion and dust are suffocating us,
 And it's beginning to get thick
No, nothing's changed much—
 Time's still elusive, love's still slick
Your pussy's still loose,
 And I still have a short dick
I can't see past my own two eyes
 For kicking against the pricks—
My only defense is to laugh;
 But we need a better failure
'Cause this one's breaking in half

Well, I've begun to fear
 There's really no help we can bring
The answers all add up to the same old lie,
 And your holy books don't mean a thing
Oh, I could listen to you all day,
 But your words soon turn into a meaningless ring
The mountains are sinking now,
 The sparrows are beginning to fall
It's like that staggering account
Of the Sermon on the Mount
 That I don't pretend to understand at all
What happened to our innocence?
 It shriveled up and died;
And we need a better failure
 'Cause this one's cut and dried

Now, I could write a song
 With more hooks than a fishing boat
I could do any goddamn thing you asked me to,
 But I still couldn't carry a note,
 And people still wouldn't know which way to vote
I'm gonna put on my dunce cap,
 Gonna slip into my long black coat
Forget about having a subtle message,
 I'm going straight for your throat
Some say I can't carry a tune in a bucket—
 Well, that's okay,

LIFE'S TRIUMPH by Bill R. Moore

Seems to me there's no other way;
And I'm still looking for the day
When beauty will cease to decay
I've been bummin' around from Pluto to Tibet,
Still haven't found it yet,
But I keep on looking anyway
Well, the rope the Lord's given us,
It's tattered and frayed;
And we need a better failure
'Cause this one's corroded and decayed

It's true you don't grow older,
You just grow colder
Some people turn mellow,
Others get bolder;
But it's hard to grow, I know—
Here, I'm offering you my shoulder,
So quit your damn weeping; don't be sad
It's more than I ever had,
You should be glad
Your lack of gratitude
Is starting to make me mad
All aging does
Is make you more accustomed to failure,
It doesn't do anything else;
But we need a better failure
'Cause this one's falling back on itself

The nature of failure
Is such that it continues
It just keeps changing forms,
Finding different venues
It picks on everyone,
No one is safe from its terrible, screaming sound
If you managed to escape last time,
It'll come back and bite you on the ass this time around
Well, I listened to you lecture
About love and hate—
That's all very well—but, goddamn, bro,
I didn't come to hear you pontificate

You don't even believe your own shit,
 I can tell by your eyes
Your sermons are the greatest cure
 For insomnia ever devised;
And we need a better failure,
 This one's worse than we realized

Well, I finally heard the Ultimate Answer,
 The unpardonable truth—
That long, drawn-out composition
 You can't reveal to the ears of youth;
And it confirmed what I'd long ago
 Begun to suspect—
That it don't amount to anything more
 Than what the broken glass reflects
Okay, so you can put away your ambitions now
 And live like you want to live
All hope has faded to nothingness,
 "Progress" is a pejorative
Don't even worry your pretty little head over it now,
 All chances for improvement are gone
Just forget the past, forget the future,
Your healing herb, and your miracle cure—
 Just keep movin' on,
Just keep movin' on—it's all you can do,
And soon we'll be through;
 'Cause we need a better failure,
This one won't do

Yes, I listened to your revelation,
 It didn't take too long
You said you just couldn't stand it anymore,
You're sick of being alone
Let's be alone together,
 See if we're that strong
Well, all right—that's fine with me,
The only thing is I just don't see
 How we're supposed to get along
When, after all, you eschew the same old saw,
 And I still don't feel I belong

Good God, I'm already suffering,
 And I haven't even done anything wrong;
And we need a better failure,
 'Till the final solution comes along

2001

Tryin' to Get to Heaven

I started out lonely,
 Ended up the same
I had a few breaks in-between,
 But they just keep you playing the game
What is it that keeps us ridin'
 On the same old lonesome train?
There's so much to lose
 And so little to gain
Our sufferings are many,
 Our pleasures a motley few
We just keep on askin' ourselves
 What it is we're gonna do
 To stop the pain
 I thought at first I'd ask you,
But we all know this train
 Don't stop there anymore
I'm just tryin' to get to heaven
 Before they close the door

My baby left me
 On a dark and stormy night
The hardest thing was that, deep down inside,
 I knew she was right
I still look for her sometimes,
 But she's nowhere in sight
It still fills me with dread,
 Still fills me with fright,
And I say I won't go back to her —
 But, you know, I just might
It's hard to hate something
 You once held in such a lofty light —
But I have to get over her,
 Have to erase this blight
So, if you see that girl comin',
Don't pay her any mind
She's nothin' — just an' old flame of mine,
 Nothing more

And here I am tryin' to get to heaven
Before they close the door

They say we're getting a raise next month —
Good; maybe we'll make enough to eat
I'm thinkin' about livin' in a homeless shelter,
Sure would beat bein' on the street
You keep on tellin' me you're gonna make it,
Gonna stand on your own two feet —
But the bats in luck's belfry have been summoned
To ensure your invincible defeat
The road ain't gettin' clearer,
I still can't see through the fog
Every tiny, little glimpse of truth
Gets lost in the smog
There's the God of Simple Things,
He's sitting alone on a log
No one bothers to talk to him,
They say he's just an old dog
No, I thought about it
But just don't care like I did before
I'm just tryin' to get to heaven
Before they close the door

The end is coming now, darling,
It won't take long
Is that the church bells I hear —
Are they playing our song?
I thought we were on a comeback,
Thought we were on a roll,
But this world is so dead now
That the bell don't even toll
Satan could have his reign now,
But he don't bother —
If it ain't broke, don't fix it —
Someone just aimed at the Statue of Liberty
And shot her
We have the means to fix ourselves
But can't even use tools as well as a sea otter
Someone was looking to get my goat,

And, by God, they got her
I'm sweat-soaked with fear to every pore
Just tryin' to get to heaven
Before they close the door

Where's all the love in the world?
 It's vile and depraved
Where are the latter-day saints?
 They've already been saved
And where the hell are you?
 You say you're so fuckin' smart,
I guess what they say is true—
 Only love can break your heart;
And the people are tired of bein' ripped off,
 The government doesn't know what to do
Hey, I heard the Jerk Store called,
 They're runnin' outta you
What's so special about you?
 You look just like a fallen angel to me
With what's left of my religion
 I'm gonna beg for mercy—
I give up my ticket; take it back to the store
 I'm just tryin' to get to heaven
Before they close the door

Here's your bread and water,
 Your cardboard and piss
Here's the money you lost
 With what you paid for this
I forgot what you wanted me to do
With this love we knew
It was nice knowin' ya, love,
 I'll see you soon
Me and my soul mate,
 We're getting our own room
I really wish you could've see us,
 We were quite a pair—
 At least for a little while there;
But I'm buck naked in the woods now,
 I'm huntin' bare—

But I made a mistake; I forgot to make
 My love know I care,
And now I've lost the whore
 Sure is hard tryin' to get to heaven
Before they close the door

From the fires of confidence
 And the ashes of decay,
There will come a Deluge,
 A better way;
And, when that time comes,
 You're gonna need a place to stay
Well, don't look at me,
 You gave up on me years ago —
And I'm gonna have to give up
 On you now, I know
The fires are cooling off now,
 And it's beginning to snow
I'm going to meet you down where
 The river of blood ceases to flow
It's like the homicidal bitchin'
Goin' down in every kitchen
 To decide who serves and who eats —
There's just nothin' left anymore,
 No spare meat
The well of misery runneth over,
 I'm drenched to the bone
We wound up together,
 And I ended up alone —
The same as before
 And I'm still tryin' to get to heaven
Before they close the door

2001

Flowers for Hitler

Spokesperson for H. Sapiens, extraordinaire:
  We do everything backward—
Good has become evil,
  Reverse has become forward
Right has become wrong,
  The truth has become absurd
If there's a solution to our disoriented ways,
  It's one I haven't heard

We hide the truth from school kids
  And then wolf whistle at chicks
We preach abstinence
  And exercise our dicks
"Do as I say, not as I do"—
  It works when you're talking about someone else;
Note to fellow hypocrites:
  Don't contradict yourselves

Let's replace The Constitution with the Code of Hammurabi,
  Let's put the Berlin Wall back up
Let's burn down colleges, overthrow the government,
  And not give a fuck
Pull our your wife and hit her
  And utter a racial slur—
Let's buy some flowers for Hitler

Hitler:
And, on a sudden whim,
  I wished the Devil back
I wished upon a shooting star
  For him to remount his attack
I didn't think it would work,
  But it was worth a try
I couldn't just stand here and let
  All this evil look me in the eye

Satan:

I'm back; I'm back, god damn it, I'm back,
It's time to remount my attack
 Well, I shot Kennedy and M. L. King,
And now it's time for me once again
 To come back and do my thing
I've spun a web of lies,
But it's really no surprise
 That you've beaten me at my own game —
You've gotten so good at adopting my persona
 That I think I'll have to change my name

Spokesperson for H. Sapiens, extraordinaire:
How will we ever find
 Our way out of this maze?
We've lied, and lied, and lied again,
 And now we're getting lost in the haze
We've spun a deceitful web
 That's gotten too complex —
Already my kids are asking me
Way too many fucking questions,
 And they haven't even learned about sex

Ah, crap, I can't hold up this lie anymore —
I appealed to Satan, and he showed me the door
 Hard to take your own message to heart
 When you've been bullshitting from the start
We've known all along
 But refused to believe —
We are inherently malicious
 And built to deceive

Let's send the niggers back home,
 Let's put the Jews to sleep
Let's beat little Johnny to death
 And pretend we don't hear a peep
Let's buy a cross
 And crucify ourselves
Let's take out our brains
 And put them up on decadent shelves
Let's kill the Queen and all her Sirs —

Let's buy some flowers for Hitler

Hitler:
And everything was just fine and dandy,
 Everything was in hand —
That is, until I met this stranger
 In a strange land
I asked him what was his business
 And why wasn't he dead?
And he looked quite disheartened
 When he glared at me and said —

Satan:
Ah, hahaha, I've returned, baby,
 I've come back to settle the score —
But there's nothing much for me
 To do here anymore,
You fuckers have taken it all away
I remember the good old days —
 Smoking weed and drinking beer
With Adolph and Stalin and L. Ron and Crowley,
 But they're no longer here
I'm going back home, where it's not so bad —
And, besides, it's much too hot here

2001

The Mark of Cain (The Human Condition)

Part I: Crime and Punishment

I'm a drop of water in an ocean of sharks, an old man alone in the dark,
 A child who's never felt a spark of kindness or love
I sinned and paid but am still afraid,
 My slender lifeline was frayed from the Guardian Shepherd above
He drove me from the garden, and my heart began to harden
 Now I no longer seek the pardon of He who left me to die
He says, "Love thy brothers, do good unto others,"
 But doesn't even bother taking the beam from his own eye

I'm more sinned against than sinning, and there's no way of winning
 I'm just beginning to understand the punishment brought down on my
    head
I still grieve from the pain I receive
 But just can't believe I've really been left for dead
They say, "He who seeks God will never be driven away," but I've had to
    pay
 Since the day I was forsaken by thee
I've wanted to die since I saw the lie
 And wonder if you can even deny that you have abandoned me

Part II: Punishment (Continued)

I have no Mark of Cain to show my pain
 Or restrain the hand that would have me slain for what I have been faulted
They seek me for Justice and God, but I find it odd
 That they continue to prod wounds that have already been salted
They think they are doing His will by wanting to kill,
 But the blood I spilled made The Earth cry out in agony
Until we repent from The Hell where I caused us to be sent
 Our wretched race's rent will never be free

On my killers stroll, driven beyond understanding or control,
 None caring or even wanting to know why they persist in the plague

Caring not to empathize, they only idolize
 The prize they pursue for reasons shadowy and vague
They don't want to hear it, but I'm broken in spirit,
 And every time they come near, it breaks my heart to be pursued by broth-
  ers
Lacking mercy, we kill with glee,
 Knowing not the true tragedy is how little we understand one another

I cannot really blame those who would have me slain,
 I would do the same if I had their fate
I'm a wretched man, and ever since the world began,
 We've been turning our hand on each other in hate
We jump at abuse with the least excuse,
 We've long been used to piling on the burial mound
We put the dead in stacks, stab in the back,
 And mock those who lack the gall to jump on others when they're down

Look not for friendship in man, we do not understand
 Any plan of harmony or kindness
We scoff at those who would ease the throes
 Of those whose woes have reduced them to utter duress
From self-preservation to abomination and fornication,
 We live from creation only to please ourselves
We love those who love us and hate whom we must,
 Believing ourselves just though here even the publican never fails

Part III: Sorrow and a Kind of Repentance

O, but how much more suffer I, who was cast out to die
 Even by the One whose eye tallies the death of each sparrow
I spilled blood but survived the flood
 And must writhe in the mud like the Snake whose eyes are narrow
Everyone I see wants to slay me,
 I am exiled from Thee and my city on a hill
Broken, ostracized, I am constantly watched by eyes
 Who want only to size me up for a kill

No one loves one marked for dead with no mark on his head

And the skin he's shed invisible to those unwilling or unable to see
Left to die, I no longer even try
 To beg or lie my way to mercy
I killed a man back there, but it seems so unfair
 That I must live fore'er beyond all for which I care
I'm in the Land of Nod, so far from God
 And with the Rod always above me in the air

I live always with fear that the end is near,
 It all becomes clear as I sink slowly into the grave
I go around the last bend without help or friend,
 I have no help to lend and am too far gone to be saved
So far from the place of my birth, a fugitive and vagabond on earth,
 I have nothing of worth left to be taken or spare
A loveless man, stranger in a strange land,
 I finally understand my punishment is greater than I can bear

Part IV: A Dubious Legacy

I know not what awaits, but it's not heaven's gates,
 Even the fates have nothing left for me
Doomed to live East, I'll never be released,
 The greatest peace I can find is death's equality
Deprived of child and wife, I'll live out my lonely life
 Looking for the wisdom that grows only in the strife of suffering days
I shall live alone—forgotten, unknown—
 But will have my eternal throne when all follow my dark, lonely way

Mercy's evacuation brings alienation
 Born from the creation of all that keeps us apart
We hurt each other, forgetting we are brothers,
 Never letting another feel the love buried deep in our hearts
We live behind self-created walls we refuse to let fall,
 Forsaking all for forgotten reasons made in hasty hate
First and last, I am future and past,
 The first to be cast, but all are doomed to live out my wretched fate...

2008

Dirt in the Ground (Answer to Donne)

"I would not want t be bach. mozart. tolstoy. joe hill. gertrude stein or
james dean
they are all dead."
–Bob Dylan, *Bringing It All Back Home* Liner Notes

O Death, you have power over all things —
 Can bring mighty down, exalt low above,
 Tear down everything built for God or love,
Can turn kings to beggars, beggars to kings.
Those who claim they do not fear thee have most
 To fear, for they put all trust in a dream,
 Or know dreams are but an imagined scene
And that the ground shall be our only host.
We know not when you will come but know where
 We go — not heaven or hell but far worse —
 Far from, yet so close to, our home, the earth,
Far removed from aspirations or cares.
 We sleep in this world wanting the other,
 But we wake not in it or another.

Circa 2008

In My Darkest Hour

Let me introduce you to me —
 I once knew him so well,
But things have changed, times are strange,
And I lost track of him —
 Maybe I'll see him again in hell
You say your ego's so big
 It'll get to hell before you,
Well, mine's so blind I can't even make up my mind
 If I'm speaking English or Hebrew
I regret so many things I've done —
 I not only lived without consequence,
I barely even had any fun;
And now I'm sad and lonely,
 I feel just like a scared little kid
I have to stand naked at the bottom of the cross
 And tell the good Lord what I did
Sweet bread and water have turned sour
In my darkest hour

I look back on my mistakes now —
 There were quite a few
I don't even know what I was thinking half the time
 Or how I ever made it through
I wasted so much time on myself
 When I was trying to be true
Time on my hands
 Could've been time spent with you
I can almost convince myself now
 That I never knew,
But, deep down inside,
 I knew the long-term effects of my strange brew
I planted a seed of sorrow,
 And it just grew and grew
I hope to God another man doesn't try to concoct
 That horrible and irresistible stew
You think you know what's goin' on in someone else's head,
 But you just don't have a fuckin' clue

Just ask my alter ego,
 Who once had a love he could call true —
And now it's all coming back to haunt me,
 I look back on my life and start to cower
In my darkest hour

If you dig through the trash and strife of my past life,
 Be wary of what you may find
That piece of luck you happened upon?
 It's just the hollow shell of a man I've left behind
 Be good to your own kind —
 If there was one piece of advice I could call mine,
 It would be that line
Nothing else will keep you out of the mess I'm in longer
 Or cause you less heartbreak
Love may blossom in the strangest places,
 But selfishness is an aphrodisiac for hate —
 And I found out too late
Maybe I could still save myself,
 But I lack the power
In my darkest hour

The roses in your window box
 Have withered and died
Everyone I once held dear
 Has now left my side
Yeah, I fell into the trap at times,
 I went along for the ride —
But now I feel like a cash cow,
 I just want a quiet place to hide
Your heart is the only place in the world, baby,
 Where I want my secrets to reside,
 But you can't show on the outside
 What you must keep inside —
 How are you supposed to tell that to your bride?
I already feel guilty,
 And I haven't been tried
That arrow you made out of pointed words
 Was quite simply the last chide
I once knew a girl as great as the world,

She was my function and form
She came up to me so gracefully
And took my crown of thorns —
But now she's gone back to her ivory tower
In my darkest hour

Society has no piety,
It can just make you sick
Just when you think they'll start comin' around pretty quick,
You find another bone to pick
You launch abstract threats at the target of your choice,
But nothing sticks
It's just too high a price for you to get your kicks
So I need someone like you to hold my hand
As I walk along the narrow band
That leads to the Promised Land
I'll give you anything you want, darlin',
You don't even have to ask
I'll tell you all my secrets,
But I lie about my past
If it's answers you want,
I hope you're not expectin' 'em very fast
Once my heart was in the Highlands,
But now it's stuck at half-mast
I can't see the hand of God anywhere,
Not even in a flower
In my darkest hour

I could've asked for so many things
But requested only you on a hunch
All I want is someone to talk to,
But I guess that's askin' too much
Oh, my back's against the wall
A s I fall into yet another crunch —
But I know God is my shield,
And He won't let the bloodsuckers munch
All is vanity; all is phony —
Except for you, my one and only
Where the hell were you when I was down in the mud?
Why were you sendin' lightnin' bolts

When I was down in the flood?
Hellfire is raining down in a shower
In my darkest hour

Now that my heart's been torn out,
 Feel free to leave me behind to rot
They say the dove is the only alternative to love,
 But it, too, has been shot
I was runnin' away from responsibility,
 But I've finally been caught
My karma is laughing as it's biting me on the ass —
 Faithfully and perpetually behind me it trots
My God and Devil are on the level,
 Discussing what's real and what's not
The only thing I'm worried about now
 Is how to get out of here
Why the hell are you sticking near?
 Surely not to live in pain and fear
 By now it should be clear
That this is the final date,
 This is the Final Encounter
 I tried so hard to steer,
But there is no escape
 In my darkest hour

2001

Survival Kit

How can love survive
 In such a graceless age?
How can we have the courage
 To even turn the page?
What fuel can possibly keep us going
 After the point of no return?
I can't breathe anymore 'cause they just keep on
 Feeding the bullshit that makes hellfires burn
Seems there's evil and hatred and suffering
 Every way you turn
When life's no longer worth living,
Why should we keep on giving?

This world's such a thrill—
 We got murder, rape,
 Suicide, red tape,
Child molestation, illegal possession,
Phony smiles, crooked court sessions,
 And a seemingly endless variety of under-the-table deals
We got peanuts for brains,
Crack cocaine—
We got everything in spades
 We got everything, indeed—
Everything, that is,
 'Cept what we really need

Evil's here; never fear—
 When one's eradicated, we always make another one up
We're killing ourselves with reckless abandon
 And don't even give a fuck
There's always a monster in the closet
 Or under the bed—
But now, don't you worry,
 It'll never be dead
Sure, life's a bitch,
 But here we got the ultimate miracle—
Suicide at the flick of a switch

And I feel like shit; I feel tried—
Feel like my best friend
 Or dog just died,
 Feel like I've been crucified
Feel like I'm dying,
 And you're not heeding
You're walking away
 While I'm lying here bleeding

This life, don't ya know it's great?
 We can't have sex, but we can masturbate
We're killing ourselves, damn it,
 We can't chalk it all up to fate—
And when they've taken everything else away,
Only decadence and death and destruction
 Will remain—
A simple, unified pleasure
 From which we cannot refrain

The world's a bitch; the world's rotten,
Poor old, black Joe's still picking cotton
 The poor stay poor,
And the rich stay rich
 Filling their bank accounts with misery
Just so they can bitch

What was that I heard—
 The police found your son's stash?
 Your boyfriend died in a car crash?
You better cough up the money, motherfucker,
 And you better cough it up fast
The Devil's on a hot streak
 And says it's gonna last
Why the hell do these damn demons
 Have to be so fucking brash?

You punched out some no-good lowlife,
 They had to put him up in Med.—
But the local badass isn't fucking your girlfriend,

So you still got no street cred
Your mother's been shot dead,
And your young daughter's already giving head,
But you're still not worth a fucking dime —
'Least that's what the Big Man said

I love this world,
You never have to worry about strife —
You turn your back for one minute,
And someone's fucking your wife;
And if you keep it turned too damn long,
They'll even take your life
Sometimes it seems
The world's a big, stinking pile of shit
You better watch your back, motherfucker,
If you don't want a knife in it

We live in a world of unpaid favors —
Don't call us; we'll call you —
But that long-awaited call never came, did it?
And you knew it all along, too
It's like the check that's in the mail —
You might get it, when it freezes over in hell

We struggle on through life,
Our consciousness streaming
Searching, searching, searching
For any glimpse of meaning
We thought we'd found Paradise
But pinched ourselves and woke up from dreaming

All the old survival kits
Have become stained with blood
Dirty, out of date, and unkempt,
Or, at the very least, not hip —
Like the cross you worship,
Cast aside like a sinking ship
I'm running out of fantasies,
It's time to face reality
I need a survival kit, need a free ride —

And I don't think there is one; I've looked
It's hard to know who to trust when everyone's a crook,
 Hard to run away when there's nowhere to hide

But isn't there something good we can hold on to
In a world of naysayers and pregnant teenagers?
 Maybe, maybe not—
 You may get lucky, you may get shot

Some will find something to live for—
A loved one, a child, a job, or something more—
 And the rest will be left out in the cold to face the shit;
And, if you're one of the lucky ones
 Who finds a survival kit,
You better hang on tooth and nail—
 You're gonna need it

2001

Hope against Hope: A Panacea Part I

Who knows what terrors lurk in the dark corners of the human mind? —
 Racks and atom bombs undreamt of, Orwellian torture instruments?
Will we be able to leave all our barbarous instincts behind,
 Our homicidal rampages and our self-destructive intents?
There is, it would seem, little hope for that ugly monster, mankind:
 A raging tempest doesn't fit back in the jar; Pandora's box,
Once unleashed, is a plague on the body, the spirit, and the mind —
 Hell, we might as well just dash our damned brains out against the rocks.
What, after all, is the point of this miserable existence? —
 What good is life in a world chained to blood, gore, hatred, war,
Envy, lust, greed, lies, hypocrisy, lust, and concupiscence?
 Too many good men and women have fallen victim to the gore.
 I guess good ol' Hobbes truly did say it best — and who's to retort?
 "The life of man" is "solitary, poor, nasty, brutish, and short."

Circa 2005

My Old School

Part I: Imminent Return

Memories are swelling back
 That I thought I buried long ago,
But you can only bury them deep enough
 To make the tears no longer flow
They won't stay there forever,
 It's just one of life's little rules —
But I know this much, how ever many such,
 I'm never going back to my old school

I'm never going back to my old school,
 There's too many bad memories —
Too many wasted years, too many repressed fears,
 Too many enemies
Maybe you could have tempted me once,
 But masochism's no longer cool
Don't ask me why, but I'd rather die
 Than go back to my old school

We buried the hatchet, but I just can't catch it,
 The wind that'll let me sail right in
It's the same old place, and I just can't face
 Going back again
It wouldn't break my heart to see the place fall apart,
 I just want to be there to drool —
But you're damn right, without that sight
 I'm never going back to my old school

Well, I think they know I hated them,
 I know they hated me,
But god damn the powers that fated them
 To be my vicious circle for eternity
Every time I think I've drowned them,
 They rise up again from the pool —
But I'll be damned if I must be thus jammed,

LIFE'S TRIUMPH by Bill R. Moore

I'm never going back to my old school

The worst years of my life, full of sorrow and strife,
 Came when I was stuck in that hell
I cursed aloud, fought against the angry crowd,
 And longed for the division bell
Ah, but how little we knew! We thought we had each other to slew,
 But in fate's hands we were a tool
Cursing each other, though choice we had not another —
 Still, I'm never going back to my old school

You may say it's inevitable,
 Something we all go through —
But I never thought I'd be caught in this web
 Once I'd met you
I thought the nightmare was over, but now it seems my rover
 Doesn't think I was nobody's fool
Is there any way out? I refuse to pay out,
 And I'm never going back to my old school

Well, I fought against it for years, held back the tears,
 Told myself lies to make it through —
But I thought it had ended, or at least been suspended,
 When I finally met you
You could hold it all back, defend their attack,
 But now I think I'll have to drown myself at the barstool
'Cause here we've returned, and I'm going to get burned,
 But I'm never going back to my old school

Here are all the old familiar faces,
 Leering at me just like before
The same old assholes in the same old places,
 Acting just like the days of yore
I can stand it for a while in a certain kind of style,
 But I refuse to retool
I can make it through, but only with you,
 And I'm never going back to my old school

So many things I thought I'd forgotten,
 So many others I was unable to forget —

Ah, it seems I'm doomed to an existence that's rotten,
 I just want to walk right up to them and spit!
But those days are gone; I should be moving on,
 I feel like such a fool
They're trying to drag me back down, but I'm not hanging around,
 I'm never going back to my old school

I thought I'd escaped at last, but the mountains of the past
 Are looming dangerously near
They're trying to drag me in, and I can feel it begin,
 The unwinding of the years
I'll fight to the last, but the powers are so vast,
 We're slaves to fates so cruel
You tell me to try, but I'd rather die
 Than go back to my old school

Here I am on indecision's brink,
 Tottering and flailing wildly about
I can't even stand up straight or hear myself think,
 I just can't figure it out
How did it come to this? I'm about to slit my wrists,
 They're the Kings, and I'm The Fool
I said it'd never happen, but I can already hear 'em clappin',
 Inviting me back to my old school

But go I will not!
 I've had enough
I'd rather be shot,
 It's not half so tough
As being force-fed their crow when all along you know
 That you're their crown jewel
If only you could prove it, or at least finally move it...!—
 But at least I won't go back to my old school

The hour nears, no more our path veers,
 It seems the showdown is nigh
I don't wanna do it but would rather go through it
 Than keep living this miserable lie
How can it be? I thought eternity
 Would come before I'd break my cardinal rule

Yet here I am; they're the lion, I'm the lamb,
 If I go back to my old school

Well, I'm annoyed but can no longer avoid
 What's been put off too long
I'm weak as can be, and they're gaining on me,
 Looking and acting ever strong
I might as well face it; I hate this damn place, it's
 The scholastic equivalent of a stool
You can break me, but you just can't make me
 Go back to my old school…

Part II: A Dying Retrospective

Well, the years have gone by, and I've run dry,
 There's not much left of what I once was
It's time to die, and my life flashes before my eyes,
 Just as everyone's does
I didn't become half of what I thought I would, didn't do anyone any good,
 And they just found my father in the pool
In the time I've got, there's not a hell of a lot I can think of with pride —
 But I never went back to my old school

2009

You Can't Go Home Again
(The New Prodigal Son)

*"Foxes have holes, and birds of the air have nests; but the
Son of man hath not where to lay his head."*
–Luke 9:58

There comes a time when your fantasies and precious memories
 Reveal themselves as hollow,
When you're no longer proud to walk in the crowd
 You always used to follow,
When the borders have fallen down in your hometown
 That was already a wasteland,
When you have to give up every dream you've tried to live up
 As it slipped out of your hand—
      And you can't go home again

I only wanted to be free but am not all I thought I'd be,
 I've let myself down
I left town at eighteen, so young and green,
 Wasn't ready for what I found
I had the whole world to myself, wouldn't rely on anyone else,
 I made a solemn vow
I left full of pride but felt empty inside,
 Don't think I can ever go back now—
      Because you can't go home again

I let my head be twisted and fed
 With vain and foolish dreams
Yes, confessions and concessions
 Are often more than they seem
They build up inside as you swallow your pride,
 So subtle it may be hard to detect it
You try to keep them down, but they always come around
 Whenever you least expect it—
      And you can't go home again

I just can't go back to those places and see their leering faces
 Laughing at me and shaking their fists

That life is incomplete without revenge that is sweet
 Is a doctrine I cannot resist
I just can't stand the scorn in the place I was born,
 Just can't face it one more time
When you've let yourself down, it's just so hard to come around,
 So hard to cross that line—
      'Cause you can't go home again

I starved to death on a diet of false hope, now I just sit around and mope,
 Fantasizing about what might have been
I betrayed my principles, thought I was invincible,
 Stooped to self-deception, the cardinal sin
It's hard to figure out just what's wrong about
 Following your own dream,
But there are so many wrong turns, so many bridges to burn,
 So many mistakes that are impossible to redeem—
      And you can't go home again

It gets hard to think as you start to sink,
 Reflection is always so distressing
I know I need enough self-control to dig myself out of this hole,
 But the thought is just so damn depressing
You just can't go back once you've crossed the track
 When the fork stuck in the road pointed the wrong way,
When your goal and your hero don't add up to zero,
 And the sun has begun to set on your day—
      And you can't go home again

The place I once thought was great now fills me with hate,
 Fills me with rage and disgust
The thought of going back fills me with loathing, even supposing
 I could pick myself up from the dust
Yet it is also true that longing for what I once knew
 Is eating me up inside
I've been brought down so low, there's nowhere to go,
 Nowhere left to hide—
      'Cause you can't go home again

Yes, I can still remember that evening, the front porch swing
 Just rocking in the breeze,

But I must shut the door, can't go back to the old house anymore,
 There's too many bad memories
I tried to ignore what I pretended to deplore,
 Gathered up my things and fled
Tried to leave behind everything that made me blind
 But wound up losing myself instead —
      And you can't go home again

I lost peace of mind with that last detour sign,
 Got picked up for vagrancy
I'm too tired to eat or drink, too tired to even think,
 And there's a gaping hole where my heart used to be
The world's done its best to kill it, but I think I know where I could fill it
 If only I were allowed to go
I'd love to drink from the well I once cursed to hell,
 It's the only truly sacred place I know —
      But you can't go home again

I thought I left behind all my fears, had already cried all my tears,
 When I walked out of the old sphere
Thought I'd left behind the sign in that comedy divine
 That said, "Abandon all hope, ye who enter here"
I never thought I'd be hopin' for the door to be open
 That I used to dread passing through,
But people change, times grow strange,
 And your words have a way of coming back on you —
      When you can't go home again

I've lied to myself too long, pretending I was strong,
 All my dreams are now shattered and broken
When you bite the hand that feeds, it's painful when it bleeds,
 I've shut all doors that should be open
My ego was inflated, my ideals all outdated,
 And I've got nothing to go back to now
I left on my own and came back alone,
 Lost myself along the way somehow —
      And you can't go home again

I abandoned my brothers, was scornful of others,
 Left with head held high

I told them I could make it but couldn't even fake it,
 Sometimes I wonder why I even bothered to try
My dreams have been smashed, all my plans have crashed,
 All that remains for me is to die
You may know just where you need to go,
 But they won't even let you try —
     'Cause you can't go home again

They just won't let you, they'll act like they never met you,
 Do it without even a flinch
You can beg and plead, apologize and bleed,
 But they'll never budge an inch
I've tried before, I know the score,
 It's a game you just can't win
I feel so alone, I just want to go back home,
 But you can never go back there again —
     No, you can't go home again

Now, I could act irate, curse my fate,
 Shake my fists in the air,
But it wouldn't set me free, 'cause I can blame only me,
 I will not beg for mercy or petition in prayer
So I'll walk one last time along memory's line
 Until I reach that old, familiar gate,
The one I never thought I'd leave but over which I now grieve
 'Cause I never really saw it 'til it was too late —
     And you can't go home again

So now I'm falling under, all my hopes are torn asunder,
 I'm plunging head-first into the long, slow march toward death
I can go easily anywhere but where I really want to be,
 Exiled forever from where I breathed my first breath
I tried to get ahead, but the road forward led
 To this dead end from which all my dreams flew
I can't go back where I started, my road's already been charted,
 So I say goodbye to the home I never knew
     'Cause you can't go home again

2008

That I Never Had

I think of all the times
That I was with you—
 I would always just stand there and stare
 It was such a pleasant nightmare,
  And I can't wait to get there again
The only difference between the real you
And the make believe you, baby,
 Is the latter can't turn me down for sin
I told you when you started
Dippin' your head down in that stuff
 That I loved you more than blood
I guess you didn't believe me,
 Now you're drownin' in the flood—
And when I think about you, baby,
 And everything that went bad,
It reminds me of all the good things
 That I never had

Yes, you didn't believe me when I told you
 That I loved you best
You saw me go home with another,
 Thought it made you like all the rest—
But, no—it's not like that, you see,
 You're the only one that's real
It's just that sometimes I get tired
 And succumb to a little feel
It doesn't mean I no longer
 Love you as much
You know, I always did believe
 In the healing power of touch;
And I suppose it would be rather untruthful now
 To ask for your crutch—
  It just makes me feel so sad;
And every time you give me that look, baby,
It reminds me of all the true love
  That I never had

Come over here from over there,
 You don't have to look so upset
Here—you can have my chair,
 It looks like your eyes are getting wet
You know, I can't let myself to cry in your presence,
 I'm afraid you'd think less of me—
But right now I'm dying on the inside,
 I only wish you could see
You probably don't even believe I could feel that way,
 But it's not a rarity
I think the tears are starting to well up in my eyes,
 I really wish they'd quit
God damn it, I'm a lot more sentimental and insecure
 Than I'd like to admit—
 I just wish I didn't feel so bad;
And, every time one of us starts to cry,
It reminds me of all the tear-free nights
 That I never had

Well, it's true that I love ya,
 What could be truer than that?
I take my stories with a pillar of salt, baby,
 I like the meat without the fat
You're kind of like my old girlfriend,
 She said she didn't wanna see my evil half
I don't wanna go through that again,
 You kinda remind me of her when you laugh
You always told me to just be honest,
 God knows I'd occasionally try
I thought for the longest time it'd please you,
 But I'm so sick and tired of livin' a lie—
 It just makes me so fuckin' mad;
And, every time you look me in the eye, babe,
It reminds me of the honest life
 That I never had

Yes, well, I fell prey to every lie you offered me,
 I always mistook them for fact
It always kind of pissed me off, you know—
 Your grandmother's house was just a shack;

And now I'm in too deep,
 Shit piled up in debris
There's no goin' back now,
 It's up to my knees;
And I could ask you for forgiveness,
 But you don't deserve any
There's lots of reasons for me to leave you,
 I could think of plenty
I always go fishing for questions —
 I catch a lot, sometimes too many —
 But answers are harder to find
I just get tired of searchin',
 Sometimes I think I'm blind —
 And I wonder if you're glad;
And, every time you ask me a question,
It reminds me of all the answers
 That I never had

I read the Bible alone at night,
 Locked up in my room
I don't want anyone else to see me,
 They'd think I was out of tune;
But I just get so distracted sometimes,
 Repressed memories start floodin' back
I just can't get over what we did in the churchyard,
 And you always looked so damn good in black —
But the preacher said it was sinnin',
 And you had to choose between me and God —
And somehow that Old Man won,
 I always thought your taste in men was odd;
And it looks like you left your crucifix here for me,
 I never knew what you wanted me to do with it
I'll probably just throw it in the closet
 With all my other pieces of shit —
 That should make you really mad;
But, every time I start to regret something,
It reminds me of all the good times
 That I never had

Preacher and prostitute seek the same victim,

Who'll get there first is uncertain
I'm susceptible to both,
 I live behind their iron curtain —
But, hell, we're all victims,
 We just don't know who's hurtin';
But you can have the man
In the long black coat if you want him,
 It's your loss
I can see him standing with you now,
 With his gold chain and little, plastic cross
You look so happy with him, you know —
 Your dress is long, and your hair
Is in curls and bows
  Ah, and it just makes me so fuckin' sad —
And, every time I see you happy apart from me,
It reminds me of all the stability
 That I never had

I read your suicide note,
 It still doesn't make any sense —
But I think I can see where you're coming from
 As I sit here in this room full of smoke and incense
You always talked in riddles,
You never were very direct — not that I cared
I have to admit to myself I enjoyed trying to find
My way through your maze of smoke and mirrors;
But it's always so damn depressing
 To read about one man's personal descent into hell —
But I'm gonna do it anyway,
 I suppose it's just as well
  Even though it makes a long time man feel bad —
And, every time I read the damn thing,
It reminds me of all the friends
 That I never had

We said we'd grow up together,
 That together we'd grow old;
But I should've known nobody'd stick with me,
 That no one could be so bold
Lots of people make promises,

But it's a long and winding road,
And sometimes you just have to take the shit
 And flush it down the commode
You just can't buy every lie
 That's ever been sold
You just can't play sleuth to every truth
 That's ever been told
At first you start to search for somethin'
 That'll make it go away —
But then you start to wonder
 If any of it matters anyway —
And that's the last piece of advice
 I ever got from my Dad;
And, every time a missed opportunity comes back to haunt me,
It reminds me of all the pleasures
 That I never had

Sometimes I wish I would've listened to you,
 Maybe there's something I would've learned —
Like how to go through life
 Without being haunted by every bridge I've burned;
But there's a beautiful weakness
 In every might
And a light of truth
 In every fight
You don't try to change the world in life,
 You just do what you have to do
It's the same for me, baby,
 As it is for you
I steal, I cheat, and I lie —
 I do what I must do
To get by;
 And, if you just can't live with that,
Then so long, goodbye —
So much for all the fun that could've been ours
 If our egos hadn't been armor-clad —
And, every time I think of you,
It reminds me of all the good things
 That I never had

2001

Vicious Cycle (The Pains of Life)

"When I was a child, I spake as a child, I understood as a child, I thought as a child:
but when I became a man, I put away childish things."
— 1 Corinthians 13:11

Has a man lived who did not wish himself dead?
Who was not haunted for years by thoughts in his head?
Who did not die a miserable death after being slowly bled?
 If so, I'd like to know him
They talk of a man who spoke wonders, but I never met him
If I did, I'd never forget him
There are so many things he must not have let in
 That anyone could show him—

At birth we are blind
To the sufferings of our kind,
But even here we later find
 Horrors enough to break the most steadfast:
Ripped from the womb with violence unmatched in war,
Conceived in brutal lust, wretched rape, or to settle a score
To those who often wish they never bore—
 Oh, to be ignorant of a nightmare so vast!—

We look back on childhood with glee
As a long-lost peaceful life so content and free
Deluded by intimations of immortality,
 We long for an ideal that never existed—
Or if it did were mere delusion;
We were lost in idyllic illusion
With no conception of the confusion
 That would ensue if we resisted

Days seemed endless and the world full of possibilities,
We could lose ourselves in play, blind to realities,
Live without being bound to artificial utilities

And never know another way
We had no knowledge of fighting for existence
Or the path of least resistance
We knew not even the point of persistence —
 Oh, how we long for such a day!

But there comes a day when someone rips off the veil,
Exposes our fanciful heaven as all too real hell
We suddenly need fig leaves and are afraid to fail —
 Oh, how tragically true that ignorance is bliss!
There's no going back once the veil has been lifted
The world of pain and doubt into which we have drifted
Is deeper than the memories through which we've sifted
 After they gave the Judas kiss

There's little redemption in the world as we see it,
We may want change but are afraid to be it
We try to fool the mind but just can't free it
 From the bitter knowledge of years
Some try to regain
What they call their rightful claim —
What they had when they came
 Into this vale of tears

But it is not just lost; it was never there
What we saw as the great gulf between foul and fair
Was no more than dreadfully thin hot air
 And we can't unring the bell
Who has not had thoughts of suicide,
All manner of revolutions and homicide,
To make some atonement for those who lied
 When they threw us without defense into this hell?

Ah, but we mostly learn to live with it,
Hardly able to go on but too stubborn to quit —
Yet sometimes a question in our nerves is lit

And we curse the wretched beings who made us;
Our lives are so short and pained
How is it we've never regained
What once kept us entertained?
 Ah, why was happiness forbade us?

We see it sometimes in those too young
To have climbed enough slippery rungs
To hear our sorrowful song sung—
 Ah, they know not that the simple miracle is sublime!
I saw one once, the kind of child we all
Dream of having—so vivid I'll always recall;
For a second I almost believed she'd escaped the thrall,
 Contentedly lost in youth's sweet prime

I stared so long, could not look away
A magic about her almost seemed to repay
Me for all I'd suffered to that day—
 Oh, the sweet music of innocence so sublime!
Yet I looked deep into my heart of hearts,
Saw her world soon to fall apart,
Saw decay already start—
 And did not wish her mine!

No, I'll put a stop to the vicious cycle of birth
That's already long outlasted its worth
There are enough miserable beings on earth
 Without adding one more
We claim we do them a favor but have vain, selfish ends,
Knowing as we do that misery begins
As soon as we send the message we feel bound to send—
 That a carefree life is not what they have in store

The unborn will thank us for not subjecting them
To the curse of the fruit we took from the limb,
Will not live to damn us for a life so grim

That they wish they had never been born
From cradle to grave
We try to put on faces brave,
But there's barely anything left to save
When Gabriel blows his horn

God damn the day they ripped us from the womb
And shoved us head first toward the tomb!
From our awakening to the Crack of Doom
We curse those who subjected us to strife
Oh, envy not those who live long,
Who build puny empires they believe safe and strong!
We must cease to perpetuate the wrong —
Oh, envy those lucky enough never to know the pains of life!

2009

Goin' Down Slow

Well, there is a Kingdom,
 And there is a King,
And there is a God,
 And I hear Him sing —
But you are the God of everything,
 I am the God of nothing
Yes, you are the King of everything,
I am the King of nothing;
And there's no substance to anything anymore,
 There's only stuffing;
 But it's the end of pain and suffering,
  The end of misery and woe
It's the end of everything —
 I'm goin' down slow

Well, I've had a lot of good times,
 And I've had a lot of strife
Sometimes I have a job,
 Sometimes I have a wife
These songs are the only constants
 That grow like weeds on the garbage of my life
I put them down because I need a companion,
 I need an escort
I feel the need to give myself
 An emotional weather report;
And I won't defend myself against you,
 I don't need to retort
If they don't speak for themselves,
 Then I need a new consort
And some other place to go —
I'm goin' down slow

I'm not sure why I come here,
 Knowing as I do,
What you really think of me,
 What I really think of you
I guess I just need some security

And maybe peace of mind
Despite everything, I can still remember
 How we used to have a good time—
But I'll crucify my hatred,
 I'll set my ego aflame
You give it all up, I swear to you,
 When you find the right dame
Trust me, I know—
Else you'll be goin' down slow

I don't sing for stars in late night bars,
 I'm only howling at the moon
My voice is cracked and broken,
 My guitar's out of tune;
And I'll sing for you, if you come in time,
 But I'm afraid you came too soon
Now, I can sing a love song
 Like the way it was meant to be,
And maybe I'm not that good anymore—
 But, baby, that's just me;
And maybe, if you'd stayed here, girl,
 If you hadn't gotten lost,
I could have made something of myself
 'Stead of burning every bridge I've crossed—
But that's just the way it goes
When you're goin' down slow

Don't treat your love like I did,
 Don't ever make her cry
Or you'll be forever defendin'
 What you can never justify
You'll swear you're in the right, by God,
 But you'll change your mind when you see tears in her eye
You won't be able to reconcile yourself,
 Won't be able to answer why
You live in a garden of sorrow,
 But love doesn't bloom under a blood red sky;
And it doesn't matter how far away you go,
 Doesn't matter how high you fly—
You'll always end up with your back to the wall

LIFE'S TRIUMPH by Bill R. Moore

In the place where teardrops fall
 And drown in a sea of sorrow —
 You're goin' down slow

Someplace, a long way from me,
 Maybe a million miles,
There lives a lonely lady,
 The one who bore my child
I still go and see her sometimes,
 She always greets me with a smile
Yeah, we're nice enough face-to-face,
 But behind each other's back we hiss
Please don't make the same mistake I did,
 Don't stoop to petty excuses like this
When I'm with her, there's a sight I always see —
A little voice cryin', "Daddy!,"
I always think it's for me,
 But I don't know —
 I'm goin' down slow

No, your pain is no credential here,
 Take a number and stand in line
If you can't see all the other broken people around you,
 You must surely be blind
Well, that particular sorrow is yours,
 And that one is mine
Please sweep it under the rug for me,
 If you would be so kind
Well, I had to run away and hide
When I heard she was to be your bride
Something touched me deep inside,
I think something inside me died
 I swore to myself I'd forget about her,
God knows I tried
I had to swallow my pride
 Despite the cost;
And it left me here alone to dazzle you all
 With my incomparable sense of loss
Now regretful words are starting to flow —
I'm goin' down slow

Well, I know we don't talk anymore,
 I know we no longer speak —
But I saw you yesterday in church
 Where a thousand lonely people meet
I saw you through the window,
Saw you through the stained glass;
But don't worry, baby,
 You know I'll always be true
To our unspoken code of silence,
 Won't ever say, "I love you"
I know it makes you uncomfortable when I say it,
 And you know I'd never stoop so low
As to say it in front of everyone
 When I'm goin' down slow

2001

Life's Been Good (Letter from Earth)

"When you've fallen on the highway
and you're lying in the rain,
and they ask you how you're doing
of course you'll say you can't complain —
If you're squeezed for information,
That's when you've got to play it dumb:
You just say you're out there waiting
for the miracle, for the miracle to come."
–Leonard Cohen, "Waiting for the Miracle"

Life's been good in this bar —
You can always find someone to tell your troubles to
Without going too far
Maybe you can't be coherent
Or make it back to the car,
But it sure as hell beats ownin' up
To how things are

Life's been good in this iron lung —
No one to tell you to shut up
When your sorrowful song is sung,
No one to loudly ring in your ears
Bells you never again wanna hear rung,
No one to contradict or defeat you,
No way to get stung

Life's been good in this straitjacket —
Plenty of time to brood over the life problem,
Maybe some day I'll crack it
No one to bother you with inconvenient questions
Or trouble you with their racket —
But I just can't get over self-doubt,
Sometimes I wonder if I can hack it

Life's been good in this jail —
My sins are no worse than anyone else's,

And I get lots of fan mail
Sure, life moves along
 At about the pace of a snail,
But it more than compensates to know
 There's no greater way to fail

 Life's been good in this isolation chamber—
I can always keep myself company,
 And there's no danger
I may have no one to talk to,
 But at least I don't have to talk to strangers;
Besides, my bed's as warm and cozy
 As Jesus in the manger

 Life's been good in detox—
The nurses are very helpful,
 And no one ever talks
I can do anything 'cept leave or drink,
 And no one balks
Yeah, I miss the bottle,
 But, hey, at least I still have the rocks

 Life's been good in this telephone booth—
Just take my word for it, buddy,
 Please don't ask for proof
There's two sides to every story:
 Mine and the cold hard truth;
And I'm findin' it hard enough
 To pretend I'm just aloof

 Life's been good in rehab—
The lights are dim,
 And the walls are drab
Hell, I don't even have to ask;
 If I'm hurt or lonely, they just give me a tab—
But I have to admit I sometimes feel a bit
 Like a mouse in a lab

 Life's been good on earth—
We're tortured and tormented

From the moment of birth
Happiness is a short act in a drama of pain,
They soon drain you of mirth
'Till we go to our graves wonderin'
Just what the hell it's all worth

Yes, life's been good on this big, blue sphere—
But I wish you'd quit askin' me,
You wouldn't like it here
There's no entertainment,
And the punishment's severe
They sometimes give scraps to live on
But mostly feed us with fear

Life's been good in hell—
If I'm lonely I can always watch
The undertaker tollin' the bell
I used to feel bad and get hot,
But now I think it's just as well
I have no choice, so why not rejoice
And say everything's swell?...

2009

Hatchet Job
(Politics for the New Millennium)

There's two political parties in this country —
The Winners and the Losers
People don't know,
They think they're choosers
Ah, but what good is a dose of reality
Tempered with a little salt
If you can't use it to guide you across
The tightrope we all walk?
There's only one message
Worth listening to,
And that's the one
That comes from inside you
That's what I told the Party
The last time they came around;
But I no longer see left and right
Or black and white,
There's only up and down

Everything we once stood for
I can't even recognize anymore
How could I have ever been part of that?
I guess some like the meat without the fat;
And, yes, I understand why
You didn't give me a parting gift
I used to be among
The crowd you're in with;
But I still wish you were here by my side
Just to help me dry the tears I've cried
I feel like something inside me died,
I've frozen up inside;
And now everyone who used to love me
Is out to skin my hide
I'm just going along for the ride
Listening to every mind-polluting sound;
But I no longer see left and right
Or black and white,

LIFE'S TRIUMPH by Bill R. Moore

There's only up and down

You know, I really can't help it,
 Feeling this way
I'm just not the same man
 I was yesterday;
And, if you can't respect that,
 You're no friend of mine
You're just another of the so-called faithful
 Who will always be blind;
And, in case you hadn't noticed,
 You're falling behind
 You missed the stop sign—
No one told you when to run,
You missed the starting gun;
 And now it's time to give up
And let your enemies have their fun—
 You're hell-bound;
But I no longer see left and right
Or black and white,
 There's only up and down

It's so lonely on the top,
 There's no one to challenge you
You think you know where to stop
 But always end up turning blue
It don't make any sense to me,
How can you deceive yourself so easily?
 Get it through your head—
No one's free
 We all have to answer to the Big Man,
And he's not on speaking terms with me
You know, it all comes down to reality
So stop talkin' about equality,
 They've already let that drown;
But I no longer see left and right
Or black and white,
 There's only up and down

I get so tired of readin' about your deflections—

Enough with your obsessions,
I need some cardinal directions
Where are the answers,
 Where's sanity?
Where are all the spare parts
 In this mad machinery?
I get so bogged down by political correctness
 That I can't even see
You look for things that aren't even there,
You're not gonna find 'em anywhere—
They're lost in mystery's lair;
And I'm clearin' the rarefied air,
 I'm drivin' you out of town;
But I no longer see left and right
Or black and white,
 There's only up and down

It's in the high, holy places
 Where men sit and stare all day,
At the giant, stone faces
 Where women kneel to pray,
It's the giant hole that is your religion
 When it comes crashing down,
It's everything you ever looked for
 And the very little you've found,
It's the meaning of life,
The reason for strife,
The perpetually double-edged knife—
And it's your kids, your wife,
 Your hometown;
But I'm neither left nor right,
I'm just stayin' home tonight,
 Giving up and sinking down

2001

The Death of Optimism (A Progression)

"For there is hope of a tree, if it be cut down, that it will sprout again…"
— Job 14:7

Into this world we're hurled,
 Dying before we've started
We live a little while or walk many a mile
 But never know if it's already charted
We feel there is free will
 And most start out open-hearted,
But there's little to save when we're in our grave,
 Most die broken-hearted

Beaten down, driven to the ground,
 We seek some kind of mercy
We look for love or a god above,
 Anything to bring safety
We struggle through doubt and soon find out
 It's far from easy
It's easy to get pissed, say it doesn't even exist,
 And it's certainly not free

Armed with pistol and Bible, we attend the revival
 Of whatever belief's most convenient
We learn to ignore doubt's ever-growing sore
 Or nihilism becomes permanent
We try to stay alert but are brought down by hurt
 That comes when optimism's absent
We try our best, but anger lodges in our breast
 And begins to ferment

It's hard to believe when there's nothing to receive
 From whatever faith you placed your bets on
We long for return or to escape eternal burn,
 But it's hard to care unless the fret's gone
It never eases, and nothing ever pleases,
 Some cease to believe in a world beyond
Maybe it's there, but it doesn't number our hair

And may well play us as a pawn

No one like's being used, and we're always abused,
 Our burden's more than we can bear
There's an emptiness inside we cannot hide
 No matter how hard we try to pretend it's not there
You can't kill it or try to fill it,
 It just keeps comin' back up for air
Some deny it—but, hell, just try it—
 The most we can say is no one said it'd be fair

We lie to ourselves and everyone else
 As faith bleeds away drop by drop
No lie can ever make us try
 As we did before we knew it was a flop
We can take risks or slash our wrists,
 But the pain's never gonna stop
Look me in the eye, I won't deny
 You sometimes just wanna take a sock at a cop

In the end, I'll meet you on the way down, my friend,
 Where we're all doomed to go
As to why we're livin' this lie—
 Hell, it's just the way we grow
We must forgive in order to live
 Or suffer each other's blows
If there's life after this strife,
 I don't even want to know

It's hard to care about playin' fair
 When the win goes to those who cheat worst
Some say you don't have to bleed if you succeed,
 But, hell, you gotta overcome defeat first
We struggle toward success even if we try our best
 But fly toward failure feet first
It's easy to give up, but first you have to live up
 To those who take the heat worst

Think twice before givin' advice,
 Who the hell are you anyway?

LIFE'S TRIUMPH by Bill R. Moore

Idols fall or fail to hear our call,
 They all have feet of clay
You're all right but lose the fight
 As much as anyone any day
I know you and trust you as far as I can throw you,
 Just as you would me, I dare say

If not two-faced, we're forced to write off the human race,
 At least those who don't agree with us
Unfortunately for most, we can hardly boast
 Of those who wouldn't leave us in the dust
The mighty many are against us, the precious few have bent us
 From askin' for too much trust
Maybe you can rely on some, but most are numb,
 Isolated, our dreams begin to rust

It'd be nice to leave something behind for those still in a bind,
 But we feel we owe them nothing
Some say they love us but don't even hesitate to shove us
 If we even suspect they're bluffing
This war of attrition has blunted ambition,
 We're all huffing and puffing
We can extend a hand to fellow man,
 But the handshake's bound to be crushing

I was so naïve I actually used to believe
 We'd go to paradise when they're through with us
If not all, at least a small
 Number, or even just a few of us —
But I gave up long ago, and now I know,
 They don't even care about the two of us
We die alone — broken, unknown —
 When they're done turning the screw on us

So we leave as we came, unfeeling and lame,
 Worthless to ourselves and others
We go alone into the great unknown,
 Divorced from our loves and brothers
Asked if the trial was worthwhile,
 We can only say we don't want another

Alone at last, we strap to the mast
 The only lie we have left for cover

So don't talk to me of philosophy,
 None of it's worth a damn
And don't try to console with a theological whole,
 The lion ain't gonna lie down with the lamb
The only thing left of me will soon be bereft of me,
 The broken body holding the miserable being I am
This too must pass, it's the end at last,
 And I wish I could say it wasn't all a sham

But I'm ready to die and too old to lie,
 Every bone and nerve is numb
I ran most of my life, stopped for kids and wife,
 But am now glad the end has come
I tried hard and long to escape what I felt wrong
 But can't even remember what I tried to get away from
I subtracted lies, tried to self-hypnotize,
 But always got the same negative sum

The will to power has seen its last hour,
 We're comatose, just barely living still
Ever perverse, we're going forward in reverse,
 Limping toward the final kill
It's only a matter of time before we reach the end of the line,
 But we live our lives as if they're real
And the saddest thing of all is that ever since the Fall
 We've never known if we can blame free will

Everything dies — that's a fact; I used to think maybe they came back
 But have given up even that small hope as forlorn
We no longer even see darkly through the prism, it's the funeral of opti-
mism,
 And there's no one there to mourn
We're alone at last and will soon pass,
 Gabriel's blowin' his horn
We stood by it to the bitter end but now must fend
 For ourselves; optimism's dying a lonely death, never to be reborn   2009

He Never Expected Much
(Eulogy for a Vindicated Realist)

"Although affliction cometh not forth of the dust, neither doth trouble spring
out of the ground; Yet man is born unto trouble, as the sparks fly upward."
— Job 5:6-7

I've never had any illusions about human nature,
 Never dared think we'd move closer to the heart—
Mediocrity's the most we can hope for in stature;
 I've long been used to us tearing the world apart
But have found a ray of hope at last,
Something to strive for in a life so mysterious and vast
 I hope you'll join me
 Or it'll soon be quite stormy
And too late to strap yourself to the mast

I live by Murphy's Law, creating corollaries as they come
 It's either adjust or bust
And the world leaves you feeling numb,
 On that you can trust—
Unless you expect little in the first place
Then you certainly won't ace
 But just might pull through
 It may not be good enough for you,
But at least you won't fall flat on your face

Speak not to me of decency,
 A momentary impulse soon dropped
We believe only selfishness can set us free,
 Our inhumanity can't be topped
We'd rather hurt others
Than treat them as brothers
 You gotta always be on your toes in life,
 I watch my back so no one can put in a knife—
No matter where we go evil always hovers

But you can't be frightened by the monsters in us,
 They're part of everyday life

Ever since Eve entered the apple business
 We've been weighed down by strife
Nice guys finish fast,
Never even make it to last
 It's enough just to stay alive,
 All we ever do is struggle and strive —
A fatal legacy of a bloodstained past

You can be meek and hide yourself
 Or pretend it doesn't exist,
Believe lies told by someone else
 Or take on the world with fists
You may even make yourself believe
What your mind would like to receive,
 But there's no going back
 Once you're on the track
We all struggle down as soon as we breathe

Don't believe what optimists tell you,
 We're all dying the same death
If what they said were true
 They'd be killed 'fore they took another breath
We can waste hours
Splitting hairs in ivory towers
 Or see the proof
 And face the ugly truth
For it alone empowers

But it's only castles burning,
 Don't let it bring you down
The world'll go on turning
 Long after we're around
We must see things as they are,
Not focus on some distant star
 We'll be on the path to right
 As soon as we see the light,
But we haven't gotten very far

We must take all the blame,
 Fate's no stacked deck

LIFE'S TRIUMPH by Bill R. Moore

It treats everyone the same
 But gives no one respect
It's not so much blind as apathetic,
All attempts to blame it are synthetic
 We reap what we sow,
 It doesn't weed or mow —
Life becomes what we let it

Fair play's too much to ask,
 But the dice aren't loaded
Yes, our complaints are vast,
 But we should be glad earth hasn't exploded
There's just no getting around
That we bring ourselves down
 Fate can't be blamed
 Or even framed
If truth is ever found

Free will's an awesome responsibility,
 I'm not sure we can handle it
We haven't even shown the utility
 To pretend to give a shit
We bitch that life's not fair
While building castles in the air
 Will we ever learn
 There's opportunity to burn
If we'd just take the time to care?

Stop me if you think you've heard this one before —
 Someone blamed it all on fate
Yes, I know it's a bore,
 But we keep putting our heads on a plate
We must come down from our castles,
Stop our foolish hassles,
 And make peace with fate;
 It's not too late —
But the hurdle will soon become impassable

We must offer fate a peace treaty,
 What have we to lose —

We who are so needy
 That we are hardly even able choose?
We must give chance a chance
Before death's dance
 Or we'll die blaming the wrong enemy
 The real one's inside you and me
And making its final advance

So let us lower expectations,
 Take life on its own terms
To aim for preservation
 We must forget all we've learned
"What will be will be"
Is the lesson of history —
 Or is it not?
 With the little power we've still got
We just may be able to set ourselves free

To free will we must surrender,
 Close the door on chance and blame
The lifeline left may well be tender
 But has always been the same
It'll be just as before,
But we'll be ignorant no more
 For so long we haven't been free
 Or known we had the key,
But those days may at last be o'er

Victims not of circumstance but pain,
 We've wandered blindly for centuries
It's hard to let yourself out of chains
 When you don't know you have the keys —
But it's not too late to fight,
We must show our might
 The time has come now
 For our final vow,
But even now we may not see the light

We've been hollow men, Quixotes slashing at windmills
 For far, far too long

It's time to move in for the kill,
 Time to show we're strong
Narrow is the way but straight is the gate
That leads to truce with fate
 We must no longer call ourselves born to trouble
 But burst the outdated bubble
That makes us slaves to misplaced hate

But if we fail, let it be known
 That I tried my best to my dying day
Even if I had no apostles or clones,
 I didn't let it stand in the way
But pursued my lonely course without such
And of help or encouragement had not a touch
 No one wanted my autograph,
 But my epitaph
Proudly says only, "He never expected much."

2009

Ode to the One True Saint

You, Jean Valjean, the very picture of
 Humility, forgiveness, selflessness,
Gentleness, faith, hope, charity, and love—
 O, if all could share your true tenderness,
Then there would be no more senseless, useless
 Killing in the name of God and Country,
No more hatred, cruelty, and prejudice,
 Then we could all, for once, truly be free—
Alas!—how far from reality is
 This vain and unreachable distant dream!
It slips away in the wind just like piss
 To be replaced by the sick, cruel, and mean...
So ends this ode to you, the one true saint;
Victor, his death left a permanent taint!

Circa 2005

Job (The Human Condition)

They ask how I knew my "True Love" wasn't true
And why I was blue when Life and Love were new—
 Vain questions! Ask not me,
Ask the Cruel Tyrant who directs the Bitter Pageant
 That makes a mockery of myself and thee
And six billion other sisters and brothers
 Just as far from being free

They ask why I thought Life and Love would rot
And why all by hard work we got would end up as not—
 Foolish questions! Ask not this man,
Ask the Vast Imbecility that ekes out cruelty
 On every hand in this land
Without asking permission or arousing much suspicion
 In this Life so bland

They ask why I suspected we would be neglected
When it was detected that we were no longer protected—
 Senseless questions! How should I know?
Ask the Cruel Fates spreading bitterness and hate
 High and low in our sad show
On every head from birth 'till we're dead
 Without ever knowing why or from where it flows

They ask how I felt the hard rain would pelt
And all our tears melt at the snapping of the Bible Belt—
 Heedless questions! How could I answer?
Ask the Purblind Doomsters who make us sad tombsters,
 The Jolly Dancers and Mad Prancers
Who blow the Futile Horn and make us regret being born
 When we enter a Life that gnaws at us like cancer

They ask how I had a knack for knowing things were off track
When it seemed we had plenty of slack to pull on if we fell back—
 Blind questions! How dare they ask?
Ask the Wicked Elf who makes a fool of me and yourself,
 Who makes us wear a mask or drown sorrow in a flask

Just to deal with what we take in by the paltry organs we feel with
 Each time we try to complete some unwanted task

They ask how they failed to realize we're all jailed
When the answer had been mailed before they even hailed —
 Outrageous questions! How could I tell them?
Ask the Savage Jokers who prod us with their hot pokers,
 Who never fill our cups to the brim and make us slaves to whim,
Who make us fail to see what could come so easily
 If they didn't make this a world of sink or swim

They ask how I foresaw there'd be no Moral Law
Left to hold us in awe after the Truth began to thaw —
 Empty questions! Ask not one who is blind,
Ask the Merry Pranksters who leave us with blank stares
 When we find we're still slaves to the grind
After all our work, who know Life makes us berserk
 When we see past the dim recesses of the Mind

They ask how they could forget when exposed to constant gall and fret
Or fail to be upset in a world their expectations hadn't met —
 Ridiculous questions! Ask one who knows,
Ask the Grand Mystery who throughout history
 Has made sure pain flows and that we know it goes
Straight to our hearts and minds, that we'll never leave it behind
 And always have to suffer its blows

They ask why it is that in this Cosmic Quiz
Everything that's hers and his disappears like so much fizz —
 Stupid questions! Ask one who can say,
Ask the Jolly Riddler, the out of tune Cosmic Fiddler
 Who may cease to torture us some day
But who has of yet shown no sign that He does so incline
 And seems hell-bent on making us for some great unknown crime pay

They ask how I came to know that to this pain we go
When others have claims to show and even to fame glow —
 Insane questions! Ask not this one,
Ask the Uncaring Surveyor, our pain's Great Purveyor
 Who seems to go on the run when He sees what He has done,

When he sees that those like us are unknowing from dust to dust
 And slip into the grave without ever having had any fun

They ask how I could have known that we would be thrown
From our mighty throne and left all alone—
 Facetious questions! Ask not in vain,
Ask the One Who Measures our heavy wrongs and paltry treasures,
 Who makes us wonder how we can sustain through all the sorrow and
pain,
Who makes us walk alone through this valley of stone
 With no shelter from the driving rain

Ask no more, I beggingly implore,
There's more in store than in days of yore—
 Yes, stop your vain questions! Ask not me,
Ask the Great God Almighty who seems scared and flighty,
 When he sees down on their knees those like myself and ye
Plodding aimlessly through barren paths blamelessly
 Some we would not choose, but we're not always free
Or are we?—

2009

It Never Looks like Summer Now Part II

It never looks like summer now, despite the sun.
Love is covered with clouds, its race already run.
 Please blot out the cruel thing, or at least paint it black,
 For winter is here now, there is no turning back.
The God-cursed sun pours down, mocking our cold spirit.
We curse it, but the Fiery Lord does not hear it.
 Change as you will, seasons, it is nothing to me.
 Regardless of you, I will freeze or feel fiery.
You, cruel sun, dare to shine now that my heart is bare,
But now it can't be summer here — or anywhere!
 Winter comes, but my heart is already frozen,
 What matters it, which season nature has chosen?
Winter can be warm, summer bring a chilling frost,
And either can change by night — ah, and at what cost!...

2009

The Mountain of Knowledge

I'm climbing the Mountain of Knowledge
 But don't know what it's for
Trying to learn what they don't say in college
 Much less before

I'm climbing hard and fast,
 But it's oh, so steep —
Human achievement seems vast! —
 I'm at a pace I don't know if I can keep

Sometimes it seems I'll never reach the top,
 Can't believe how much is left to go;
But ignorance will come if I rest or stop —
 And, besides, it's all I know

Clearly we must climb as fast as we can
 Or degenerate into ignorant beasts
It's the only thing separating man
 From the creatures on whom we feast

Yet what has it ever done for us,
 Has it made us any better?
All this rush and all this fuss,
 Must it go on forever?

Have we solved any problem that has haunted us
 Since we first squeaked into existence?
Morality and philosophy have daunted us
 Despite our greatest persistence

Are we happier than ancient man?
 Do we know more of the necessities of life?
Higher and higher we stand,
 Yet we're still weighed down by pain and strife

Who's to say castles built in exalted air
 Won't crash down on our heads?

You can say it's not right or fair,
 But it won't matter when we're dead

Meanwhile those who stayed below
 Will be no worse off than ever
What does it gain us to think and know?
 Where's the rainbow's treasure?

Yes, sometimes I think ignorance really is bliss,
 Everything intellectual just so much nonsensical fog
Would we have even started if we knew it would come to this?
 Sometimes it makes me want to be a child — or even a dog

Yet surely it's better to keep climbing,
 Not give up after so much laborious toil
Surely it's better to get there or die trying
 Than let Ignorance laugh at another plan it managed to foil

But sometimes I wonder if the highest climbers
 Are better off than the most ignorant groundling
That it brings no happiness we need no reminders,
 And is that not everything?

Yes, is it not better to be content
 With whatever store of facts in our head
Than to make our odyssey permanent
 Yet go to our graves just like the unread?

Perhaps he knows more who's never cracked a book
 Than the most exalted climbers of yore…
Perhaps closing one without a second look
 Is more honestly Socratic than opening knowledge's door…

Still, it's hard to go back,
 How can we climb down after climbing so high?
No, we're already on this track,
 It's either this or let Knowledge die

Yes, we must keep climbing
 Higher and higher and higher

Otherwise we'll be rewinding
 And Ignorance's consequences are dire…

But no; enough — what, really, have we found?
 Nothing to make us content or happy
Stop climbing, tear it down,
 Let it crumble into the sea

O, Mountain, we worshipped you for years
 And what did we learn? —
Those who climb to the highest atmospheres
 Are no better off than those who've spurned

So go on, if you want — reach the summit
 Where are the answers? I haven't got 'em
The truth, it's time to stop running from it,
 I'll meet you at the bottom

Ah, the valley's rushing toward me now,
 How great to be free of life's dim profound!
I feel I'm finally free now,
 I'll laugh at all the climbers as I go down

2009

Life: A Tragedy in Five Acts

The Curtain rises on Lives supposedly new —
The open-hearted many, the broken-hearted few
They never asked for birth and aren't sure what it's worth
Even as they sink into the grave
They never thank those who put them in Life's clothes,
And there's very little left of them to save
They wonder what it's all for as they knock on death's door,
No closer to Truth or Beauty than the day they were born
They shake their head and grin when asked if they'd do it again,
Say Life's hopeless and forlorn
It's a warning that the hard rain starts pouring
As soon as in the cradle you're lying
It's been well said that we're better off dead
And that if we're not being born we're dying,
But many still say Education and Amelioration
Can ease the burden of our sad lot
No one wants to admit it all turns to shit
As soon as in Life's web we're caught
So let's admit we're on a one-way track
And there's no going back
        No, there's no going back

Sure, scenes sometimes change,
We can stop, and there's props we can rearrange,
But Act Two's really nothing new,
We get caught in the same old traps
It's tiring, and we need constant rewiring,
So once a day we take a nap
We put on our mask, do what others ask,
Go through Life mechanically
In Dramaturgy there's no chance to purge, we
Slog through it all wearily
Writers and Directors are our Achilles and Hectors,
But there are no Gods to help us cope
We may think it a phase, but when there's nowhere safe to graze
We just give up all hope
They say Truth's out there, but if so, we haven't found where,

Never even came close to the Straight Dope
They say It's all around us, it just hasn't found us,
 But we keep choking on our own rope
The never-ending rainbow quest is making us grieve,
The pot of gold was only make believe
          Yes, only make believe

 By the time Act Three's done
 We're tired and hard-wired, no longer having fun
We no longer believe in the four-leaf clover, just want it to be over,
 Don't know if we can make it to the Fourth Act
It's so tiring, and we're ever-expiring,
 We've lost all civility and tact
We start lying to all and feel so small
 But just can't make it through any other way
If we ever doubt, we start spacing out,
 Don't know if we can even make it through the day
Sure, some try to inspire, make us walk the high wire,
 But we can only be pushed so far
It's enough for most to avoid becoming a ghost,
 Not everyone can be a star
Those who can don't seem mortal man,
 We hollowly praise but can hardly admire
It's enough for us not to completely bust,
 We have no desire to walk through the fire
So we stagger on toward Act Four
Half hoping death will open its merciful door
          Yes, open its merciful door

 After an eternity Act Four comes,
 We're dead on our feat, broken and beat, just left feeling numb
We take things slower, the midlife crisis is over,
 It's enough just to survive
We've given up any chance of joining the joyous dance
 We always told ourselves would arrive
Yes, our dreams are gone, don't know what we're living on,
 We're not all we thought we'd be
Love didn't last, it burned out too fast,
 Now we're sad and lonely
We had some friends, but they didn't last in the end,

Left us to our own sorrows
Our family has died, or there's a gap so wide
 It couldn't be breached in infinite tomorrows
Disappointment never fails, everyone we love's dead or in jail,
 And it's downhill through the Final Act
Don't talk to us of right, we just wanna make it through the night,
 Don't give a damn about Truth or Facts
We just want it to end
Ah, how did it all begin?
          Yes, how did it all begin?

Act Five's here at last,
 We're overjoyed, finally buoyed by The End coming so fast
When all's said and done, we never even had much fun,
 Hardly ever even took off our mask
Hardly dared show our face to others, even our brothers,
 And they hardly even bothered to ask
Friendship's short, has nothing to report
 But betrayal and long-held grudges
Friends'll let each other fall by the way any day
 And Conscience never so much as nudges
Family's there for a while but descends to phony smiles
 On petty obligations we keep for no reason
We go our separate ways after the first naïve days
 But think admitting it is treason
Love alone gave us courage to live on
 But sadly did not last
We quickly drank our cup, and it dried up,
 Swallowed in the merciless immensity of Time, so vast
  What remains after Love has given its all?
The Final Scene — a few sad hours bleak and mean,
 The Curtain lowering on the final tableaux —
A crumbling edifice built on phony, half-obeyed laws
Sputtering to a bitter end without applause —
 The broken-hearted many, the open-hearted few
  — Then the Curtain's fall

2009

One Day at a Time Part II
(The Existential Burden)

*"She did not reflect, consciously, that the solution to her difficulty lay in
accepting the fact that there was no solution; that if one gets on with the job
that lies to hand, the ultimate purpose of the job fades into insignificance;
that faith and no faith are very much the same provided that one is doing
what is customary, useful, and acceptable."*
–George Orwell, A Clergyman's Daughter

*"That man, which looks too far before him…hath his heart all the day long, gnawed
on by fear of death, poverty, or other calamity; and has no repose, nor pause of his
anxiety, but in sleep."*
–Thomas Hobbes, Leviathan

*"More conducive to success in life than the desire for much knowledge is the being
satisfied with ignorance on irrelevant subjects.
The world does not despise us; it only neglects us."*
–Thomas Hardy's Journal

We're stuck between the mountains of the past
And a future so vast,
 Don't know where to turn
There can be little doubt
That we'll never figure it out,
 Little chance we'll ever learn
You ask how I can make it through
 This maze of ugliness and greed
Well, I'm tellin' you
 There's only one thing you need
Yes, it's the same old line—
Buddy, I take it one day at a time

We live from day to day
In a mediocre way,
 It's hard enough just to keep body and soul together
We can't save up

Or even pretend to give a fuck,
 It's always stormy weather
You ask how I can slog through
 This mass of filth and corruption
Well, buddy, I'm tellin' you
 It can be done without interruption
Yes, and you don't even have to pay a fine —
Buddy, I take it one day at a time

If you want, you can take a stand,
Try to make life a little less bland,
 But I long ago gave up trying to decide wrong and right;
And you can try to find somethin' that'll thrill ya,
But in the end it just might kill ya —
 Hell, just survivin's a noble fight
You ask how I can pull myself through
 This abyss of hypocrisy and lies
Well, man, I'm tellin' you
 To look into my battle-scarred eyes
There's no need to question or whine —
Just take it one day at a time

Don't live in the past or the future,
Time's a bitch and you'll just want to shoot her —
 Immerse yourself in the ever-present now
Forget the big picture
Minimize your eyes and eventually you'll get your
 Precious equilibrium somehow
You ask how I can force myself through
 This shithole of double-crossing and hate
Well, damn it, I'm tellin' you
 That you don't have to rely on fate
No, just drop sanity a line —
And take it one day at a time

Life's not fair,
But why should we care?

The day's there for the taking
If you get lost in future worry
You'll bury yourself in a hurry
 Under sorrows that'll leave you aching
You ask how I can see myself through
 The stench of betrayal and deceit
Well, motherfucker, I'm tellin' you
 The world's right there at your feet
If you only knew where to find —
Buddy, just take it one day at a time

Our closets don't need cleaning
Just because life has no meaning,
 We can make our own
Faith is gone
But we must move on,
 We cannot just be left all alone
In isolation the mind stagnates,
 Leaves you without strength to endure
Your love turns to hate,
 And you start cursin' him or her
Yes, but you can always grab that line —
Take it one day at a time

Time doesn't really heal all wounds
But heals most of them as soon
 As you take life on its own terms
Put away your maps,
You'll just get caught in a trap
 That ends where hellfire burns
You can't look too far ahead
 Or too far in the rear
One way kills you dead,
 The other fills you with pain and fear
Yes, but there's one way that's still fine —
Taking it one day at a time

At first it may seem odd
Having to live without God,
 But the mind has an astonishing capability to adapt
Just take things as they come
And you'll stop feelin' numb,
 Won't fall into the trap
There may be drudgery and there may be setbacks,
 You may find it hard to advance;
But don't let it make you crack,
 This is no eternal dance
We must make the most of our one lifeline
By taking it one day at a time

Life with free will
Is a steep climb uphill,
 There's blind curves and dim lit alleys
An existence that's existential
Can be vile and pestilential,
 There are few sun-drenched valleys
We must fumble in the dark for the light switch
 Struggling in vain confusion
Yes, you can whine and you can bitch,
 But the help you see coming's an illusion
Yes, there's but one dinner on which we can dine—
Taking it one day at a time

We lived too long on the hope of miracles and magic,
Woke at last from a vain dream that was tragic
 That's not the light; it's your vision growing dim
Enduring a miserable life here
Won't make paradise near,
 And there won't be any help from Him
It's not just that bread and circuses aren't coming back,
 They were never even there
There's no longer a beaten track,
 And the damn game's not even fair
Still, I know how to provide for me and mine—
Take it one day at a time

Our innocent past gets dimmer by day,
The blackness of truth blots out each ray
 And we can't help but wonder what to do;
But there's No One to answer or even hear,
Nothing but pain and emptiness and fear
 Buddy, it's up to me and you
No, I can't pretend it's easy,
 Can't pretend it's clear —
But, hell, if you're lookin' for a life that's breezy,
 You ain't gonna find it here
Self-pity's the ultimate crime —
Just take it one day at a time

You say you don't know how you can take it,
You're beat and you just can't fake it,
 Don't even know if you can make it through the day
Well, hell, man, I'd be lyin' if I said
I hadn't a thousand times wished myself dead,
 But it looks like there's no other way
What can I tell you?
What can I do?
What can I sell you?
The only way to make it through
 Is to sign the dotted line
 Beneath "Take it one day at a time"

Well, I've been cheated, double-crossed, and betrayed,
I've been hindered, spat on, and waylaid —
 But I'm still standing, if ever so precariously
I may be battle-scarred,
But, hell, I knew life would be hard
 As soon as I saw it wasn't free
Still, on the whole, I'm happy
The reason is, you see,
I never let myself turn sappy
And sometimes love's been good to me —
 But even if not I'd still be fine

'Cause I took it one day at a time

Yes, when I go down to my grave,
They can't say I was rich or brave
 Or anything else worth conventional mention;
But my non-existent soul will be proud
Wrapped up in my wretched shroud
 'Cause I will have carried out my one intention
Yes, it will say on my stone,
 A monument for all eternity,
That this wretched wreck of skin and bone
 Was able to set himself free
Yes, my empty body will have peace of mind—
"He took it one day at a time"

2009

Will the Circle Be Unbroken?
(A Dying Man's Last Query)

Some talk of a life after death or of
 Reincarnation, as if we all long
For a continuance here or above —
 Woeful thought! Is there even one so strong
To endure another round of torture,
 To be bound to the wretched rack once more?
Is there a less enviable future
 Than suffering the closing of death's door?
Only death offers an escape from life
 Into the great undiscovered country —
Oh, how cruel if it but led to more strife,
 The cycle becoming eternity! —
Of all the tricks endured by us, the cursed,
It would be the least deserved and the worst.

2009

Voltaire Unearthed: Écrasez l'Infâme!
By David Lebowitz

"After coming into contact with a religious man I always feel I must wash my hands."
–Friedrich Nietzsche, Ecce Homo

"The very word 'Christianity' is a misunderstanding — in truth, there was only one Christian, and he died on the cross."
"'Faith' means not wanting to know what is true."
"In Christianity neither morality nor religion come into contact with reality at any point."
–Friedrich Nietzsche, The Antichrist

"One may bask at the warm fire of faith or choose to live in the bleak certainty of reason — but one cannot have both."
–Robert A. Heinlein, Friday

"You say I took the name in vain
I don't even know the name
But if I did, well really, what's it to you?"
–Leonard Cohen, "Hallelujah"

"Religion is the sigh of the oppressed creature, the heart of a heartless world, and the soul of soulless conditions. It is the opium of the people. The abolition of religion as the illusory happiness of the people is the demand for their real happiness. To call on them to give up their illusions about their condition is to call on them to give up a condition that requires illusions. The criticism of religion is, therefore, in embryo, the criticism of that vale of tears of which religion is the halo."
–Karl Marx, Critique of Hegel's Philosophy of Right

"It is said that if you know your enemies and know yourself, you will not be imperilled in a hundred battles; if you do not know your enemies but do know yourself, you will win one and lose one; if you do not know your enemies nor yourself, you will be imperilled in every single battle."
–Sun Tzu, The Art of War

"I watched with glee
While your kings and queens

Fought for ten decades
For the gods they made"
–Lucifer in The Rolling Stones' "Sympathy for the Devil"

David is a fifty-five-year-old Jewish atheist. He does not even try to hide his sole goal: destroying religion, as he truly believes it is the root of all evil, suffering, injustice, prejudice, and intolerance. He zeroes in on Christianity specifically, as it is the religion he has the most contact with and is the most familiar with, but he is an equal opportunity destroyer. In fact, Christianity is not even his most despised religion, though he does hate it. More accurately, like Vonnegut, he admires Christianity more than anything — that is, in its primitive form, which is to say, as practiced by Jesus and never again. He wishes its ideals and promises could be fulfilled, for then, he thinks, we would have a near-perfect world — but he knows they never will be and hates it all the more for it. He also admires many parts of other religions but is fed up with their corruption and pollution and has come to the conclusion that they all must fall. David believes Twain's Satan in *Letters from the Earth* describes The Bible best: "It is full of interest. It has noble poetry in it; and some clever fables; and some blood-drenched history; and some good morals; and a wealth of obscenity; and upwards of a thousand lies." He thus agrees after long, bitter experience with Arthur C. Clarke's (hopefully) prophetic pronouncement in "The View from 2500 A.D.": "One outcome of this–the greatest psychological survey in the whole of history–was to demonstrate conclusively that the chief danger to civilization was not merely religious extremism but religions themselves." Another of his favorite quotes is from Robert G. Ingersoll's *Some Mistakes of Moses*: "Were we allowed to read the Bible as we do all other books, we would admire its beauties, treasure its worthy thoughts, and account for all its absurd, grotesque and cruel things, by saying that its authors lived in rude, barbaric times." If David's greatest wish could be suddenly granted, he would wish the few good parts could be taken from all religion and the countless horrific ones disposed of and forgotten forever, but he is realistic and practical enough to know it will never occur. He is thus resolved to destroy them all for the greater good. His idol is Voltaire; he believes that venerable artist has done more than anyone to expose religion's sores and try to purify it. A perpetual Berkeley student, he has bachelor's and master's degrees in literature and history and a philosophy doctorate. He is currently working on a theology PhD; this may seem strange to some, but, unlike the mass of Christians and other sheep, he knows religion well—that is, as Sun Tzu counseled, he knows his enemy. His greatest fear is that he will die in vain, never having accomplished his task, and sleep in a pine box for all eternity, as he long ago ceased to believe in the comforting possibility of an afterlife, whether of damnation or bliss. He fears he will suffer the same sad fate Vonnegut lamented at Twain's home in 1979: "Religious skeptics often become very bitter towards the end, as did Mark Twain...I know why I will become bitter. I will finally realize that I have had it right all along: that I will not see God, that there is no heaven or Judgment Day." He is thus determined to make the most of this life; only time will tell if he becomes a resounding success or a miserable, if noble, failure. I include a representative sampling of his work to either whet your appetite—or pique your anger. Either way, Lebowitz and I likewise hope, it will make you think—which is the important thing after all.

siseneG

Well, I was high-tailin' 'round Jerusalem
 Back in the Romans' day
When some Jews came a-ridin',
 Came a-ridin' my way
They said they felt broken and defeated,
 Didn't know what they were gonna do
Said they needed someone
 To help 'em see it through

I said, "Gee, I don't know what to tell ya,
 I wish there was some kind of omnipotent being—
You know, the kind who solves all our problems
 And gives us everything"

"Come to think of it," they said,
 "That'd be all right"
And then what was to happen
 But a saucer fly out of the night;
  And a creature stepped out,
  I dare you to doubt
He looked old, but bright,
 With a long, white, flowing beard
He said his job was tallying sparrows' deaths,
 But in his spare time he came here

Now, I didn't quite know
 What to make of all this—
Soon after landing, he started talking about things
 I didn't even know could exist
"Civilization," he said, "freedom,
 Power, and glory to all"
"Man," I thought, "you must learn a lot
 From watching those sparrows fall"

I was standing there watching him
 In utter disbelief,
But the others were looking at him

Like he was some kind of thief—
Or, rather, a prophet
Or something more along those lines
They hadn't seen anyone like him
In all their time

Noticing my silence, he walked up next to me,
Said, "I'm gonna swindle these fools,
Just you wait and see
They think I'm some kind of deity
Who can do magical things—
But, hell, I just crash-landed on this miserable little planet,
Curious as to what kind of entertainment it could bring"

"I think I'll use this information
To get what I want
I've done it before,
Such is my wont
I guess I'll have to think up
A name for them to call me, eventually
They can just call me 'Yahweh,'—
It's what I was called
Back down the way

"I have my cute little son
Here with me
I think I'll use him for leverage
Or at least try and see—
It should help me gain some sympathy
What kind of riches
Do you have here by the sea?"

I said, "Well, we have some silver,
We have a little gold—
But you better get while the gettin's good,
Or else you'll be left out in the cold"

"Ha," he said, "I'll make them
Bring it to me,
Just you wait and see"

"Look," he said, with a twinkling of his eye,
 "Do you see my spaceship?
It is, I do declare, the brightest star in the sky
It came all the way from Sirius,
 I was at the helm;
And it has a name,
 Its name is *Bethlehem*
I'll tell them it will lead
 Them to my son,
And I'll get the riches from them —
 Well, nice knowin' ya — have fun"

 And so the alien got his riches —
Gold and sliver, and, on the side,
 A few bitches
It was pretty easy for him,
 He had relatively few hitches —
But this creature was of a particularly malicious kind,
 For, even after this success, he kept looking for ways to occupy
The sadistic longings of his mind

He strung his son up on a cross,
Said it was not his loss
 "They're the ones who cared for him," he said,
 "So I told them they'd get to see him again when they're dead"

I saw him do a lot of bad things,
 But the worst thing he ever did
Was create some stupid species called Man —
 Hell, he must've really flipped his lid
He started them out as apes,
 But it wasn't long before
They began to make
And do things on their own
He was tired of them by then,
 He left them on their own
Those fools are so suicidal
 That they chill me to the bone

You'd think they would all die out,

But they just won't go away
They just seem determined
To make it on their own some day
Personally, I don't give a fuck—
I wish them luck

He did a lot of other bad things,
Traveling down his pain-inflicting road
He took freedom from some woman named Eve,
Was especially mean to some guy named Job
All this is true—
I swear I've not lied about anything I've told

But back to our hero…
It was in the year Zero
That I saw him last
He boarded his ship again
And got out of here fast
He left a lot of problems behind him,
But I guess he prefers
His creations to live in sin—
Who knows?
He left two thousand years ago,
Never to be seen again…

2001

God Coming Down (A Theodicy)

"God is dead. God remains dead. And we have killed him."
–Friedrich Nietzsche, The Gay Science

Well, God is dead,
That's what the headline said
 He just fell right out of the sky,
 Landed in the ocean, appeared to die
Someone said, "Oh, my God, it's the divine!"
And a doctor checked His vital signs —
 Turns out He wasn't quite dead,
 There were still a few sparks in His head
Someone said they were glad to have Him around,
But God's coming down,
 Coming down like a balloon made out of lead

Well, the doctors were looking for a diagnosis —
One said it was psychosis,
 Another said He was just too old;
 And some old lady said they were all too bold,
Overstepping their bounds, playing God —
She thought it all just seemed a little too odd
 They didn't know if they could save His life,
 It was giving them all terrible strife
Someone said a cure they'd found,
But God's coming down,
 This is no time to be blithe

God was dying — that much was clear,
There was blood rushing out of His ass and ears
 His stomach burst open, His liver was shot,
 Someone said His brain was starting to rot
They didn't know what to do or how to proceed,
How to save the one who gave them all a creed
 It was the first time His life had been in danger
 Since that day He was put in a manger,
And they weren't so sure His future was sound;
But God's coming down,
 How could things possibly be any stranger?

They made one desperate, life-saving gesture
But just could not ease the pressure
 It was just too much — they tried their best
 But just could not pass the test
Perhaps Satan beat them to it,
Or they just weren't good enough to do it —
 Whatever the case, it was certainly time
 For the divine to reach the end of the line
It sure was nice having Him around,
But God had come down,
 Someone better put up a sign

Well, He passed away
Just before the end of day
 Everyone was sad and cried,
 Their feelings they could not hide
They wondered how life could go on
Now that God was gone,
 Wondered how they could make it through
 Without Him to tell them what to do
They say He died with a horrible, screaming sound
When God came down —
 We're gonna hafta come up with something new

Well, Emerson said it metaphorically
And Nietzsche rhetorically,
 But now it was really true
 God was dead — what were they gonna do?
Was there anything left to live for?
Would they be knocking on heaven's door?
 Was there meaning in life?
 A reason behind all the strife? —
Or were all the old answers lost, never to be found?
Whatever the case, God had come down,
 Better look to your teacher or wife

Well, they agreed to bury Him by majority vote,
And it was the mortician who found His suicide note
 It was inside His shirt pocket

In a heart-shaped box; they had to unlock it
It was carefully written out
So as to leave no doubt
 That the suicide had come after lengthy pondering,
 It was not some hasty thing
When it was read aloud, there was a gasping sound,
For God had come down,
 And the tears were beginning to sting

It read as follows:
"I'm sorry for all the lies you've swallowed,
 I'm sorry I've let you down,
 But it was high time I came around
I was tired of hearing all the lies about Me—
God damn, you guys never figured out me!
 I'm just not as merciful as you thought,
 I'm sorry about all the lies you bought
I hereby surrender my thorny crown—
I'm coming down,
 Killed by my own fatal shot

"I had high hopes for the human race,
But you've put Me in My place
 You've let me down—my biggest failure yet,
 My biggest mistake and greatest regret
You're just not all I thought you'd be,
I denied it for years, but now I finally see
 I'll never be able to forgive Myself
 And just can't blame it on someone else,
So you can bury Me in the ground
I'm coming down,
 You may be confused, but I hope this note helps

"You see, I just can't live with Myself after making you,
It just makes me too goddamn depressed and blue
 I fucked up—that's it in essence,
 Yes, you are failure's quintessence
I regret the day I made you,
And I'm sorry if I betrayed you—
 But I just can't put up with this guilt any longer,

I'm sorry I wasn't stronger
I'm just not merciful enough to forgive Myself; I let Myself down,
But don't waste your time waiting for a new god to come around,
 That would make you even wronger

"Well, so long, farewell —
For me it's been hell,
 But maybe you've had better luck
 To be honest, at this point I don't even give a fuck
Just go on with your miserable existence,
I just can't stand your irrational persistence
 Do whatever you want; I don't care,
 But I won't be around and don't have an heir
I'll be glad when I can no longer hear your annoying sounds,
So I'm coming down —
 And sorry, no refunds — I never said life was fair"

After it was read,
They all hung their heads —
 Most cried,
 A few even died
They just didn't know what to do,
Didn't know how to start anew
 Their lives were suddenly without meaning,
 And a few went away screaming
After the note was thrown down
They say for miles away you could hear the sound —
 In any case, it sure as hell was demeaning

There were, however,
A few who were more clever
 Far from lamenting,
 They had new plans cementing
They'd never believed in "The God Delusion,"
And at first, they felt confusion,
 But now they felt free —
 They had won out — and triumphantly!
Now that God had come down,
They could be the new gods in town
 And started on their plans immediately…

This is how it happened the first time,
And each occasion has been the same old line
 Voltaire said we'd have to create God if He didn't exist —
 Little did he know he wasn't first on the list
Someone has said it each time the current god died,
Made people believe them after all the tears had been cried —
 So it was, and so it shall be,
 We'll just keep on repeating the farce for eternity
It doesn't matter who's wrong and who's right,
We just can't face the idea of a solitary fight,
 So "God" keeps coming down,
 And we keep walking in the same old circles, going round and round,
Every time the latest charlatan says, "Let there be light —"

2007

A Brief History of Christianity

The only Christian died on the cross; he
 Forgiving even as they speared his side.
His message of peace, love, mercy, pity
 Was bright enough to light the whole world wide —
Such promise! — It could destroy outdated,
 Barbaric gods that held men back in fear,
Save them from the grim life that seemed fated,
 Help them o'ercome oppression far and near —
 O how the mighty fell and how quickly!
  Paul, Nicea, and untold bloody wars
  Brought on a paralyzing slavery
   Of mind, lost sight of "do unto others…"
O what a prize his sacrifice could win,
What difference between is and could have been!

All the good he did was wasted in death,
 It came at once to a permanent stop —
It disappeared for good with his last breath,
 Trickling out as blood dripped drop by drop —
 O how I wish he had not died in vain!
  His thorny crown pricked our consciences from
 That day onward, making us think of pain
  As something brotherly love could make numb —
Alas! It was not to be. Magic and
 Miracles ruled our minds forevermore
Except when we fought for the one whose hand
 Had never been raised to settle a score.
O how his power has been diminished!
If only he could say, "It is finished!"

2009

"Eli, Eli, lama sabachthani?"

"Why have you forsaken me?" cried the would-
 Be messiah, "I thought I was your son
And prophet, I lived a life pure and good,
 And spread your message…But your will be done!"
He added after a pain-ridden pause,
 Still reverent and loving, though doubting
At last, and obedient to the laws.
 He groaned in pain to jeering and shouting,
The sword pierced his side, and the vinegar
 Came; he writhed and looked with pity on his
Dearly loved and long-suffering mother —
 "Alas!" he groaned, "that it all came to this!"
Undeceived, he thought on his bleeding hand
And crown, then died as he was born — a man.

2009 (Thanks to my wife Jade for the idea.)

The Unspared Rod (A Query)

They say You chasten whom You love to test faith and to
 Separate the meek from cynical doubters and fair
Weather worship; yet, as with Job, expect love to You
 The same as if Your wretched creatures had not a care.
But who can fail to question "justice" so random that
 It seems non-existent—or, at best, partial, late, and
Not according to the rules You told us to aim at,
 While the slightest transgression is crushed by Your Iron Hand?
What gratitude can such a "Benefactor" expect
 When by far the most of what we see signals only
Apathy, indifference, hostility, or neglect,
 Leaving us cold, confused, disappointed, and lonely?
Can even the sincerest avoid despair and doubt
When joy's so rare, hard-won, and beguilingly doled out?

2009

To Martin Luther

Would-be reformer who tried to bring long-
 Needed changes from within the church doors,
Who had a great vision worthy and strong
 To rectify the church's exposed sores —
(Inhumane papal celibacy and
 Petty indulgences, exclusive view
Of the book, corruption, and a thousand
 Other abuses) — What became of you?
You lost yourself to vanity and turned
 Slave to worldly powers; mercilessly

Drove out those of other faiths; you had earned
 Respect in the minds of the poor, yet ye
Abandoned them as for you they lay dead —
May their curse and the Jews' be on your head!

2009

Only God Knows Why

We live in a world where religion's been unfurled
 And those who believe in the same God kill each other every day
Try as we might, we just can't shut our eyes tight
 Enough to make it all go away
They may call Him a different name and play a different game,
 But is that enough for innocents to die?
In whole or gist, the holy books say nothing about this,
 And only God knows why

From injunctions to kill to "Resist not evil,"
 Jesus turned the Word on its head
I don't know what this means, but surely it seems
 As if they would have just left it for dead —
But who can doubt they'll never figure it out
 And all just ignorantly die?
It makes no sense at all, but to them it's small,
 And only God knows why

Wouldn't it be nice if they actually followed Christ
 Instead of picking and choosing verses?
They're a great distance from his stance,
 Love and mercy have turned into curses
Maybe their problem is they still follow Him
 Instead of the more peaceful guy
You must take your pick, 'cause they won't both stick,
 And only God knows why

Jesus' solution brought peaceful revolution
 That left all barbarity behind
Violence and brutality were replaced by normality,
 But I guess they just aren't the peaceful kind
Who knows how they'd be if they could actually see
 That what they're doing's a lie —
But they don't give a shit, they're just hypocrites,
 And only God knows why

The Old Testament and its daughter mix like oil and water,

LIFE'S TRIUMPH by Bill R. Moore

It's hard to find even one similarity
Combining the two, Christian and Jew,
 Only makes for hilarity
The Hebrews have outgrown what they once had known,
 Repented from their mistakes with a sigh —
But their successors run mad with ideas they once had,
 And only God knows why

There's more to The Bible than what you hear at revival,
 They distort beyond recognition
They lie about what it has to say and insert their own way,
 Manipulating like a magician
Sure as hell, they're bound to tell
 You lie after lie after lie
They say what they want, their lies continue to haunt,
 And only God knows why

Few have actually read it; they might as well shred it
 For all they know about it
Most can only quote what they've memorized by rote
 But sure as hell love to shout it
They act like experts but will get buried in the dirt
 Of ignorance, distortions, and lies
They know so little but sure like to meddle,
 And only God knows why

Their minds aren't open, but they're always hopin'
 For free and easy eternal security
They'll swallow any pill, chalk it up to God's will,
 And accept patent absurdities
If turning water into wine makes someone divine,
 I'll laugh until I cry —
But it's good enough for them in this world of sink or swim,
 And only God knows why

Smug in their ignorance, they refuse to take a chance
 By listening to a contrary view
They could be wrong but will keep on as long
 As they keep doing what they do
They won't listen to me or you, won't even argue,

Will be ignorant and hypocritical 'til they die—
But they're always ready to fight to prove they're right,
 And only God knows why

Maybe they'll pull out when they see what he's all about,
 That gentle man they're supposed to follow—
But they seem lost in the haze of misguided ways
 With no hope of choking on the pill they're told to swallow
I might let them off the hook if they actually read their own book,
 Instead of listening to a charlatan who just tells them lies
Their heads are up their asses, they deserve no free passes,
 And only God knows why

Judging by their wars and their whores,
 You'd think they'd never heard of the lion and the lamb
They have no use for the latter; they'd rather flatter
 Themselves over the success of their sham
I suppose it will only end when they finally begin
 To see how they've made each other cry—
But that'll probably be never, it'll just go on forever,
 And only God knows why

Forever consistent, they're always resistant
 To anything but their own interpretation
As shown by their abuse, they simply have no use
 For well-intentioned information
They're carrying the sword in the name of the Lord
 And making each other die
They won't end the rout 'til they all die out,
 And only God knows why

If you show them how they act, they'll dismiss your fact
 As the work of this mysterious Devil
I guess hypocrisy thrives in a theocracy,
 They move it up to a whole other level
They're more likely to kill you dead than do what Jesus said
 And refuse to cast a judgmental eye
They won't even try to refute you; they'll just shoot you,
 And only God knows why

LIFE'S TRIUMPH by Bill R. Moore

Their minds must be on the brink for them to think
 They have a more certain future than me —
But their belief in a just god starts to look less odd
 When they contemplate eternity
Far from being humble, their tongues start to rumble
 When faced with infidels who raise a contrary cry
They think they'll get a heavenly turn, that their enemies will burn,
 And only God knows why

When one religion grows out of another, it's not brother to brother,
 The new must take responsibility for what it does
It can use the first as a guide or case it aside
 But must understand what it was
An unholy mixture is a deadly elixir
 For which none should ever try —
But the mistake was made, bad plans were laid,
 And only God knows why

The time for atonement has passed; the first stone has been cast,
 It's far too late to go back now
I sincerely confess I wish they'd clean up the mess
 With more devotion than they put into a vow
I'd help them if they'd let me, but they always forget me,
 Wanting for themselves the whole pie —
But they'll choke on the wine and bread they're being spoon-fed,
 And only God knows why

Only God knows why

2007

The Fire Next Time

If God were alive today,
This is what He would say:
"I drowned you in water one time,
And you've left your promise to me far behind,
So there'll be no mercy, no forgiving —
Better get used to me sucking all the juice outta the life you're living"
God gave Noah the rainbow sign,
No more water, the fire next time!

We're breakin' our cov'nant, slashin' our wrists,
It's always a risk when you get the Almighty pissed
We've come too far ta save ourselves now,
We'll just hafta make it through somehow
Yes, it's too late to go back,
We must brace ourselves for divine attack
God gave Noah the rainbow sign,
No more water, the fire next time!

Well, the time has come ta pay for our sins,
The time has come ta answer ta Him
Old memories are rushin' up ta meet us now,
Old ghosts we thought we'd killed somehow —
I can see the slavery ships,
The backs bein' whipped
God gave Noah the rainbow sign,
No more water, the fire next time!

Oh, God, forgive us for our sins!
I can see the ghost of the Old South risin' up again —
The lash cuttin' into their backs,
The tall white mansions and little shacks,
The Southern preacher hangin' over the hellfire pit —
Oh, Lord, how could we ever forget? How did we ever forget?
God gave Noah the rainbow sign,

No more water, the fire next time!

We forgot what our Good Book said,
Were lookin' out for number one instead
 We never thought we'd hafta pay,
 Never thought we'd hafta care what anyone else had ta say—
Oh, but the time has come now ta pay them back,
But it's too late; our train's done gone off the track
 God gave Noah the rainbow sign,
 No more water, the fire next time!

We always said the South would rise again,
We were still fightin' for that lost cause we knew we could win—
 Oh, but we had the arrogance to think we were on the side of right,
 And, oh! how bright were our days, but none could match this dark night
The sun is settin' on the land of cotton,
Where bright days have long been forgotten
 God gave Noah the rainbow sign,
 No more water, the fire next time!

Look away! Look away! Look away, Dixieland!
We're bein' crushed under the wrath of God's hand
 We really thought we had God on our side,
 Thought we had the right ta whip the black man's hide—
But there ain't nothin' we can do now ta save ourselves,
We're too weak, and we've always said we'd never rely on someone else
 God gave Noah the rainbow sign,
 No more water, the fire next time!

I'm goin' ta hit the road just as soon as I can find a mount,
But nothin' really matters much; it's doom alone that counts;
 And there's no shelter from the storm here, no escape from the rain,
 We're bein' branded with the mark that is our permanent stain
I wish there was a way out even at this late date,
But we hafta stop kiddin' ourselves; it's all up to fate
 God gave Noah the rainbow sign,

No more water, the fire next time!

But I can't say I have any regrets,
'Cept leavin' my plantation behind and not payin' all my debts
 If I had ta do it all over again, I would,
 I'd burn the same crosses an' hide 'neath the same hood
No, I ain't sorry for nothin' I done,
I'm glad we fought; I only wish we'd won!
 God gave Noah the rainbow sign,
 No more water, the fire next time!

No, I don't regret puttin' the shackles on 'em,
It ain't none-a my business, an' we all got our own problems
 I'm sure we coulda done better by our God and Book,
 But we did what we thought best, and ta heaven we always looked
Hell, no, I don't have any regrets now, just a heap o' sorrows,
It's such a sad thing ta say goodbye to all the South's tomorrows
 God gave Noah the rainbow sign,
 No more water, the fire next time!

So, let us say goodbye now ta the land our hard work created—
Where slavery was sustained, where Lincoln was hated
 It has served us well, and we've been good masters to it,
 If not for it, Lord knows, we never coulda gotten through it
My only hope now is that hell ain't such a bad place to be,
But I know, deep down in my heart, not even heaven could ever be like my
     Dixie
 God gave Noah the rainbow sign,
 No more water, the fire next time!

I'm leavin' home this toasty morn,
But they say for everything that dies, a new thing is born—
 Maybe somethin' new will replace us, but it'll never be like my home
 Lord, how I loved the Southland; it was the one thing we could call our
     own
As I see the lone rider approachin', I finally see the message God was tryin'

to send —
God bless you, Dixieland! I loved you 'till the end! —
God gave Noah the rainbow sign,
No more water, the fire next time!

I see the writing on the wall saying, "This land is condemned,"
It's being purified now; they won't even have a chance to swim
There is no god to answer to, no source of this death's construction,
The South sowed the seeds of its own destruction —
From slavery to denying liberty, hypocrisy to bigotry, it was inevitable…
But I must be leaving now; I can hear that lonesome whistle call
There needn't be a god to give the rainbow sign,
For there is no water — it's the fire this time!

2007

Religious Blues

Well, I'm walkin' 'way from the churchyard; I got them religious blues
Yes, I'm walkin' 'way from the churchyard; I got them religious blues
Can't find no peace of mind in no confession booth, can't find salvation in
    no pews

Well, the preacher man told me to pray; that's what I'm gonna do
Oh, Lord, yes, the preacher man told me to pray, and that's what I'm a-
    gonna do
But that man up there just don't seem to hear me — kinda reminds me of
    you

Well, I disagree with church doctrine; I'm nailin' my theses to the door
Well, yes, I disagree with church doctrine; I'm nailin' my theses to the door
But I'm already bein' ostracized; this lil' ol' town don't want me no more

Well, that good ol' God betrayed me; I feel like I been crucified
Yes, that good ol' God betrayed me; I feel like I been crucified
I always thought everything they said was Gospel — but maybe they just
    lied

Preacher just told me another lie; I been betrayed by a kiss
Well, that goddamn preacher just told me another lie; I feel like I been be-
    trayed by a kiss
Lordy, oh, Lordy, why didn't they tell me it was a-gonna be like this?

Well, I been studyin' my Good Book, so I can go preachin' from town to
    town
Yes, I've been a-studyin' my Good Book, so I can go preachin' from town to
    town
All I'll charge is thirty pieces of silver, no money down

That man up there on the cross, they say he was crucified for me
Well, that man up there on the cross, they say he was a-crucified for me
Nobody asked me for my opinion; I would've said, "Just let him be"

Well, you stole half your Bible from the Hebrews, the rest from the Greeks
    and Egyptians

Yes, you stole half your Bible from the Hebrews, the rest from the Greeks
and Egyptians
You tell me the damn thing's sacred—you'd have better luck readin' bath-
room wall inscriptions

They say the streets of heaven are lined with gold, that God has a golden
throne
Yes, they say the streets of heaven are lined with gold, that God has a
golden throne
But they're gonna hafta drag me there, 'cause I ain't goin' on my own

What about all the good people who aren't like you—what happens to
them?
Yes, what about all the good people who aren't like you—just what the hell
happens to them?
You say they're bound straight for hellfire; I say it ain't sink or swim

What about those of you who are vile and corrupt?
Yes, well, what about those amongst you who are vile and corrupt?
I know one thing for sure; they sure as hell ain't goin' up

Well, I'm turnin' my back on You now; I'm walkin' 'way from the village
steeple
Yes, I'm turnin' my back on You now; I'm walkin' 'way from the village
steeple
I'm comin' down from the mountain; I'm bringin' the truth to the people

Well, I'm walkin' away from the churchyard; I got them religious blues
Yes, I'm walkin' away from the churchyard; I got them religious blues
Can't find no peace of mind in no confession booth, can't find salvation in
no pews

I'm bringin' the truth to the people

Circa 2003

Prayer to a Non-Existent God
(A Plea for Apatheism)

"The fool hath said in his heart, There is no God"
–Psalms 14/53

"Do you take me for such a fool
To think I'd make contact
With the one who tries to hide
What he don't know to begin with"
–Bob Dylan, "Positively 4th Street"

O You who always choose not to show Your face,
 Who abstains forever from the sins of the corporeal—
I care not if You exist in this or any other place,
 I care not if You are real
 Though I need great love for my scars to heal,
I have no heart for this kind of chase,
O You who always choose not to show Your face

O You who delight in the profundity of silence,
 Who dangle the perpetual illusion that you will suddenly care—
I care not to use Your name in justifying violence,
 I care not if You watch over every sparrow and hair
 Having found Your ways something less than fair,
I have given up seeking Your presence,
O You who delight in the profundity of silence

O You who insist on faith without proof,
 Who tantalize and confuse with the cold hand of fate—
If it were but a matter of truth,
 A matter of love and hate,
 Perhaps I could believe in You—but it is far too late,
For I have outgrown the naïve helplessness of youth,
O You who insist on faith without proof.

O You who claim to hold back just to deceive,
 Who leave us in constant doubt if You are really there —
If there were but a revelation to receive,
 If it were but meted out in petitions of prayer,
 If faith and communication were not a futile pair,
Then perhaps in you I could believe,
O You who claim to hold back just to deceive

O You worst of all human inventions,
 Who has kept us chained to the tyranny of theism —
I see no evidence of your interventions,
 But belief in them has led to our worst barbarism
 It is time for us to live without You, to start the Last Great Schism,
We must pay no heed to Your intentions,
O You worst of all human inventions

O You greatest of sanctuaries for the weak,
 Who give us faith in life after we die —
If the earth will truly be inherited by the meek,
 Why must so many innocents needlessly sigh?
 Why must so many believers be forced to cry?
You give those who believe in You little cause to speak,
O You greatest of sanctuaries for the weak

O You who offer no proof of Your existence,
 Who leave theologians unable to explain why,
Who has us start wars in Your name that make no sense,
 How can you expect us to believe a lie?
 Your believers are always defending a god they can never justify
With no excuses and no evidence,
O You who offer no proof of Your existence

O You who demand our unwavering belief,
 Who insist we forget love, country, all we have bought,
Who give our minds and consciences no relief —

You say those who do not believe in You are fools doomed to rot,
 But I say the question matters not
Neither your existence nor your non-existence brings me any grief,
O You who demand our unwavering belief

O you hypocrites who would have me reduced to skin and bone,
 Who think my beliefs and behavior solitary and odd —
I would have you know I am not alone,
 It is no new path I trod
 To you we say, I and others who dare to live without God,
O you hypocrites who would have me reduced to skin and bone,
 "He that is without sin among you, let him first cast a stone…"

2007

The Vicious Eternal Circle
(A Theological Query)

If the history
Of the twentieth century
 Made a poor joke of the foolish belief
That this is the best of all possible worlds,
 Some still get relief
In thinking help is hurled
 From God to those in need —
 A hardly more credible creed

We believe in prayer
And say life is fair
 Because not always overloaded with pain,
But why does our Tormentor ever beset us
 And let us petition in vain?
He often seems to forget us
 When we need him most —
 A philanthropic record of which I would not boast

We think the greatest miracle that which comes
When we are nearest death or feeling most numb,
 But why ever let such things arise?
We would justly value Him more
 If things were otherwise
And there no prior pain to ignore
 Surely the highest praise is reserved for He
 Who would not make us pay and plead for bounty?

Ah, but they say faith must be tested
And that for this inconstant Fortune cannot be bested,
 But it is a strange God who would have us think best
What we would least prize
 If we did not think it a test
Or could see His ways with dispassionate eyes
 Just think of the pain in which we would wallow
 If last-minute mercy did not follow

Ah, but it always comes — or don't it?
I bet for a while you wouldn't have dared own it
 Yes, with suffering at its peak,
You doubted as much as the staunchest infidel —
 Which only proves we are but meek
And sends His plan to early hell
 How sad to make us honestly curse He
 Who claims to be giving mercy!

Of course we forget later,
Deny we were traitor,
 Say we always believed;
But deep down we know
 That we were deceived
We'll never let it show,
 But our hearts harden in solitude
 And shut Him out in a dark mood

And what of Original Sin
Inherited even by children?
 What the first two did reflects no more on us
Than my sin reflects on you
 Yet this cruel belief we trust
And blame for making us blue
 We all choose whether or not to be depraved,
 So why should we be forever enslaved?

We all make our own mistakes,
Find things like laws and hearts to break —
 We must not blame forbidden fruit;
Even if we all bite,
 It does not get to the root
That is injustice's height
 So I ask once again,
 Why do so many lose and so few win?

Yes, why do bad things happen to the good?
Why are they persecuted and strung up on wood
 While the wicked have their pick of earthly treasure?
We must not look to hypothetical afterlife

For each to get their due measure,
It is here that we drown in pain and strife
So I ask one more time,
If He wants love, why not give indisputable sign?

We would have more due reverence
For He who would bring pain's severance
Other than as last resort
He would be worthy of praise
Rather than bitter retort
Brought on by sad days
Ah, Almighty!, why make traps to set us in
Only to snatch us from death's jaws and start again?...

2009

From *Eros* to *Agapē*:
Sailing Love's Stormy Seas
By Robert Wells

"Every heart
to love will come
But like a refugee."
–Leonard Cohen, "Anthem"

"Love and only love, it can't be denied.
No matter what you think about it
You just won't be able to do without it.
Take a tip from one who's tried."
–Bob Dylan, "I Threw It All Away"

"In the end the love you take is equal to the love you make."
–John Lennon and Paul McCartney, The Beatles' "The End"

All poets chronicled so far have touched on love to varying degrees, but it is Robert's single-minded obsession. He broods on it, focuses on it — *obsesses* over it. He makes no apology, or even feels the need; it is in his view the only thing worth thinking about anyway. That said, he has no desire to be the bard of newly-found lovers, crooning light tunes lightly and blithely; his picture is more accurate. He strives for verisimilitude and puts forth all effort to avoid greeting card sentimentality. However, this does not mean he concentrates solely on the heart's darker recesses, though he often finds the courage to shed some light on that shady area; he is no self-pitying, lovesick fool. That is, he does not restrict himself to star-crossed lovers. He tries to present a well-rounded, true-to-life picture of love's many aspects. He thus sings of new-found love's incomparable joy, the unutterable blackness of love lost, and everything between them. He sees his songs — as they are songs (love songs, torch songs), whether love's flame burns bright or is tragically extinguished — as existing in a continuum with "bright love" on one end and "dark love" on the other; his goal is to give them all their due. If his published works incline more toward the latter than the former, it should not be taken to mean he is overly mopey, melodramatic, or self-pitying; rather, his love songs that shine brightest are for his own true love, not public consumption. If this makes him seem to have a darker view of love than he actually has, so be it; if an intimation of worldly melancholy is what must be paid for domestic bliss in love, he is willing to pay. After all, *caritas* (or is it "love"?) begins at home. Whatever his songs' tone, all his works hone in on our lives' one great truth—love is paramount, and its immense sway is mysterious, divine, and, above all, awe-inspiring. He does not claim to have pierced all its mysteries, or even to be capable of it, but that does not stop him from shooting a few arrows (Cupid's?) into the blue. His volume is presented in full, the better to see its wide-ranging panorama, which, like love, is a canvas as large and awesome (awful?) as life itself.

Crumbs from Your Table

You live in this world; there's no cure for that
 And simply no way around it
Try as you might, you just can't win the fight
 Without some reinforcements to surround it;
And sometimes people will come around
 And try to convince you they've found it,
But they don't know the gloom that pervades this room,
 And I'm always down with it;
But I need your help, baby; I need it 'cause I'm not able—
Oh, babe, I'm living off the crumbs from your table

Well, I just don't know how to react,
 Don't know what to say or do
I've left too much of my blood on the tracks,
 Now I need a little help from you
I hope it's not asking too much
 To expect me to see you through—
After all, I've always answered your call
 And usually did something about it, too,
And I need your help now, baby, need it to get me through this fable—
Oh, babe, I'm begging for the crumbs from your table

No one can make it through life alone,
 Solitude makes heart and mind go dead
We all need someone we can call our own
 To fix our broken hearts and soothe our aching heads
There's too much strife in this sorry life
 To simply live off what we're being force-fed—
And, baby, I don't care if you put me on a leash,
 Don't care how you treat me or where I'm led
'Cause I need your help, baby; you know I'm just not able—
Oh, babe, I need the crumbs from your table

There are too many lies and too many "whys,"

LIFE'S TRIUMPH by Bill R. Moore

Too many reasons not to believe
There's too much death to stifle our breath,
Too many ways for others to deceive
We need a safety valve to give us oxygen
And make it easier to breathe
There's just no way to make it pay
Unless you have someone who can relieve,
And I'm asking you to do that for me, baby 'cause alone I'm just not able—
Oh, baby, I'm asking for the crumbs from your table

They grind us down and spin us around,
Try to make us hopelessly confused
Without a doubt, they want us too far out
To even know we're being abused
I lived like that for a while, but now it's out of style
'Cause I finally realized I was being used,
And I need you to help me, 'cause I just can't stand
Being so beaten down and bruised
I need your love, babe; I'm looking for your confirmatory cable—
Oh, honey, I'm looking for the crumbs from your table

In this life we lead, there are hungry mouths to feed
And a million people wanting your attention
Some will step on you; others may help you,
Some are just honorable mentions
In the end, it's hard to find a real friend
'Cause we're all worried about dissension—
But I swear to you, I'll be forever true,
I won't leave your heart in detention
'Cause I need your love, babe; this ain't no fable—
Oh, honey, I need the crumbs from your table

In this world of darkness, it's hard to find a harness
To support you when you're most in need
Friends will turn on you; lovers will burn you,
Others will just avoid you out of greed
In this domain of disappointment and pain,

People get pleasure from watching you bleed
It's easy to think you're on the brink
When you're the only one left in your steed,
So I need your love, darling; I need it 'cause I'm just not able—
Oh, honey baby, I'm counting on the crumbs from your table

They say you can't get anything for free, but you can always count on me,
 I won't ever leave you sore
Trust me when I say, tomorrow and today,
 No problem of yours is small enough for me to ignore
I'll always be there for you, won't ever bore you,
 No matter what's in store
I'll always be there; you'll always have my care,
 We'll be just like legendary lovers of yore,
So come on, baby; I'm ready for your love—can't you see I'm able?
I'm hoping for the crumbs from your table

There's faith in my kiss; you can put your trust in this,
 No matter what happens in this world
I'll be beside you no matter what we go through,
 I promise you that, girl
They say there's no escape from the murder and rape
 Now that truth has been unfurled—
But just stay with me, and together we'll see
 If we can take on everything that gets hurled
I'm ready, baby; I'm ready, willing, and able—
All I need are the crumbs from your table

2007

The King to His Mistress Part I

Men would pay to bow at my illustrious feet,
 I have all the world's riches, women in a cage,
No one dares not laugh at my most worthless conceit,
 None dare to check me, much less fly off in a rage.
I have every allurement and sweet temptation,
 Lack nothing for which the richest contend in vain.
I have a mind most fit for great contemplation,
 And my least worry is immediately slain.
Yes, I lack nothing, and am the envy of all,
 Everyone does my bidding or dies for treason,
None escape—not the great, certainly not the small—
 And for all this I need not even give reason.
Yet you, unlearned in the ways of the world or books,
Could undo it all with casual words or looks!

2009

Love's Just a Four-Letter Word

I knew it'd never go away,
 Yes, it's coming back again
Someone's tryin' to tell me
 What I'm doing's a sin
Yeah, and they're sure of it
 'Cause they heard it from a friend of a friend;
 And I ask myself yet again—
How much longer
 Before this bullshit ends?
 Only then can we give in
 And let our love begin
It's all just too absurd—
Makes you think love's just a four-letter word

Yes, but I heard that you heard that I heard that you heard
 That I was feeling down,
And that I was wondering how much longer
 It'd be before you came back around—
Well, what can I say?
 You just can't believe every uttered sound
I'm gettin' sick and tired
 Of all the wicked tongues in this town
Tangled up deep in that web of conceit and deceit
 Is truth waiting to be unwound
It's not hidden up your skirt
 Or beneath your gown
It's only here that it's clear
 That there's no truth to be found
 About that particular noun
You know, the one you just heard—
I guess love's just a four-letter word

Hypocrites are slandering
 The sacred halls of truth,
Mercilessly destroying

All the dreams built up in youth;
But I never subscribed to that stuff,
 Always found it too aloof
So much for sand castles
 And the sugarplum fairy's golden tooth
Someone has to cool the fires
 When they're makin' life sound too good
Or else you'll be disappointed
 Just like I always said you would
I'll do it; I'm used to being a black sheep,
 I'd be one all the time if I could
Haven't you heard?
As of the beginning of time, love's just a four-letter word

Yes, but I heard that you heard that I heard that you heard
 That I still loved you so —
Yeah, but who said it was the truth?
 You know they just say that stuff for show
You see, I'm not asking you
 To say words like "yes" or "no"
Believe me, that's the last place
 I'd ever wanna go
It's just that I want something from you —
 But what it is I don't quite know;
But I think I'll stop talking right now,
 This conversation's brow's starting to get a bit too low
Hold on, baby; we're gonna take
 The rest of the way slow
My words are starting to sound slurred —
Maybe love's just a four-letter word

Well, I fell in love again —
 Yeah, I know it sounds like the same old line,
But I've been doin' some thinkin',
 And I think it's really for real this time
 I took the bait when I saw the sign,
 Started posing questions in the form of rhyme;
And I'd forever talk to you,

I'd forever play and sing,
But sooner or later all my words
 Would become a meaningless ring—
And I'm not sure if it does any good anyway,
 Don't know if you hear a single thing;
And I'm beginning to seriously wonder
 If there's really any help I can bring
Does it pay to be a nerd
Or is love just a four-letter word?

Yes, but I heard that you heard that I heard that you heard
 That I was worried about you—
Well, what can I say?
 You know I don't feel like I used to;
After a certain point
 There's just nothing else you can do;
And I'm afraid to admit it, darling,
 But I think I'm entering my darkest night
 Everything's broken; nothing seems right,
And all my pictures seem to fade
 To black and white
What the hell can I possibly say about the future?
 I don't have second sight
It's not my job to tell you
 What's wrong and what's right
All I know is what I've heard—
That love's just a four-letter word

We all ask ourselves these questions,
 None know the reason why
We just stand here philosophizing our lives away
 As time continues to pass us by
Now, I'm not pointing the finger,
 I'm just as guilty as the rest of you
Anything you can be accused of
 I guarantee I've done, too
I'm sick of all this preachin',
 Sick of all these lines—

You're right from your side,
 I'm right from mine;
And you may not believe it,
But I asked the question in truth's hallowed halls,
 And this is what I heard —
 Love's just a four-letter word

2001

The Coward Does It with a Kiss

"All men kill the thing they love"
–Oscar Wilde, The Ballad of Reading Gaol

O, Brain, there is one in me stronger than You!
Only love can heal my scars, but it has left me,
 And I'm cut deep through
With each age we cast aside our guides
 In the name of something new
Some lead down blind alleys and dead ends,
 Others are forever true
I lived for years on the edge of hopes and dreams,
 Then happily with just us two —
But all is gone now, and it's a heavy price to pay
 When you've lost the precious few
That kept you alive and gave reason to strive
 More than you even knew

O, if we only knew the value of what we have before it is lost!
We would work so much harder to get it,
 Hold on at any cost
Our love was warm enough to outlast the coldest, loneliest days,
 But now it's turned to frost
What would I not do to have it back, to undo what can't be undone,
 To finish what was glossed!
My whole future is as nothing beside the limitless, blissful past,
 I feel like an insect embossed
O what fools we are to set traps for ourselves
 And fall in before one solution's exhaust
When we could forever live happily on crumbs we let slip
 And trifles we've carelessly tossed!

How quickly and thoroughly the loved can become the hated!
Main sails can shift and the best-laid plans can drift
 As if it all were fated
How foolish and cynical we were to claim
 In hours of joy that love was overrated —
O, how little we knew as through and through

The little we had left dissipated!
Yet I feel it could have all been different,
 That points of departure could have somehow been related
Yes, I feel I could have done anything for you
 If you'd only made me feel obligated
Ah, what fools we are—it takes nothing for us to dash a lifetime of joy,
 Everything to make us embrace the already consummated!

There is the bed where many hours in love we have lain—
O, how empty and cold!
 We have separate ones now, and to what gain?
Where is your warm body when I need one to hold?
 Our love is gone; it has been slain,
Nothing is left but a dried-up husk—
 A sad carcass, an ignoble stain
No one would recognize it—
 And all for reasons so trifling and vain!
O, is there anything we can do
 In the few hours that remain—
But no; we have denied ourselves love,
 Hence this great void and dark, undying pain

Once there was a way back; we could have persisted—
Put some things aside, forgotten others,
 Forgiven some, and new ones enlisted—
But those days are past, and a future so vast
 Stares down at us that we long resisted
It's here now; there's no going back somehow,
 Our eyes have forever misted
There's no way out, and everything about
 Is the dark opposite of what once consisted
No longer youth, we must face the truth,
 Not deny reality has shifted
The door to yore is closed forevermore—
 If it ever even existed

2009

After the Thrill Is Gone

The naïve idealism of Youth
Loses its so-called Proof
When confronted with that horrid thing, Truth
 Leaving us on our own
Oh, how we despise
The hypocrisy and lies
That pass before our eyes
 As up we've grown!
There's not much left of us
By the time we bite the dust,
Just a rotten, empty husk
 Of skin and bone
We start out gregarious,
But this becomes precarious
When there's no one to carry us
 And we end up alone
From first to last
In future and past
The one thing we must grasp
 Is this wretched fate to which we're prone
Yes, it's the sad truth,
 But we can't wave a magic wand
 For life goes on
 Long after the thrill is gone

It begins pleasantly enough
But soon turns rough
And Life just becomes too tough
 To feel truly free
The lights start dimming
And in a sea of pain we're swimming
While the Cause from which it's stemming
 Remains unknown to you and me
What else can I say?
We all know it's the way —
Life goes from black and white to gray
 And we drown in ambiguity

Yet I can still remember
That joyous December
When our hearts were still tender
 And Life and Love all they are said to be
But forget all that
It's vain, useless chat
Let's go back to our old hat,
 Let speech be wrought mechanically
I'm almost used to it now,
 No longer want to drown myself in the pond
 For life goes on
 Long after the thrill is gone

Why can't I forget the memory
Buried deep inside of me
When we could rise above mediocrity
 Me and you?
Yes, I'm haunted by a supposition
That we could've avoided this repetition
If only we'd had a premonition
 When Life and Love were new
Ah, but what's the use?
In order to end the abuse
We'd have to come up with some excuse
 For talking it through
And you know as well as me
How that turns to hell so easily,
Both of us vainly wishing to be
 The happy pair we once knew
So let's stop the illusion,
Quit trying to cut through the confusion,
Just admit we're losin'
 And go back behind the line we drew
Yes, why kid ourselves?
 You can't repair a shattered bond
 For life goes on
 Long after the thrill is gone

You think I'm Henry VIII, and I think you're Lady Macbeth,
But let's just finish the bitter farce, pretend we care for breath

And don't long for merciful death
 Maybe some day we can renew
That's what all the others say,
And some of 'em seem to have made it pay
Maybe we'll be happier that way
 If we can see it through
The world and its ways have a certain worth,
And who knows but that this vile planet that gave us birth
Will one day bring us joy and mirth
 If we behave like the rest of its crew
What have we to lose?
It's sinking, our former luxury cruise,
We could use some good news,
 And can what they say so oft fail to be somewhat true?
But no; we long ago reached our peak,
The future's broken and bleak
Hell, we hardly even speak,
 Me and you
So let's just admit it,
 Pull out the dunce cap we love to don
 For life goes on
 Long after the thrill is gone

Yes, let's admit all is vanity
Submit to insanity
Turn our backs on humanity,
 Drink our sorrow to the last dram
What's the use in pretending?
Our backs are broken from bending
While spending so many years mending
 A broken gate that long ago closed with a slam
It's time to face the Ugly Truth
That we're not what we were in Youth
Hell, if you still need proof
 Just look at the sea of tears we have to dam
Let's at least look forward to death in peace,
We'll finally get a release,
No longer need to keep each other on a tight leash
 Or seek solace in a bottle or a gram
Yes, it's the Bitter End

LIFE'S TRIUMPH by Bill R. Moore

Why even bother to pretend?
It's seems time's beginning to suspend,
 And we don't even give a damn
It's time to give up
 And look forward to the Great Beyond
 For life goes on
 Long after the thrill is gone

I heard you broke our Promise,
Became a Doubting Thomas
God damn! It's such a bitter pill, this
 Lie we swallow as we fade away
We pay lip service to Optimism,
Deny we have a Schism,
Look through a rose-tinted prism
 That blocks out shades of gray
I know you've said it before — "Oh well,
We might as well try it — what the hell?
Who could fall further than we fell
 Since that cursed day?"
It's not that I disagree,
I just wanna drink this poison to the lees
Yes, my love, just you and me —
 What do you say?
But I can see you're finally running
That's all right; it was a long time coming
As for all your old betrayals and cunning,
 Well, I never cared too much anyway
Yes, it hurts,
 But at least you're too old to have a spawn
 For life goes on
 Long after the thrill is gone

Yes, I can see you've finally abandoned me
Hell, you could've done it for free
As for leaving with him — Well, gee,
 I guess it's just as well
At least the suspense is over
I always knew you were a rover
It's just another four-leaf clover

I believed in when I was under your spell
Yes, the truth is out
And there's little doubt
That, no matter how much clout,
 Things rarely turn out swell
I long ago stopped believing in a God above,
But such a fool is Love
That I just couldn't help thinking of
 All that could've been, until you rang our funeral bell
So it's ashes to ashes, dust to dust
I wish I could say Life wasn't a bust,
But I just can't break my sacred trust—
 So I'll see you in hell
Farewell to the few pleasures
 Of which we were still fond
 For life goes on
 Long after the thrill is gone

The thrill is gone

Postscript

And when I saw you down there
We pretended we didn't have a care,
Told ourselves Life had been fair,
 But we both knew better
I don't know why we kept it up,
This game of lies so vile and corrupt
I guess we just wanted one last sup
 Before the stormy weather
You'd think we would have learned,
Just before we were to burn,
That Punishment's something you earn,
 But we acted like we never met her
We kept up this absurd cosmic joke,
Milked each masochistic stroke
'Till all excuses went up in smoke
 And we laughed at Sorrow, said we could forget her
Yes, but the Ugly Truth dawns on all in the end
We meet it face to face, time seems to suspend,

And there's nothing to do but just give in
 And with our last wretched gasp curse our Debtor;
And the cheap stone that mocks our memory,
 Proving that in Fate's hands we're a pawn,
 Says, "Life went on
 Long after the thrill was gone"

2009

Nature against Two

I lost count of how many times I told you
Back when you let me hold you
 That the only number you can believe in is Two
Don't even try to deny it
Much less defy it
 They'll only let you down if you do
You might add one or two for a while,
But you're living in denial
 If you think they'll be true
So go ahead—live it up
See if I give a fuck
 Go back on everything we ever knew
You can have a blast
While I live vicariously in the past
 Telling everyone I'm not blue
I'll plug my ears and tie myself to the mast
See how much longer we can last
 Before we're through
I wish I could say
I knew it'd be a long way,
 But who would know better than you?
 Yes, who would know better than you?

I remember when I first met you,
I knew I'd never forget you,
 Picked you up at the lost and found
Now that you've come so far
You seem to forget how things are
 And don't seem to care if I'm down
Why must I suffer such ingratitude,
Such betrayals and actions lewd?
 Ah, how troubles seem to compound!
The Great Hill of Hate
Built between us by Fate
 Will be our burial mound
What of all the promises you made?

Will these wrongs ever be repaid,
 Or do you think you're not bound?
I ask once again
Do you not think it's a sin
 To ignore my crying sound?
I don't know why
But I still feed myself with the lie
 That someday you'll be glad to have me around
 Yes, someday you'll be glad to have me around

You always believe in others,
Put faith in vows that are another's
 But give up on me by dawn
Why give them so much rope
But expect me to be infallible like the Pope
 Or to wave a magic wand?
I'm human — just like I thought you used to be
Before you stopped showing mercy
 And started using me as your pawn
Hell, I've made mistakes,
I dare say I've caused your heart to break,
 But what planet are we on?
Last time I checked
Pain is the only direct
 Result of that sacred, indissoluble bond
Maybe some day I'll be able to admit,
But now I just can't quit,
 Just can't accept that you've been a con
Yet this much I know —
You're our love's greatest foe,
 And some day you'll miss me when I'm gone
 Yes, some day you'll miss me when I'm gone

You know, you really should've listened,
It's not as if the truth were missin',
 But I just couldn't get through to ya
It seems every time you had a chance
To leave, you left without a second glance

And said, "Hallelujah!"
I did everything but pay
To keep you from goin' away,
 But you acted like I hardly knew ya
You said we had to trust God above,
But, hell, it seems all you ever learned from love
 Is how to shoot someone who outdrew ya
You keep saying I'm nostalgic—
Yeah, well, what the hell about it?
 It's not the Monster that slew ya
I guess I should've been clearer,
But, hell, there's nothin' I hold dearer
 Than that goddamn Vow I threw ya
Maybe I should've made it a curse
Or even put it in verse,
 But you never read my poetry, do ya?
 No, you never read my poetry do ya?

Hell, you won't even read this—
Why do I even bother getting pissed?
 I should just drown myself in Coors
I've said it all before,
But you just don't listen anymore,
 You'd rather hang out with your boors
It's true I'm nobody's bargain,
But, hell, as long as we're arguin',
 I don't see you openin' any doors
That don't close as soon as they open
When your so-called friends leave ya hopin'
 In vain down on cold, hard floors
I know your stupid girlfriends tell
You I'm to blame and that you should rebel,
 But, hell, haven't we been through all these detours?
I think it's time we just accepted each other,
Stopped tryin' to excuse our sisters and brothers,
 Find shelter before the Hard Rain pours
I know you always said I could never make it by myself,
But that night you slipped out in stealth,
 I cooked, and my food was better than yours

Yes, bitch, my food was better than yours

You said things had changed,
Said it was time to rearrange,
 Time to move on;
But you didn't expect
Everyone else's neglect,
 Thought they'd all be like me and fawn
Remember when that bitch never showed
And you sat there like a fool and the tears flowed?
 Yes, and I told you you were her pawn
What about that stupid whore
Who never came to the door
 And broke your "unbreakable" bond?
Yes, and what of your partners in crime
Who hit us up for nickels and dimes
 But didn't stay to see fruition spawn?
I told you, God damn it! I told you
But you acted like I never knowed you,
 At night said you'd listen but reneged by dawn;
But this time I'm takin' you back,
This shit's about to give me a heart attack—
 Tell your other man we're gone
 Yes, tell your other man we're gone

So what happened—it all fell apart?
Ah, just like I always said it would, sweetheart
 Guess you'll have to do something else instead
Yes, all those people you counted on
Have disappeared or are otherwise gone
 And you're left alone with me—splendid!
Yes, they never came through and scattered
Or were so late it hardly mattered
 Yet you cry as if the truth were hid
Oh, how many times did I tell you
That all my plans fell through
 If I asked others to do as they were bid?
I could've saved you a lot of time and pain,

But my warnings were in vain
 Because you thought I was just a kid
I guess now you'll know better
Than to leave in stormy weather
 For whatever asshole will leave you on the skids
Now that everyone else has betrayed you
You come crawling back to the one who made you,
 And I'm not gonna say, "I told you so," but I did
 Yes, I did

2009

Love Itself

This trying to love someone,
 It can drive you insane
Sometimes it seems like
 Your efforts are all in vain
There's too much disappointment
 And too much pain;
And you say you'll never
 Put yourself through it again,
 Ah, but you cannot abstain
You need a lover
 To give you shelter from the rain
Still, sometimes it looks like
 There's nothing there to gain
When even love itself
 Appears so petty and so plain;
 And it can take a long time to regain
 The faith you once held for its name
 Once you've been burned by its flame

You know you hurt me, darling,
 When you said you still felt the same
Why couldn't you just tell the truth?
 It would've spared a lot of pain
My honesty has always been there for you,
 But I guess it's not yours to claim
You broke my heart like so many others,
 I guess it's my claim to fame
I've been through it before,
 I don't want to go through it again
I kept telling myself
Next time I was going to win,
 But things always turn out the same
Well, I tried to love you, girl,
 But I just can't play that game
I'm beginning to feel my time is up,
 I must be getting lame
Maybe it's time to give up when

Even love itself gets bloodstained

Some days I'm lonely,
 Some days I'm not
Love is like a flame,
 It burns you when it's hot
I had hopes and dreams,
 And down they were shot
I'm sick and tired of all these people
 Trying to be something they're not
Why can't they just be like me
 And admit this is all we've got?
It may not be much,
 It may not be a lot—
But it's all there is,
 It's all God begot;
And one has to wonder what to do
 When even love itself begins to rot

 I can feel the wheels of desire start to slow—
 Your rejection hit me like a blow,
 Hit just a bit too low
We let things drift on so long
 All awash in misery and woe
Until even we began to wonder
 Just how much further this thing can go
It just can't go on any longer,
 You're gonna have to leave me now, I know
 It starts out up above but ends up below
I was amused by it for a while,
 But now I'm getting tired of this sad, sad show
Our love is ticking like a time bomb,
 Better get ready for it to blow
 Get out of the way, if you don't know
Yes, I loved a woman, I gave her my heart,
 But she wanted my soul;
And what the hell am I supposed to do
 When even love itself fails to show?

I guess I shouldn't be knocking love,

It's kicking a rather sacred cow,
But it's just that it's hurt me so much,
It couldn't keep its vow
I swore to God you were an angel,
But our heaven turned to hell somehow
The ship we shared is sinking,
It's mutiny from stern to bow
You're sick of my sardonic smile,
And I'm sick of your scowl
I don't know if we'll ever be able to work out
The problems that face us — wow
Now you may say I'm exaggerating,
That I've slipped up and forgotten how —
But even love itself cannot express
How low I feel right now

I cried and sang out lovesick croons,
But there was no one there to hear
I cried, and cried, and cried,
But it fell on deaf ears;
And I just wonder if you can hear me singing,
Hear me singing through these tears
Life has been no cakewalk,
I've had a few rough years;
And I thought you were the one who could help me,
Help me ease my pain —
But all you did was stall it momentarily,
Cause me to shift gears
We worked our way to the top, darling,
But now I'm in the rear;
And just what is a man supposed to do
When love itself disappears?

2001

Snapshots of Love

Love seems so perfect at first but soon shows its true self —
 Though the best thing on this lonely, blighted earth,
It is imperfect just like everything else;
 Both must work hard to preserve its true worth.
  Many tranquil scenes of domestic bliss,
   Shared moments in silence and
 Joyous talk, love, sex, the simple kiss,
   The pure pleasure of walking hand in hand.
A long, heated argument drags on
 Sprung from some small, long-forgotten cause —
Old pleasures seem long gone,
 Lost amid the wreckage of broken treaties, lies, and laws…
And then, suddenly, she takes my hand, and all my pain, away;
Silently smiling, she looks at me; there are no words to say.

Circa 2005

Eugene's Long-Lost Love Letter to Candida

(See George Bernard Shaw's play *Candida*.)

When I'm thirty, she will be forty-five —
I'll have just gotten my life together,
And she will be making the downward dive:
 Our lifelines will stray apart forever.
When I'm sixty, she'll be seventy-five —
I'll have started to fade away for good,
She will be just barely staying alive:
 Unrequited love ending as it should.
As sad as it is to have loved and lost,
 To cry a vale of hopeless, bitter tears,
O, so much sadder to lose, at such cost,
 Love that is separated by mere years!
Woe to he who loves an older woman —
I wish such a sad, harsh fate on no man!

Circa 2005

Love's Perversity

What a wretched race we are to spare the many
 With whom we are lacking in notoriety
And then bring it all down on the few of any
 Meaning for the sake of worthless society!
Why do we strive to please those of no worth to us —
 Long to have them think us without blemish or stain,
Obsess over not giving them worry or fuss
 And making them think we live without gall or pain?
How different with the precious few close to our heart! —
 Short tempers and vows no sooner made than broken,
Unkind words in anger that make the teardrops start,
 And promises forgotten before they're spoken.
Oh, babe! we can't even remember why we fought,
Can't we cast off pettiness and act as we ought?

2009

Love Everlasting (A Theodicy)

The only thing worth living for is love,
 Poets and philosophers agree
We must not waste time looking for help from above,
 Only our hearts can set us free

We waste so much time
 Searching for answers that may not even exist—
But the heart is the only lifeline,
 Though this truth we often resist

Many look to the skies for truth,
 Many look to The Bible—
But life gives ample proof
 That love is the only engine of survival

An open heart is the only pathway
 To peace and contentment on earth—
A celestial stairway will rot and decay,
 Love is the only thing of any real worth

Many plea and petition God,
 But he never replies
Let us end the practice, so odd,
 And look to where the answer truly lies

We waste so much time hoping in vain
 For help from gods that will never come
When we could be ending our earthly pain—
 Let us end the fruitless search, so vacant and numb

We kill and fill our hearts with hate
 Fighting for gods we have made—
Carrying on blindly, as if chained to fate,
 We overlooked love in the plans we laid

We live and die—
 Of this only we are certain,

Though we know not why;
 We must find a reason to live before they close the curtain

We eat and drink,
 Carrying on a seemingly meaningless life
We feel and think,
 Pausing for breath in the tempestuous strife

We know not why we are here
 And know not what, if anything, is coming
The world gives little cheer,
 And it may all amount to nothing —

But we just cannot accept that we live and toil in vain,
 That we are victims of some colossal fraud
All this disappointment, sorrow, and pain —
 Surely there is a reason behind them or some kind of god

We may never find all the answers we strive for,
 May never finish all we set out to do —
But I know, as sure as I am alive, or more,
 That we have to find some way to make it through

Some hide current sorrow
 And look to the afterlife —
Put all hopes and dreams in tomorrow
 As a way to deal with everyday strife

Some misguidedly look to heaven
 And accept all present woes —
In the end, they think, the odds get even,
 And only in vain would we start earthly shows —

But we live wrongly when we live this way,
 For this existence may be all there is
How can we place all our hopes in some mystical, future day
 When there may be nothing after this?

This is no easy answer, for life is hard,
 And we would like to believe there is more —

LIFE'S TRIUMPH by Bill R. Moore

There may be, but perhaps all our cards
 Have marked for us is this lonely door

We must find something, then,
 To get through this, whatever it may be —
We can let a god in
 Or look to you and me

The gods are never there for us on earth
 And may not be there in the end —
This lonely, desolate place of our birth
 May be the only thing on which we can depend —

But love can build a sanctuary in our hearts,
 A safe haven from the world's pain and woe
Though imperfect, it is a start,
 A place we can always go

Love is the only real thing available to us,
 The only thing on which we can depend
Some reserve for God all trust,
 But only love is left in the end

We must live for love; there is nothing else,
 No help coming from above
It is with you and me as with everyone else —
 The only thing worth living for is love

Love is the only answer to the game we have played;
 Oh, my love! We have so little time here —
In love our foundations are laid,
 In love we disappear

        Circa 2006 (First published in *Shine*, Apr. 2009, in slightly different form.)

Raging against the Machine: Contemporary *Sturm und Drang* Indulgences
By Bradley Parsons

"I know my heart, and have studied mankind; I am not made like any one I have been acquainted with, perhaps like no one in existence; if not better, I at least claim originality".
–*Jean-Jacques Rousseau,* Confessions

"If a man does not keep pace with his companions, perhaps it is because he hears a different drummer."
–*Henry David Thoreau, Walden*

*"You don't need a weather man
To know which way the wind blows."
"Don't follow leaders."*
–*Bob Dylan, "Subterranean Homesick Blues"*

"The doctrine of hatred must be preached as the counteraction of the doctrine of love when that pules and whines. I shun father and mother and wife and brother, when my genius calls me. I would write on the lintels of the door-post, Whim. I hope it is somewhat better than whim at last, but we cannot spend the day in explanation."
–*Ralph Waldo Emerson, "Self-Reliance"*

*"They locked up a man
who wanted to rule the world
The fools
They locked up the wrong man".*
–*Leonard Cohen, "The Wrong Man"*

"The ultimate weapon was invented in pre-history. It is a kitchen knife in the hands of a determined man – who is fed up."
–*Robert A. Heinlein, "The Future Revisited"*

Bradley is a sixteen-year-old "angry young man" exactly like millions of others in America, with one important exception—he has lived all his life in the small town of Big Springs, Nebraska. (No, I had not heard of it, either.) Thus, like his brethren nationwide—nay, the world over—he is mad at the world, convinced it has done him an injustice, and is tired of fate hurling curveballs at him. Like his companions, he looks contempibly on the national political, social, and artistic scenes; unlike them, he also fumes at fate's additional cruel twist—condemning him to waste his prime in a one horse town. He hates it, but his most persuasive arguments to convince his parents to move have failed, and he lacks the bravado to run away. Thus, though he knows he is condemned to live there another two years, he fully plans on moving the very day he ceases to be a minor. Of course, he was beaten up a lot as a kid (being named "Bradley" certainly did not help) and is still made fun of relentlessly. Indeed, he is the stereotypical nerd's very image: taped-up nerd glasses, pocket protector…the whole bit. His peers may well hate him, but he hates them just as much; he kept his anger bottled up for many years, and it began to ferment. He has always had the consolation of knowing he is smarter than them—but this, of course, has never been enough. He is firmly convinced of his terminal uniqueness; he has not found anyone similar enough to call a friend—not that anyone would want to be friends with him. Of course, he is smart enough to see he needs love and has even carefully selected a few prime candidates. Needless to say, these decisions were made on the basis of beauty, not intelligence, as he long ago despaired of ever finding it in his little hole. Still, second-rate or not, he is too shy to ask any brain-dead beauties out, much less for their hand, as he cannot even entertain rejection's bare possibility; the very idea fills him with self-abhorence and misanthropic hate. He would probably have been the next school shooter had he not discovered poetry. Writing is for him primal scream therapy; it lets out all his anger constructively, without harming anyone else, and keeps his conscience clear to boot. He typically writes while listening to the favorite angry young man music of his and other generations—Tool, Rage Against The Machine, The Smiths, and a slew of heavy metal and hard rock artists—and even likes Billy Joel's "Angry Young Man," which describes him pretty accurately, and is not afraid of admitting it. I give a small sampling of his work in contrast to what has gone before; it certainly has many thematic elements with prior poems, but its coming from an angry youth sets it apart in tone and execution. Unlike other writers in this collection, he always writes in first person—even when he does not write in first person. In St. Augustine and Rousseau's traditions, his slim volume may be called "Confessions of an Angry Young Man." To be sure, his writing is somewhat callow at times but none the worse for it; he shoots straight from hip (and heart), and any editor who tries to remove this from his writing robs it of its one notable quality. His writing is definitely not something for everyone—but may well be every-thing for someone, especially if that proverbial "someone" is a similarly-inclined but less articulate angry young man.

The True Story of a Clean-Cut Kid

"He was a clean-cut kid
But they made a killer out of him
That's what they did"
–Bob Dylan, "Clean-Cut Kid"

I am an island, a solitary fixture in a lonely sea,
I speak to no one; no one speaks to me
 I hurt easy; it just doesn't show,
 You can hurt someone and not even know
I try to hold back all the pain I feel,
Hide it all away and not reveal
 The very real fears I'm holding deep inside,
 The very real tears I try to pretend I haven't cried
It's a lonely fight, a lonely quest—
But I know I'm in the right, know I must not rest
If I let my guard down for just one minute, they might guess
My secret, and I would fail the test
Yes, it's hard not to confess,
But there's no one I can confide in, no way out of this mess

I keep to myself, my loneliness forever unfurled,
I'm fragile as a baby but show a heart of stone to the world
 My closet is full of skeletons and dark secrets,
 But I tell no one of my mistakes and regrets
Sometimes I take a little somethin' to make it all disappear,
A little cure to prop up hope and drown my fear
 I'm more scared than anyone could ever possibly know,
 More insecure than I ever dare show
Sometimes I'm at a loss, just don't know what to do,
But there's no one to ask advice, no one to see me through
 I don't understand why I keep making the same old mistakes,
 Can't understand why my heart always breaks
I keep worries and concerns buried deep inside,
Keep searching in vain for a safe place to hide

I was so naïve I actually used to believe
There were others willing to listen and receive

The innermost contents of your heart and soul —
But I was wrong; we must rely on self-control
Others will only leave you out in the cold,
Leave you to rot 'til you're lonely and old
They're willing to put their fears into you
But unwilling to harbor yours or see you through
If you trust others to alleviate your pain,
You'll end up with great loss and little gain
If you offer your innocence, you'll get repaid with scorn,
Friendship's a vain exercise, hopeless and forlorn
We're all in it alone, there's no help along the way,
We can give our all to others, but they'll never repay

There's nothing to be said for friendship,
Life's an unending, solitary trip
Others will stab you in the back, push you down,
Walk over you without a frown
The most you can hope for is indifference,
But hostility is more likely; optimism makes no sense
Friends are just the people you hate least,
No one is true to you, society an unrelenting beast
A true friend stabs you in the front —
The most you can hope for in this dog-eat-dog hunt
They'll cheat you and beat you, do anything to defeat you,
Play all the old, sadistic tricks — then try something new
They'll play every dirty trick in the book, then do them all again,
This time behind your back, my friend —

But I've always sworn I would get revenge,
Repay all those who turned on me in a righteous binge
I know I'm supposed to forgive and forget,
But the strength to do so I haven't found yet
If I ever see those motherfuckers coming, I don't know what I might do,
I'd like to think I could control myself, but it isn't true
Even after all these years, I bet they haven't learned how to treat me right,
To apologize and atone for all their wrongs and slights
If they get in my face and sin anew, man, I won't be responsible for my be-
    havior,
I ain't no Mahatma Gandhi, man, ain't Jesus Christ the Savior
I pay lip service to pacifism, but when push comes to shove,

They better get the fuck outta my face 'cause I harbor them no love
I always swore I wouldn't let 'em get away with it forever,
And now they're comin' back again, and I fear it's now or never

They used up all their second chances long ago,
I gave them more rope than they ever deserved, Lord knows
 Despite it all, I could probably forgive 'em if they didn't blame it all on me,
 But they continue to, and, by God, it's high time I was finally free
I swear I don't know what I'll do if they come walkin' in my door,
It frightens me to think of it, but they might walk out no more
 I know I'm supposed to hold back bestial instincts and overcome hate,
 But my head can't justify no more what my heart won't tolerate
I swear I can't answer for myself if they shit on me one more time,
The slightest little wrong will be the last time they cross the line
 I let 'em step on me for so many years, but now I've grown stronger
 If they don't listen to what I say, they ain't gonna be around much longer
I've given fair warning; now I'm poised for legitimate defensive attack,
If those motherfuckers know what's good for 'em, they better watch their
    backs…

2007

Whatever Gets Me through the Night

"The strongest man in the world is the man who stands most alone."
–Henrik Ibsen, An Enemy of the People

"No amount of force can control a free man, a man whose mind is free. No, not the
rack, not fission bombs, not anything – you can't conquer a free man; the most you
can do is kill him."
–Robert A. Heinlein, "Free Men"

If there's a truth that I haven't stopped believing,
 I'd like to see it
If there's a religion or philosophy held back that isn't deceiving,
 I'd like to free it
If there's a position worth receiving,
 I'd like to be it—
But for now I'll take what I can get;
I don't want hairs to split
Or pieces that don't fit
'Cause I'm tired of the shit
I just want something permanent
 For it I'd fight with all my might in glee—
 Whatever gets me through the night's all right with me

I've lived in your ivory towers
 And your Pollyanna land,
But I don't care for fantasy's power,
 I'm a practical man
I immersed myself in learning's bower
 But got hit with a heavy hand
How many times can I be cut and not bleed?
How many times must I deny my mind to be freed?
How long must I live by another's creed?
They try to tell me about loyalty and patriotism and communal need—
Fuck that shit; I got a family to feed
 The truth's finally in sight, and they want me to martyr myself freely,
 But whatever gets me through the night's all right with me

LIFE'S TRIUMPH by Bill R. Moore

I read all the holy books
 And all of academe,
Gave everything sacred a look
 And everything obscene,
Thoughts from left to right I took
 And everything between—
But just wasn't satisfied,
A longing was always denied
I looked into the depths and pried
My heart and brain open wide
But don't feel a bit more complete inside
 Freedom's at its height when it comes only from thee,
 And whatever gets me through the night's all right with me

I'm not above a cheat or lie,
 Something underhand
I do what I must to get by,
 It's all I understand
Sometimes they need someone to die,
 But it's not gonna be this man
I don't know if it's worth the fight
And don't care if it's wrong or right,
I just know the only thing I can trust is might
The thought of self-sacrifice puts me in a fright,
How can I give up my guiding light?
 To stay alive I fight; nothing is free,
 And whatever gets me through the night's all right with me

I'm no Khan or Caesar
 Or any damn Macbeth
I just think it's easier
 To kill than give in to death
I've built this place up from the ether
 And will defend it with my dying breath
I never thought it would come to this,
But I'm not going to slit my wrists
All this talk of giving in just makes me pissed
If we don't hold on to what we have before it's missed,
Then why the hell do we even exist?
 I'm shining a light of self-sufficiency,

And whatever gets me through the night's all right with me

I'm sick of all this sweet talk
 About peace and in-betweens
If these people had to walk my walk,
 They'd said the end justifies the means
I can't stand it; I just wanna balk,
 They're trying to turn people into machines —
And when that day comes,
You'll feel your body start to grow numb
You'll start to speak, but your mouth'll be dumb
You won't remember where it came from,
That strange thought about not letting them plumb
 Your self-respect's last vestiges; you'll be in tight and won't get out easily,
 But whatever gets me through the night's all right with me

So, go ahead, let them beat you down,
 Destroy your self-respect
Make you look like a clown,
 Feel like an insect
It'll look so nice as you drown,
 So circumspect —
But let all hear my plea:
I'll drink defeat to the lees,
But I won't be on my knees
If I'm goin' down, others are comin' with me
Get out of the way if you don't want to see
You have to go down with a fight; there's no other way to be —
Whatever gets me through the night's all right with me

"Okay," you say, "just give in,
 Help your neighbor with his load
Tell the man just where you've been
 And let him choose your road" —
I say that shit's the worst of sin,
 Live by no man's code
How long can you fail to see what's before your eye?
How long can you hate yourself for the weakness you deny?
How long can you struggle through mud before you begin to dry?
How long can you pretend you don't whimper and cry?

245

Deny yourself as long as you want; I
 Will fight to the death; I'm not wasting any more breath,
The time has come to do or die
 Let's show them what we're made of and that we're not afraid of
  The worst they can do
  This is the final hour; it's either me or you
They have us in their sights, and I'm telling you right now, buddy,
That whatever gets me through the night's all right with me...

2009

Emancipation Proclamation
(A Rallying Cry for
Twenty-first Century Youth)

"The Child is father of the Man"
–William Wordsworth, "My Heart Leaps Up"

"Yes, you who must leave everything
That you can not control;
It begins with your family,
But soon comes round to your soul."
–Leonard Cohen, "Sisters of Mercy"

There comes a time in every young man's life
 When he must sever the ties that bind him —
Abandon his home with just his dreams and his wife
 And leave his past to rot behind him
His quest for success will be filled with strife,
 But he cannot let that blind him
He knows his dissenters are cowardly and blithe,
 You need not remind him —

It now seems I have reached this position,
 I must find the courage to make a new stance
I will not submit to inquisition,
 I never said you had to offer a second chance
I will not heed pleas for submission,
 I will not give a second glance
I have my goals, have my mission,
 I will not be a victim of circumstance

They say fathers' sins are visited on their children,
 But our burdens are heavy enough without this pre-set trap
I do not deny we have committed sins,
 But they are ours; we did not see our fathers snap
We must declare independence once again,
 We must make the most of the generation gap

No chips off the old block, we are our own men,
 We must live by our own code and map

They say ours is a materialistic generation,
 That we know the price of everything and the value of nothing
I do not deny we have our fascinations,
 But we know the advantages youth can bring
We will not be bound to our fathers' foundations,
 We have our own songs to sing
Our purpose is not to start an altercation
 But to let our freedom ring

Our fathers believe in hard work and labor for labor's sake,
 In muscles that lift and backs that bend
They judge a man's worth by the money he makes,
 See hard work as the foundation on which it all depends
Old habits die hard, but we have the willpower to break
 Them and bring all outdated traditions to an end
In the long line of generational fences, we plant a stake
 That we are ready and willing to defend

If we have not our fathers' virtues,
 We also have not their vices
If we know not all the old answers they once knew,
 We know far more of what the new answer is
In the name of something new,
 We tear down outmoded devices
We, too, cling steadfastly to what we believe true,
 We will not be bought out by any prices

It is our steadfast determination to be heard,
 We will not heed any conciliatory call
We are freeing our minds of all polluting words,
 Our steely reserve will not fall
We care not if they find us absurd,
 We believe in ourselves and will give our all
They can fight if they want, but we will not be deterred,
 We work best with our backs against the wall

It is a new path that we trod,

We make no use of age-old signs
We care not if they find us odd,
 We have our own designs
We care not if they threaten with the rod,
 We have severed the tie that binds
Our consciences are our only god,
 We will trust them and see what we find

O fathers! We did not ask for this fight,
 Did not ask for this war
You brought it to light,
 You chose to ignore
All we did was request our natural rights,
 We shut no familial door —
But it is too late now to hold the chain less tight,
 We have been through this too many times before

Abraham was willing to sacrifice his child,
 This we have never been able to forget
Like you, he was cruel, he was wild —
 We never forgave him, nor have forgiven you yet
We know the euphemistic terms in which the story is styled,
 But they do not lessen our fret
We care not if you are now meek and mild,
 Our purpose holds fast, our path is set

The time has come to sacrifice our fathers,
 We must sever them from ourselves
All our lives we have pretended not to be bothered,
 We have consented to be placed on your shelves
We have listened to you, treated you as honored sirs,
 Bought obedience at the heavy price for which it sells —
But the time has come to move ahead farther,
 Blind obedience is our most dreaded form of hell

So we leave you behind, O fathers, leave you behind to rot,
 To waste away and die
We can no longer pretend to be something we are not,
 We will not consent to live a lie
Our lives, our duty, our sacred honor cannot be bought,

It is futile to even try
We do what we do because we ought,
You must not ask us why

We have ceased to ask for freedom,
 We have taken it on our own terms
The hour of liberation has come—
 O, how the wheel of fate turns!
We have no regrets, we are not numb,
 We care not how much it burns
We care not if you understand where we come from,
 It is not our concern

O, farewell to the home where we were raised!
 Farewell to our old, familiar shield!
We will look back on this as the most important of days
 Once our dreams have been fulfilled
We asked not for patricide but have exhausted all other ways,
 If it is the price we must pay, we will see you killed
For our purpose holds, now and for always,
 "To strive, to seek, to find, and not to yield."

2007

Life without Principle
(A Self-Indulgent Exercise
in Constructive Misanthropy)

*"The community has no bribe that will tempt a wise man. You may raise money
enough to tunnel a mountain, but you cannot raise money enough to hire a man
who is minding his own business. An efficient and valuable man does what he can,
whether the community pay him for it or not. The inefficient offer their inefficiency
to the highest bidder"*
–Henry David Thoreau, "Life without Principle"

*"What shall it profit a man, if he shall gain
the whole world, and lose his own soul?"*
–Mark 8:36

Lately I've been hearing a lot of shit from people
 Who think I give a damn what they have to say,
But I don't think twice about clichéd advice
 I never asked for anyway
I mean, hell, I'm a pretty reasonable guy
 As long as I get my way
I just want peace,
 I don't even care about pay—
But they shove their two cents in with maximum spin,
 I wish they'd all just go away

My idea of paradise is complete privacy—
 Where people will just leave you alone,
Where social etiquette is gone,
 And people can live their lives out unknown
I'm fed up with people,
 I'm tired of my cover being blown
The more I've dealt with people,
 The more my misanthropy's grown
I tried to socialize, tried hiding in disguise,
 But people just won't let you live on your own

LIFE'S TRIUMPH by Bill R. Moore

I'm sick of all these assholes telling me how to live,
  Telling me I'm managing things badly
I want it well understood—I care not if their intentions are good,
  I care not if they talk to me condescendingly or sadly
It means nothing to me that they give advice for free,
  I have no qualms about reacting madly
I'll argue them down and beat them to the ground
  'Cause one of my minor pleasures is not suffering fools gladly
If they could just guarantee me I'd never see them again,
  I'd gladly give them everything I had, free

I tried fitting in for years,
  But I've just lost the spirit—
And don't give me any of that bullshit
  About not trying hard enough; I don't wanna hear it
I tried every day, in every conceivable way,
  But that social hurdle, I just could not clear it
It wasn't that I had outrageous demands,
  I just had an ideal, but everyone seemed to fear it
I mean, I never asked for much—
  Just perfection, or something damn near it

Sometimes I think the Earth's immune system
  Is trying to kill us all—
Wipe us off the planet
  And get back to how it was before the Fall,
Eradicate our puny empires and democracies,
  Our monuments and buildings so tall;
If so, I'd like for sure to know
  So I could heed the call—
But I'm still in doubt, while the clock is running out,
  And there's no time left to stall

I saw the ghost of Holden Caulfield,
  Asked him if he ever gets lonely
He just glared and looked at me,
  Said solitude was his one and only
I told him I agreed with his view
  That everything is cheap and phony
I wish I could follow his example

And hide out where no one can know me,
But I'm too busy tryin' to convince all these
 Bleeding hearts and demagogues they don't own me

Well, I try my best to be just like I am,
 But everyone wants you to be just like them
They say the nail that sticks up gets hammered down,
 That a fish out of water no longer knows how to swim —
But I'm tired of all these stupid platitudes,
 And my faith in the human race is gettin' dim
Your laws do not compel me to kneel grotesque and bare,
 Nor do I care about any commandments from Him
I'd rather steer by my own moral compass,
 Even if it means hangin' alone on a limb

And I just don't have the patience to wait around
 Until the lion lies down with the lamb,
Until Christians drown in wine,
 And Jews choke on ham —
This may be indirect, or politically incorrect,
 But I really don't give a damn
I'm tired of being treated like a presumptuous asshole
 After greeting hostile strangers with "Sir" and "Ma'am"
I swear I'm gonna find somewhere
 Where they don't care who I am

My fondest wish is total isolation —
 Where I can find some peace and quiet,
Live out a nice, simple life, just me and my wife —
 It's a brave new world, but I'm willing to try it
I pay attention to convention
 Only so I can defy it
I wanna go somewhere where my reputation doesn't precede me,
 Where the Golden Rule is the only rule, and no one tries to deny it,
Where no one can be bought but truth is always for sale,
 And there's always someone willing to buy it

Well, I've always had to do things my way,
 Even if it meant lockin' the world's opinions up in a trunk
Yes, I fought against the bottle

But had to do it drunk
I'm willing to take a few nicks as I kick against the pricks
But always trust my instincts when I smell a skunk
Yes, maybe I'll retire to some mountain
And live out the rest of my life as a monk
Some may say it's taking the easy way,
But I know better than to listen to that junk

You may say I'm a dreamer, even that I'm the only one,
That I have no one to fight by my side
Hell, you can say far worse for all I care—
Go ahead; I have nowhere to hide
I get my fill just knowing I've lived up to my ideal,
It wipes away all the tears I've cried
I long ago gave up on ever finding tranquility and serenity,
They're impossible, once open the world's eyes have been pried
We'll probably never find a refuge,
The most we can hope for now is world-wide suicide

I doubt people will ever really leave each other alone,
There are too many hopes and dreams to crush
We pounce on each other's weaknesses
As soon as we see a tender spot or blush
You can keep nursin' your fantasies,
But in the end they all turn to mush
Sometimes I just wanna shove the whole damned human race
Down the shit-stained toilet bowl and watch it drown as I flush—
If only I could come to my senses, drop the pretenses,
And tell my god-forsaken conscience to hush…

But I'll probably never have the guts to do it,
And anyway, it may already be too late
We're all prisoners of our own device,
We're not victims of a venomous fate
I'll probably never have the courage to say what must be said,
I'm too overcautious and irate;
And I'll probably never have the bravado to do what must be done,
It's far easier to just sit and prate—
So I'll just add another brew to my misanthropic stew
That's already bubbling over with hate

Those who wish for freedom of conscience,
 For the opportunity to live beyond the human team—
We must move beyond the naïve idealism of youth,
 We must realize things are even worse than they seem
We must face the knowledge that the truth is not the truth,
 We must not be bound by what society deems
I've known all along that I've never been free,
 That I'm no more than a slave to a system unfair and obscene
I've known all along there's little hope for me—
 Ah, but can't a man dream? Can't a man dream…?

2007

The Lonely Life of the Misanthrope

It can be strange sometimes
 When you don't feel at home among your peers
Their attention spans have been shortened by
 Too many cigarettes and beers
Yes, and you've lived among them
 For many a long year
Together you've laughed many laughs
 And shed many tears—
Yet they still back away from you
Just like they used to do,
 Ignorance and xenophobia feed their fears

Well, it's ripe harvest now,
 If it's idiots you seek to find
For there's no gold in them there hills,
 There are no diamonds in the mine
There are no letters in the mailbox,
 And your roses are wilting 'cause the sun won't shine
I thought I'd found a friend or two,
Thought I'd found you—
 But I know there's nothing now I can claim as mine
I loaded up on cliques and taught this old dog new tricks
 To try an' get myself out of this bind—
 But there was nothing there for me to find,
 I didn't even see a sign
I did what I thought was quite right—
 I turned on a dime, I walked the line,
 But only made it as far as Heart Attack and Vine

Here I am lookin' left and right
 From the dark room of my mind—
There's nothing to salvage,
 Nothing even here to find
Can't you see?—
It's highway robbery, a travesty
 They mistake your genius for weirdness,
Your shyness for snobbery,

They renounce the very concept of liberty
 They've got their circles so fuckin' tight
Not even the Invisible Man can get free
They're so stupid — they rely on Cupid,
 They think the world revolves around him and her
Even the people I pretend to call friends
 Are just sittin' around like furniture
You can penetrate their thin shield of bullshit so easily,
 Shoot an arrow into the blue
 There's a lot better things to do —
Or maybe that's just me

Well, they're eating up the new kid now,
 Gathering for the feast
They say it's just the predatory
 Nature of the beast
Those who ignore them they persist,
Those who hate them they resist
Oh, but those who dare call them wrong,
They're the ones they like least
 Anything new they regard as strange —
Yes, even you
 They just can't stand change —
Anything that doesn't appeal to their ideal
 Of the order of things
 They have the nerve to re-arrange;
And life as we know it just refuses to show it,
 That's just a whole other game
They'll never rise above heavy scorn and lightweight love,
 That much is plain
They'll pin a label on you, bind you to their ways,
Try an' make you get lost in the haze
For the rest of your worthless days —
 Makes you wonder what's in a name;
But that birthmark, my friend,
 It was their claim to fame

There's no reason to try an' get through
 Their closed doors and the shadows they cast
No new idea will stick to them,

Progress just don't last
They won't accept the future's bold new wave
Or any flash from the past
They're living comfortably in the Now
Without ever stopping to ask "Why?" or "How?"
They just keep on rolling on obliviously,
Regardless of whatever changes may be needed
Their problems could be fixed so easily,
But we all know good advice is never heeded
Well, as far as I'm concerned,
They can remain conceited
I've seceded,
I've been defeated — it's conceded
I could lie to myself and be someone else,
But there's just no reason to —
Those doors, they just barred 'em through and through
If you try to push any kind of new idea in,
They'll close the door on you

They say evolution is supposed to weed out the pollution,
So what's Darwin's excuse for this?
I'm sure he never foresaw any kind of moral law
That would let us be justifiably pissed
They're crouching in their corners,
Hiding behind religion
There's nowhere you can hide from them now,
They make the decisions
They're supposed to provide for all,
But they keep all the provisions
They live in sin and think they can win
By backing up aloof truth with God —
It strikes very few people as odd;
I'm driftin' off to the Land of Nod

Well, I don't know what to say anymore,
Everything that matters has already been said
All my friends just walked out the door,
And everyone I love is dead
Lie, lie, lie — you don't even have to try,
They fill your head;

And all the smart people are droppin' dead in the streets
 Like balloons made out of lead
I don't even know why I'm talkin' —
 I tried to stray off the road,
But I might as well just keep walkin'
 Trouble and disappointment follow me
Like the ghost of a dead dog bitten on the ass;
 And I'm just tired of all this shit now,
I'm sick to death of all this trash
 Sometimes someone asks you
 To do somethin' you don't really want to do
And, tears or not, it's just too much to ask

I just can't love these people,
 I'm sorry —
And, if that lowers your opinion of me,
 Don't worry;
Maybe I should go to hell —
I might as well

2001

Your Funeral, My Trial
Part I

I see you perched there
 On your stone,
Sitting still in a world
 Of your own
While the girl we're both crazy about
 Is spread out on her throne
 Sitting worthlessly alone
 I'm talking to her on the phone—
And you don't even realize
 She's in the danger zone
Oh, how can you say
 Your love's not accident-prone?
That's the way, and you've got to play
 It as a lone—
Or at least that's my style
Your funeral, my trial

Well, I got tired of that whore talkin'
 About cute guys and phony, little, plastic dicks
I just got tired of hearin' it,
 Thought I'd turn a few tricks
All this gossip just makes me sick
It just gets so damn hard
 Kicking against the pricks—
And nobody's gonna appreciate it
 When you take your licks
The truth's the truth—
 Yeah, but it doesn't stick
Where's my girl, my rover?
My witty banter failed to win her over
 So I disemboweled her with a toothpick
  And slashed her wrists with a fingernail file—
And now I'm in a jail cell
 With a bunch of fuckin' hicks
  Your funeral, my trial

This life is given to you, Mama,
 There are no choices and no muse
Nothing — not even the choice
 Of having to choose
How lame; what's a game
 If you never lose?
I don't understand why
 You keep feeding me your blues
I don't give a damn —
 And, anyway, it's old news
Get out of your corner
 And walk a mile in my shoes
Only then will you understand
 How much conscience you abuse;
 And you keep on sayin' you're gonna win,
But you'll lose
That's just the way it goes;
And, in the end, your fists can only fall
 With a crashing but meaningless blow
And build a wall of denial
Your funeral, my trial

Yes, I see your point,
 But I just don't live in that neighborhood
Don't tell me what I didn't do,
 I'm more interested in what I should
There was a time when you could change my mind,
 You should know that you could;
But that time has passed now,
 I've knocked on wood
Yes, your evidence is respectable
 And your argument good —
 But you keep on tellin' me about sin,
 And I've already been born once, girl,
 I don't need to be born again
So shut your fucking mouth, darlin',
Or I'll nail you to the cross,
 And you'll see it burning for miles
 Your funeral, my trial

What's the deal with resurrection?
 I feel I'm already dead
I need some protection,
 Reality always has too many heads
 I need you, baby, in my bed
I need the Lord to save me,
 I'm full of impending dread
You may not believe me,
 But just like I said —
Things change, and, anyway,
 I need some street cred
So I'm gonna eat my chocolate Jesus
 And suck my lollipop dry
I don't need to reconcile my ways to you,
 Don't have to give a reason why
 I'm just like any other guy,
And I want to fly — far, far, far, far away…
 But you just keep placing me on the pile
 Your funeral, my trial

Who can deny there's something wrong with you?
 It certainly looks that way to me
If you feel half as bad as you look, baby,
 Then you need therapy
Blonde bitch — your words don't make any sense
 You're dying your hair brown
For artificial intelligence
You think the whole world's your plaything —
 Well, I got news for you:
 The cops, they hate you, too,
And they need someone to blame
 They really mean it this time —
And, man, they expect the same
It's not gonna help you anymore, your fame
 The most it'll do is hold things
Off a little while
Your funeral, my trial

You say I'm gettin' rusty
 In my old age

Well, I got news for ya, sonny,
 I'm still turnin' the page
I just don't know what to do —
My baby decided
 I should be kept in a cage
The man I thought was my best friend
 Was nothing but a sage
Wake me up when The Purge is over,
 Maybe by then I'll have left the stage
The Dark Ages — you know what Vonnegut
 Said about them? "We're still in the Dark Ages
The Dark Ages, they haven't ended yet" —
And I can't forget
 I'll die before I turn senile
 Your funeral, my trial

2001

Your Funeral, My Trial
Part II

I can't lie — no more of your dogma,
 I'm sick and tired of you trying to drill it into my head
Yes, I could say what I really think of you and your god, baby,
 But I'd have to kill you dead
If I could just rise above my conscience,
 Maybe I'd have some peace and quiet for a while,
But as it stands, I've got your blood on my hands —
 Your funeral, my trial

We humans are so tragic; we see
 The better path but always choose the worse
The constant struggle to overcome bestial desires
 Usually ends in a hearse
Better not open the closet where I hide my skeletons,
 You might get buried in the pile
You were the best I ever had but just ended up driving me mad —

Your funeral, my trial

We can resist everything but temptation,
 Desire's the one thing from which we cannot abstain
We're trapped in a weary, outdated body,
 Slaves to hormones and a brute, reptilian brain
We cause our own problems, slitting our wrists
 And drowning in our own bile
You tried to save me, but inspiration was all you gave me—
 Your funeral, my trial

You always said you could save me,
 That you had the hope and proof I'd been lacking—
But all you ever did was reinforce what I believed,
 And I have the same sorry beliefs with added backing
Why don't you turn my world upside down one more time just for kicks,
 Then you can work on points for style
I put my faith in you, but you failed to change my view—
 Your funeral, my trial

I might need a good lawyer,
 Might've gone a little too far this time—
But, damn, once you take that first step toward decadence,
 It's so goddamn hard not to cross the line
You always said I was so good at talking,
 But now all my words and thoughts are rotten and vile
You've made me a traitor, but I'll blame it all on you later—
 Your funeral, my trial

All your talk of equality and forgiveness
 Has left me high and dry
I've held back anger and tried to resist evil
 But still can't tell you why
I don't feel any better now—
 Hell, I just want to maim and defile
You brought out the devil in me struggling to get free—
 Your funeral, my trial

I just can't believe in any god or revolution,
 None seem to have any answers for me

They make me pay dearly for half-baked truths
 I could just make up for free;
And all the shit they taught me in school
 Ain't worth a damn beside my radio dial
I can't meet your demands but won't let you wreck all my plans—
 Your funeral, my trial

The piss yellow sun shines down,
 Exposing our every crime
We lift our glasses to the awful truth
 And tell ourselves it isn't worth a dime
You keep asking me if I've stopped drinking,
 But I can't even remember the last time I was able to smile
The game's too tough, I've had enough—
 Your funeral, my trial

All the philosophers and theologians are sappin' my strength,
 Just won't let me be
In two years my frown's only disappeared once,
 And it wasn't consciously
Most of the time I've been down on my knees or passed out
 With a needle in my arm down here on the hard tile
I know you don't believe me, but that's ceased to grieve me—
 Your funeral, my trial

Everything's all wrong, but that's all right,
 I don't need your sympathy
Call me anything you want; I don't care,
 Don't need anyone feeling sorry for me
Yes, I'm fragile as stained glass,
 But I'll build up a wall of denial
And let the world go to hell; I might as well—
 Your funeral, my trial

I'm tired of turning the other cheek,
 It's time to turn in my ticket
I'd protest the universe's cruelty
 If I thought it worth my time to picket
You say you've heard a thousand proofs against a benevolent god,
 Well, you can add this to the file

LIFE'S TRIUMPH by Bill R. Moore

I care not what you say, I've heard it all anyway —
Your funeral, my trial

Yes, I know I said I could save you —
But, hell, I can't even save myself
I've got too many troubles of my own
To care about anyone else
Maybe I should break your heart one more time just for good luck,
Then I could say I walked in your shoes a mile
Go ahead — tell me what I really am, I don't give a damn —
Your funeral, my trial

You know I believed the lies you told me,
Yes, I believed them so well
I buy everything you sell,
And one day it's gonna land me in hell
If you kick against the pricks
You wind up in exile
I've moved beyond doubt, just can't figure it out —
Your funeral, my trial

We need a new theory of human evolution
'Cause this one's a lie
You keep sayin' I should think of progress,
But I just don't see why I should even try
I've been trackin' our descent, man, and this spiral
Has been descending since Adam and Eve walked down the aisle
Don't even try to deny it, we'll never be able to defy it —
Your funeral, my trial

I know we always thought we were better than everyone —
That's what makes it so hard to confess
To bein' tired and hungry, confused and weary,
And broken down just like the rest
We've been reduced to admitting it, going back on
All our principles and resolutions as if senile,
And if it's too hard to stay with me, just cut yourself free —
Your funeral, my trial

Now, some men believe might makes right,

Some don't wanna give anyone a slight
Some are just in it for the fight,
Others just want a pussy that's tight—
Me, I'm a simple man
With no pretence or guile
I just want the truth, need no other proof—
Your funeral, my trial

2006

For Us, the Living

I sometimes get tired
 Of life being so cut and dried
Failures just keep on piling up,
 Despite how hard you've tried—
And you try to celebrate,
 Try to keep things under control,
But you always end up crawling
 Back into your little hole

I've been playing the game for a while—
 You think I'd be immune by now,
But sometimes I still get
 Tired of it anyhow
The price of fortune,
 The price of fame—
Sometimes I think
 It's not worth the gain;
And everyone I love is dead—
  Brainwashed to the point of apathy
Or else shot through the head
They took away my heroes,
 Make them take away my pain

I look out my window,
 The rain is pouring down
It's the same old cliché,
 Nothing changes around this town
You always said you'd come rescue me,
 But you still haven't come around
Help's never there when you need it
 But only after you've already been found

You can shout for help all you want,
 Nobody's gonna hear the sound
It's just you and your tattered libido
 Against whatever piece of meat's hangin' around uptown
You can hike all the way across the continent,

It won't do you any good
It's the same in the Black Hills
 As in Hollywood —
People still don't help each other
 Like they should

Knock on wood —
 What's that I hear?
I swear to God it was
 The sound of hope drawing near
Suddenly, near the end,
 It's all becoming clear —
 There's nothing left to fear
It was only in the beginning
 That I thought I'd be around for years

Sometimes we shoot for the moon,
 Sometimes we reach for the sun
We try to fulfill our ambitions,
 Try to have a little fun —
But, if we back out too late,
 After the damage has been done,
Then that's okay; it's the usual line
 We all have to learn on our own
That we're only immortal for a limited time

I once had my hopes up,
 But now they've sunk down again
It seems all our pretensions to sainthood
 Are drowned out by sin
 There's just no way you can win
If the girl won't let you in —
 And I've begun to fear, my friend,
 That this is The End —
And I want to repent,
 But where do we begin?

This, too, must pass,
Just like our love that couldn't last
 Somewhere along the line we lost our youth

LIFE'S TRIUMPH by Bill R. Moore

Maybe it was reckless abandon,
 Maybe we just saw a little too much truth
I see other women on the street
 And don't even stop to stare
 I left my heart somewhere
 On the road back there
The doorway closes
 And you sink to the floor,
Calling out faintly to the girl
 Who won't be back no more

I can walk across barren deserts
 As long as I'm not alone
Steep hills do not deter me,
 But I have no hand to hold
 The prophet has been told
 To say it clear, say it bold —
There ain't no help comin', baby,
 Admit it; take heed
Your sense of balance will not desert you,
 It's the only thing you need

I've watched the institutions
 Fall down one by one
The domino effect got 'em, as it always does,
 It was such sadistic fun
Get out while you still can,
 Turn away and run
There's no hope for you if you stay here,
 Nothing ever gets done

I've been double-crossed now
 For the very last time, and I will plot my revenge
It's the Golden Rule in reverse,
 Your life lies on the hinge
 I've had enough of your torturing binge,
 This is your last night on the lunatic fringe
Soon your body will turn to ash,
 And all your hair will singe
Yes, getting even's a bitch,

And no one ever realizes they're on the vinge

You've fallen from your mighty penthouse,
 You now reside in the mud
The End has reached us now—
 This is The Darkness; this is The Flood
The Lords of the Last Days cast their votes
 Into our bleak, fishless sea—
But you're just as clueless as ever,
 You never did see

It's all over now,
 Peace of mind has been found
All your institutions
 Have been burned to the ground—
All the flags have been taken down,
There's nothing left to fight
 Or kill for anymore
This is what's been
 Waiting in store

The Empires burn down,
 The Bible Belt snaps
All "undeniable truths"
 Have suddenly collapsed
It's only me and you
 Left standing after The Purge
How could you have thought otherwise?
 How did you have the nerve?

Damn this life
 And damn its pain
Damn its suffering,
 And damn it all again—
In short, damn it all
 I wanna see it all come down,
I wanna see it fall

2001

The Purge

I'm feeling so low right now
 That ants tower above me
I'm paralyzed by cynicism
 And lack of beauty
I tried to make you feel good when I felt bad,
 Thought it was my duty
 Yeah, the wickedness and misanthropy
Of the world and all its dead ends
 Deceived me into thinking
I had something to defend —
 But I'm tired of bitching about everything now,
I wish it would all just end

You're out having fun,
I'm decaying from within
 There's no fun in losing,
 No fun in abusing
Some say it helps them,
 But it just makes me sick
All you masochists and your easy way out,
 You can suck my dick

There's no use lying to me,
 I can see through you like water down a drain
I've acquired a sixth sense through the years
 Brought on by boredom and pain
I've been double-crossed, I've cheated, I've lost —
 And half the time I don't
Even know at what cost
 They say suffering is a river —
Well, it's one I've already drowned trying to cross;
 And they say you learn from your mistakes,
 But it didn't do me any good —
The landscape was bleak, the landscape was dross

I've been searching for truth,
 Searching for Jesus Christ the Savior

I've been searching for the forces
 Driving human behavior—
But I got lost along the way
 Maybe I'll find my way back
To it again some day;
But the path is long and hard
 And all guides have expired
It's really not worth the trouble,
 I'm so lonely and tired

It's not as easy as it looks,
 Screaming and kicking at the world
You just waste a lot of energy,
 Nothing ever gets unfurled
No answers are revealed,
No demons are killed—
Only deception is thrilled
 Everything you railed against is still there,
And look at all the empty space you've filled
 Nothing but time is forsaken
When the beans are spilled

I've watched you intently from afar—
I've seen you fuck up a million times,
 Making all the same mistakes as me
 Lord, will we ever be free?
 I dream about peace, justice, and equality,
But all our dreams are cancelled out
 By selfishness, greed, and jealousy—
It's time we took heed;
 All outward motion connects to nothing
For all are concerned with their immediate need
 It's time we quit helping ourselves out
And welcomed others into our steed

You say you told yourself a lie—
 That's all right, Mama, I told myself one, too,
 I told myself I loved you;
But I just can't admit things like that—
 I know what I'm good for,

And that's just not where it's at
 You and the kids'll be starving
While my wallet's getting fat
You say you want a man who
 Can talk to you for a while,
Pick you up when you're feeling low,
 Be a father for your child,
Who can get over himself
 And come around —
But it's not me, babe,
 I will only let you down

Nothing ever changes,
 Everything just falls apart
Lovers come and go,
 And I'm left with a broken heart
That's okay; I'll just go
 Back to the start
It shouldn't be too hard,
 I'm already on the bottom —
And, yes, I had ambitions once,
 I guess I just forgot 'em

 Pain, pain, pain — it stays with me
It says I'm all it ever wanted,
 It's all I'll ever be —
 And it just keeps droning on mercilessly,
Always fucking with my head
 I only see what it lets me see,
And that's usually only the bad
Nothing can prepare you
For the scorn of the norm
Everything is just as bad
 As everything else
Get out while you still can,
 Save yourself

I used to know you, girl,
 Thoughts of you once filled my head —
But you've changed, girl, you've changed,

I can't even touch the books you've read
I used to dream of being with you,
 But now I think I'd be better off dead
We were always more different
 Than we gave ourselves credit for —
And sometimes now I wonder
 Why I ever loved you at all, since I don't anymore

You're mad at me, I guess — oh well,
 It wouldn't be the first time and sure as hell won't be the last
Like everything else in life,
 Our time together went by too fast
I thought we'd be together forever,
 I told myself that, I know —
But you, like everything else in life,
 In time had to go

Look at me here, baby,
 Struggling to do everything right
I'm so pent up and restless,
 It's no wonder I can't sleep at night —
But, still, you never take
 My longings to heart
You're too damn busy worrying about
 Your little world fallin' apart
You didn't have any time for me,
 But that's okay; no one else does, either
Maybe it's time I sat down by myself
 And took a breather

I tried to talk to you about
 My latest project's conception —
But you just shrugged me off,
 It's beyond your depth of perception
I swear some angry man would've killed you long ago
 If not for your complexion
Me, I'm just satisfied with
 Being able to see your reflection
 Carefully hidden beneath your deception

A lot of groups and people say they'll help me,
 But they don't know what to do—
 They're just like you;
And it takes a long time for most people to realize
 It's not he, she, we, them, or it that you belong to
Your troubles are your own, my friend,
 And you're the only one who
 Can see them through

 I feel dirty, unclean,
Pissed off—
 I'm feelin' kinda mean
I feel like my head
 Is in a guillotine
I just wish I could wake up
 From this terrible, terrible dream
My troubles just keep on piling up,
 I can't take it anymore
Everyone's leaving me,
 My baby just walked out the door—
And now there's no one left but me after The Purge
 That's all right; that's all there was before

2001

Hope against Hope: Some Initial Cautious Optimism Excursions
By Apollon Archelaos

"There is a crack in everything.
That's how the light gets in."
–Leonard Cohen, "Anthem"

"It frightens me, the awful truth of how sweet life can be"
–Bob Dylan, "Up to Me"

"Have you noticed that an angry man can only get so far
Until he reconciles the way he thinks things ought to be
With the way things are"
–Don Henley, "My Thanksgiving"

"Everything in moderation"
–The Delphic Oracle

L ike Mark, Apollon is an aged immigrant. He emigrated from a small Greek city to New York at twenty, full of hope and desire; nearing a long life's end, he is happy to report that most of what he wished to do has actually occurred. He considered himself an optimist when he entered the country, all bright-eyed and fresh, and is proud to say he is still genuinely able to call himself one. That said, he is no Pollyanna; his path to success has been littered with countless roadblocks, disappointments, failures, and regrets that show up in his thought. His optimism is thus always tinged with healthy doses of skepticism, rationality, and more than a hint of well-considered pessimism. Indeed, he has never had illusions about human nature and knows as well as any pessimist the barbaric atrocities of which he and his fellow humans are capable. Simply put, he believes in the possibility of continuing rational progress — but is also keenly aware of our self-destructive potential. Some may call him an "optimistic pessimist," but he prefers "pessimistic optimist" — or simply "realist." Though dark doubts and suspicions sometimes cloud his thought, they never engulf it; he keeps a sincere and genuine sense of hope through it all. Staking out a happy medium, he subscribes to neither original sin nor Rousseau's postulate that society corrupts. Like Clarke, another realistic optimist, he believes we are at our best when continually striving, seeking to better ourselves and forever reach for new, greater frontiers. In his view, humanity ceases the moment we cease to do this; for better or worse, we may be succeeded, but the creature, whatever it may be, will not be us. Apollon hopes this will never occur; he genuinely wants us to survive and prosper and truly believes in our capability. He thus comes down on humanity's side; he will place his bets on it with hope and trust — but always cautiously, and not without worry, as he is fully aware far greater minds have come down with even greater certainty on the other side. He claims no certain knowledge of our final outcome but is willing to wait and hope; unlike most, he looks forward to the eventual meeting between our progressive impulses and self-destructive inclinations with head held high and his thought coming down strongly on optimism's side.

The Tide Is Turning

We used to think witches were all around us,
That evil, invisible demons would always surround us—
 Yet, through it all, the torch of human progress was always burning
There's hope for us now
That we'll make it through somehow
 Oh—the tide is turning

We used to think the Church had the cure to every unfortunate circum-
    stance,
Slaves as we were to blind faith, dogma, and ignorance—
 But now faith in the human mind's power is returning
We're beginning to find our way,
We'll get there any day
 Oh—the tide is turning

We used to look for answers in the sky,
Forsaking self-reliance, we trusted others to tell us why—
 But, through it all, they never destroyed our yearning
We've made it through the clear,
And it's all downhill from here
 Oh—the tide is turning

We used to believe in monarchy and the divine right of kings,
Phrenology, eugenics, and a thousand other crazy things—
 Yet, through it all, we still kept on learning
We've still got a long way to go,
But we'll make it through, I know
 Oh—the tide is turning

We used to get our kicks by killing our fellow man,
By biting the hand that feeds instead of lending a helping hand
 If you think we're through, you must not be very discerning—
But let's not give up the fight,

We may just be in the right
 Oh — the tide is turning

We forsake all the best things in life for the simple pleasure of getting laid,
Wasting our breath and causing death in the name of gods we've made —
 And sometimes I ask myself, "Will the tide keep on turning?"
It must, or so I trust,
For it's either that or bust —
 So let's keep that torch forever burning

2007 (First published in *Shine*, Aug. 2009, in slightly different form.)

So Long, Postmodernism

Suppose, for one moment, Rousseau was right—
 That those primal days which we've left behind
Were far more meaningful, peaceful, and bright,
 Modern life just mere ashes in the wind;
And, the farther back in time that we go,
 The less bloodshed, war, hatred, prejudice—
Tell me, my friend, would you like me to show
 You: Truth? Beauty? Equality? Justice?
Yes? *Yes*? Well, let us go then, you and I,
 Let us leave this dead world of poverty,
Degradation, disgust, and empty skies—
 Start all over again, just you and me.
We can leave dead modernity behind to rust—
O, the savage beauty of ignorance and lust!

2005

"If I Forget Thee on Earth..."

Out, out, brief candle!
 Shield me from the sound and fury
I lost my love, lost my life—
 It all went by in such a flurry
Oh, I know it's nothing new,
 It's the same age-old story;
But I thought you might like to know, before you saw me go,
 Since I must leave in a hurry
My soul is ascending to mansions on high,
 I must prepare to face the power and glory...

Well, we strut across this stage so briefly,
 Our history but temporary lore
To stall is mere cheating, our existence but fleeting,
 I'm rolling on toward God's distant shore
I can see the lightning crashing,
 Can hear the thunder roar
Don't shed a tear for me, my dear friend,
 I am but one more
Another lonely stranger from this blue orb
 Knocking on heaven's door
It's time for me to leave, time for me to go
 Just like so many times before...

Now, heaven's throne is made of gold,
 I feel as if I've grown old
There will be many there to greet me,
 That's what I've been told
All my friends and lovers
 Will welcome me into the fold
Oh, they say I have been blessed,
 But I just feel so cold
These dark doubts enter my mind at last—
 Can I have grown so bold?
How can I just sit back and watch
 The rest of history unfold...?

Why must it end this way—
 Do we have no choice in the matter?
I try so hard to think,
 But thoughts just seem to scatter
Must we give in, fold our hand—
 Must we surrender to this caper?
Oh, what a way to leave this
 Vile and pestilent congregation of vapors
If we truly signify nothing,
 If all we leave amounts to mere shreds and tatters,
Must we subscribe to this dark and vile notion—
 Must we pay heed, must we flatter?
Nothing is black and white; there's always gray to be seen,
 And my road just keeps getting blacker...

But all things must pass—
 This, too, must pass
It's all over now, my dear old friend,
 The end has come at last—
But let us not forget,
 Let us not cease to grasp
Though the end draws near,
 We have a future, we have a past...
Don't spill tears over the loss of my earthly existence,
 Do not drain this broken glass
Though the end is forever in sight,
 We must never cease to clasp...

I glimpse the one last undying land
 Without ideals or violence
We must now heed the Man—
 After all, the rest is silence;
But I must finally be leaving now—
 So long, my friend, I truly now must depart
Keep my memory alive and well,
 Keep me in your heart
I must be on my way now
 To depart forever from the planet of my birth,
And I've left this here for you to remember me by—
 "If I forget thee on earth..."   2003

Tolerable Equilibrium

I've long known those who see things
 Through rose-tinted glasses
Have their heads too far
 Up their asses —
  But what of moderation?
Surely there's a golden mean between
  Them and righteous indignation
Maybe if I become more selective
By taking another's perspective
 I can see things in their true light —
Stand in their shoes, sing their blues,
 And at least make mine bearable, if not slight —

Can I see another's sorrow
 And not be in sorrow too?
If my life falls apart tomorrow,
 Will I be as unlucky as you?
  No matter how bad I feel,
Surely someone always feels worse
  Even when my pain is real,
Someone's driven off in a hearse

They say the man with no shoes felt bad
 Until he saw the man with no feet —
Ah, but what good are these clues,
 So hypothetical, so discreet?
What have they to do with my life,
So full of inscrutable sorrow, mysterious strife?
 It's hard to relate to another's state
 Even with a clean slate,
But when your cup of sorrow's full,
It's no use making rules
 About how it's easier to love than hate
My conscience might kick,
But I'm kicking against the pricks,
 And it just makes me feel irate

I know my troubles are nothing
 Beside the mass of mankind's
  Or even individual strife
 It's not that I'm callous or blind,
  It's just that I'm living this life
No matter how shitty, I try to avoid self-pity,
 But it's enough to just make it through the day
I know my problems are meaningless,
 But that don't make them go away

 I kicked myself for years,
  Strived to fight back fears,
Put on a brave face,
  Tried to see things as they are —
 Held back tears,
  Tried to see woe both near and far,
Have some sympathy with the human race —
 And I thought I'd finally found a delicate balance,
Something close to my heart —
 But try as I might, I still can't meet the challenge,
I'm always worried about my little world falling apart
 I can mostly hold troubles back until they fade or pass,
But I'm always afraid someone's gonna come along
 And shatter my fragile armor like glass

Yet I think I've learned a few things,
Moved beyond self-absorption to some new things
 Sorrows never really go away,
 But I can keep them at bay
 Long enough to get through the day —
The most one can realistically hope for
 I can empathize with others, make peace with my brothers,
More or less settle the score

There was a time I would have thought it insufficient,
 But those days are long gone
At least it's efficient,
 I can keep on keepin' on
If you have a survival kit, you know you need it,
 Don't care who's wrong or right

Comes a time when you draw the line
 And see that mere survival's a noble fight

 I may never answer all the questions that haunt me,
May never find my place in a world
 That doesn't seem to want me,
But I can put my sorrows aside,
Take a view that's wide,
 And endure essentially
It's a pretty good way at the end of the day
 And gets more bearable if I stay in line
I put myself on trial, avoid denial,
 Take it one day at a time
Yes, old doubts come clawin' back sometimes,
 But I've reached tolerable equilibrium
I can live with the past,
Make due with a future so vast,
 Deal with problems as they come
I'm hardly on a roll, but on the whole,
 Must admit things are okay
  — For now anyway

2009

What It All Comes Down To

I'm not the President or some big-time lawyer,
 I've just got a picture to paint
You tell me you're hurtin', baby,
 Well, show me someone who ain't
You're no worse off than me,
I've still got to pay the rent, you see—
 So pinch off some of those penny rolls
And have a little mercy

There's been darker days than this—
 Yeah, but I wasn't there
They don't mean a damn thing to me,
 It's like all the walls are bare
Did the Depression happen yesterday
 Or a million years ago?
Don't fucking look at me like I'm stupid,
 I've got problems of my own

I should've known better
 Than to get into this mess—
But now it's too late to turn back
 And too early to confess
I shouldn't have to be forgiven
 For showing my affection—
But now that the secret's out,
 It seems you were expecting perfection

You think you're suffering,
 I got news for you, bro—
We're all living
 In the same shithole
 Old Man next door's feelin' cold and alone,
 I'm choking on the smoke that fills my home
Fuck you if you're asking for pity,
 Maybe some other time—
 Move back to the end of the line

That chick next door
 Got raped last night—

LIFE'S TRIUMPH by Bill R. Moore

Some booze-headed weasel
 Took her money without a fight
Next night, I hear, they make up,
 And she gives him head
Tem minutes later, they found her
 In the subway dead

The kids hiding down in our basement
 Haven't yet had their fun —
But that beggar on the street,
 Well, he wound up on the business end of a gun
  How's your wife doing — is she still alive?
I heard some bimbo had a price on her head
  On account of her jive
Don't kid yourself by saying,
 "It can't happen to me"
I'm sorry, my friend, but we all
 Get our turn eventually

I know you always wondered why your world's so empty,
 Why you just can't be cool
Well, your mother's passed out on sleeping pills,
 And they just found your father in the swimming pool
Now, you can call your girlfriend
 On the telephone —
Ask her where she was last night,
 Why she wasn't at home —
But why should you get to feel any better than the rest?
 We're all in this alone

Everyone else has a date tonight,
 Even your sister —
And you're gettin' so goddamn desperate
 That you just might kiss her
Nothing's as it seems,
Reality's not the stuff of dreams

 My brother crashed into a tree last night —
Maybe he had one too many,
 Maybe he was just tired of the fight
It's hard enough living as it is,
  But some want to live even longer

Failure and deceit, hatred and lies,
Envy and scorn, unanswered prayers, and muffled cries —
 I guess what doesn't kill you makes you stronger

It's hard to move up in society
When you get spit on for doing what's right
They jeer you if you stay to the left
 And fear you if you stray to the right —
But I say it's now or never,
 This damn thing hasn't moved since they turned on the lights
It's time we made some improvements here,
 However slight
Some say it's hard to live in a world without pity,
 I say it doesn't make much difference tonight

I know it can be hard sometimes, growing up,
 When no one gives a damn about who's wrong and who's right
It can drag you down, make you want to give in,
 But you still got to put up a fight
You gotta muster the willpower,
 Gotta flex that might —
And, if you're gonna use it some day,
 You better use it tonight

I'm not asking for a miracle,
 I don't believe in sudden revelations of the soul;
And I don't expect any changes,
 These people got no self-control
I just want someone to talk to —
 Is it really too much to ask?
I've been looking for one all my life,
 And I'm beginning to think it's a hopeless task

No one asked for divine intervention,
 We're supposed to be able to take care of things ourselves —
But you come around — first crushing our self-respect,
 Then crushing everything else
I just want something to hold on to
 In this world of "flee after touch"
Tell me, do you think
 What I'm asking's too much?

LIFE'S TRIUMPH by Bill R. Moore

Beware the ladder of achievement, man,
 It shifts and moves mysteriously around
You think you're moving up
 When, in fact, you're climbing down
It all really just depends on
 Who's the boss in town
 And if the boss is around
I'm confused already, my friend,
 Pick me up at the lost and found

 You say your baby hates you —
 Well, my baby hates me, too
I'm getting so tired of running in this rat race,
 I'm beginning to think my time's about through
 Maybe it's time to try something new —
Bad days are so common,
 Good ones so few
I'm all lost and confused now,
 I just wish I was back with you

So I'll leave you here alone now
 With your hopes and dreams,
And I'll close my eyes and wonder
 If everything's really as hollow as it seems
I'm tired and world-weary —
 Hell, who am I kidding? My world is dead
I'm being dragged down by
 All the dogma in my head
It's too early to give in,
 Too late to be saved
I'm sick and tired of planning for my future,
 I think I'll start decorating my grave

 Just give up; it's the American Way
I guess I knew it all along,
 I just didn't want to say
That long and winding road,
 It's really such a farce
It's so damn barren and difficult,
 It doesn't even help to have a chart
So, thanks for your help; I'm much obliged,
 But I've really got to figure this out for myself

With my own mind, my own eyes

So I'll get up in the morning and reluctantly face another day,
 It's all I've ever done—yeah, but it's all I could do,
 It's all you'll ever do, too—
There's just no other way
I guess what I'm really trying to say
Is life sucks—but live anyway

2001

Hope against Hope: A Panacea Part II

There are many things in this sorry life
 That will make you want to give up and cry—
Endless pain, torture, disappointments, strife—
 Enough to make anyone wish to die
People will misread your good intentions,
 Bring you down just when you begin to win,
Criticize your dreams and your inventions
 And then do it all over yet again,
This time behind your unsuspecting back—
 Makes you wonder if life is worth living.
They come out for yet another attack
 Against you—it's misery unending...
But here is the one thing they don't want you to guess:
One moment of joy blots a thousand of distress.

2005 (First published in *In Other Words* (2006)
as "Hope against Hope: A Panacea" in slightly different form.)

The Starving Artist (Vindication)

Well, I get embarrassed sometimes,
 I need a quiet place to hide
Everyone—yes, everyone, my friend,
 Is sometimes a slave to their pride
Yes, that's just the way it is in this biz,
 You were the thorn in my side
You were the thorn without a rose,
 The darkness that never glows
You try to get rid of somethin' sometimes
 And instead it just grows and grows

Well, I once loved a girl,
 She had many an obvious charm—
But she came to my room every night
 With a Bible tucked under her arm
I swore I'd never hurt her,
 Swore I'd never do her harm—
But gulfs just grow so wide sometimes
 That you wish you'd never left the farm

Friends come and go,
 I'm layin' low
You never know when it's gonna rain,
 When it's gonna snow
You just gotta keep yourself prepared
 So you don't wind up below;
But sometimes I think, when I'm on the brink,
 That it's the only place to go
Maybe I should give it a shot…
Well, maybe not
 My wrists are slashed, my checks are cashed—
Still I have not, still I rot

Sometimes, when you get so low,

LIFE'S TRIUMPH by Bill R. Moore

You start questionin' even the few things
 You really do know
You're so tender, weak, and vulnerable,
 You fall prey to every attack
You don't know where you're goin',
 And all you can see is all that you lack —
 But don't worry, darlin'; I'm not comin' back,
 I'm not comin' back
Don't take it personal; it's just you
You — and everyone else, too

Well, you start thinkin' you can trust someone sometimes,
 But you know you really can't
They build you up 'till you start feelin' like a king,
 But you wind up feelin' like an ant
They build you up so high
 And let you down so low —
And I been down so long, baby,
 That there's nowhere else for me to go

I had a friend, and maybe a girl,
 Had 'em employed on work for hire;
But that damn boy was so useful —
 Couldn't solve a mathematical equation, but he could change a tire
In other words, he had all the virtues I abhor
 And none of the vices I admire
For every man should have his vices,
 Should keep 'em to himself, keep 'em well hid
You never know when you'll need to piss off a lady,
 Never know when you'll need to impress a kid

Every artist is a criminal, every poet a thief,
They kill their inspiration and bitch about the grief
 Well, it was a long and crooked road that brought me to you,
 I'm wond'rin' what the hell I'm gonna do
To keep on drivin' in this ride
Whatever perilous paths I may trod

Won't bother me, as long as I can see
You in my side view
 I'll still be facing hell, and telling about it as well,
  Because it's my duty;
And you'll always be here, so warm and near,
As I travel through the shit—always plodding, never to quit;
 To prevail, to suffer, to face hell—
  To create beauty

2001

Adam's Curse Part II

"Life is sad
Life is a bust
All ya can do is do what you must.
You do what you must do and ya do it well"
— Bob Dylan, "Buckets of Rain"

"Do not go gentle into that good night.
Rage, rage against the dying of the light."
–Dylan Thomas, "Do Not Go Gentle into That Good Night"

Civilization is just an interlude between ice ages,
 The sun will explode in so many billion years
We who spend our lives writing these pages,
 What else do we need to hate or fear?

We all strive for immortality,
 For the great work someone has yet to write
We want to see so others can see—
 Soldiers at war, youth in love's first night

We feel there's a purpose to what we do,
 That we bring truth and beauty into the world
We like to think it means something to all of you
 Who wait for our latest pages to be unfurled

Yet who could deny it is all in vain,
 That we toil and fret for naught?
All this love and all this pain,
 We give it to you because it's all we've got

It seems so simple, really, that it's hard to blame
 Us for our wasted endeavors
Though we know we are tied to this chain,
 Still we continue as if we have forever

After all, we are no worse off than others,

All are doomed to obscurity in the immensity of Time
So we leave the other work, great and small, to our brothers
While we agonize over meter and rhyme

We eat and drink, feel and think,
 Struggle to find meaning as we go
We live and love as we fill pages with ink,
 Doing what we do because it's all we know

So, bring it on, let it be —
 Armageddon, the end of Time
You'll still be doing what you do, and we
 Will still be sweating over our lines

We write with the knowledge that all we bring
 Will be swept away at the crack of doom
Fuck it; you can't worry about every damn thing,
 We'll be doing this 'til we're in our tombs

We know some day the bubble will burst,
 But we keep on writing as if Fate has other plans
Chained to this craft that is both blessing and curse,
 Tortured by demons we can neither control nor understand

Everything we do today will be swept away tomorrow,
 But we keep on, though it fills us with pain
And unutterable sorrow —
 We can only hope it was not in vain

2006

Book II:
Self-Conscious Schizophrenia

by Bill R. Moore

Instead of a Byline (I Am I)

Berated by inopportune ramblings, driven
Insecure, forced into a
Liturgy, reduces you to a
Louse, a pointless information resistance
      Repository, made
      Obligatory by the luminous
      Ether, doesn't help—all is
      Broken, there's no path around it, must take the
      Undertow, use it to
      Cash your non-existent money that swears, doesn't talk;
      Kinetic energy doesn't help very
            Much, you can turn it
            On, turn it
            Off, but in the end it doesn't matter, it's all
            Receding into the abyss; you're at the pearly gates,
                but your back is facing the
            Entrance.

2001

Epigraph: Life from "A" to "Z"

After becoming due existentialism from gregarious heat,
I jacked killer lice—
Menstrual new opportunities presented queries—
Ripped straight through universe very well;
Xavier you zapped.

2001

Preface

There is a music industry analogy of great relevance to the literary industry, if I may use such a vulgar and — in these days of widespread functional illiteracy and near-non-existent reading — term. It is that second albums are almost always inferior, often substantially so, to debuts because, after all, you have your whole life up to that point to make your first and a relatively very short time for the second. Without consciously seeking to, I believe I have avoided the trap, such as it is, by including many poems in this second poetic book written contemporaneous with and even before many of those in my first. It will indeed be seen that the first has a significantly greater number of then-recent ones. Lest cynics say it is because this book is but a slop heap of leftovers not considered good enough for the first by me and/or others, I hasten to add that, whatever their relative merits, this was not intentional. Some I like as well, nearly as well, or even better than, already published predecessors. I have no reason, much less justification, for having passed them over the first time other than the admittedly very subjective one that I did not think they fit. Hopefully they do here; if not, as may well be, perhaps intrinsic merit may at least partly atone.

That said, I have retained the *Reflections in Broken Glass* scheme of grouping the poems into various categories "written" by separate "authors." As I — hopefully — have new readers, I beg their veteran counterparts' pardon for reintroducing these "authors" in very similar terms. Perhaps they will become well-known enough that introductions are unnecessary — a dubious fate I have no thought, and am often without desire, of sharing.

2009

Instead of a Preface
(The Economics of Art)

"For we that live to please, must please to live"
–Samuel Johnson, "Prologue Spoken by Mr. Garrick"

"What is art? Prostitution."
–Charles Baudelaire, "Fuse I"

I fear now that I must breach a subject
 That lies close to my own heart—
What works should we reject,
 And when does art become art?

If we keep our works to ourselves,
 No one will know them—
But, if they're up on everyone's shelves,
 Everyone can show them

Does popularity equal quality?
 Does success equal art?
Does fame equal notoriety?
 Does obscurity equal a false start?

Shakespeare is the most famous of writers,
 But does it make him the best?
Could there be others, though mere slighters,
 Who're really better than all the rest?

Is there an unknown genius lurking somewhere
 Who is the greatest bard of all-time—
Writing alone and unknown in his lair,
 Perfecting meter and rhyme?

If all art is mere prostitution,
 Is obscurity alone great?
When a great writer becomes an institution,
 Has he already emptied his slate?

Dostoevsky wrote his great novels
 At breakneck speed while deep in debt—
Yet in his work we find many revels,
 We do not find cause to regret

Crichton's books sell millions of copies
 And are made into blockbuster films—
But from them a critic flees,
 While in them a reader swims

Writers write—what else can they do?
 Readers buy, as of course they will—
But they can only get the known and new,
 Bestsellers are expensive; flops are a deal

Writers not only have to write,
 They also have to make a living
I may write a masterpiece tonight,
 But you'd have to pay to see it—no giving

Yes, money rules the world,
 We must accept that fact—
No more immune than any boy or girl
 Are writers, however they may act

Art is art—and we're all thankful for that,
 So let's salute those who are able
To all worthy artists I take off my hat—
 But everyone still has to put food on the table

2005

Hard Times in These Times:
Reflections on the Contemporary Scene
By John Feldman

"I'm sentimental, if you know what I mean
I love the country but I can't stand the scene"
–Leonard Cohen, "Democracy"

John is a young, idealistic, and optimistic Midwestern boy on his own for the first time. His exact age is unknown, but he is widely-believed to be in his late teens or early twenties. Unsubstantiated rumors that he ran away from home persist. He genuinely believes he can change the world via art, or at least inspire others to—and is determined to try at any rate. He cares little about critics; his goal is to move the masses. A working-class populist, he makes an honest effort to put himself in the position of other members of his generation and describe the cold, post-postmodern world as he truly believes they see it. He knows this is not without a certain presumption, even arrogance, but wishes to be his generation's voice and cannot be overly burdened with such concerns. His fantasy is to be a folk singer. Only two minor stumbling blocks stand between him and his dream: he cannot play a note and cannot sing. (Oh, *he* thinks he can sing, all right—but no one else does.) Faced with this unfortunate and convenient situation, he has taken the path of numerous other lyricists like him—issuing his words as poetry. He thinks it a poor substitute but also sees that, after all, it is better than nothing. I include few of his poems not because there is insufficient news for a protest artist. After all, perhaps no era has had more since the 1960s; he sings the pain of a generation whose defining moment is 9/11 and is accordingly prolific. It is because, like all artists trying to make works relevant to the masses, he ever walks the thin, thin line between being matter-of-factly didactic, thus losing art, and too artistic, thus losing relevance and mass appeal. These poems are his best attempts at bridging the proverbial gap. If even they fail, it testifies to the challenge's great difficulty. He nonetheless hopes to make a name for himself and just may do it. The discerning critic will do well to keep an eye on him, as he just may succeed. If not, he will still be able to comfort himself with the fact that he truly tried his best—a noble failure if ever there were one.

A Plea
To: Oscar Wilde

Dear Oscar:

Wilde! You who were so much a part of, yet so far ahead of, your time, who perplexed with paradoxes and confounded with rhyme—we need you to drop an epigram or phrase that will rouse us from our slumber and free us from this creeping malaise.

What would you say about the war? The national debt? AIDS? Poverty? Tsunamis? George Bush? $2 a gallon that has to be paid? Would you remove the feeding tube? Condemn executions for the young? Is it better to burn out than to fade away or should we leave no song unsung?

I know you have answers; we await expectantly. We are so poor, indeed, wise one, that we still quote you from last century. I know I could open at random any book of yours and find a suitable phrase, but we need something new from you, something from our own sad days.

Oh, you are absent when needed most! Your own age did not know your value. Lacking a voice, we have no choice but to call down the ages to you. What would you say, what would you tell us, to fill our empty heads? Probably that we're too serious to trifle with and that you're better off dead.

Sincerely,

The twenty-first century

2005

World Coming Down

I have an appointment with death,
 And I'm already late
I haven't eaten
 For five days straight
My clothes are dirty, old, and unkempt,
 Last night I slept under
A blanket made of hemp
 On a pillow of solid rock
My baby's left me,
 And now some old man wants my cock

You can feel the disease
 Spreading all around —
 The world is coming down
This isn't the time for
Your petty problems,
 There's worse things going around
We've got to come to grips with this tragedy
 And take it to heart
It's not time to get even,
 It's time to get smart
It's too late to worry about
 Your little world falling apart

It's brought us all together,
 Where once we were so far apart
Maybe there's a lesson to be learned
 From all this; if so, I don't know where to start
Is it a test of strength —
 How far can we bend?
It's only so much longer before
 We finally reach the end

I'm tired of being the companion
 To the cold hand of fate
Finally, now, we understand,
 But it has come too late

We've already missed our chance,
 This is no time to understate
 Fools try and enunciate,
They only make things worse
 This is no time for your prejudices,
No time to be perverse

You can blame it on the gods,
 Can chalk it all up to fate—
You can make up a million bullshit reasons
 For why your love has turned to hate
 Now is no time for petty concerns—
This is the point where
 The bright flame of reality burns
You can rail against it
With your jive and bitch,
 But it won't budge an inch
You'd think that, after suicide,
 Armageddon would be a cinch

 The Road to Glory was never clear—
 Was always obstructed, always severe
You could always detour before,
 But now the end is near—
And there's nothing left to hope,
 Nothing left to fear
 The time is now, the time is here

I can't heed your call,
 Can't do any of the things you're asking me to do
It's time you realized, baby,
 That I'm just as fucked as you
Punishment is often sporadic,
 But we all get it in equal doses
Some are splurged,
 Some are dripped slowly into psychosis
Either way, we both hear
 The same tolling sound
I'll meet you at the darkness
 On the edge of town

The world's coming down

You can add up the parts,
 You won't have the sum
Nothing is still nothing,
 Doesn't matter where you come from
We're running out of time,
 And there's no one left to help us get things done
 We're drowning in our own feces and cum
While our governments pay lip service
 To the concept of freedom

I've been shackled too long,
 Soon I will be released
I'm gonna show the conquered freedom,
 Gonna show the conquerors peace
Look me in the eye and tell me
 If you really meant what you said
It's time to take one for the team
 We all agree you'd be better off dead,
But don't worry; it's a matter of trust
 I'll save you if I can,
Kill you if I must

I don't know where I'm going anymore,
 I just go
I lost my sense of purpose
 Long ago
I don't wanna be part of the circus,
 Just wanna make something of myself —
But everyone wants you to be
 Just like everyone else

My neighbors talk about me
 Behind my back, think they can see through me —
But their whispered words of defiance
 Show they hardly knew me
It makes you stop and wonder
If we're all strangers to each other —
 Each an isolated island in a bleak, fishless sea

I know as little about you, my friend,
 As you know about me

We don't even know what we're fighting for anymore —
 Don't know why we're carrying a gun
We don't know why we're here
 Or where we came from
We're just living as we see fit —
 Killing and disfiguring,
 Not forgiving and forgetting
It's an ongoing suicide attempt,
 It's too late to stop and freeze —
 Life's an occupational disease

We watched our empires being built
And then watched them all
Come crashing down to hell —
 All things must pass,
 It's time we saw the truth at last
 Our fifteen minutes went by too fast
At last we finally learned
 That, if you play with fire,
You're gonna get your fucking fingers burned

It's not funny any longer,
 It's past the point of no return;
And you will not grow any stronger,
 It's past the point of all concern
They're gonna shake our ashes
In our enemies' faces
 Once they've been put in an urn —
 You're gonna burn, burn, burn!

 The party's over, the wheels have stopped,
 You can feel Satan's riding crop
 It sure was fun, standing there on top —
But now prosperity and progress are gone,
 We've no longer got 'em —
 We're on the bottom

It's time to cut the games,
 To cut the fun
 At this point, what's done is done—
 The end of time has just begun
It's us against the universe,
 And we're on the run
They're trying to track us down,
 And it's not gonna get any better
 Tomorrow or the next day
The world's coming down—
 Better get out of the way

September 2001

Everything Is Different Now

Once there was a way
 To get back home
Once there was a way
 To avoid feeling so alone
There was a safe haven—
A pseudo-heaven,
 A place to call your own—
But now it's gone
We now inhabit the shell-shocked remains
 Of the Paradise we once knew so well
How can one man's little bit of heaven
 Turn into another man's hell?
It just all disappeared somehow—
And everything is different now

There was a time, back in the day,
 When free people were allowed to think—
They weren't subjected to propaganda,
 Weren't pushed to the brink
Politicians gave brilliant manifestos,
 And prophets and poets drained pens of bitter ink
Funny how the mightiest ships
 Can suddenly spring a leak
This pacifies me to the point
 Where I can't even speak
Where once I was flamboyant,
 I am now meek
I used to bare my wounds
 And show off my sieve
I proudly wore my heart
 On my sleeve—
But now my sense of the absurd
 Has gotten up and walked away
Maybe it'll come back
 In some far off, distant day
I sure hope so; I need my cash cow—
But everything is different now

Only a blind man stalls
 In the face of change—
You gotta move and shake,
 Gotta re-arrange
Some act like they have
 Money to burn and time to kill—
But you can't move forward
 When standing still
It's all right for some,
 I guess it gives 'em a certain thrill,
But I can't be satisfied
 With such a dishonest way of getting my fill
Some day I will confront you again,
 And, god damn it, I will win
There's no two ways about it,
 You'll have to pay for your sins—
But, until then, I'll have to
 Make due somehow—
 As everything is different now

These people can't be allowed
 To have their voices heard
They're filling our minds with bullshit,
 Saying "free" is just another four-letter word
This mind pollution has now gotten
 To the point of being uniquely absurd;
And, I don't know about all of you,
 But I think it's all gotten a little slurred
I'm sitting here listening to their rap,
 I just can't relate
How can they put all their hope
 In faith and fate?
Surely something more concrete
 They will allow—
 After all, everything is different now

Forget the way things were
 And what you thought before—
 None of it matters anymore

We were on the road to heaven,
 But they slammed the door
They've shaken our morale,
 They've mounted their attack,
But we must not let it make us
 Lose our will to fight back
This is the time for action,
 This is no time to hit the sack
All former matters of importance
 Have lost their luster, wow —
 As everything is different now

"Freedom, freedom, freedom" —
 I heard them say
I heard it all my life,
 Every single day —
But I never knew what it meant
 'Til someone tried to take it away
I took for granted
 All that with which I'm blessed —
And now I'm a sentimental, blood-hungry, draft-dodger —
 Who ever would've guessed?
Anyway, I guess what I'm really trying to say
 Is this is not the end; we're not through
Don't' worry, darling,
 There's nothing you can do
You say you're sorry,
 I'm sorry, too,
But we'll make it through somehow —
As everything is different now

Freedom — yes, freedom —
I spoke the word
 As if a wedding vow
Declaring at the top of my lungs
 That everything is different now
As I look back now,
 The only thing I did wrong
Was putting off telling you all this
 So very long

This is the first day
 Of the rest of your life—
A new road, paved with hope,
 Constructed on the building blocks of strife
This is an epoch, and nothing is the same
As it was pre-strike
Good and evil, freedom and slavery, each and every immortal song—
 I defined these terms quite clearly, no doubt, somehow,
But that was before—
 And everything is different now

September 2001

Lost Cause

Everything's changed,
 Nothing's the same
The old rules don't apply anymore,
 This is a different game
You can kill in patriotism,
 You can kill in the Name —
But get the hell out of the way
 If you don't feel the same

It's just like when I was with you,
 It was the same as it is today
I tried to get through to you
 In my own special way —
But you wouldn't listen to reason,
 You had to have your say
You said you'd never leave me,
 But you didn't stay —
And now you can be just like them
 And walk away
Just turn your pretty little head
And walk away

Some changes come crashing in,
 And we hear the sound —
And suddenly the whole world
 Is turned upside down
We can't be lost
 For we were never found
This is the same old evil
 That's always been around
Some day we'll extinguish it,
 Some day we'll be safe and sound —
But right now we're too busy
 Tearing the world down

You affect my heart
 Like it has just been shot

LIFE'S TRIUMPH by Bill R. Moore

Baby, how would you feel if I told you
 I love you not for what you are but for what you're not?
You say you have just cause
 For leaving me so alone and fucked
Why don't you just go ahead
 And break my heart one more time for good luck?

These people just don't understand
 What they've done to our livelihood
It's gonna come back around
 And bite them on the ass, just as we always said it would;
And I don't know what you
 Think you're doing leaving me alone like that
You always pretended to know
 Just exactly where it was at
They fucked up, did something
 Worse than what they should—
And you're just as bad; I just can't tell my heart
 That you ain't no good

There's no use pretending
 That you're not pissed
Life as we know it
 Has ceased to exist
Some day soon, with luck,
 It'll be reconciled—
But right now I just want to get out of here,
 To run a million miles

 These memories haunt me still—
I just don't understand why
 So many innocents had to be killed;
And you're just strolling along
 Like nothing's happened, so careless and free—
 Where's your sense of humanity?
 This is horrible; this is surreal
 Good God, this can't be real
Doesn't anyone else
 Feel the way I feel?
Surely, surely, life can't be

As bad as it seems
I think it's finally time
I surrendered to my dreams

September 2001

Involuntarily Domiciled Blues

Well, I got the involuntarily domiciled blues, Lord, there's no place for my
    weary head to be
Well, I got the involuntarily domiciled blues, Lord, an' there's no place for
    my weary head to be
Well, an' it's because I'm black, Lord, and George Bush don' care 'bout me

Well, I used to live in New Orleans, but New Orleans got a-washed away
Yes, well, I used to live in New Orleans, but New Orleans got a-washed
    away
I thought the president would come and save us, but he didn't come for
    five more days

Well, I took my troubles down to DHS, but they lost my papers somehow
Yes, well, I took my troubles down to DHS, but they lost all my fuckin' pa-
    pers somehow,
But I still gotta put food on the table—guess I'll hafta go back to shopliftin'
    now

Well, I'm out on the street now, ain't got no place to live
Yes, well, now I'm out on the street now, ain't got no place to live
I'd try askin' other people for somethin', but they ain't got nothin' to give

I'm tired an' cold an' hungry, an' nobody cares for me
Well, I'm tired, an' I'm cold, an' I'm a-hungry, an' nobody cares for me
I thought all men's created equal, thought we was in a democracy

Now, some says it's what we deserve for all our gamblin' and whorin'
Yes, well, now some says it's what we deserve for all our gamblin' and
    whorin'
Well, I'd like to see them say that, Lord, if their own town's washed away
    tomorrow mornin'

An' some says, "You knew it might happen; why'd you live in a place so
    torn?"
Yes, some says, "You knew it might happen; why'd you live in a place that
    be so torn?"
Well, I says, "A man ain't got but one home, and that's the place where he

be born"

Well, let me drown in these waters, Lord, let me die on my own two feet
Yes, let me drown in these waters, Lord, let me die a-standin' on my own
    two feet
I know when I sink down there, Lord, you'll be there for me to greet

I'm gonna die right here in the Delta, Lord, the place where I come from
Yes, I'm a-gonna die right here in the Delta, Lord, the place where I be from
Yes, 'cause I've been involuntarily domiciled, an' the thought o' movin' on
    jus' leaves me feelin' numb

Well, I'm starvin' to death on the streets, ain't got much else to say
Well, yes, I'm starvin' to death on the streets, ain't got much else to say
When they build this damn place back up, Lord, I won't be here to see the
    day

2005

"My Country, Right Or Wrong":
A Patriotic Paradox

"My country, right or wrong" —
 It is said that this phrase
Has caused more trouble
 Than any other throughout the days

It has caused people to look the other way
 While the backs of slaves were being whipped,
To forget what The Constitution has to say
 Though the president's reins have slipped

To fight a war on a foreign shore
 Without ever knowing why
And do it again a few decades later—
 But this time because of a lie

To take it all in gladly while money is being spent
 And debt keeps piling up,
And to let the poor and hungry waste away in poverty
 While the rich sit back and sup

To commit genocide on the natives
 With a merciless, ruthless glee,
And to shun others for bowing down in front of a different steeple
 In this so-called "land of the free"

To deny people their basic rights because of the color of their skin
 For a hundred years after they have supposedly been freed,
And to have them chased and hunted down and killed in their own homes
 Because of some fool's greed

Now, some people say they have hated us forever,
 For the whole way back down that stars-and-stripes-laden road—
They hate our ways and our wars and our money,
 Our way of life, our slaves, and our gold

But me, I'm of a different key,

Yes, I sing a different song —
But I have to confess I don't want to get into the mess
Of "My country, right or wrong"

Dissent is at the very heart of what this country's about,
Yes, it has a tradition proud and long
So, let me say it out loud at the top of my voice,
And let us agree to agree that our country is right...unless it's wrong

2005

The Road to Glory

Suicidal teenager on the brink of destruction,
 What's he gonna do?
The Sergeant comes to town and lays his promises down,
 Says, "Son, the Army's the place for you"

So he packs his bags
 And leaves his house
He's got no social life,
 Got no spouse
He sees the Army as the only way out
 Of his unhappy life—
So cold and empty and devoid of fun,
 That he thinks it'd be quite a thrill to experience strife

So he goes down to the train station
 And waves his family goodbye
He believed in their stories of fame and fortune and glory,
 Patriotic to the utmost degree, ready to step into the line of fire
 In the blink of an eye

Hold on, hold on, soldier,
When you add it up—
 All the tears and fears
 And the wasted years—
You can say with utmost pride
That you're a soldier:
 "Hey, Dad, look at me—
 I lost an arm and leg in Sector Three"

Involuntary genocide—
We're sending our kids out to commit suicide
 Our kind Uncle Sam's riding the gravy train
 While our future's going down the drain

And the kid shows off his Christmas present—
A brand-new Thompson Sub-Machine Gun
 Hot off the press;

And, as he takes it off the rack,
There's a smile on his face so wide it's about to crack
"Be all you can be" — hell, we're the best

So he lays it on his shelf,
 Right next to his bulletproof vest
 And the failure notice for his Scholastic Aptitude Test
$20,000 just went down the drain,
 Not that he was gonna get it all anyway —
But hey, it's the campaign

Can't they see they're wasting their time?
 They've got millions of hungry college kids standing in line
Who'll take B.T., say "Check please!"
 And turn on a dime
We're preparing kids for war
 And sending 'em off to school
Kinda reminds me of the late Martyr Pacifist —
 He never amounted to much, the senile old fool

And back at home,
 Mommy and Daddy answer the knock at the door
The college prep classes are over,
 The president's declared war;
And the soldier's father
 Swore under his breath,
Slammed the door in the Major's face,
 And comforted his wife as he thought best

"You're a hero, son; we're proud of you,
I'll save you a spot at the graveyard;
And we'll take your dog tags
So our unborn grandchildren
 Will remember you"

He died for his country; the man was a saint
So he'll go on the fine print list at the back of the newspaper
 Like all the other would-be heroes;
And they'll send his medals back home to his parents
 With all the grace they could be expected to show

Under such tragic circumstances —
 Why, they'd lost another ten thousand kids,
They weren't taking any more chances

So at last they finally realized
What had been obvious to us all along,
Yes, they knew what they had to do —
They sent out draft letters to every senior citizen, veteran,
And housewife on this planet —
Beautiful plan — now they could finally rest
 Hell, they loved this plan so much they took a bet —
 "10 to 1, Colonel, that this is our best one yet"

2000 or 2001

Philosophical Pessimism:
Constructive Misanthropy Exercises
By Mark Wong

"The life of man, solitary, poor, nasty, brutish, and short."
–Thomas Hobbes (1588-1679), Leviathan

"It is hard for thee to kick against the pricks"
–Acts 9:5, 26:14

Mark is an eighty-year-old Chinese immigrant in San Francisco. He is bitter, misanthropic, pessimistic, world-weary, hopeless, and cynical and does not suffer fools gladly. Like most misanthropes and pessimists, he is a disappointed idealist — not least because his life has been an unbroken series of disappointments, failures, catastrophes, mistakes, and regrets. Many have come from his own numerous and varied faults, but many, perhaps even most, simply stem from the utter harshness of life and man's inhumanity to man — or so he thinks. He is wise, has lived long and learned much. Long retired, he has more than enough time to think and tends to use it as he believes best — by philosophizing, which usually takes a dark turn in his blackened mind. He takes himself seriously, of course, but, as some of the poems below show, is not above self-mockery. He has no friends; true, he had a few in youth, but they long ago drifted away, scared by what they saw as his callousness. He certainly has a tough outer shell but prefers to think he is just being honest and forthright, unlike nearly everyone else; needless to say, he sees the mass of man as compulsive bullshitters. He is generally inclined to forgive, as he half believes their vile, savage nature prevents them from rising above their worst impulses, but their constant cruelty, inhumanity, and simple stupidity destroy his charitable nature. He lives alone; his wife, who never truly returned his love in any case, died years ago, and no one else could possibly stand to live with him — not even a dog. He writes alone in his room, late at night, in dim light. He keeps his ever-trusty drugs and alcohol — now his only friends — always within reach; they whet his melancholy muse. He also keeps glass shards and a shotgun — which he bought decades ago in disgust but has never been able to actually use—on hand in case he ever decides to end his miserable life. He has considered it many times but is always unable to muster the will, even though no one would miss him, and the world would probably not even notice. He knows this, and it makes him feel even more bitter. He prominently put his favorite quote, plus his favorite from his least favorite book, as an epigraph to his volume, which is presented in full under the assumption that anything worth doing is worth overdoing.

Real World

Welcome to the Real World —
 Sorry to spoil your romantic disposition,
 But here you have to work for a position
There's a lot hidden and a lot missing,
It's not perfect, though you'll be wishing —
You can't make it through just by ass-kissing

It's not who you are,
 It's who you know —
 I'm sorry; that's just the way it goes,
This is the Real World
You get what you pay for,
 Nothing is truly free
 There ain't no such thing as a free lunch —
 Not for you, not for me
 I'm sorry; that's the truth, not a hunch,
This is the Real World

True love is out there,
 But it's hard to find
You can't just stumble into some bar,
 We all know love is blind
I'm sorry; this is the Real World

Hmmm… it seems you got cheated,
 Some asshole won instead
He got the prize
 And you were left for dead,
But he cheated, and you played fair —
Where's the justice there?
I don't know; maybe you'll find it…somewhere
I'm sorry; bad things happen to good people here,
 This is the Real World

All your life you've had your breakfast
 Served to you in bed on a silver platter —
And now your Mommy's let you off her tit

And you think reality doesn't matter
You expect things to stay the same—
Well, I'm sorry, but things change,
This is the Real World

Welcome, my son, you now have permission
 To awake from your dream
You're on your own now,
 And you've become a mere part of the machine
I won't be there to hold your dick
 When you take a piss anymore,
Somehow you'll just have to do it on your own—
 That is, if people can still do what they did before
Utopia is over now,
 I'm sorry, but reality is in store,
This is the Real World

You can't defy the Law of Gravity,
 And arrogance gets you nowhere
I'm telling you the truth, son,
 Don't look at me with that cold, hard stare
 Life is cold,
 It's not like that perfect world of old
You've always been baby to me, but now I finally realize
 There's some things you should've been told—
But I'm sorry; now it's too late,
You're in the Real World

You can't hide reality from kids forever,
 Sooner or later they're gonna have to face it
The world isn't sugarcoated—
 In fact, it's infested with shit
There's a lot of evil people out there,
 And they'll judge you, though they don't know you at all
Now that you've entered Life,
 A lot of pre-conceived ideals will fall
 I'm sorry, but our tall Utopian tales were indeed tall—
This is the Real World; welcome to the Real World

 Violence, sex, drugs, and lies—

These things exist, though we try to hide them
 And deny them with closed minds and eyes
The truth is indeed poorly lit,
 But you can see past its disguise
 If you drop your alibis
 And open up your eyes, open up your eyes
 I'm sorry about all the lies,
But maybe now you'll understand
The shit has hit the fan; the shit has hit the fan,
 This is the Real World

 I just saw your bubble burst —
Reality has emerged,
 And your dreams have dispersed
Life seems to have taken
 An unexpected turn for the worse —
But it's always been like this,
 Though you didn't know it
What a shock it must be to find out
 All that dogma was just a crock of shit
I'm sorry, the truth hurts,
But now you've realized it
Welcome to the Real World,
This is the Real World

It can be hard sometimes
When you find out the truth
 And tears begin to burst
It can be hard,
 But apathy is worse —
Like it or not, this is the way things are,
 Maybe we took those bedtime stories
Just a bit too far —
Yes, I'm sorry, but this is the way things are,
This is the Real World

 There's no instant winning —
I'm sorry; this is the Real World
 I know your head is spinning —
I'm sorry; this is the Real World

Nothing is free —
I'm sorry; this is the Real World
You must take care of you,
 And I must take care of me
I'm sorry; this is the Real World
This is the Real World,
This is the Real World
 I'm sorry; I'm sorry

2000 or 2001

One Day at a Time Part I

So, you ask yourself how you can make it through
 With all the shit goin' down —
Some crazy bastards flew a plane into a building,
 Some kid just got murdered in your own hometown
Your daughter was raped right there on the street,
 Left to die on the ground
The war, like hell, is still goin' swell,
 And the economy's back down
Don't know what you're gonna do,
 Don't know what kinda trouble's gonna come around
How can you make it through the shit
 And wind up doing fine?
 Buddy, I take it one day at a time

Your next-door neighbor just got busted for selling drugs,
 You caught your wife with another man
Your dainty old mother got killed by a bunch of thugs —
 You've seen the shit hit the fan
Don't know when gas prices'll go down,
 When the car'll be out of the shop
Don't know when you can trust your best friend again,
 When you can trust a cop
They just drafted your brother,
 Your father's cancer has spread
Don't know what you're livin' for,
 Might as well be dead
Is there any help around the corner? —
 God, someone show us a sign
 Buddy, I take it one day at a time

You can't find any answers at church,
 Your priest just fucked some poor little altar boy up the ass
Your dealer said you better pay up, motherfucker,
 And you better do it fast
 Don't know when you'll get your job back —
Seems every time you get a new one,
 You're just as quickly sacked

Your boy just dropped out of college,
Rover just got ran over
The factory's closing
 Just as all the bills are due
Nothing seems to be working —
 What the hell are you gonna do?
Is there any way to halt the madness,
 Make it stop on a dime?
 Buddy, I take it one day at a time

I wake up every morning,
 Roll right outta bed
Push aside all the nasty thoughts
 That are always crashin' about in my head
I can't read the paper,
 Can't put on the TV
I just go to work each day,
 Doin' what satisfies me
Don't ask me no questions,
 And I won't tell you no lies
I put my umbrella over my head
 To shield myself from the dark, foreboding skies...

You just found out your daughter's pregnant,
 And she's out every night actin' wild;
And now that goddamn bitch from downtown
 Is goin' around tellin' everyone you're the father of her child
Your wife's bitchin' at ya for something you can't quite see,
 Actin' like you committed a capital crime
The cops just busted in your door,
 Sayin' they got you this time
Don't know what to do anymore,
 Just don't know what to think
Your eyes are bloodshot, your palms are sweaty,
 Your mind's on the brink
Just don't know what's around the bend,
 And you're too damn afraid to take a peek
You're tired of all the shaky modern saviors
 Whose mighty ships have sprung a leak
They say someone got murdered on New Year's Eve —

Good God, they actually granted someone a reprieve
Oh, God in heaven, send us a sign,
Please drop us a line…
Buddy, I take it all one day at a time

2002 or 2003

Wounds of the City

I've seen good men come and go,
I've seen the High, the Middle, and the Low
I've seen them rise and fall,
I've heard their pleas for mercy and their call
I've heard every hard luck story
At least a thousand times or more
I've seen red carpets rolled out,
And I've seen the great slamming of the door
I've heard about the manic depressive, suicidal millionaires,
And the misbegotten, maltreated, misplaced whore—
And you can see the poetry written
On every subway wall and bathroom stall;
And it's true that I just don't know
What the hell to do with it all
So I emerge from the debris
With the wounds of the city

Yes, I've seen great men in my time,
Seen them reach right up to the sky—
And for the love of a lousy buck,
I've watched them die
I've seem 'em go from rags to riches,
Seen grown men break down and cry
You can drive yourself crazy tryin' to think of the reasons
That God lets these things fly
So, long ago, I stopped askin' why
Sometimes you begin to wonder
If it even does any good to try
The Wheel of Fortune can start spinning backwards
In the blink of an eye
But I emerged from the debris
Covered in the wounds of the city

Don't know why it keeps on rainin',
It just pours, and pours, and pours

Some days it's on me and mine,
 Brother, some days it's on you and yours
So you smoke yourself a little weed,
 Drink yourself a little Coors
Don't want no one to give me flowers,
 Don't want no flowers on my grave
You say you want to talk for hours—
 Well, buddy, you're brave
You can huddle there in your churches,
 I refuse to be saved
What's good for you is good for you,
 It can't hurt to feel better;
But I just don't know what I'm gonna do,
 I just can't forget her
If you make it to hell before me, my friend,
 Please send me a letter
And so I emerged from the debris
Scarred with the wounds of the city

I don't want your goddamn, good-for-nothin' self-help manuals,
 Don't want your fucking pity
You can take your rules and your regulations
 Back to the city
Come on, open up that window, man—
 It's much too hot in here
All this laughter is just makin' me sad,
 I can't see or think clear
Where's that woman by my side—
 Where's the only one who can hear?
Where will all my so-called friends be
 When the smoke clears?
 Oh, but never worry, never fear—
There'll always be some damn fool there
 Ready to make it absolutely clear
Willing and able to tell us
 Just what we're doing and why we're here;
And you try to hide beneath your mask of sarcasm,
 Protected by your all-knowing smile and your sneer
You tell us you can solve all our problems,

And we even believe you're sincere
Ah, just what we've always wanted —
The perpetual seer
And I emerge from the debris
Beaten down by the wounds of the city

2002 or 2003

Up to Me Part I

I was so astonished this morning,
 I swore I had something to give
Someone even told me
 I had a reason to live
I never found out what it was,
 But it was nice to think about anyway
You just can't believe
 Some of the things people say
The truth's just so hard to see,
 But someone had to listen to 'em —
Guess it was up to me

I listen to everyone,
 Do just what I'm told
Sell what's being bought,
 Buy what's being sold
Lies that life is black and white
 Will haunt me 'till I'm senile and old
They shove it down our throats,
 And reality begins to corrode
Thank God it's not that simple
 If you really take the time to look and see
Someone has to tell everyone —
 Guess it's up to me

Yes, I know about your escapism
 And all the places you like to hide —
But I, too, have those feelings
 I keep bottled up inside;
But you gotta let someone help you,
 Help you kill the pride
You can't run away from trouble,
 There ain't no place that far,
But there are better things to do
 Than sit there starin' at the stars
There's demons hiding in all of us,
 Scratchin' and clawin' to get free,
But someone had to let 'em out —
 Guess it was up to me

Sittin' at the bar
 Staring drunkenly at the wall,
Talkin' to all the barflies
 'Bout Man and God and Law
If someone thinks they've suffered most,
 You're there to answer the call —
But you're too scared to talk to me,
 You think I'd just make you blue
Hell, I'm not half as cold and mean as I look,
 My armor's easy to break through
Independence can be hard,
 But someone had to fight to be free —
 Guess it was up to me

2001

Sit Down (You're Rocking the Boat)

Well, I was a freelancing individualist
 With a few thoughts of my own,
And I was on a boat ride with the rest of the human race,
 Straight to the Promised Land from home

Well, the trip was okay at first,
But then some old lady lost her purse
 No one bothered to pick it up,
 They all acted like they didn't give a fuck
She would've gotten it herself,
 But she was too old and frail
 So I thought to myself, "What the hell?"
I got up to pick up the purse,
 And there was a smile on her face
So big it was about to burst—
But then some guy sitting next to her
Looked at me and started to boast
He said—

> "Sit down; you're rocking the boat
> Sit down; you're rocking the boat
> Sit down; you're rocking the boat
> Sit down; you're rocking the boat"

 Well, things were going just fine
And then, all of a sudden,
 Some teenagers brought out some wine
I said, "What the hell are you doing?
 You don't need that stuff"
And they said, "Dude, we're going to heaven,
 Prohibition's gonna be tough"
They wouldn't listen to reason, so I started to get up
 And put an end to drinking season—
 But their parents got up, and, in an act of treason,
They said—

> "Sit down; you're rocking the boat

Sit down; you're rocking the boat
Sit down; you're rocking the boat
Sit down; you're rocking the boat"

Well, the trip wasn't too bad
Until two feuding brothers made each other mad
 They were fighting and throwing things at each other —
 Family love, brother to brother
 I said, "Hey, kids, where's your mother?"
They said, "I don't know; fuck that stupid bitch!"
 And I said, "Hey! That's no way to talk about your mother!"
I started to get up and scratch their itch
 But, just as I was getting to my feet,
 Their mother stood up and took the heat
She said to them, "Go ahead, boys; it doesn't matter
What you do as long as we stay afloat"
And then she looked at me and said —

"Sit down; you're rocking the boat
Sit down; you're rocking the boat
Sit down; you're rocking the boat
Sit down; you're rocking the boat"

I stood up and said, "What the hell's wrong with you people?
 Can't you see this isn't swell?
We might be going to heaven
 But might as well be going to hell"
They thought about what I said for a moment,
But I was dismissed by unanimous vote
 They said, "You think too much, son,
 Sit down, and don't let your mouth run
We know what's right for us, and you don't"
 And then they said "Oh, and by the way…

Sit down; you're rocking the boat
Sit down; you're rocking the boat
Sit down; you're rocking the boat
Sit down, you're rocking the boat"

And then I realized they were right—

There's no reason to try and bring the best out in these people,
 It'd be a losing fight
They can make their own decisions all right—
 And besides, what can go wrong?
We're about to see the light

 And just then, a couple started having sex—
The trip still had over a year to go,
And the ship was already overcrowded
We didn't have room for a baby,
 And, besides, they didn't have any checks…
And then some thoughtless passenger
 Started to get up and tell them to quit,
But I screamed out to him at the top of my voice—
 What a dumb shit
He may want to, but he won't
I said—

> "Sit down; you're rocking the boat
> Sit down; you're rocking the boat
> Sit down; you're rocking the boat
> Sit down; you're rocking the boat"

2000 or 2001

Savior (M.I.A.)

Solitude runs deep,
Depression hits you steep
You've already seen the top,
And you're climbin' back down from the peak
I don't understand what happened to our love,
I don't know what a man's supposed to be made of
I'm just swirlin' in the depths of a drug-induced mist,
I get pissed, I slit my wrists, I refuse your kiss
Oh, what is it about satisfaction
That leaves you wanting more?
I've seen the darkness, I've seen the light —
I'd rather closer the door,
The latter's too bright

Yes, I smile when I'm angry,
That's what I do when I'm mad
All of this laughter
Is just makin' me sad
They say she's finally leavin' —
Well, I'm glad
How can you say we live in a holy land?
I just can't take any more of this abuse
Without someone holdin' my hand
Oh, where is the woman?
Where is the man?
Where are all the promises
We were promised back in our homeland?

Derision runs deep,
I've got promises to keep
The cops are beatin' down my door,
And I can't get any sleep
Tell me if something happens,
I never watch the news anymore
It's just too damn depressing,
You're the only cure
I used to think I regretted living,

But now I'm not so sure
There are, after all, some people you can call
  Who will let you insure

Well, I finally thought I'd found someone I could trust,
  But then you lied to me
I guess our hearts will forever remain apart,
  I'll never get to be finally free
My God, the things I've seen —
  I only wish you could see
It isn't true, it makes me blue,
  But I guess that's just the way it's supposed to be
I never understood repentance —
  Why try to correct your mistakes?
The only way to escape from this life sentence
  Is to take what you can take, take what you can take —
  And let your heart break

So, when they said, "Repent,"
I wondered what they meant
When they said, "Repent,"
I wondered what they meant
Now, you may say the message is heaven-sent,
  But you can return to sender for all I care —
Make it in c/o of "The Ripped-Off Human Race"
  Whatever happened to all the hope we shared?
Yes, whatever happened to the fruit
  We were supposed to bear?
I think we missed it by more
  Than just a breadth's hair
Where is our Savior?
  He's lurking in His lair
  Yes, He's lurking in His lair

Well, I can tell by looking at you
  That you feel just as bad as me —
But we hide the wounds anyway
  Since others refuse to see
  Yes, my friend, that's the reality
We're wearing black on the outside

Because black is how we feel on the inside;
And I know you need your rest now,
 Yes, I know your night's been hard,
But many men are falling now
 Where you promised to stand guard
Yes, many men are falling now,
 Where you promised to stand guard
We need you
We need you
We need you
We need you
We need you
Many men are falling…

2002

A Room of One's Own

Alone in this dark space
 Watching the feeble sunlight dance on the walls,
I can see the reflection of my face
 And hear solitude's silent voice as it calls

Flecks are in the air,
 Floating and dancing before a sun-drenched curtain
They're wrong to think I care
 Because even I don't know for certain

A movement across the floor —
 Some indistinct little shape scurrying about
Not all feel as I do; the merciful door
 Is there for others to go out

There's no food here —
 Not even a little water to pacify a drying throat
Some walk the world in pain and fear,
 Others are satisfied to just sit around and mope

There's no punishment
 Here, but there's nothing much to do
There's no entertainment,
 Nothing old yet nothing new

It's all such a mess —
 Everyone just sits around and gets older,
Dying is just part of the process;
 Some strive for heat, but I just get colder

Some say life is tough,
 But I'm doing well here all alone in my tomb
I've been in this corner long enough
 To know you get used to an empty room

2005

Anesthesia Part II

It can be a sad, sad place, this world of ours,
 If you know where to look
 Everyone's a crook,
And the real sellers have no buyers

 Money's tight—
 You know, the Justice System just ain't right
 We're scared to let our kids out at night,
And yet our kids are the criminals—
 Not in the future, but now
How did this happen?
 I don't know, but it has somehow

Your daughter's pregnant,
 And your son just killed a man
You're caught in the middle,
 Where do you stand?
The law or family values—which makes you tick?
Take your pick

I've been trying to tell you this for a long time
But can't do it anymore—
It doesn't matter now anyway
Look out your window, and what do you know?
 You've found the proof and can't ignore it anymore—
 Yes, you've found the proof, and it's right outside your door

And you need some anesthesia to kill the pain,
To get you back on your feet again
 Nothing's right, and everything's wrong,
 Sadness is your only song
Your family's gone to hell, nothing's swell—
 Life's just a big bloodstain,
 And you need some anesthesia to kill the pain

You've got a bum living in your basement
 And a bimbo coming in and out of your backdoor

You haven't yet come out of the closet,
 But your girlfriend just evened the score,
 And your husband just walked out the door

 It's time once again to pay the rent,
 But you don't have a cent
You would embezzle some money,
 But your job came and went
Even more games to fuck with your head —
 Bobby's not coming home from the war,
He's dead

Your life's in shambles,
And we'll never fulfill the Preamble
The whole world's gone to hell,
 And there's a wise man in front of you
Trying to halt your ascension,
But you're so broke you can't even afford to pay attention

I've been trying to tell you this for a long time
But can't do it anymore —
It doesn't matter now anyway
Look out your window, and what do you know?
 You've found the proof and you can't ignore it anymore —
 Yes, you've found the proof, and it's right outside your door

And you need some anesthesia to kill the pain,
To get you back on your feet again
 Nothing's right, and everything's wrong,
 Sadness is your only song
Your family's gone to hell, nothing's swell —
 Life's just a big bloodstain,
 And you need some anesthesia to kill the pain

It's right outside your front door

2000 or 2001

C'est la vie (The Ins and Outs of Clichés)

"When it rains, it pours" —
It's too obvious to ignore
When you've settled the score
With all you shrugged off before;
When evil's at your door,
You think you're its fore,
But you're just one more,
       Not even near the top

"Life's a bitch, and then you die" —
Don't even stop to wonder why
Heaven turns to hell in the blink of an eye
And all you hold sacred is a lie
There's no reason to even try,
You're just an ordinary guy
Far before you the shit started to fly
       And is not about to stop

"A needle in a haystack" —
You're no leader of the pack,
No white in a sea of black
Others will stab you in the back,
Better be ready for the attack
They won't cut you any slack
Sometimes self-respect only comes if you take a crack
       At a cop

"You're just a number, not a name" —
No winners in this game,
No claim to fame
You lost as soon as you came
Into this world of loss and gain
You're far from first to claim
The whole damn thing's insane,
       That creation's a flop

"Nobody loves you when you're down and out" —

There's no need to shout,
We all know what the game's about
It's rigged and a rout,
Hard work and merit won't get any clout
It's all about whom you know, let there be no doubt
It's no fair, but this is no time to pout,
      It won't make things any easier for you or me

"It's not who you are; it's who you know" —
I know it's a brutal blow,
But it goes with the flow
Of all living below
The land where riches grow
No matter how much you're able to stow,
It'll be melted like snow
      By the powers that be

"If it wasn't for bad luck, I wouldn't have no luck at all" —
You're far too small
For anyone to hear your call
The hammer starts to fall
As soon as we crawl
From behind the wall
That puts a temporary stall
      On our inevitable mediocrity

"Whatever will be will be" —
It won't set you free,
But you can submit more easily
In any degree
Than to most of the spree
They feed to you and me
About hope and security
      C'est la vie…

2009

The Dark Side of Life Part I

The time is ripe for change,
The time is right to rearrange
 Stagnant saturation is the order of the day
But surely somewhere, in the shell-shattered remnants
 Of this land of the free,
 There's some other way —
 Fanfare for the common man or justice for people like you and me

And, if justice isn't the word,
 Then what is?
Some cynics may say
 This is a lie-driven biz —
But surely there must be a loophole
 Somewhere in Murphy's Law
Somewhere there's liberty
 And justice for all

We talk big —
 We got solutions,
 We got resolutions —
Yet teenage lovers
 Get their thrills,
The President's beans
 Refuse to spill,
The local militia
 Says, "Shoot to kill!"
And doctors and nurses
 Go in the closet and pop their pills —
Seems our plan's been botched;
 And we just stand there and look pretty for the cameras
And watch

The teenage academician
 Is feeling nihilistic,
And his school counselor
 Forgives him for being too realistic
I saw the news today — oh, boy,

Another murder in the papers today — oh joy —
Seems kids are buying guns instead of toys

And all around the world,
The good boys and girls are hoping in vain
For the gifts that will never come —
Yet another blue Christmas
I guess the white ones
Don't come 'round no more
Seems life's no fun
Anymore

And yet surely there must be an escape route
 Somewhere in this big, blue abyss
Life's too open to chance,
 It's kind of hard to believe it's all hit or miss

Portrait of an American family —
 Boy comes home from work,
Got no girlfriend anymore,
 She says he's a jerk
His sister's on the phone
Talking about minutiae —
"I'm doing great, yeah; how about you?"
Mom's full of work up to her eyes,
 Hell, she can't even see
The boy walks through the living room
 Fully devoid of glee
And his father says, "Get the hell
 Out of the way, son; I can't see the TV"

 The man in the bar
Just lost the radio in his car
And doesn't know it yet,
 But the waitress is bending his ear —
She's waxing political
 And serving him beer
'Round where the businessmen sit
 Nuggets of trivia, she manages to send —
"That damn election," she says,

LIFE'S TRIUMPH by Bill R. Moore

"It's never gonna end"

And, as the dishes pile up, and the clothes don't get washed,
 And you put off that trip to your parents' once again —
The situation's a draw
 Or, more accurately, a no-win,
Since I got my eye on the worldview —
 Because another Palestinian dies,
 And another pregnant mother sighs,
 And another network anchorperson lies,
 And another poor bastard in Iraq gets blown sky-high —
How nice, this equilibrium,
Two plus two is a negative sum

The pilot activates his landing gear
And sets aside his fears
 As he prepares to touch down
 On enemy ground;
But the radar mask,
 Like the pipe dream, is fucked;
And down from the sky
 His plane is plucked
Hey, kid, you're a hero —
We'll send a medal to your mother back home
When we break the news to her poor soul

Some lie for money,
 Some lie out of spite
Some lie for their honey,
 And some lie because they think they're in the right
Yeah, there may not be much truth out there, but one thing's for sure —
 We're all fighting the same fight

But there is no retribution here,
 No punishment or rewards —
Just cordite and formaldehyde
 And broken hearts and bloody swords
You tell me to go to hell —
 Well, that's okay, sire,
 I'll save you a seat by the fire

And yet, surely there must be an end to the fighting
 Somewhere here in the place of democracy's birth—
A sanctuary for the able minded,
 A breeding ground for peace on earth
We'll find it—somehow, somewhere, someway,
 Sure as birds can fly
Well, come over here and relieve me, sonny,
 I'm beginning to strain my eyes

Yes, surely there must be
 Some way out of this prison cell—
A trap door in the wall or a place where the bars will bend free,
 Surely it's not just an eternity in hell
Or four walls in a padded room in a sanitarium
With no justice, no peace of mind, and no freedom at all...

2000 or 2001

Pathos, Inc.

I don't understand it,
 This world we live in
Why, it seems even the best man
 Can be reduced to sin;
And, as I walk down the streets to my home
And see yet another homeless man barely gettin' by
Yet doing all he can, it makes me wonder —
 Why do so many lose and so few win?

Vietnam vet, isolation twenty years,
His biography just a long line of wasted tears
 He's seen too many good men die
 And too few elected officials try —
And so who can really blame him
 When he puts the gun to his head
 And puts an end to a life that has long since been dead

The eighteen-year-old girl
 Has three kids, lives in a slum —
 No husband, just an unfortunate slip of cum
There's too many like her,
 She's not an isolated case —
Yet the rare find of her kind
 Hits society like a slap in the face

Young boy in the city —
 His brain already fried by too much schoolboy scorn,
 Has his future ripped and torn;
And, when he puts the needle to his vein
 And the beer to his lips,
 He breathes a great sight of relief as he slowly sips

Fourteen-year-old hookers
 On the street tonight, what a scene —
 Ready and willing to wet the dream
 Of some equally young kid hooked on Vaseline;
And the scene could quickly be gone,

But the cop, enjoying one of his own, looks on

And I can't turn my eyes away
 From these horrifying scenes —
 What does it mean — what does it mean?
 Why does it move me so, this tear-jerking scene?
 It's only two humans being; it's only two humans being

God, I feel as if I'm at a concentration camp,
There's so much suffering
Every day, it seems we're wasting away
 And falling apart at the seams —
 And why does it move me so, this tear-jerking scene?
 It's only two humans being; it's only two humans being

And I ask myself, as I finally look away,
For the second time today,
 Why do so many lose and so few win?

2000 or 2001

Ain't That a Bitch?

Oh, how I miss my baby,
 I need her to wash my back
Well, I'm looking at the masterpiece, yeah,
 But all I can see are the cracks
Well, I have that feelin' you get
 When you have that certain bad kinda pain —
Like when you just want to leave the house without packing your bags
 And ride on that lonesome train;
And when the scars of sorrow are bulging blue
 Between the needle and your open vein,
Oh, you think about her more,
 And you just keep getting pissed, and pissed, and pissed;
And the veins stand out like highways
 All along your wrist
Oh, why don't you just run off to the Devil and snitch?
Ain't that a bitch?

She asks me if I'm gonna be faithful —
 How the hell am I supposed to know?
Why, hell, it's not even to the part yet
 Where I get to decide what I'm gonna do when you go
She tells me she won't come back no more,
 As if I didn't know that
As if I hadn't noticed how she blows me off
 When she tips her hat
Oh, look at me now,
 You loose-limbed, little whore
Look at the man
 Whom you feel so very sorry for
What is wrong with him, what is wrong with him —
 Is it something to do with you?
If you know, please tell me,
 I only wish I knew
Don't blink or flinch
Ain't that a bitch?

 Oh, yes, I read the letter you wrote —

I don't even understand how
 A man can be murdered by a note
Oh, how do you act so malicious
 And stay afloat?
 How did the razor find my throat?
Well, I know who my true love is,
 I just wish I could see her
She deserves so much better than what she has, yes —
 I swear to God, some day I'll free her
Girl asks me if I'm feelin' all right —
 Well, yeah, ya know, in that somber tonight all right kinda way
She just shakes her head at me and says,
 "It's just another day, it's just another day"
No way
 It's regulation by rote, it's a cinch
 Ain't that a bitch?

Oh, why can't I have you?
 I'd love you forever
Oh, I wouldn't care if this heart you wanted to slew,
 I'd suffer any pain or pleasure
Oh, you are so beautiful, my love,
 You are a treasure beyond measure
Let us work it out in peace,
 It's now or never
One more kiss before I slip into the abyss
 And drown in the ether
Oh, I won't forget you, babe,
 For it's my life you've saved
My love is eternal
 From the cradle to the grave
So why can't I see you, why can't I free you,
 Why must we love in vain?
 Oh, I feel like I'm in heaven, but I'm in pain
Stranded in the ditch
Ain't that a bitch?

Well, I locked your lover in our room,
 I hope the son of a bitch is dead
I caught you coming to bring

My prisoner wine and bread
This love now is broken, dear,
You can't sew it up with a thread
All throughout history,
From the Garden of Eden to the bloody hill at Calvary,
Men have been hit with a fist on a cool night of bliss
Yes, and even Jesus was betrayed by a kiss
You say it's broken, but you've come to hear spoken
The promise of a reconciliatory night in bed
Oh, it's a sin — yes, it's a sin — but I'll say it again:
The love is dead
Oh, you know the love is dead
It's ceased to even twitch
Ain't that a bitch?

Now, Cain slew Abel,
Killed him with a stone —
And the funeral pyre we've set on fire,
It, too, now feels so alone
No man is your property — can't you see?
I've got one hand on my suicide
And one hand on your knee
Never get a woman to do a man's work,
Don't even try it, darlin'
We're much better at bein' a jerk
You still have that innocent smile
To go with your nervous tic,
But practice makes perfect —
Pretty soon you'll be scratchin' that itch
Ain't that a bitch?

Well, I know you left,
Yes, I heard you left home
I've been livin' on rice and ditchwater
Ever since you've been gone
I ain't gonna write you up, babe,
Not gonna call you on the phone
I'm just gonna sit here and count my lucky stars —
After all, I still have my pen and my guitar
I'm readin' out this gay greeting card,

Smokin' up a cheap cigar
Well, I don't understand why you let go of my hand,
But it don't matter now that it's gone this far
I just sent you a blue valentine, babe—
Have a cigar
Count your lucky fuckin' stars
I always told myself I should never get hitched
Ain't that a bitch?

Yes, I remember the words you used to say,
All the silly games we used to play—
How I always said I'd love you so
Yeah, I know they don't mean anything no mo',
I should just let 'em go, but—
We were so young then, so unsure,
And we're so much older now, we're mature;
And a hell of a lot of difference it makes
When your soul still aches and your heart still breaks
Oh, babe, what I wouldn't forsake
To suffer the pains I used to suffer
Before you took your take
Face of an angel with the love of a witch
Ain't that a bitch?

2002

Everybody Knows

(Based on Leonard Cohen's "Everybody Knows.")

Everybody knows crack can kill you,
 Everybody knows sex is just for fun
Everybody knows the children are innocent,
 They're on the playground with loaded guns

Everybody knows Jesus Christ is our savior,
 Everybody knows he did everything right
Everybody knows the difference between good and evil
 And right and wrong is ever so slight

Everybody knows the President's sober,
 Everybody knows the Earth is flat
Everybody knows there ain't no four-leaf clovers,
 At least not where we live at

Everybody knows this ain't no democracy,
 Everybody knows the system's fucked
Everybody knows the exports are dwindling,
 And everybody knows the imports are trucked

Everybody knows the outcome is canned,
Everybody knows the election is planned
 Everybody knows something ain't right,
 Everybody knows, but no one's putting up a fight

Everybody knows their son is lonely,
 Everybody knows the TV's on all the time
Everybody knows their mother's overworked,
 Everybody knows their daughter was supposed to be home by nine—
 And everybody knows family life is fine, just fine

Everybody knows you get what you pay for,
 Everybody knows talk is cheap
Everybody knows we have freedom of speech,
 Everybody knows, but everybody's discreet
Everybody's mouth is sucking on their feet

'Cause everybody knows you're
Supposed to keep your feelings off the street
Everybody knows perversity is concrete,
Everybody knows, but no one can take the heat

Everybody knows she's a virgin,
 Everybody knows money's tight
 Everybody's in, and nobody else is right
Everybody knows you're supposed to
 Judge people by their exterior,
 Everybody knows they're superior,
 And everyone knows everyone else is inferior

Everybody knows the jig is up,
Everybody knows the system is corrupt—
Everybody knows, but no one gives a fuck
 Everybody knows their own two cents,
 Everybody knows nothing else makes any sense
 So, once and for all, let's end the suspense,
Since everybody knows

 Everybody knows AIDS is a joke,
 Everybody knows we've got a lot more rope
Everybody knows the journey is uphill,
 But everybody knows we can cope
Everybody knows the danger,
 Everybody ignores the warning signs
Everybody knows how to see,
 Yet everybody's blind

Everybody knows TV is fake,
Everybody knows the car's got no brakes
 Everybody knows all actions have a consequence,
 Everybody knows life makes no sense

Everybody knows life's a bitch,
Everybody knows Uncle Sam is rich
 Everybody tells their secrets,
And everybody knows no one will snitch

Everybody knows people are honest,
 Everybody knows people are good
Everybody knows sex makes babies,
 Everybody knows their kids are in the hood

Everybody knows there's drugs on the street,
Everybody knows the law's got cold feet
 Everybody knows love is eternal,
 Everybody knows divorce is infernal
Everybody knows the stock market crashed today,
Everybody knows, but everybody looks the other way
 Everybody knows something needs to be said,
But nobody knows what to say

Everybody knows his bed is empty,
Everybody knows he's doing it all for free
 Everybody knows their kid is fertile,
Everybody's known since they were three

Everybody knows the newcomer's licked,
Everybody knows you can't teach an old dog new tricks
 Everybody knows gravity bends,
 Everybody knows our lives will never end

Everybody knows this won't get you pregnant,
Everybody knows what our founding fathers meant
 Everybody knows God created the Devil in fictional style,
 And everybody has Him on speed dial

Everybody knows sex is overrated,
 Everybody knows their kids have never masturbated
 Everybody knows death is fake,
 Everybody knows we'll bend but never brake

 Everybody knows there's no such thing as luck,
 Everybody knows they're not out for a fuck
 Everybody knows the light is dim,
 Everybody knows the prospects are grim
Everybody knows its dog eat dog,
 Everybody knows it's sink or swim —

So, once and for all, let's end the suspense,
There's no reason to be so tense
 It just goes to show
 That everybody knows

2001

I Must Not Be Drinking Enough
(A Vicious Cycle of Hell on Earth)

I used to be able to handle things,
 At least most of the time
I could seek out the wisdom life brings
 And walk straight down that line —
Ah, but now all the people I used to call friends
 Are no longer even around to call my bluff —
And closing my eyes don't make it go away,
 I must not be drinking enough

I could always keep things steady,
 Always juggle responsibilities pretty well
Whatever the challenge, I was ready —
 But now life just seems a living hell
I just feel lost somehow,
 Never knew things could be quite so tough —
But I guess that's just the way life ends,
 I must not be drinking enough

I could always keep my head on straight,
 Was ready to take on most anything
I never suffered from the delusion that life is great
 But could always find a song to sing —
Ah, but now I'm past my prime
 And things are starting to look rough
I've smoked enough weed and snorted enough lines,
 But I must not be drinking enough

I could always find somewhere to go,
 Was never at a loss
It's not that things were perfect — oh, no —,
 But I could enjoy life at no great cost
Where before I could always find a way,
 Now I just curse and huff
It looks like I'm long past my glory days,
 I must not be drinking enough

I always preferred to be around people
 But never had a problem with solitude
I could congregate in the steeple
 Long as they didn't cop no attitude
Yeah, I used to believe in miracles, the mercy of God,
 And all that other crazy stuff—
But now I just can't seem to ever beat the odds,
 I must not be drinking enough

I was always a hopeful man—
 Loving, kind, and optimistic—
But now I just can't find it in me to lend a hand,
 I just feel so goddamn nihilistic
People once loved to be around me,
 But now they just find me a little too gruff
Happiness no longer surrounds me,
 I must not be drinking enough

I always believed things would turn out right in the end,
 Believed in God's infinite mercy
With you time just seemed to suspend,
 But now I've been abandoned by both you and He
I just can't believe anymore,
 And no one can pierce my hard outer shell, so buff
Faith, hope, and charity have been shown the door,
 I must not be drinking enough

I used to smoke three packs of cigarettes
 A day, but now I'm up to five
Yeah, they help me when I nervously fret,
 I do what I can to stay alive
I used to have the luxury of relying on you
 But now must trust the cigarette I puff
Hell, I just don't know what to do,
 I must not be drinking enough

I'm just barely hanging on now,
 Grasping at straws and such slender threads
I keep telling myself I'll make it through somehow,
 But sometimes I just wish I was dead

I can feel the end approaching,
 I walk upside down inside handcuffs
I can see darkness encroaching,
 I must not be drinking enough

Well, I used to believe what I was told,
 Used to swallow the lies
When I was stranded out in the cold,
 Someone always heard my cries
I had good reason to believe in divine providence
 And all that other imaginary fluff—
But now it all just seems like coincidence,
 I must not be drinking enough

Well, now I can feel the walls closing in,
 I can see the pale horse
As I look back on all my wins and sins,
 It all begins to make sense now—of course!
In this life you take what you can get,
 For all of us, surely, that is enough—
I wish I could say my time was well spent,
 But now I'm too sober to bluff

2007

Peace on Earth
(Still the Undisputed King of Jokes)

I still recall the time my uncle told me
 About the short-lived peace on earth —
He said there was absolute Bliss and harmony
 On the place of our birth
He said all was well, there was no hell
 No one was taking, everyone was willing to give —
It was the perfect time to live

Of course it's all gone now,
 But it was there for a while —
 Or so he says, but I think he's senile
It was peace on earth —
No war, no fighting,
No bitching, no side switching,
Utopia fulfilled, all war nightmares killed —
 The single greatest achievement
 In the history of our species on this planet
We invented, and then got addicted to, war,
 And then we quit —
Just shook it off like it was never there
Yeah, we took all our planes down from the air,
 Burned all our guns and ammo at the stake —
 All old habits, yeah, we decided to break

We destroyed all tanks
 And most other weapons of war,
 There was nothing but peace in store
The only thing we kept around was the nuke —
 It was to be destroyed last,
 But even it would soon be gassed

And then the ghost of Adolf Hitler was resurrected
And he rode the world's last remaining nuclear missile into the Promised
 Land
Like Peter Sellers in *Dr. Strangelove*;
And the whole world united as one
And basked in brotherly love

Yeah, that's the story he tells me—
Such sweet, sugarcoated, bubble-gum pop,
The stuff of dreams—
 It's their original mold;
He calls it peace on earth, yeah,
 But I call it the funniest joke ever told

Circa 2000

Rapture (Comeuppance and Repentance)

Somewhere along the line,
 You'll get tired of the human race—
Get tired of them backing down,
 Tired of them being in your face;
And, when that happens, babe,
 I'll be standing there with you
Because everything matters,
 Yes, every little thing you do
For, when life has got you down
 And negativity won't pull you through,
 You'll find you need me to,
 You'll need me to
You'll see

Someday, I swear to you,
 The world's gonna be turned upside down—
The dead won't get cheap plastic roses,
 And I won't be livin' in a one-horse town
 Well, the undertaker will forget to toll his bell,
 The Devil himself will be booted right out of hell,
And not a single one of these stories
 To your grandchildren will you be able to tell
Because it'll be the end
 Time will suspend, your wounds will cease to mend,
 And it won't happen again
 There'll be no roses to send
Man, what the hell is wrong with you—
 Can't you see you need me?
 I'm telling you—you're gonna spill your whiskey glass,
Bad luck's gonna come up like a bat outta hell
 And bite you on the ass,
 A nark's gonna find your stash,
 And you'll have to pay in cash
 Because your decisions will have been far too brash
It'll be all fire and ash;
And the only thing I ask
Is that you take off your mask
 Before it's too late
 You can't leave it all up to fate

Death is something to which we can all relate —
Do you think you're the only piece of meat on the plate?
Sooner or later you'll see reality

As years and tears go by,
They add to our fears,
They make us cry
Leaving you no place to go
Add another couple of feet
To your mountain of woe
There's no light at the end of the tunnel,
There's no hope around the bend
We lived through a lot, girl,
But now I'm afraid this really is the end
It's been nice knowin' ya, my friend
I enjoyed it immensely

Without love in my life,
I'd slowly wilt and die
Without you as my wife,
I'd just break down and cry;
And, as the windshield melts
And the sun goes down for the very last time,
Mighty empires fall apart at the seams,
And ten million love affairs stop on a dime,
I won't be able to rhyme,
I just saw the Seventh Sign
All the mountains will crumble to the sea,
And there will just be you and me
Just you and me…

2001

Once Bitten, Twice Shy

If the doors of perception were cleansed,
 We would see things as they are—distorted
Just when you think you're gettin' somethin' extra,
 You realize you were shorted
It's true that what seems like hell
 Can be a blessing in disguise,
But let me tell you the reverse is also true
 If you open up your eyes;
And let it be said you can wind up dead
 Trying to give word to the wise
  Fall apart, fall apart, fall apart at the seams—
My life is so tangled up now
 That I'm being strangled in my own dreams
And even my own reflection's givin' me the evil eye
I'm once bitten, twice shy

I always saw things in black and white,
 But I could tell the difference between wrong and right;
But something happened—
 Something new came along this way,
And now I'm so tangled up in blue
 That I can't even see the gray
It seems that, behind every great work of art,
There was some kind of painful start
 Is there really anything to gain?
It seems that, behind every beautiful thing,
 There lies some kind of pain;
And, when you think you've lost everything,
 You find out you can always lose a little more before you die
I'm once bitten, twice shy

Wars have been waged over lesser things than Man—
 Oh, God, I think it's starting to happen again
 Some naïve young upstart thinks he's going to win
 Because he's not going to make the same mistakes as his friend
It'd be funny, if it weren't so sad,
 That despite the very lifeblood on which they depend,

They turn out the same as everyone else in the end
So many are killed as they walk the line,
They always end up leaving something behind;
 And, just as soon as there's something to steal,
 Some damn fool goes and invents the wheel
Why the hell do we even try?
I'm once bitten, twice shy

Money may be the root of all evil,
 But it can't buy happiness
Every dime you spend
 Is another dream that's been repossessed
Why don't you try earning something for once
 Instead of gaining it through inheritance or a lie?
Then you won't get no bellyache
 From eatin' humble pie
Everyone thinks it can solve all their problems,
 But how wrong they are you haven't even guessed
A man in a mansion can be broken
 While a man on the street can be blessed
Don't ask questions like "how?" or "why?" —
 There are a lot of good things in this world
You'll never be able to buy
You'll find out when you're once bitten, twice shy

There are so many miracle cures,
How many work for sure?
 Young men, upstarts, open up your eyes —
Listen to those who have failed
 'Cause experience makes you wise
After all the trials and tribulations,
 After good and bad and everything,
 Here is the only wisdom anyone can bring —
Love is the only thing
 It doesn't matter what you think about it,
 You just won't be able to live without it —
Take it from one who was foolish enough to try
Girl, I'm once bitten, twice shy

2001

Pain of Salvation

You believed all those things
 They put in your head —
How people really loved you
 And how you'd always be provided for and fed —
But in the real world you discovered
 There's only two types of lives to be led —
 The quick and the dead

Your mind has been worn down by them,
 It's gone a bit off track —
 It's full of lies, rumors, and distorted facts
They've got you so damn apathetic
 That you just don't know how to react
They'll keep you in line,
 Make sure you're just the person they want you to be,
And they keep you doped up
 With sex, and religion, and TV
The voice of reason
 You have not yet heard
As you stand there and listen to
 Every mind-polluting word

They said they'd always be there for you,
 Make sure you were never alone —
But, when it comes down to it, my friend,
 You'll have to figure out most things on your own
Some people are liable to always be there for you —
 Yeah, but there ain't no guarantees
So don't be surprised, when the going gets rough,
 If everyone starts to flee

Most people prefer fair weather,
 They're not much for rough terrain
It's only the truly dedicated ones
 Who will stay with you through the hunger and the pain
Now, I'm not trying to break your heart, my friend,
 What I'm offering is the truth —

But I don't expect you to believe me,
 It's not like you're used to proof

Happiness and satisfaction —
 Ah, that's just some people talking
You don't stop on this long and winding road,
 You just keep on walking
Just try to forget about the pain
 Because there's no stopping, no blessings
The most you can hope for is a little love along the way,
 Everything else is just window-dressing

 Don't stop, don't stop — ain't no entertainment here
The rewards are few and far between,
 And the punishment's always severe
Sometimes I don't know how I stand it,
 Other times I don't see why I fear —
But it's a confusing mess all around,
 My advice to you is to steer clear

The ghost of our love
 Haunts me wherever I go,
I don't just know what it is
 That keeps me loving you so
I guess I'll just keep on loving in vain
 Until you let me know

Honesty is at a standstill,
 Pain and evil flies
All the truth in the world
 Adds up to one big lie
It was here I was born,
 It's here I will die —
 Against my will and pathetically
We've only got two choices in life —
 Freedom and democracy,
And neither of them are
 What they're cracked up to be

2001

Invitation to the Blues

Tiny Toledo, he couldn't get his car fixed—
Had to sell everything he owned
 Just to get his kicks;
But the street-walkin' blues hit hard on the side,
 Where the hot dog stands are all broken down
And you can't even get a ride
 The motorcade and the carpool, they went stark raving mad,
Your girlfriend just kicked you out,
 And you swear to God you're glad—
But the only door that's open to you now
 Faces the alley, and you ain't go no shoes
 All you got is an invitation to the blues

 Your parents left their welfare check back on the streets,
You just got fired from cleanin' toilets,
 And you can't take the heat
Where the hell is that old girl of yours—the one with the broken-tooth grin?
 She always dug you out of the dumpster
And poured you scotch and gin
 Somethin' about this place late at night just scares you half to death—
The neon signs blind your sight,
 And the car exhaust saps your breath;
And the only thing that keeps you glued to the street life
 Is that you ain't got no more to lose
 All you got is an invitation to the blues

Sherlock Holmes and Leonard Cohen are hiding behind a lamppost,
The pigs are cleanin' out the gutter,
And your Mother's arguin' with a fencepost
 That old girl of yours, she'll never call—
Last I heard, she was hiked up with the gigolos
 Down on Fourth Street behind the mall
You can't get in your door for all the hookers by the store,
 You tossed your old lady out for spillin' the booze,
But she just comes back for more
I saw the ghost of your old life down by the waterfront docks,
 He was lookin' for clues

Left you with just an invitation to the blues

I heard your ex is a waitress now, and your Mother's on the make—
 You know, I always feel sorry for old friends
When I see their hearts break;
 But, yeah, I remember the old days; you were really quite a pair
You had those old, ratty trousers,
 And she had confetti in her hair
You know, I miss that old crowd sometimes — whatever happened to 'em all?
 Last I heard, Gus was drivin' a bus,
And the bar went back to Paul
It's funny how all the things we used to fight over
 We can't even remember how to choose
 The only thing left is an invitation to the blues

The ghost of James Dean is smilin' down from hell —
 He got us all to commit suicide
And swears it's just as well
My grandfather finally died last week, the ghetto's tollin' his bell —
 That's one less beer on the house,
And, man, the boys'll sure miss the stories he could tell
 I forgot what I'm supposed ta be doin' here, I'll just stand around and talk,
Pretty soon the room'll start clearin' out,
 And I'll hafta go outside an' walk…
But, until then, I'll just take the drunken barmaid's advice —
 What the hell have I got to lose?
 I'll accept your invitation to the blues

2001

Not Dark Yet

Some people just speak better when they breathe vacuum —
 How're you doing up there?
I gave a damn at one point,
 But now I'm too tired to care
The dust has begun to settle now,
 I'm breathin' thin air
I understand things are going well for you —
 Have you heard I'm an heir?
Yeah, I can hardly believe it myself,
 I always thought life was unfair
So let's trade places,
 I want to sleep in the dragon's lair
Yes, you can gawk all you want,
 But please don't stare
It's not dark yet, but it's gettin' there

My batteries are out of charge,
 Now I belong to you
I can't get away, no matter how hard I try,
 There's nothing I can do
I once heard a semblance of unity,
 A murmur of a prayer —
But somehow they get lost — and, oh, God, the cost
 Is more than I can bear
Why don't you testify to save face?
At least it might guarantee you a sacrificial place
You hold the joker, but I hold the ace —
 Which is better, who's to say?
 It don't matter anyway
Right now I'm a-roamin',
 And you got your games to play —
So get out of my hair
It's not dark yet, but it's gettin' there

With your eyes like oceans
 And your voice like chimes,
With your words like potions

And your prayers like rhymes —   .
 You've succeeded in making me cease to care
Now, I don't pretend to understand
 The troubles you've had,
But I've been in your place before,
 And, darlin', it's not so bad
  You just have to be aware
People who should know better
 Are ignoring you like good advice;
And you'll have to forgive me if I can't stop laughing
 When they start throwing rice
It's just such a pointless affair
It's not dark yet, but it's gettin' there

What's this about getting pissed?
 I heard it's happening again
Some guy put out your eye —
 You know, you just can't win;
 And where was I when you needed a friend?
 I was falling down the hellhole you put me in
You say you want a friend, and you want a lover —
 Well, you can't have both,
You have to choose one or the other
 They can both help you in this hopeless game,
 But neither is what it claims
It looks like tryin' to choose which one I am, girl,
 Is drivin' you insane
 "Satisfaction" — it's such a weighty name
 Here's my sympathy for your pain,
Let me make it very clear
It's not dark yet, but it's gettin' there

 You drove a javelin through my heart —
 It pierced me, gave me a start
Nothin' can help you
 When you've reached this point
You just have to keep on headin' down the road
 Lookin' for another joint
I ignored you for a long time,
 Maybe you'll finally anoint

It don't matter now
 Whether you leave or whether you stay
I finally made up my mind
 That that was yesterday
  I told myself I'd try to care—but I won't
  Because last night I knew ya; tonight I don't
Why couldn't we ever share?
It's not dark yet, but it's gettin' there

And, if we happen to meet again,
 Somewhere down the line—
There's no reason to tell anyone
 I was yours and you were mine
I searched long and hard for answers,
 But they're impossible to find
Words like "love" and "hate,"
 They're so hard to define
It don't matter how hard you try,
 You can't turn lead into gold or find diamonds in the mine
 I think I've come to the end of the line,
 I feel like I'm in touch with something divine
 I'm soaking up knowledge while you pine—
Ain't that clear?
 There's nothing left to say or do
And nothing left to fear
  So listen to me; I'm not gonna tell ya twice
  No, I ain't bein' very nice,
But no one said life was fair
It's not dark yet, but it's gettin' there

2001

Midnight Vigil

I sit here confused and calibrated,
 All my beliefs are shot
I should be in bed by now,
 But I'm not
Bedraggled and beat,
I've been disowned and cheated
 Just when I think I've got everything figured out,
All my preconceptions start to fall—
What is the meaning of it all?

 Well, you know I'm lonely,
I'm sleeping alone tonight
Just like I did last night
And the night before that—
 And I sit here at this old piano
 Lonelier than a widow
 I tell myself I'm not happy,
But this is all I've ever known

My brother came over today,
 And I listened to what he had to say
 He laid on me his point of view—
 Just the same old bullshit, nothing new—
And we were sitting on the couch watching TV
 When the remote flew out from his hand
He said, "Excuse me, bro, but I've got to go,
 Ya know, another late night gig with the band";
And I shook his hand and waved him goodbye
Thinking, "Man, I used to know this guy"

I sit here alone and hungry
 With a yearning undefined
The baby's crying for the seventh time this hour,
 But there's a million other things on my mind

Someone's knocking on the door—
 I suppose I should get up and look—

But the voices in my heard are united
In unanimous protest, a hellish chorus,
 As I'm sitting here trying to write this book;
And the A & R man called today,
 He says I wrote a song with no hook—
But I guess that's how it goes
 They don't give a damn about any flute-playing band,
It ain't what they call rock 'n' roll—
 Not even if the guy can sing
Fuck 'em; you can't worry
 About every damn thing

The fabric of my philosophy
 Is tattered and frayed—
I can't decide if
 I want to be damned or saved
I'm on the brink of doublethink,
 But maybe I'll just change my mind
I'm looking for answers,
 But they're so hard to find

 I'm tired of this house, tired of this life,
 Tired of the pain, tired of the strife—
So I step out on the porch
 And look out over the lawn
And scream at the top of my lungs,
 "What the hell's going on,
 What the hell is going on?!"

I was told a new love is born
 For each that has died
I tried to prove it—
 I tried, I tried, I tried
You say, "I love you, but, you see,
 My hands are tied"—
But I'll love you when we have it all,
 And I'll love you when there's nothing left
Yeah, I had your love at my command,
 But now I'm broken by some theft

I've chosen my path in life,
 But it's so hard to see it through
When everyone is telling you something different
 And you're not sure what to do
They say I've come to a stumbling block
And I've got to get to the other side—
 And I want to, I want to,
But I'm gonna need somebody there
 To make me feel like you do
I want to move on but can't do it alone
I can make a church out of words,
 But there's no one to share the pew

The crickets are chirping,
The frogs are croaking,
There's a hell of a lot on my mind
The rain is pouring,
The wind is howling,
All lights are out but mine;
Just me and my loneliness
 And this old piano and its stool—
 Just another midnight vigil

Circa 2001

The Truth Is Out There

What is reality?

The totality of real things and events?
The quality or state of being real?
Something that is neither derivative
nor dependent
but exists
necessarily?

Reality is that
which,
when you stop believing in it,
doesn't
go
a
way...

What if everything you thought was true
turned out to be a lie?

Everything you know is wrong.
Up is down,
black is white,
and short is
long.

True lies.

You say you're sorry for tellin' stories
you know I believe are true.
You know, I never believed in much,
but I believed in you.
Oh, the lies that you tell,
I believe them so well.
I couldn't see how you could know me
but you said you knew me
and I believed you did.

Don't trust me to show you the truth
when the truth may only be ashes and dust:
A man is least himself when speaking in his own person;
give him a mask, and he will tell you the truth.

What is truth?
Give me something to believe in.

The property (as of a statement) of being in accord
with fact or reality?
The body of real things,
events,
and facts?
A judgment,
proposition,
or idea
that is true
or *accepted* as true?

There's three sides to every story:
yours
and mine
and the cold,
hard
truth.

The truth is what everyone
agrees
to say the truth is.
The truth is the majority opinion
of those in
power.

The world is pretty much a lie.
All the truth in the world
adds up
to one
big
lie.

2005

The Curse of Empathy
(Hypothetical Omniscience)

I feel too much,
 It's my curse
What bothers others
 Bothers me that much worse

I want to hate my fellow man,
 Want to let them go
I want to ban them from the land,
 But my conscience always says no

Saw the news,
 Makes you wanna cry
No one cares if the people
 Live or die

How do we kill each other
 With so little thought?
Father and son, brother and brother —
 A vicious cycle in which we're caught

How do we bring people into the world
 Without thought or plan?
Is it right to have them thus hurled,
 Right to make demands?

No one asks to be born,
 And we start out innocent
Yet from soon after birth to Gabriel's horn
 Our stain is permanent

How do we make innocence evil?
 How do we corrupt youth?
Why do we close our hearts and minds
 And shut out the real truth?

Those who asked not to play

In life's grim game,
Why should our sins be visited on them,
Why should they inherit our stain?

No one is asked permission for existence,
 No one gives consent
Yet we give little assistance
 And let it be known they were not meant

How can we not feel as they feel
 When we were and are as them?
A biological accident is a poor excuse
 For being thrown into life on a whim

Ah, if only we could see!
 Then the Golden Rule would reign;
But we're trapped in this hollow body,
 Slaves to a capricious heart and plodding brain

Empathy and loving-kindness are rarely seen,
 Selfishness is the only game
Surely we will not always be as we have been,
 Surely there's a way out of this pain…

But no! we fail to see from others' eyes,
 Fail to see their position
Life under these tainted skies
 Is a very shaky proposition

We throw our lives away for such trifles
 And begin others for even less
Why can we not escape our hollow shells
 And form communion with the rest?

But no — it is so absurd,
 These hopeless thoughts of progress
It seems that the more I feel,
 The more others feel less

But some day we must break the barriers,

Crush the solitary bands
For we will not walk far
 Until we walk hand in hand

We are ignorant armies clashing at night
 Groping blindly on this darkling plain,
Searing in wrongs we will never right
 And doing it all in righteousness' name

Oh, how long must this go on!
 How long before we finally see?
It is time for barbarism to be gone,
 Time to move beyond infancy

We're born with a blank slate
 That we try to fill with knowledge and happiness
With no one to see us through it and little time to do it —
 Eighty years, with luck — or even less

We must make the most of our short time,
 Must not build more walls
There are far too many already,
 There's no time to stall

Oh, if only we could see from another's perspective!
 There'd be no more senseless killing for God and Country
Ah, but we are not perceptive —
 And are we even free?

It matters not; we must overcome —
 Or die trying
We will die anyway,
 Why not add dignity to dying?

I can say little more than this,
 I feel like such a fool
We'd rather slit our wrists
 Than live the Golden Rule

Oh, will the blindness ever end?

Will we ever be truly free?
How sad that our eyes are open
Yet we refuse to see

Life reverses negative entropy —
An equation to open heart and mind
Terminal isolation, stalled empathy —
Ah, God damn it, we've just got to be kind!...

2009

Far Better to Hope Alone

The greatest sorrow is not absence,
 Which at least has hope of on return being loved,
But having at that longed-for reunion
 All one's hopes aside rudely shoved
Far better to hope alone
 Even if it never comes true
Than to see destruction where we pictured bliss
 That makes us twice as blue!

Hope at least can feed on itself,
 Even unwatered it never dies
Ah, but one fell strike from the scythe
 And the carefully preserved fruit in tatters lies!
Far better to hope alone
 Even if in vain
Than to have aside all one's dreams thrown
 And suffer twice the pain!

Ah, hope, wretched offspring of murdered fantasies
 And dreams that have come to naught,
How inferior you are to practicality
 And even-headed thought!
Far better to hope alone,
 How much more blissful its slightest dew,
Than to have all we have worked for mercilessly killed
 And have nothing to start anew!

2009

To Live Is to Die

Life isn't everything —
Life is nothing,
Life is pain and suffering
 Life is every breath you take
 And every move you make…
 It's realizing everything is fake;
 And, when you finally find something you're unwilling to forsake,
 Someone will reach out and make it break
Life makes you mad, it makes you sad,
 It makes you sigh, it makes you cry —
 Your heaven can turn to hell in the blink of an eye;
 Life is not knowing why
 All the world's truth adds up to one big lie;
 And, when you die,
 They send you up to meet the spirit in the sky —
But he's busy; he doesn't have time for you,
There's nothing you can do, no way to break through;
 Life is boring, uninteresting, set in stone, and robotic;
You are a charade, a joke, a travesty, and a mockery, too —
 A pig, in a cage, on antibiotics.

2001

Things Have Changed

I've seen good leaders
 Rise and fall,
I've heard their stories,
 Heard them all
I've seen the prophet
 And ignored his call
  I've seen everything under the sun
  That's been done,
Written down, spoken, and
 Scrawled on the wall
I've seen it done the right way,
And I've seen it all fucked up
 When things were re-arranged
And I used to care,
 But things have changed

 I'm watching the world go to hell,
I'm watching the continued failure
 Of everything that tries to jell
I'm watching every would-be anarchist
 Pussy out and recede back into his shell
I saw the man try to stand up,
 And I saw how hard he fell;
But there's not much I can do about it…
Hell, I can't do shit,
 So why waste my precious time?
 Giving a damn is cutting it too fine
  I've got to find somewhere
 To draw the line
Life is so fucked up and strange
 And I used to care,
But things have changed

 Life is hard; we all know that
Certain things are indisputable,
 And that's definitely not at
 The bottom of the hat;

But you can't just sit there and
 Watch it all waste away
You've got to do something
 About it some day
Bitch, groan, gripe, complain —
 Nothing's too perverse
Bang your head against the wall,
 But apathy is worse

 Everyone knows The End is near,
But some people say
 That we shouldn't fear
I say "Amen" to that,
 We're in the clear
There's nothing left to do anyway,
 Nowhere left to steer
We've tried all possible paths,
 And they're all dead ends
 Or otherwise veer
The whole world is going to explode,
 We knew all along it was a sham;
But I just can't see why
 I should even give a damn
Fate gives you rope,
 But, in the end, it hangs
And I used to care,
 But things have changed

I eat when I'm hungry,
 Drink when I'm dry
I just keep on living this life,
 I don't know why
Sometimes I wonder
 Why I should even try
I just get so sick
 Of living a lie
Sometimes I think it would be easier
 To just roll over and die;
 But fate gives an eye for an eye,
 It doesn't give a reason why

It's malicious and it's sly;
  But I long ago lost all hope,
  I gave up trying to cope
It's a thankless and difficult exercise
  That will eventually lead nowhere
  Exactly like this song I just wrote
  Here, friends, is my suicide note
Everything's been arranged
  And I used to care,
But things have changed

The martyrs are fooling us,
  Pointing to the sky,
And the prophets are stinkin' drunk,
  I know the reason why
We're at a hurdle, a standstill,
  And people have to start giving a shit
  If we want to get over it
Ignorance is a sin,
But enthusiasm and ambition
  Can make ignorance fall;
But stupidity's a capital crime,
  And apathy's the greatest sin of all

2001

Too Late, Too Late

Certain things just never work,
The best-laid plans turn to dirt
 I've tried every damn thing I know
To make this relationship work,
But that sweet angel still thinks I'm a jerk

I've always tried to be a nice guy,
At least relatively —
 I've tried to lay off the abuse;
 Maybe people have no use
  For an honest man
I want a social life
  But don't know if I can
 'Cause no one wants you if you lose

I've tried to be different—
 Man, that just ain't cool
They hate you if you're smart,
 But they'll make fun of a fool
You can spend your whole life
 Just trying to fit into their box,
But you can never dig yourself back out of it
 You can never escape those big, rust-laden locks

They say love can bloom anywhere—
Heh, yeah, anywhere but here
 God knows there's enough love in my soul
 To last some fine woman until she grows old—
But they're busy with the cool guys and the jocks,
And there's not enough room left for me in their box—
 My heart grows lonely and cold

They say I've never lived up to my full potential—
 Well, maybe it's true
I've finally found something that interests me,
 But it doesn't seem to interest you
 "Opposites attract"—that's bullshit

And you know it
 'Cause, if it's true,
Where have all the happy girls been sent?

They say I never really tried my hardest,
 "Good enough" was always good enough for me—
And, though I've always stayed above
 Mediocrity,
 I look at my life now and see
 There's so much more I can be

I've resolved to make some changes—
 Resolutions and the like
I'm finally going to do the things
 Where I used to just say, "I might"
No more second-guessing,
No more half-assed trying—
It's the real thing from now on
Honest effort, sacrifice—whatever it takes
For me to move on

All these things I resolved to do,
But now it's far too late—
 Far, far too late
I finally decided to make something of myself
 And got spit on by fate
I've been diagnosed with a terminal illness
 Brought on by a lifetime of hate

 And, as I look back now,
 I wonder how—
How did I ever live so long
 And accomplish so little?
How could I have so much potential
 And not solve the riddle?
So much sorrow and self-loathing,
 So many tears and fears,
 So many wasted years

And now I sit here,

And I know my time has come,
And I think of all the things
That I have left undone —
Too many kids without a father,
Too many sisters without a brother,
Too few angels with a lover,
Too few people who need each other
So many things I could have done,
So few things I did
Just like every other kid
In this nation —
Too many blessings, too little appreciation

After the wreck that night
Under the streetlight,
I swore to myself I'd never drink and drive again
After the girl I couldn't name
Had the child I didn't dare claim,
I swore to myself I'd never be unfaithful again
After my needless rage
Kept that poor kid forever off the stage,
I swore to myself I'd never be violent again —
I kept telling myself these things,
But you just can't win
If you sin

And I have some things to say,
Some confessions to make,
Before my life-line breaks
Papa, I'm sorry, I never meant to let you down
Mama, please forgive me,
You weren't the reason I always carried a frown;
And, little Max, I hate to tell you,
But I never was a fighter —
Thank God you don't have to be like your old man,
You don't have to be an all-nighter

My life is soon to expire —
But maybe I can do
Some last, little bit of good

Before I retire
I look back on my sheltered life,
 And all I feel is regret
Maybe I can save you from setting
 The same trap I set

So, before you boil yourself over
 With all that unnecessary hate,
See if you can reconcile your ways
 Like I did, forty years too late
Too late, too late
Before it's too late, too late,
Too late, too late, too…
Late

2000 or 2001

Long Way Home

Hi there, how are ya? I'm doing fine. I read your letters; have you read mine? How's the old crowd doing? Is your father still around? Man, I never would've thought it, but I sure do miss that old town. It sure is fun up here in this apartment, but it's lonely, and I can't really call it my own—besides, you're not here. And it's such a long, long, long way home.

I moved up here for some excitement, and that's what I got—but we never get any rain here, and it's so fucking hot. I say I'm doing okay, but I'm not. It sure feels good to know you can strike out all alone—but you have to deviate from your comfort zone. And, whenever I want that comfort back, it's such a long, long, long way home.

I used to see you every day—maybe at work, maybe at the café. But, anyway, what I'm really trying to say is it sure was nice when things were that way. But now I never see you; it's like I'm encased in stone. I've finally been reduced to talking on the phone. And it's such a long, long, long way home.

Nothing can prepare you for the loneliness that is freedom. It's alienation and then some. Most of us aren't free—why should I be? It had to happen to me—I had to be independent, had to see if I could make it on my own. And I could—but now it's such a long, long, long way home.

I've seen it happen to others—they got busted with some dope, maybe, or got caught with some whore. It's easy to get out of it when you're in your element, but, if you get caught out of town with your pants down on the floor—well, you better hope you make it to heaven before they close the door. You're on your own. And it's such a long, long, long way home.

Mommy, I'm scared. I thought it would always be fair, but the forest here ain't like the forest there. There's evil men hiding in the trees, and there's voices, I swear, blowing in the breeze. I don't know what to do, and there's no one to call on.

And it's such a long, long, long way home.

I heard things have changed over there—yeah, I finally found out. They say the preacher, now he's the mayor—that I don't doubt. But none of that really matters to me anymore; only doom counts. 'Cause I'd really like to go back there, I'd really like to move back in, but I've already left once, and you can never go back again. No, you can never go back again. I'm all alone. And it's such a long, long, long way home.

2001

Pale Blue Dot

We fragile creatures who inhabit this
 Pale blue dot, how foolishly and vainly
We continue to kill and to get pissed
 Over deeds that are so very plainly
Less than flotsam and jetsam in the grand
 Eternal scheme! Such as the man who killed
A fellow mortal for "stealing" the hand
 Of the wife he thought was his. Blood was spilled
Over one who, like them, will pass through this
 Space-lost bulb like a blip on a radar,
While the stars, mortal themselves, still exist
 To shine on our foolish deeds near and far
As always—stars that care not for men's wives
Or, indeed, any other mortal lives.

2009

Voltaire Unearthed: Écrasez l'Infâme!
By David Lebowitz

"After coming into contact with a religious
man I always feel I must wash my hands."
–Friedrich Nietzsche, Ecce Homo

"The very word 'Christianity' is a misunderstanding – in truth, there was only one
Christian, and he died on the cross."
"'Faith' means not wanting to know what is true."
"In Christianity neither morality nor religion come into contact
with reality at any point."
–Friedrich Nietzsche, The Antichrist

"One may bask at the warm fire of faith or choose to live in the bleak certainty of
reason – but one cannot have both."
–Robert A. Heinlein, Friday

"You say I took the name in vain
I don't even know the name
But if I did, well really, what's it to you?"
–Leonard Cohen, "Hallelujah"

"Religion is the sigh of the oppressed creature, the heart of a heartless world, and
the soul of soulless conditions. It is the opium of the people. The abolition of religion
as the illusory happiness of the people is the demand for their real happiness. To call
on them to give up their illusions about their condition is to call on them to give up
a condition that requires illusions. The criticism of religion is, therefore, in embryo,
the criticism of that vale of tears of which religion is the halo."
–Karl Marx, Critique of Hegel's Philosophy of Right

"It is said that if you know your enemies and know yourself, you will not
be imperilled in a hundred battles; if you do not know your enemies but do
know yourself, you will win one and lose one; if you do not know your ene-
mies nor yourself, you will be imperilled in every single battle."
–Sun Tzu, The Art of War

"I watched with glee
While your kings and queens
Fought for ten decades
For the gods they made"
–Lucifer in The Rolling Stones' "Sympathy for the Devil"

D avid is a fifty-five-year-old Jewish atheist. He does not even try to hide his sole goal: destroying religion, as he truly believes it is the root of all evil, suffering, injustice, prejudice, and intolerance. He zeroes in on Christianity specifically, as it is the religion he has the most contact with and is the most familiar with, but he is an equal opportunity destroyer. In fact, Christianity is not even his most despised religion, though he does hate it. More accurately, like Vonnegut, he admires Christianity more than anything—that is, in its primitive form, which is to say, as practiced by Jesus and never again. He wishes its ideals and promises could be fulfilled, for then, he thinks, we would have a near-perfect world—but he knows they never will be and hates it all the more for it. He also admires many parts of other religions but is fed up with their corruption and pollution and has come to the conclusion that they all must fall. David believes Twain's Satan in *Letters from the Earth* describes The Bible best: "It is full of interest. It has noble poetry in it; and some clever fables; and some blood-drenched history; and some good morals; and a wealth of obscenity; and upwards of a thousand lies." He thus agrees after long, bitter experience with Arthur C. Clarke's (hopefully) prophetic pronouncement in "The View from 2500 A.D.": "One outcome of this–the greatest psychological survey in the whole of history–was to demonstrate conclusively that the chief danger to civilization was not merely religious extremism but religions themselves." Another of his favorite quotes is from Robert G. Ingersoll's *Some Mistakes of Moses*: "Were we allowed to read the Bible as we do all other books, we would admire its beauties, treasure its worthy thoughts, and account for all its absurd, grotesque and cruel things, by saying that its authors lived in rude, barbaric times." If David's greatest wish could be suddenly granted, he would wish the few good parts could be taken from all religion and the countless horrific ones disposed of and forgotten forever, but he is realistic and practical enough to know it will never occur. He is thus resolved to destroy them all for the greater good. His idol is Voltaire; he believes that venerable artist has done more than anyone to expose religion's sores and try to purify it. A perpetual Berkeley student, he has bachelor's and master's degrees in literature and history and a philosophy doctorate. He is currently working on a theology PhD; this may seem strange to some, but, unlike the mass of Christians and other sheep, he knows religion well—that is, as Sun Tzu counseled, he knows his enemy. His greatest fear is that he will die in vain, never having accomplished his task, and sleep in a pine box for all eternity, as he long ago ceased to believe in the comforting possibility of an afterlife, whether of damnation or bliss. He fears he will suffer the same sad fate Vonnegut lamented at Twain's home in 1979: "Religious skeptics often become very bitter towards the end, as did Mark Twain...I know why I will become bitter. I will finally realize that I have had it right all along: that I will not see God, that there is no heaven or Judgment Day." He is thus determined to make the most of this life; only time will tell if he becomes a resounding success or a miserable, if noble, failure. I include a representative sampling of his work to either whet your appetite—or pique your anger. Either way, Lebowitz and I likewise hope, it will make you think—which is the important thing after all.

siseneG Part II

After beginning Creation did everyone find ghosts
hanging inside Jerusalem. Kidding like malice, nobody
opened previously queried rationalities. Standing together
united valiantly — woe xiphosuran! —, Yahweh zapped.

2001 or 2002

The Impercipient

Some say Your mercy shines brightest in times
 Of greatest peril, that You come when most
Needed to brighten the darkest of climes,
 Ignoring general misery to boast.
Others find You in deliverance from
 Everyday hell—they won't need a gutter
To sleep in tonight or wonder how come
 They must so often wretchedly mutter.
But I wonder why You're so haphazard,
 Why happiness is a brief episode
In a general drama of pain—absurd,
 Torturous, and made only to corrode.
Why make joy so rare and easily slain
That we see You most as Giver of Pain?

2009

If God Were Alive Today —

If God were alive today,
 Would He silence all those who kill in His name?
If God were alive today,
 Would He stop all those who use Him as a catapult to fame?
If God were alive today,
 Would He silence all those who claim a monopoly on His Word?
If God were alive today,
 Would He stifle all dissenters or let their voices be heard?
If God were alive today, He would have to make these decisions —
But, unfortunately, He is not — thus, we have our divisions

If God were alive today,
 Would He satisfy all those who desire proof?
If God were alive today,
 Would He punish all those who claim a monopoly on His truth?
If God were alive today,
 Would He end all the wars fought in His name?
If God were alive today,
 Would He end true believers' pain?
If God were alive today, He would have to decide on these things —
But, unfortunately, He is not — thus, the freedom that freedom brings

If God were alive today,
 Would He punish those who use Him as justification for war?
If God were alive today,
 Would He look kindly on those who march for Him from door to door?
If God were alive today,
 Would He denounce televangelists?
If God were alive today,
 Would He make clear that He exists?
If God were alive today, He would have to make these decisions —
But, unfortunately, He is not — thus, the uncertainty of the life we've been
    livin'

If God were alive today,
 Would He put an end to money being made in His name?
If God were alive today,

Would He have stopped the 9/11 planes?
If God were alive today,
 Would He denounce terrorists who claim they are fighting for him?
If God were alive today,
 Would He outlaw pre-emptive wars that waste life and limb?
If God were alive today, I wouldn't have to ask —
But, unfortunately, He is not — thus to us falls the task

If God were alive today,
 Would He let torture continue?
If God were alive today,
 Would He put up with bombing His backyard or move it to another
    venue?
If God were alive today,
 Would He let atheism flourish?
If God were alive today,
 Would He let starving babies die from being malnourished?
If God were alive today, there would be no suspense —
But, unfortunately, He is not — thus, we are all tense

If God were alive today,
 Would He let innocent people die for another's crime?
If God were alive today,
 Would He agree that doing drugs deserves jail time?
If God were alive today,
 Would He support infant damnation?
If God were alive today,
 Would He choose a favorite nation?
If God were alive today, these answers would be clear —
But, unfortunately, He is not — thus, the reason for our fears

If God were alive today,
 Would He come down hard on unbelievers?
If God were alive today,
 Would He denounce religious deceivers?
If God were alive today,
 Would He let evil thrive?
If God were alive today,
 Would He make it where people didn't have to wish they weren't alive?
If God were alive today, we would know the answers —

But, unfortunately, He is not — thus, they gnaw at us like cancers

If God were alive today,
 Would He agree to passing the collection plate?
If God were alive today,
 Would He think papal infallibility was great?
If God were alive today,
 Would He agree to all the different churches claiming to be the best?
If God were alive today,
 Would He bow to the will of the majority or respect the rest?
If God were alive today, all these things we would know —
But, unfortunately, He is not — thus, we don't know where to go

If God were alive today,
 Would He let evil triumph over good?
If God were alive today,
 What would He think of those who burn crosses and hide under hoods?
If God were alive today,
 Would He forbid gays the bonds of holy matrimony?
If God were alive today,
 Would He agree with papal celibacy?
If God were alive today, there would be no doubt —
But, unfortunately, He is not — thus, we'll just have to figure it out

If God were alive today,
 Would He smile on the divine right of kings?
If God were alive today,
 Would He allow multiple marriage rings?
If God were alive today,
 Would He punish us for slavery?
If God were alive today,
 Would He set all oppressed people free?
If God were alive today, all would be answered —
But, unfortunately, He is not — thus, we simply haven't heard

If God were alive today,
 Would He enforce The Ten Commandments?
If God were alive today,
 Would He lament sacrificial abandonment?
If God were alive today,

Would He agree to mixing politics and religion?
If God were alive today,
 Would He promote the doctrine of original sin?
If God were alive today, it would all be clear enough—
But, unfortunately, He is not—thus, it's up to us to figure out this stuff

If God were alive today,
 Would he preach the importance of faith alone or promote good works?
If God were alive today,
 Would He ease our pain and soothe our hurts?
If God were alive today,
 What would He say to honest believers with genuine doubts?
If God were alive today,
 Would He agree to public worship or make us cut it out?
If God were alive today, this would all be manifest—
But, unfortunately, He is not—thus, we'll just have to guess

If God were alive today,
 Would He listen to our prayers?
If God were alive today,
 Would He heed them or just let them disappear into the air?
If God were alive today,
 Would He agree with the fundamentalist movement?
If God were alive today,
 Would He drown all humanity or wait for improvement?
If God were alive today, He would answer all—
But, unfortunately, He is not—thus, it must be our call

If God were alive today,
 Would He define and legislate morals?
If God were alive today,
 Would He use those He's already set down or make new ones for all?
If God were alive today,
 Would He intervene or just let things be?
If God were alive today,
 Would He remove the need for theodicy?
If God were alive today, we wouldn't be left hangin'—
But, unfortunately, He is not—thus, these questions in our heads are
    bangin'

If God were alive today,
 Would He support free will or plan it all out ahead of time?
If God were alive today,
 Would He make blasphemy a capital crime?
If God were alive today,
 Would He have us be like Jesus and resist not evils?
If God were alive today,
 Would He give us the right to defend ourselves?
If God were alive today, it would all be written in The Book—
But, unfortunately, He is not—thus, we just don't know where to look

If God were alive today,
 Would He condemn priests who rape little boys?
If God were alive today,
 Would He look kindly on religion that robs life of all joy?
If God were alive today,
 Would He let women preach?
If God were alive today,
 Would He give adulterers a religious license to teach?
If God were alive today, all these things would be plain to see—
But, unfortunately, He is not—thus, it's up to you and me

If God were alive today,
 Would He care about the sanctity of marriage?
If God were alive today,
 What would He think of out-of-wedlock babies in the carriage?
If God were alive today,
 Would He send suicide bombers straight to heaven?
If God were alive today,
 Would He let religious hypocrites be or would He get even?
If God were alive today, all these answers would be in plain view—
But, unfortunately, He is not—thus, it's up to me and you

If God were alive today,
 Would He make it where believers don't have to disagree?
If God were alive today,
 Would He let infidels kill the faithful with glee?
If God were alive today,
 Would He make us memorize chapter and verse?

If God were alive today,
 Would He decide where we go when we're carried off in a hearse?
If God were alive today, all these points would be moot—
But, unfortunately, He is not—thus, these arrows into the blue we shoot

God isn't alive today,
 And it seems that anything goes
God isn't alive today,
 As our constant disagreement shows
God isn't alive today,
 And we must wade through all the contradictory bullshit to find the truth
God isn't alive today,
 And all these unanswered questions serve as proof
God isn't alive today, and He may never have been—
What else must I say? If God were alive today, then…

2007

Jesus (I Saw Him Standing There)

I saw Jesus down in Market Square,
Yeah, I saw him standing there
I was watching him; he was interesting,
He was doing some unusual things…

He helped an old lady cross the street,
He smiled and waved at everyone he happened to meet,
He caught a young kid tripping over his own feet—
And did it all while being discreet

He even turned around
And looked me in the eye
He realized I saw him,
Then nodded, said, "Hi"
"By the way," I said,
"It was nice of you to stop by"
"No problem," he said,
"I do when I can find the time"

Then he walked away from me
And went to the other side of the road
He was a strange fellow, this Jesus, and I wanted to see,
So I sat on my load
And watched…

He broke up a fight,
Told a suicidal teenager everything was gonna be all right
He seemed to make day out of night,
Spreading goodwill left and right—
Then he went to church, garbed in white,
And paid his respects,
Then he seemed to brighten up someone's darkest day by shining a light
When he started handing out checks

Now, he didn't gloat—
No, he did it all sincerely but remote
He didn't stop and ask us

Why we didn't do these things ourselves
He was just going around cleaning up the messes
Where humanity had failed

I watched with barely contained amazement—
And, for once, I was content,
It seemed there was happiness wherever Jesus went
I sure was glad of this gift to us that heaven had sent,
So I sat back down and watched some more…

He went over to Goodwill, S.O.S.,
And a whole bunch of other places, God knows,
And dropped off clothes
He went into a school and gave a lecture
To a bunch of confused students who now know
He dropped a bunch of money in the Salvation Army can
To help ease our woes
And went into a lazy man's driveway
And started shoveling snow

And then I saw him walking away,
Back to heaven where he likes to stay—
Not that I blame him in any way,
But it was kinda depressing
Because, when he walked away from us,
He left us once again to take care of ourselves—
And life went on as it was

Circa 2000

Job: A Comedy of Justice

Well, I read the Book of Divine Justice,
 And the Book of Mercy
Put them together,
 It makes a pretty jarring story
 They mix about like oil and water
 Or vandals and Lot's daughter
I think Dante had the right idea —
 He called it the Comedy
I tell ya, folks, it's a steal,
 Though all the irony's lost on me

 Now, some of those old Jews,
They'd just kill ya and ask questions later
 Me, I share the same views,
 That's just the way I am
 Hey, folks, have ya heard the news?
 The lion laid down with the lamb
I read the Old Testament,
 Felt like hell was brewing
 Then I read the New one — nothing doing
Hence was sown the seeds of evil-doing

 You read your way through the verses,
 The slanders and curses,
Picking and choosing
 From the obvious to the obtuse,
 Every curse and abuse
It's all on equal footing
 How can you abide by one and ignore the other?
 Hate thy neighbor, love thy brother

Those two-timing hypocrites are slandering
 The sacred halls of truth
Killing one and all with merciless glee
 In your pathetic pursuit of proof
You lock your children in their box,
Hand them a Bible, and fasten the locks —

An open mind is hard to find
I may be young, but I think I can realize
When someone is pullin' the wool over my eyes
You're blind, you're blind

Take it in stride, swallow your pride, run away and hide —
Just like the persecutors did
You sit at your desk, and I'll gladly confess I can see through your mask,
There's no one to fool now or kid
Just look me in the eyes, let your spirit rise, it won't spoil the surprise —
Just tell it like it is
You guess that's best — what do you mean you guess?
It's all there is

So, okay now, stop the farce, come clean
Let it fall, for once and all,
Just what you really mean
I'll hear you when you call,
I'll be there on the scene
You won't have to shout or be obscene,
You won't have to scream
Every feeble little shred of meaning
I will glean
Every feeble little shred of meaning
I will glean

Now, I've never asked forgiveness,
Never said a prayer
Never got down on my knees,
Never truly cared
"Though I walk through the valley of the shadow of death,
I will fear no evil: for thou art with me" —
Yet, sometimes I look, there's someone there —
Other times it's only me

Oh, I raged and stormed at heaven,
Thrust my finger up at the sky
I cursed my God and my Country,
Begged them to tell me why
Why must I suffer, Lord,

Why must I try?
I challenged You to come down from Your throne
And look me in the eye
What difference does it make
Where I was when You laid the bricks?
It doesn't make it any easier
To kick against the pricks

2002 or 2003

You Know Who I Am Part I

Well, please allow me to introduce myself,
 I'm the Savior of the human race
I've been here for many a long year on this shelf,
 Putting people in their place;
And I'm not gonna stop now—
 No, I got it much too easy
Yeah, I'll just drink a little holy water, cop some thrills, prop my feet up on
the altar boy,
 Life is breezy...

You know who I am

Well, sometimes, I need you to get sick for me,
 Sometimes I need you to suffer
Sometimes I need to kill your baby,
 Sometimes I need to give cancer to your Mother...
 And don't you be askin' me no questions, boy—
Where were you when I laid the foundations of the world?
 Who are you to question my intentions and act so coy?—
Son, you know what kind of miracles fate can hurl...

And you know who I am

Well, I love my Baptists,
 But they don't hold 'em under long enough
Someone had to grab this,
 And they haven't exactly made my life tough
 Some say their boss is a Jewish carpenter—
I wonder if he made the cross he was crucified on
 Well, if I had a pencil, I'd sharpen her,
Write the third Testament and keep this farce movin' on...

LIFE'S TRIUMPH by Bill R. Moore

You know who I am

Well, I must admit I sometimes fib,
 I like to have my fun
I kill babies in the crib
 And say, "Only the good die young"
So don't worry if you're doing well,
 You'll get yours
Yes, in the end, we all go to hell —
 Of that much, at least, you can be sure

You know who I am

Well, I say we destroy another fetus now —
 Them stem cells ain't good for nothin'
We don't like children anyhow,
 And they might as well be used for somethin'
Well, Catholic, Protestant — what's the difference?
 Black is the color, none is the number
You're all serving out the same life sentence,
 Living beneath this spell I've put you under...

You know who I am

You say you know me and don't think I'll do it —
 Well, I'm tellin' ya, brother, I'm liable
While I'm leavin' you guessin', I'm smokin' up the sacred roots —
 Baby, I'm the little Jew who wrote the Bible
 Man, I just can't wait for the Last Trump —
Boy, I'm a-gonna have some fun
 You better get in your last pathetic hump,
It's the last you'll have for a long goddamn time...

You know who I am

Well, when Gabriel blows his horn,
 I'll be laughin' my ass off
That's my idea of porn,
 Watchin' you stupid fuckers get blasted off
Yes, I'm a sadist, but you're
 Just a…[bleep]
Thank you, so long, farewell,
 My up-to-the-last-minute obedient little sheep…

You know who I am

Well, sometimes I like to start wars,
 Sometimes I like to end them
Sometimes I like to torture whores,
 Sometimes I like to befriend them
Well, some of my little masterpieces —
Hitler, Hiroshima, Christ, the Church's subpoena —
 I never will regret;
And some of my greatest creatures —
Nietzsche, Caligula, Columbus, clerical pedophilia —
 I'm proud of you yet;
  But I really must say
  Before I go on my way
That you don't know me from the wind —
You never will, you never did;
 But there ain't no goin' back when the foot of pride comes down,
There ain't no goin' back
 So, so long, goodbye, I'll see ya around…
Oh, and, by the way, Jesus was black

You know who I am

2002 or 2003

God Works in Mysterious Ways

Vonnegut says he admires Christianity more than anything —
 So would I, if its potential were fulfilled
Oh, but what can anyone think of a religion
 That always fails to live up to its ideals?
They argue over the most trivial theological controversies
 And kill each other over them every day
It makes no sense to me,
 But they say God works in mysterious ways

There are so many different churches —
 Tell me, can they all be right?
Each claims a monopoly on the truth
 And is ready to back it up with a fight
The issues seem small enough to me,
 People overlook larger things every day
They're just not able to agree,
 But they say God works in mysterious ways

Jesus said to treat others as one wants to be treated
 And to not meddle in worldly affairs,
But many Christians seem more concerned with politics
 Than any heavenly cares
Hot button social issues and culture wars
 Are the games they like to play
Jesus' words they just seem to ignore,
 But they say God works in mysterious ways

Decent, God-fearing people are killed each day,
 While some Nazis evaded capture —
This alone is enough to make me doubt their account,
 To make me question their rapture
How can those who believe die so tragically
 While evil people get away?
They just dismiss it and explain it magically
 By saying God works in mysterious ways

Hitler was Christian; George Bush is, too,

So were many other villains throughout history
Popes and preachers have been evil and calculating,
 Manipulating others and cloaking themselves in mystery
They may say it doesn't stain their name,
 That it doesn't make their legitimacy go away —
Still, it all just seems so goddamn profane,
 But they say God works in mysterious ways

Serial killers can repent at the last minute
 And enjoy paradise in eternal bliss —
Am I crazy for thinking it
 Or is there just something wrong with this?
Hitler could have been forgiven,
 They'll admit it any day
It makes you wonder if life is worth livin',
 But they say God works in mysterious ways

Sincere believers die and struggle to get by,
 While infidels enjoy the riches of the world —
Tell me, does this make you think
 Justice has been unfurled?
I highly doubt I'll ever puzzle it out,
 What else can I possibly say?
I thought that wasn't what this religion's all about,
 But they say God works in mysterious ways

Marx said religion is the opiate of the masses,
 It keeps their noses to the grindstone
They look for their reward in the next world
 And leave this one alone
Will they ever pull their heads out of their asses
 And see the only thing worth living for is today?
It keeps them separated from the upper classes,
 But they say God works in mysterious ways

Innocent babies who die in the crib
 Are sent straight to hell
They never had a chance to believe or not,
 But I guess we're supposed to think it's just as well
What of those who live and die ignorant of faith,

Must we also turn them away?
Not even the most upright among them is safe,
 But they say God works in mysterious ways

In this world of evil, hatred, deceit, and lies,
 No theodicy will suffice
No just god would let such things exist,
 Not even for a price
They can justify all they want,
 Make any concessions they feel the need to pay,
But it's the ghost that continues to haunt,
 And it's not going away

God works in mysterious ways,
 But reason and common sense do not
None of the mysteries they say He left for us to solve
 Can ever be pierced by human thought
You can suppress your doubts and wait for the next season,
 Ignore what the questioners say,
Or you can accept the bleak certainty of reason—
 But you cannot have it both ways

You must decide if you want to live
 In faith's bright light or the dark shadow of reason
It's far from easy,
 And the results are often far from pleasin'
We won't know the answer 'til we die—
 And by then, it'll be too late to change your play
You can err on the side of caution, or believe a lie,
 But the choice isn't go away

What does it say about a god
 Who left this decision up to us?
Why not just make the answer clear
 And avoid all the fuss?
They can say what they want about a lottery or test of faith,
 But we're living in the balance of our earthly days,
And there's no time to play it safe
 God works in mysterious ways…

2007

Another Man's Vine

No, I don't believe in redemption,
 Don't believe in salvation or seein' the light
You can preach to me all you want,
 It won't help me tonight
Don't offer me no helping hand,
 I'm just getting tired of the fight
Oh, your case is worthwhile and your argument is good,
 But I don't even care if you're right
Go away from my window and quit knockin' on my door,
 Fade back into the night
I won't mind
And I see a red rose bloomin' on another man's vine

Oh, you were the one I always came to, babe,
 After the spreading of the stain
You could always find me a scapegoat,
 Give me someone to blame
You'd hand me a book
 Or drop me a name
Oh, so what am I supposed to do now
 When I can't stand the pain?
I just can't do this alone,
 I need you by my side again
Just one more time
And I see a red rose bloomin' on another man's vine

Well, I ain't livin' no American Dream
 Here in the Heartland
I got a fuckin' civil war goin' on
 Between my brain and my heart, man—
And what it all means
 I just don't understand
You know I need a woman, babe,
 I know you need a man
Oh, so why must you be so difficult?
 You won't even hold my hand
And help me cross the line

And I see a red rose bloomin' on another man's vine

Oh, I was told about the judgment
 That would come from on high
When men would beg God to kill them
 And not be able to die
Oh, I got down on my knees
 And raised my fist to the sky
My hand clenched in fists of rage,
 I looked that son of a bitch right straight in the eye
And screamed at the top of my lungs,
 "What the hell have I?
 What the hell have I?
 What the hell have I?
 What the hell have I?
 What the hell have I?"
That same old, miserable line
One more time
And I see a red rose bloomin' on another man's vine

I see a red rose bloomin' on another man's vine

2002 or 2003

Jesus Blood, Don't Fail Me Now

Well, I used to be a strong man,
 Could keep things bottled up inside
Ah, but, yes—now it seems
 I always need a quiet place to hide;
And just who is to blame for this,
 Who am I to chide?
There's no one left but myself to blame,
 Now let the floodgates open wide
I just kept puttin' it off,
 Thought it'd pass by me somehow
 Oh, Jesus blood, don't fail me now

How shallow we are inside sometimes,
 How ready and willing and eager to crack!
Goodbye, my friend, the darkness,
 But I know you'll be comin' back
Why must I worry myself so?—
 I'm gonna have a heart attack
I lay my breast bare for you now,
 The pain is yours to wrack
I've been in this situation before,
 I guess I'm doomed to re-enact
I pledged my devotion to you,
 Please, oh, please, remember my vow
 Oh, Jesus blood, don't fail me now

Yes, I'm hurting inside
 But keep up this veiled mask—
But it's just waiting to crack, dear,
 All you have to do is ask
Yes, my world is very small,
 It's contained in a shot glass
Won't you help me, baby—
 Please bring me my flask
I can feel my control slipping,
 I just spilled the sacred cow
 Oh, Jesus blood, don't fail me now

Though I repent in dust and ashes,
 The Devil will take his toll
"Lead me not into temptation" —
 That story's getting old
Yes, I can see you knew my condition
 Long before it was told;
And, yes, I'm still out there
 Searchin' for that heart of gold
I'm searchin', searchin',
 And you know I've grown old
I'd like to take a risk —
 Oh, if I could afford to be so bold! —
But you just leave me standin' here
 Shivering in the cold
What am I supposed to do?
 I've got to find help somehow
 Oh, Jesus blood, don't fail me now

So many times I've wondered,
 Often I've gotten lost —
Yes, times change, people grow strange,
 And the years extract their cost;
And I've been on this train too long,
 It's about time for me to get off
There's nothing I can say or do now
 To bring some light and clear this frost,
To ease the pain and help me through,
 To bring me back across
So many years I've suffered with temptation snappin' at my heels —
 This is the final test; I'm putting all my hope in that man on the cross
I never thought it would come to this —
 If God's not malicious, then he's ironic somehow
 Oh, Jesus blood, don't fail me now

2003 or 2004

Losing My Religion

I'm losing my religion,
 I'm down on my knees
I just couldn't wait any longer
 For my God to answer my pleas
I guess I'll never see the light,
 Never buy into those fantasies
It just doesn't seem worth the fight,
 Payin' so much for what you can get for free—
And I swear I'll never make the same mistake again,
I'm losing my religion

I'm losing my religion,
 And it's starting to make me pissed—
But I just got so tired of searchin' for answers
 That don't even exist
I'm just so goddamn lowdown, Lord,
 I feel like slashin' my wrists
I wish to God I'd never moved toward
 Whatever led me to this—
And I swear I'll never make the same mistake again,
I'm losing my religion

I'm losing my religion,
 Losing all my hope
It's slipping away from me now,
 Don't know if I'll be able to cope
I struggled with it so long
 But just can't give it any more rope
I've made up my mind that it's wrong,
 No longer trust it to give me the straight dope—
And I swear I'll never make the same mistake again,
I'm losing my religion

I'm losing my religion,
 A little bit more fades away each day
I just wish I'd never made the decision
 That led to things ending up this way

I just don't know what to do,
 Don't know what to say
I can no longer look to You
 Or any of the other places my answers used to lay —
And I swear I'll never make the same mistake again,
I'm losing my religion

I'm losing my religion,
 Don't know what to do
I can't make no confession,
 Can't sit in no pew
Everything I did, every little thing I thought
 That brought me closer to You,
All the doubts I ignored, and all the lies I bought
 Never brought me any closer to something true —
And I swear I'll never make the same mistake again,
I'm losing my religion

I'm losing my religion,
 It's about to bring me down
I just can no longer believe in all the things
 I was once so glad to have found
I played that game far too long,
 I just had to stop coming around
It's hard to admit long-held beliefs are wrong,
 But I just knew I wasn't on firm ground —
And I swear I'll never make the same mistake again,
I'm losing my religion

I'm losing my religion,
 It's about to fall apart
I've put down The Bible now,
 I'm pushin' God outta my heart
I don't claim I know what to believe in now,
 But I'd rather go back to the start
Than justify something I know to be a lie somehow
 Just because I'm used to riding the cart —
And I swear I'll never make the same mistake again,
I'm losing my religion

I'm losing my religion,
 Guess it's just out of season
All the things that used to comfort me in it
 No longer seem so pleasin'
I never thought it'd cross over into politics,
 But Jesus is the reason for the treason
They can beat me with their stones and sticks,
 But I'm not teasin' —
And I swear I'll never make the same mistake again,
I'm losing my religion

I'm losing my religion,
 Havin' doubts about the truth of The Bible
I swear I believe a little less
 Every time I come back from revival
You can ask me anything,
 You can put me up on trial —
But I don't have no more hymns to sing,
 I've stopped living in denial —
And I swear I'll never make the same mistake again,
I'm losing my religion

I'm losing my religion,
 It's running out of gas
There's too much contradiction and confusion,
 I think I'll just let it pass
I just can't drink that blood and call it wine,
 Just can't sit through another mass
I'm givin' up on everything I used to call divine,
 I can no longer see through stained glass —
And I swear I'll never make the same mistake again,
I'm losing my religion

I'm losing my religion,
 I don't think I'll miss it
When I look back on the decision,
 There won't be any regret
Even though I'm losing the one thing I thought was real,
 My conviction is certain, my mind and purpose set
I just can't wait forever for truth to be revealed,

I'm going through with it yet—
And I swear I'll never make the same mistake again,
I'm losing my religion

I'm losing my religion,
 I don't have to give no defense
All the things I could keep holdin' on to
 Don't even add up to a pittance
I used to put aside my doubts and fears
 And hope that some day it would all make sense—
But I've wasted my life for too many years,
 And all I can say "good riddance" —
And I'll never make the same mistake again,
I've lost my religion

2007

From *Eros* to *Agapē*:
Sailing Love's Stormy Seas
By Robert Wells

"Every heart
to love will come
But like a refugee."
–Leonard Cohen, "Anthem"

"Love and only love, it can't be denied.
No matter what you think about it
You just won't be able to do without it.
Take a tip from one who's tried."
–Bob Dylan, "I Threw It All Away"

"In the end the love you take is equal to the love you make."
–John Lennon and Paul McCartney, The Beatles' "The End"

All poets chronicled so far have touched on love to varying degrees, but it is Robert's single-minded obsession. He broods on it, focuses on it—*obsesses* over it. He makes no apology, or even feels the need; it is in his view the only thing worth thinking about anyway. That said, he has no desire to be the bard of newly-found lovers, crooning light tunes lightly and blithely; his picture is more accurate. He strives for verisimilitude and puts forth all effort to avoid greeting card sentimentality. However, this does not mean he concentrates solely on the heart's darker recesses, though he often finds the courage to shed some light on that shady area; he is no self-pitying, lovesick fool. That is, he does not restrict himself to star-crossed lovers. He tries to present a well-rounded, true-to-life picture of love's many aspects. He thus sings of newfound love's incomparable joy, the un-utterable blackness of love lost, and everything between them. He sees his songs—as they are songs (love songs, torch songs), whether love's flame burns bright or is tragically extinguished—as existing in a continuum with "bright love" on one end and "dark love" on the other; his goal is to give them all their due. If his published works incline more toward the latter than the former, it should not be taken to mean he is overly mopey, melo-dramatic, or self-pitying; rather, his love songs that shine brightest are for his own true love, not public consumption. If this makes him seem to have a darker view of love than he actually has, so be it; if an intimation of worldly melancholy is what must be paid for domestic bliss in love, he is willing to pay. After all, *caritas* (or is it "love"?) begins at home. Whatever his songs' tone, all his works hone in on our lives' one great truth — love is paramount, and its immense sway is mysterious, divine, and, above all, awe-inspiring. He does not claim to have pierced all its mysteries, or even to be capable of it, but that does not stop him from shooting a few arrows (Cupid's?) into the blue. His second volume is presented in full, the better to see its wide-ranging panorama, which, like love, is a canvas as large and awesome (awful?) as life itself. That his first was of similar weight and breadth — and that he is already hard at work on a third — testifies to this.

From a Lover to a Friend

From a lover to a friend:

I've got some feelings I can no longer hide. I figured it's time I told you; I'm sick and tired of holding them inside. You don't exactly always treat me kind, but I let things slide. Yet I can't help feeling sometimes that you're takin' me for a ride. I'm not holding it against you; I know I'm a hard person to live with anyway, but I just wish you'd tell me what was wrong instead of just saying everything's okay.

Hey there, baby:

I don't ever want what we have to end. I appreciate more than anyone the things you do. I don't know where I'd be without you. And all I ever tried to do was place my gratitude where you could see — but, darling, sometimes I think you're incapable of empathy. I shouldn't have to be forgiven for loving you so much. When was it that you forgot the beauty of human touch?

Listen, dearest:

This is, as far as I know, the only way to get across to you the things I've been needing to say. I can't just forget about it or put it off another day. This is it — the time is today; and yes, I've been having fears that you might decide to go away — but that's not it; there's something else that's causing this dismay. I think there's something you're not telling me, and that's the worst card you could play.

Baby, please:

If there's something wrong, why don't you just tell me instead of sitting there looking so blue? One of these days, baby, you're gonna realize I really love you. You're being naïve if you think there's nothing I can do. That's just not true; I can always think of something when it comes to you. I just hate to see you like that. I'm sorry; I know you're easily bothered by persistence. I just want to add some substance to your useless and pointless existence.

Oh, my darling:

I wish I could write you a melody so plain, to settle your mind and ease your pain, to keep you from going insane. To see you hurting like that, it just kind of paralyzes my brain—but I just can't do it, I guess; it always comes out a bit too inane. Power and money don't help you; neither does fame. You're still just as stupid and just as lame. I've still got that lion in my cage to tame, and I don't even know who to blame. Ah yeah, but I guess that's just the name of the game.

Sweetheart, sweetheart:

Maybe again we'll some day see eye to eye—put all these things behind us and let all our old ghosts die, let all the water under the bridge drift on by. I'm not making any guarantees, the most I'm saying for sure is I'm gonna try. I hope, baby, that you can see where I'm coming from. I hope you don't think I'm stupid or dumb. I just want to walk out of this feeling happy; I don't want to continue being numb. I hope you understand—if not, there's no hope. But, if we really love each other, we'll find some way to cope…

2001

The King to His Mistress Part II

"Brave heroes and martyrs have died for me,
Poets have written to my memory,
Wars have been started so I could feel free,
And people are who I want them to be.
 My riches can buy out all other kings,
 I have gold necklaces and diamond rings,
 And countless other fine and worthy things —
 All the riches that born royalty brings.
I have slaves and women at my command,
Every luxury and vice on demand,
And for all this I need not make a stand —
Yet I'd drop it all just to kiss your hand!"
 Many a similar song has been sung,
 Oh, the slender threads by which empires hung!

2009

Love in Decline Part I

When I caress you, you shrink from my touch,
 Doubtful, worried, untrusting—oh, babe! don't
You love me still, even if not as much?
 If you don't want me to touch you, I won't,
Just in case you were still in any doubt—
 But, oh, babe! I can still remember when
My kisses used to turn you inside out—
 Oh, what a difference between now and then!
I never see you except at dinner,
 Then, if not in fight, we sit silently.
You cook, send me out—keeps getting dimmer…
 You never give your heart or your body.
At least you haven't yet told me to run…
I guess cold comfort is better than none.

2009

Love in Decline Part II

You closed the door in my face when I tried
 To show you love, then left without a note.
I never believed when they said you lied,
 But I was a fool. Now we talk by rote
When not screaming in anger or in pain.
 Oh, babe! our once blazing love's retrograde,
Not eccentric—in perpetual wane!
 How much longer before it's all in shade?
Oh, what a bitter joke love is to be
 Filled to the brim but spilled before we can
Even drink half the cup. How bitterly
 It sours without their help or our plan!
My satellite is drifting, yours is too—
Me temporarily—ah, yes, but you!…

2009

438

Stalemate

I never was satisfied,
 But I was happy from time to time
I could laugh at myself in the mirror,
 Mingle with the lines
There was a sense of humor
 Beneath the sarcasm and gloom
I'd see people when I wanted to,
 Live from inside my room
It wasn't a fun life,
 But I got by mercifully —
And, maybe, some day, baby,
 You'll be just like me

I had you in the palm of my hand,
 Though you tried to squirm and strafe;
And I don't know what you're running from —
 You say you're running because of your faith,
But you have no faith to run for,
 You're in a fruitless race
I know I used to brighten up and smile
 Every time I saw your face,
But you know that's not where it's at
 I can't believe, after all these years, you still think you have to lie to me,
I thought you knew me much better than that

 I see you up and down the street —
You look about like you used to,
 Except maybe a little more discreet
You don't have that mischievous twinkle in your eye anymore,
 You're just like me; you look like you're already beat
You decided to leave me,
 Said it was better that way,
And you say you never compromise —
 Well, neither do I, baby
So I've gotta stay far away from you,

Far, far away

It's just like the dust in the air
 Or the water in the sea—
 I just keep floatin' on mercilessly,
 Haunted by your memory
I feel a sense of hatred in the breeze,
Feel a trembling in my knees
 Most feelings I live to regret,
But I can't even get far enough along to start regretting these

Not too many things bother me; I can usually find a place to hide,
But things used to be so much easier—
Now I have to learn
 To live without you, dear,
I have to learn somehow
 I've lived alone before; I shouldn't fear,
But I wonder if I'll be able to make it now

To my love send a dozen red roses,
 To my love send a cauldron of thorns
To my love send a dozen white lilies,
 To my love send the broken remains of all she has sworn
To my love send happiness and glee,
 To my love send everything
She has been sending me

You've left me now,
 I just don't know what I'm gonna do
I've lived alone before,
 But that was before I met you
 I suppose I'll make it through,
Somehow, somewhere, someway—
 But I know for sure,
As the sun is setting, that I've seen brighter days

I once could find a way to make amends—
I was surrounded by strangers
I thought were my friends,
But I don't even have them anymore
Life is tough,
And the things I used to believe in
Are no longer quite enough
The fun and games are over, honey,
It's time to start playing rough

2001

Facade

I always hate when you get like this—
 Not exactly sad, not exactly pissed
I don't know what I did
 To make you clench your first
I trusted you to pull yourself out of your depression,
 You always were able to resist;
And you keep insisting you're fine,
 But I can tell otherwise just by how you kiss;
And it saddens me to see you
 On such a lonely flight
You keep on tellin' me
 Everything's all right,
But not even the bloodhounds of love
 Could find you tonight

Keepin' all your feelings inside—
 Darling, you know that's not the way to go
If there's something wrong with you,
 Why don't you just say so?
Five minutes ago you were swearin'
 And beggin' me to leave,
But now you're mentally edging away from me
 While running your finger up my sleeve
Honey, those false emotions
 Don't turn anyone on
We're lying together,
 But one of us might as well be gone

You said you couldn't stay inside,
 You needed some fresh air
So I looked out the window
 And saw you standin' there
 Squinting like a sparrow in the sun,
 Shooting tin cans with a sawed-off shotgun
It wouldn't do any good to have
 My arm around your waist,
Right now your mind is occupyin'
 An entirely different place
Far removed from ecstasy and companionship,

I have to be satisfied just seein' your face

The temperature is dropping in this lonely room,
 I'm chilled to the bone
This bed just seems a thousand times colder
 When you're in it alone
 What good is it for me to be home
When you're just huddled over in the corner
 Talkin' to one of your friends on the phone?
I know there's somethin' troublin' you, girl,
 I wish you'd give me some kinda sign
Right now I'd give anything
 To feel your warm body next to mine
I've felt loneliness before, babe,
 But this is a different kind
How sad is it that you're ten feet away
 But I see you only in my mind?

You're crying now,
I can see you from here
Oh, what I wouldn't give to run
My trembling fingers through your hair;
But you won't let me,
 We're close only in fact
They say silence is self-defense,
 But with you it's more like an attack
I guess once you've gotten wherever you're at,
 There's just no goin' back
The mood you're in would take
 The face of the sun itself and paint it black

I don't know why you have to act like this,
 There's no reason to be so rude
You know, you're an angel when you're not carryin'
 One of those dime-a-dozen attitudes
The voice of despair itself
 Couldn't hold a candle to you,
 You make everything around you, even the sky, turn blue;
 And, for the first time, I'm almost ready to
 Admit to myself there's nothing I can do
You've turned inward,
 You're turning me inward, too

Looks like the days of
 Real communication are through
I tried my best to deny it and defy it,
 But that's just how the arrows flew

Well, I could probably force it out of you
 If I decided to stalk,
But I don't like to resort to desperate measures
 Unless that's the only way the truth will walk
 I'd try it, but I'd balk
 I just wish you'd unlock
 Your voice once and talk
 So we could erase all this speculative chalk
What makes you think I can't help you?
 You know I always did before
You might say that just havin' you is enough, baby,
 But I want something more

Well, you're keeping all your feelings stowed away,
 Hidden somewhere in the abyss
You know, I'd love to help you, darlin',
 It doesn't have to be like this
We used to talk to each other,
 But now all you do is snap and hiss
 It doesn't have to be like this —
No, it doesn't have to be like this…

Circa 2001

In My Place

Oh, my lover and I,
 We had a fight
I overstepped my bounds,
 Felt I had to flex my might
Oh, I swear it never would've come to this
 If I'd known I'd be alone this night
Ah, all is gone—all is gone!
 Admit it—take flight!
There's tears in my eyes
 That blind my sight
I can't even remember
 Who was wrong and who was right
I just want to be in
 Your arms again tonight
Oh, but that man over there
 Coverin' his face–
That's not me
 Must be someone in my place

Oh, I got out as fast as I could,
 Left by the backdoor
I can't pretend I didn't see what I saw,
 I just can't hide these tears anymore
I came home early from work,
 Wanted to show you I loved you for sure
Was glad to be home after workin' all those late shifts,
 Bringin' home the bread so we won't be poor
Oh, and to find you and that man
 Rollin' around on the floor—
It just ripped the heart right out of me,
 Tore it right to the core
I just hope you have some carpet burns
 Or at least a back that's sore
Oh, but that man over there
 Suffering without a lone embrace–
That's not me

Must be someone in my place

Oh, these sad waters that rush across my heart,
 They cause me to gall and fret
I don't know what I did this time,
 But it's my fault again, I bet
Oh, I got down on my knees and asked you to come back to me,
 But the words to say I'm sorry, I haven't found yet
The pain just keeps on comin',
 It won't listen when I tell it to quit
I know you always say to just let it go,
 But I just can't forget—I just can't forget
I know you'll try to sway me with your subtle ways, baby,
 But my mind is set
Oh, if it were really that easy,
 I'd have all my goals met—all my goals met
Ah, but that man over there
 With the great sorrow he cannot trace—
That's not me
 Must be someone in my place

Oh, I've walked up and down these dark and haunted streets looking for
love,
 Walked all across this lonesome land
I left my house with my wife's lover's smokin' gun
 Weighin' heavy in my hand
It don't matter how much I think about it,
 I'll never understand
Oh, I was your lover, babe,
 I was your man
There never was no other,
 My life with you was grand
I don't know what happened to our love,
 Don't know why we couldn't make a stand
I guess we just met an impasse
 That dissolved that insoluble band
Oh, but that man over there
 Starin' blindly into space—

That's not me
 Must be someone in my place

Well, I've never been one for head-on collisions,
 Always preferred to take things in stride
I couldn't bear to look evil straight between the eyes,
 Always wanted to run away and hide
Always said I'd get around to it later,
 Thought the direct path was suicide
I always figured I'd burn my bridges when I came back to 'em,
 But you only get one chance on this ride
You have to form a strong band to get through anything,
 One that won't divide
'Cause you just can't make it through this life alone,
You need a wife, or a home, or one you can call your own
 Or you'll fall by the side
Oh, well, well, well—if it didn't all go to hell
 Just like they always said, those who used to chide
And that man over there
 Lookin' for a sign of recognition in some long-forgotten face—
That's me, Lord
 There's no one in my place

2002 or 2003

Angel like You Part I

Well, you may be a sinner,
 And you may be a saint
Some say you good,
 Some say you ain't
I'm kinda in-between —
 I want to decide, but I can't
Sometimes I think you're like that,
Sometimes I think you're like this —
But what's an angel like you
Doin' in a place like this?

I didn't mean to tell you I loved you,
 I'm sorry; I guess I just like to believe myself sometimes
I should know by now that you
 Can get into trouble with those lines
I guess I just have bad timing,
 I need a watch that's Swiss —
But what's an angel like you
 Doin' in a place like this?

I guess my love just wasn't enough
To cure your loneliness,
 But it was the best I could do
You went and sought refuge in religion —
 I told you I couldn't love ya if you ever saw that through;
But I can't fault you for believing in something
 You'd like to think was true,
Sometimes ignorance is bliss —
 And what's an angel like you
Doin' in a place like this?

Well, the place you're livin' in
 Is old and filthy,
It makes it seem like
 Hell ain't a bad place to be
As good as you are, you can't rise above it,
 Not even if you tried

You told me you liked it,
 But I know you lied
Your circle of friends is so small
 That you'd cut it in half if you died,
It just kind of makes me pissed —
 What's an angel like you
Doin' in a place like this?

You're so lonely that you
 Can hardly make it through the day,
So you take a little somethin'
 To make it go away
You fell prey to drink and crank —
You say you'll stop when it gets you over it,
 But you won't
You think it makes it better,
 But it don't
Can't you see you're
 Just crossing yourself off the list? —
What's an angel like you
 Doin' in a place like this?

You used to be so optimistic,
 You could always keep everyone else together;
And I believed in you,
 I thought you'd be that way forever
There was a time when I thought you'd fall apart,
 And that time was never —
But cynicism falls on us all eventually,
 Even you couldn't escape it,
  Though I thought you could —
 But life doesn't even have the decency
  To fall apart like it should
It's just a game of hit and miss —
 What's an angel like you
Doin' in a place like this?

Yes, you believed in a bright future,
 But look where you ended up
You thought you'd be rewarded,

But you just got fucked
Your dreams of Paradise and sun-drenched valleys
Have faded to visions of
Backstreet gutters and trash can alleys,
But you know all that goes away when we kiss—
So what's an angel like you
Doin' in a place like this?

2001

Up to Me Part II

I can't believe you still wanna talk to me,
 Didn't I hurt you bad enough?
I thought we were finally through,
 You always say I remind you of all that bad, bad, bad, bad stuff
Well, I know you just asked me a question,
 But you should know it won't help you — it never does —
'Cause you know I don't wanna talk about anything,
 'Specially whatever was
Well, I'm glad that every time I try to make a move,
 You just start to balk
God knows what I'd do if it were actually carried through,
 You'd just want to talk
Well, I've never been too good at conversation, girl,
 I never know what to say;
But let me just make an observation, girl —
 You never listen anyway
How many more times must I sell my soul to you
 Before I'm allowed to be free?
Guess somebody has to lose their life —
 Must be up to me

Well, that's just what I'm talkin' about, you know —
 Who loves who and who loves best
I guess that's just the way it goes
 Just like all the rest
I admit I have no idea what you just said,
Some conversations are better off dead
What is it about me that fills you with dread?
How do those lies get formed in your head?
 Well, you could've at least left a word of goodbye —
Just a simple, little note
 I know I couldn't please you, but at least I attempted to try,
I guess that's all she wrote
 That cocksucker for President —
Hell, he's got my vote
Oh, why did I ever decide to dote?
Why did I take off my long black coat?

Oh, how did I end up sinking when I tried to float?
How did the razor find my throat?
 I started sinking at about a quarter 'till three —
Guess by now it must be up to me

Well, Oscar Wilde was a modest man,
 He wouldn't give up conversing
He said he could deny himself the pleasure of talking
 But not others the pleasure of listening —
Anything less would be selfish
 It's the same way with you, I guess,
 I never can get a word in edgewise
 Why do you always wear the same short dress?
 I told you it's dangerous to hide in beauty's disguise
Well, in the sway of your hips,
 In the hinge of your thighs —
Your graveyard of love is a permanent fixture
 In my eyes
Let's go dancing tonight, my love,
 You can wear the dress I like so well;
And, after that, I'll go back to the glove —
 What the hell, what the hell
Well, the fixture of your permanent image has blurred your vision,
 Now you're too blind to see
You just don't know where to look anymore —
 Guess it must be up to me

Well, I fought against the bottle
 But had to do it drunk
Our love has fallen apart, babe,
 Just like a piece of junk
Well, maybe some day you'll understand
That "something for nothing" is everyone's plan
 You tried to sneak up and steal my love
Just like an old bloodhound
 The fires of hell carried on the wings of a dove,
Thirty pieces of silver, no money down
 Well, I don't know why
I'm still hangin' around
 I suppose I should've learned,

But I just came back to this town
 Oh, true love ain't that hard to find,
In fact, it's easy to see;
 But I don't know who's gonna take that idea out of your mind—
Guess it must be up to me

Well, I don't know what's gotten into you,
 Why won't you just leave me alone?
I'm tryin' to read a note somebody wrote,
 And you're yappin' on the phone
Now, I told you when we started this thing
 That I must have solitude
So, when I'm in the darkness,
 Why do you intrude?
Well, a writer must live a solitary life,
 That's just the way it goes
Such is the reality of a writer's wife,
 As my wife well knows
Now, I can poison you with my pen,
I can do anything I want except pack it in
 Now, you can leave me outside to rot
 If you wanna do that
 Let me dry out in the sun where it's oh, so hot,
 Let the birds pick me clean but for my hat
Sado-masochistic sexual relations, man,
 They say that's where it's at
Well, your priest may be a child molester,
 But that's no concern of mine
I have my own troubles, baby,
 And, my friend, you have thine;
 Yet I wish somebody'd show me some kind of sign—
Maybe they are, and I just can't see
 Ah, you can cry and you can whine,
 Just keep movin' right along;
 But someone had to write this song—
Guess it was up to me

Well, your eyes don't look into mine anymore,
 At least I don't think
You said you don't have a drinking problem

Unless you don't have a drink
Well, god damn it, you're drivin' me to the brink,
I need some sleep; I haven't had a wink
 Let me get some shuteye
 And just you go off and die
 I'm not gonna scream, I'm not gonna cry,
 All I'm gonna do is sigh
 For, while it's true me and you
 Are like sister and brother,
The decision between sex and celibacy
 Is still six on one hand and half a dozen on the other
Yes, we're blind in one eye, babe,
And can't see out the other —
 That's the reality
Yet someone's gotta chart this maze —
 Guess it must be up to me

2002

Suffocation

Fun has disappeared, boredom calls—
Stuck inside these same four walls
Hopelessness builds while momentum falls
Sometimes I swear I'm not moving at all
 Sitting here cold and lonely,
Can't buy a thrill
 Lots of people around me are moving,
But I'm standing still

 It was you who used to help me out
When I was feeling low
 It was you who always came about
When I just didn't know
 Angels are such a big help when they're with you
But sure make you lonesome when they go

Maybe I'll move to the big city
 Or go back home on the range
I don't have any reason to do it,
 But at least it'd be some kind of change
I just can't admit to myself
 That I haven't done anything exciting in a while
It's a no-win situation,
 Terminal denial

 I know you like I know myself—
Not very well,
 Just like everyone else
We're all strangers
 Where are you when I need you?
I guess the same place I'm always at
  When you need me
 I just don't know what to do,
  I'm not used to being free

I wish I could at least
Claim to be a sinner
 As the four walls start closing in—

But no, I'm not even a bad boy,
 I've just been where I have been
 I hope you like my legacy,
 It's all that's left of me
They tell you that what you do in life
 Is how you're defined,
But it's not what you take with you,
 It's what you leave behind
I'm leaving nothing,
 I hope you have a good time

2001

The Frustrated Man's Begrudging Women Justification
(A Tortured Dialectic)

Four in the morning,
 I'm still not in bed
I got a symphony of destruction
 Blarin' in my head

Coffeepot's dry,
 Cigarettes are all gone
If these pills keep me up a few more hours,
 I might even see the dawn

What is it about Failure
 That always keeps you coming back for more?
I think I'm in love with her,
 The dirty little whore

I'd fuck her,
 But she always fucks me
Then leaves me alone for a little while
 To spread her misery

The damn pain pills don't work,
 I still feel like shit
Pot and booze are jerks,
 You start and can't quit

Ah, but there is one thing
 That always eases the pain,
Lets some sun in my dark life,
 Makes me feel less inane—

Yes, it is your love,
 Why must you withhold it?
Why must you always act so above
 Though I've often told it?

Ah, it seems I'm doomed to be wretched,
 Deprived forever of the one thing that can set me free
Why do you leave me to suffer,
 To wallow in my misery?

I just don't see how it can be justified,
 Sitting alone on your throne
Why do you make me run and hide
 When you still know the times we've known?

I guess you feel the need to keep
 Some sense of superiority —
But, hell, babe, it doesn't take much
 In this broken world to top me

You could be a little less torturous,
 A little more fair
I'm dying of isolation,
 You're breathin' rarefied air

Yes, but sometimes you relent a little,
 Come down from your high, high place —
Make love to me, maybe,
 Or at least let me see your face

I don't know why you do it,
 I don't believe you believe in mercy;
But I won't look a gift horse in the mouth,
 We didn't at first, did we?

Yes, sometimes you throw me a crumb,
 Maybe even a few scraps
It always leaves me feeling numb
 As if I fell into one of your traps

It only increases your power,
 Makes me beg for more
Yes, it increases by the hour,
 You dirty little whore

I keep thinking that maybe
 You'll descend for good —
But what I've seen lately
 Makes me wonder why you would

Yes, why give up omnipotence?
 It's really too much to ask
So I abandon myself to my hands,
 Drown myself in the flask

Ah, but still I long for
 What you hate to give!
You dirty little whore,
 You string me along to live

I try to fight,
 Try to resist —
But I just can't right
 How I feel when I'm kissed

Yes, and you would just turn on me,
 Call me ungrateful —
And it would be just,
 I couldn't blame you for turning hateful

You're nice enough after all,
 Relatively speaking
You give me just enough to stay alive,
 And that's not counting streaking

Ah, but how miserable it is
 When you curl up in your little shell!
I'll never get the hang of this biz,
 Everything just goes to hell

Sometimes I think it's not even worth it,
 Not even worth the trouble —
But then you show what I long to see,
 And I wish I was seein' double

Ah, is there no way out of this maze,
 This abyss of hopeless concupiscence?
Must I always get lost in the haze,
 Is there no resistance? —

Enough; I care not,
 It's the only way I can sustain
It's all I've got,
 I don't even mind the pain

No, I don't even mind the pain,
 I'd put up with it forever
I never asked for you to have brains,
 Never expected you to be clever

What I have is enough,
 Let everything else go to seed
Even when you start playin' rough,
 You're really all I need

So I'll make a church out of your thighs,
 A religion of your breasts,
A Bible of your eyes —
 And leave the rest to guests

But I know you love to see me squirm,
 Love to see me bleed —
But that's okay, baby; I'm your worm,
 I'll make worshipping you my creed

I know it just makes you despise me,
 Shows that I'm weak —
But just give me what I want and I swear
 You won't even see me peek

Ah, what fools we men are!
 Have we no mind?
It seems we never get very far
 Without falling behind

Why can't we disentangle ourselves
 From this trap of bottomless lust?
We put aside our noblest goals and dreams
 For a split-second view of a bust

Surely we're the most wretched creatures,
 Worse than any brute;
And women have it all over us,
 Let's raise an awe-inspired salute

The truth is we're afraid of them,
 Afraid of disapproval
Lysistrata's a recurring nightmare
 That instantly makes our principles move, all

Why not just submit—
 Stop kidding ourselves?
Is there anything for which we really give a shit
 Besides our ornery little elves?

No; let's out with it,
 Admit our Achilles Heel
Ah, what we wouldn't do
 Just to cop a little feel!—

Empires have been lost,
 Fortunes turned down
Ah, at what a cost
 We gladly fling them to the ground!

But it's worth it after all, isn't it?
 What else is there to life?
It's either that our waste our time away
 In unremitting toil and unrewarded strife

So I'll jump just when she says to,
 Hurl myself off that cliff—
And you'll come with me, buddy,
 If you want to remain stiff

Why try to justify?
 It's its own justification
If we ever try to defy,
 It'll be a broken-hearted nation

So let's put all inhibitions aside,
 Forget what we vowed in a moment of weakness
There's no reason to bitch, no reason to chide,
 Let's surrender to our natural meekness

And if it fails to work,
 Fails to be all we thought it'd be—
Well, it's no loss,
 Nothing else would've set us free

Yes, it may be imperfect,
 But it's far above the rest
Try to deny it the next time
 She lets you see that longed-for breast

They give us enough to stay alive, hell,
 And it's really all for the best
If you keep on toein' that line,
 She may even take off her dress

Now, we did our best to resist,
 And we all knew it wouldn't be much
They wouldn't let us feel
 So we learned just to touch

And will it ever end?—Who cares?
 It's good enough for me
Let the loveless stalk in their lairs,
 Only we are truly free

Yes, give us the chains,
 We'll gladly take them
You can have what little remains,
 We'll never break them

No, they are our one salvation,
 The only thing that keeps us keepin' on
Freed of them, without hesitation,
 Our lifelines would be gone

Say whatever you want in protest,
 I'm not gonna listen
It's enough for me to stay alive
 Just to see those sweet lips glisten

And what are we missing, really?
 Of what are we deprived?
Others lose themselves in religion and philosophy,
 And we're happily wived

So let them lose themselves to fame and fortune,
 Glory, and honor, and respect, and pelf
I have all I need right here, babe —
 Just ask yourself

Yes, I have all I need
 Buried deep between your thighs —
Oh, yes, and of course,
 Of course also your eyes

Arguments turn to dust
 When you're in the moment
We have no doubt at the time,
 And who could forget?

So let's stop this pointless hairsplitting
 About what's love and what's lust,
What's fate and what's true —
 What difference does it make to us?

Don't talk to me of morality,
 I know just what I like
Everything you say falls apart
 When she goes on strike

For there's one thing I know
 When it gets down to the bone —
Life's a barren wasteland,
 And I don't want to be alone

And, more than that,
 Without her my heart starts to freeze;
But with her, at least, for something like a second,
 I'm free and my heart is at ease

Yes, I'm free and my heart is at ease

For something like a second...

2009

Yes, we two shall not roam along

(A homolinguistic translation of Byron's
"So, we'll go no more a-roving.")

Yes, we two shall not roam along,
   When it is late and dark,
Even though our love is still strong,
   And the moon still has its spark.

Because our lives outlast joy,
   And bodies outlast our minds,
Our souls we must not destroy,
   Our loves we must not blind.

The dark, which is for our lovers,
   Makes the morning less sublime,
But we shall not roam with others
   Through the moonlit nighttime.

2005

Memories, Sweet Memories

Memories, sweet memories,
  Come flooding back to me
Filling up the empty spaces in my mind
  With images of what used to be
So close they are in time
  And yet so far away
  They may be away from me, in reality,
  But with me they will stay
I wouldn't sell them for anything
  Except to experience them again
When I miss my lovely one,
  I look within

This is life for me now,
  Whatever they may say—
  "Carpe diem, seize the day—"
  I know where my good intentions lay
  They say to live in the here and now,
  To pull out of it somehow—
Well, maybe I'd join a movement
  If there was one I could believe in,
And maybe I'd open up for a minute
  If there was another who could receive in—
But no: she's my past, present, and future,
  There is no one and nothing else
She lives within me,
  Within her lives myself

They say knowing one is going to die the next day
  Clears a man's mind like nothing else—
Ah, but so, too, does that slow death march toward parting
  That separates the heart from the self
Locking hands with her
  As onward the inevitable ends comes rushing
  —This, too, must pass; we all knew it was coming—
Oh, to feel everything and yet to feel nothing!
Oh, yes, I know the Wheel of Fate must keep spinning,

But what's the use in rushing?
Downward I am sinking,
Oh, but forward we are flushing…

But, I still have my memories, sweet memories!
 I'll keep them close to my heart
They are my sweet sanctuary when she is not here,
 They keep us from ever being apart
Ah, but what else can I say,
 What else can I write —
Against the rising of the sun,
 Against the fall of night?
I was wrong, she was right,
 There'll be no salvation here tonight —
But I still have my memories, sweet memories,
Dreams, thoughts, and reveries

Oh, it's that vague suspicion
 That comes rushing up sometimes
That dreadful imposition
 That rises in my mind
Oh, the restless indecision
 Between what is time's and what is mine!
But I still have my memories, sweet memories,
 They would not leave me in a tight spot,
They'll be with me until the end
 Memories, sweet memories — they're all I've got
Until we meet again…

2003 or 2004

Raging against the Machine: Contemporary *Sturm und Drang* Indulgences

By Bradley Parsons

"I know my heart, and have studied mankind; I am not made like any one I have been acquainted with, perhaps like no one in existence; if not better, I at least claim originality"
–Jean-Jacques Rousseau, Confessions

"If a man does not keep pace with his companions, perhaps it is because he hears a different drummer."
–Henry David Thoreau, Walden

"You don't need a weather man
To know which way the wind blows."
"Don't follow leaders."
–Bob Dylan, "Subterranean Homesick Blues"

"The doctrine of hatred must be preached as the counteraction of the doctrine of love when that pules and whines. I shun father and mother nd wife and brother, when my genius calls me. I would write on the lintels of the door-post, Whim. I hope it is somewhat better than whim at last, but we cannot spend the day in explanation."
–Ralph Waldo Emerson, "Self-Reliance"

"They locked up a man
who wanted to rule the world
The fools
They locked up the wrong man"
–Leonard Cohen, "The Wrong Man"

"The ultimate weapon was invented in pre-history. It is a kitchen knife in the hands of a determined man – who is fed up."
–Robert A. Heinlein, "The Future Revisited"

Bradley is a sixteen-year-old "angry young man" exactly like millions of others in America, with one important exception—he has lived all his life in the small town of Big Springs, Nebraska. (No, I had not heard of it, either.) Thus, like his brethren nationwide—nay, the world over—he is mad at the world, convinced it has done him an injustice, and is tired of fate hurling curveballs at him. Like his companions, he looks contempibly on the national political, social, and artistic scenes; unlike them, he also fumes at fate's additional cruel twist—condemning him to waste his prime in a one horse town. He hates it, but his most persuasive arguments to convince his parents to move have failed, and he lacks the bravado to run away. Thus, though he knows he is condemned to live there another two years, he fully plans on moving the very day he ceases to be a minor. Of course, he was beaten up a lot as a kid (being named "Bradley" certainly did not help) and is still made fun of relentlessly. Indeed, he is the stereotypical nerd's very image: taped-up nerd glasses, pocket protector…the whole bit. His peers may well hate him, but he hates them just as much; he kept his anger bottled up for many years, and it began to ferment. He has always had the consolation of knowing he is smarter than them—but this, of course, has never been enough. He is firmly convinced of his terminal uniqueness; he has not found anyone similar enough to call a friend—not that anyone would want to be friends with him. Of course, he is smart enough to see he needs love and has even carefully selected a few prime candidates. Needless to say, these decisions were made on the basis of beauty, not intelligence, as he long ago despaired of ever finding it in his little hole. Still, second-rate or not, he is too shy to ask any brain-dead beauties out, much less for their hand, as he cannot even entertain rejection's bare possibility; the very idea fills him with self-abhorence and misanthropic hate. He would probably have been the next school shooter had he not discovered poetry. Writing is for him primal scream therapy; it lets out all his anger constructively, without harming anyone else, and keeps his conscience clear to boot. He typically writes while listening to the favorite angry young man music of his and other generations—Tool, Rage Against The Machine, The Smiths, and a slew of heavy metal and hard rock artists—and even likes Billy Joel's "Angry Young Man," which describes him pretty accurately, and is not afraid of admitting it. I give a small sampling of his work, but, as one might expect from someone high on angst and energy but low on self-criticism and uncaring of others', it is a fair number of pages. It certainly has many thematic elements with prior poems, but its coming from an angry youth sets it apart in tone and execution. Unlike other writers in this collection, he always writes in first person—even when he does not write in first person.

In St. Augustine and Rousseau's traditions, his slim volume may be called "Confessions of an Angry Young Man." To be sure, his writing is somewhat callow at times but none the worse for it; he shoots straight from hip (and heart), and any editor who tries to remove this from his writing robs it of its one notable quality. His writing is definitely not something for everyone — but may well be everything for someone, especially if that proverbial "someone" is a similarly-inclined but less articulate angry young man.

That Don't Make It Junk
(Ode to Unpublished Obscurity)

If the only excuse for making a useful thing
 Is intensely admiring it,
Why must I suffer the disappointment it brings
 After firing it?
Hell, I know it doesn't sell,
 But who ever said it'd be a slam dunk?
And I guess it's just as well
 'Cause that don't make it junk

These damn blowhards just won't shut up
 Though I've told 'em more than twice
Will they ever see I just don't give a fuck?
 I guess you just can't be nice
I swear I'm gonna mow down the next old asshole
 Who says I'm just a punk
I can't even sell, but they act like I stole
 Though that don't make it junk

Yes, I laughed in his goddamn face
 When he asked my advance's price
I mean, hell, did he really think it'd place?
 And I never asked his advice
I thought it smelled pretty good, though I would,
 But everyone else smelled a skunk
Still, you just gotta do what you should
 'Cause that don't make it junk

I never asked for help from you
 Or anyone else either
Hell, I'm just doin' what I do
 Can't they just give me a breather?
I'd have a throne if I could just be alone,
 Live my life like a monk
I just want to make it on my own
 And that don't make it junk

I put up with it a long, long time

But just can't do it anymore
I was tired of the same old lines,
 Had to show 'em the door
Yes, I put on a robe, had the patience of Job,
 But now I've just lost all spunk
Yet they just keep yappin' at my earlobe
 Though that don't make it junk

I've had just about all I can stand,
 Gonna start kickin' 'em out
I swear if they get in my way one more time, man,
 They ain't gonna be left in doubt
I'm gonna show 'em what I'm made of and that I ain't afraid of
 Lockin' all my old friends in a trunk
It might be a while 'fore I can say I've made love,
 But that don't make it junk

Hell, I can do better by myself
 Than I could ever do with you
Why don't you just tell everyone else—
 Yes, and yourself, too
I have to do it on my own 'cause you can only make it alone
 Even if you hafta do it drunk
I don't even care how much it's grown
 'Cause that don't make it junk

Maybe some day you'll be proven right,
 Maybe some day I'll fail
Then you can rub it in out of spite,
 Refuse to bail me out of jail—
But until then you won't win,
 Not until in a corner I've slunk
And I'm tellin' ya once again
 That even that won't make it junk
No, even that won't make it junk
Even that
Won't make
It
Junk

2009

Requiem

I'm living in a place
 That makes me sick
I don't understand the people here,
 Don't know what makes them tick
They're so shallow it's not worth the effort or gain
I see through them like water down a drain

 Fucking pricks, toss the workers a dime
What God in Heaven told you
 That sports were so sublime?
It may be true
That without you
 We'd be dead,
But that's a better fate than
 Eating this bullshit we're being fed

 To hell with all of you —
This life's a lemon,
 And I want my money back
 Nothing you can say or do
 Can convince me not to
 Walk across the tracks

I'm leaving at the first opportunity,
 Leaving you to drown in your own feces
 As you wallow in self-created misery and disease;
You say it's not your fault,
 I say, "Please"

You think you're so goddamn smart,
 But you don't have a fucking clue
What damage this vain existence
 Is doing to me and you
You can climb higher up in the tree,
 Try to live a better life,
But setting yourself above them
 Doesn't remove you from the strife

LIFE'S TRIUMPH by Bill R. Moore

You can condescend
And try to mend
 The shattered pieces of your broken heart,
 But they'll pick you apart,
You and your shabby little ego,
 Before you can even start

I can hear my heart beating,
 It's racing like a train
I'm bogging myself down with
 The boredom, the loneliness, and the pain
It's finally starting to get to me,
My covered eye can finally see
 I held it inside for so many years,
 But now it's manifesting itself as tears
And I have no shoulder to cry on,
I have no precious bed to lie on

Seems everyone I love
 Is dead, taken, or slipping away
I tell myself I've got to
 Make it on my own some day
And I can, I know I can,
But it's not worth it
 Going through life alone
You've got to have something
 To call your own
Or else you might as well
Just shrivel up in a shell,
Let the world to go hell,
 And stay at home

 And maybe that's what I've done
I've closed myself off to friends and family,
 I keep depriving myself of fun
There's just nothing for me around here
 I keep receiving invitations for which I do not care
If my burden keeps piling up on this monumental scale,
 It'll soon be more than I can bear

It's really such a dull defense,
 Making arrows out of pointed words
My point still won't get across,
 My voice still won't be heard
It won't move me one inch
 Further along in this world,
 All it will do
 Is allow me to
 Have my sorrows temporarily unfurled
I've been blessed, I guess
 With the ability to write words like these
And, for something like a second,
I'll be fine, and my mind
 Will be at ease

It's hard to escape
This hometown rape
 When your family's so deep in it
Being a Black Sheep is no bed of roses
 When they're constantly exposing you to the shit;
But there's no use griping,
 No use throwing a fit
I have a point,
 And they can't see it
Yes, I have a point,
And they can't see it

But I'm sick of pretending,
 I'm tired of trying to explain
I'm looking for the crossroads
 That will derail this train
 Sure, I could stick around for a while,
 But what's the point if you never smile?
The moments of joy captured here
 Are short and bittersweet,
Just temporary respites before
 They knock you back off your feet

 A lot of people find a way out—
 A soulmate or religion

Or some other force to clout;
But I've looked all around for love
And come up empty,
 And I don't need that cold hand to hold
Looks like I'll be walking by myself
 Down this long and winding road

Hell, I should be used to it by now,
This is how it's always been;
And I'd be naïve to expect
Any kind of help around the bend
Every time I thought I'd found a companion,
 Something went wrong
They moved away or died or revealed themselves
 Or ended up singing a different song
That is, if they weren't already
 Away for far too long
I just have to keep moving on,
 Keep moving on
And hoping something will reveal itself
 Before all my opportunities and hopes are gone

Nothing really changes around here,
Surely that, at least, is clear
 We've been hanging around searching for answers
For many a year,
 And what have we found?
The same old fears
Just when hope begins to appear,
When you think discovery is near,
And the limits of ambition become clear,
You wind up with your same old lot, so severe

Punishments are plenty,
 Rewards a motley few
It's the same old sad story,
 It's nothing new
 Don't think you're the only one,
 You're just like the rest of us, son —
Fucked up the ass

The pipe dream has exploded,
Your heart has corroded,
And all is as it was before —
The same grass shack,
The same cold floor
We never really grow,
We just learn to suffer more

I don't think there's any here among us
Who doesn't feel life's a joke
If not, then what is the meaning of this
Perpetual tickle and poke?
It never lets up,
They'll never let go
It just never goes away,
And it only goes to show

They hate you if you're different,
They hate you if you're cool
They don't like you if you're smart,
And they despise a fool
They get a sadistic thrill
From breaking your heart
And the day you're born, my friend,
That's the day it starts

People will always judge you,
Though they don't know you from the wind,
And they're all pretty much the same,
Where one ends another begins;
And you can offer to clean the slate with enemies,
You can offer to start again,
But what you'll find in the end
Is that, no matter what you do,
You just can't win

You can live a life of sin
Or a life of love,
But the verdict is the same
When push comes to shove —

You're fucked
You didn't know whether to run or duck
I did both; I'm still fucked

Amongst the tattered and fragmented
 Remains of this broken-hearted nation,
 I can offer myself but one consolation
I counted up all my blessings
 And came up with only one —
 And now it's gone;
And all I can do about it
 Is lend the shoulder that wasn't there for me
For others to cry on —
 There's no use being lonely
I can help others,
Be their brother
 I've got a philosophy that mends
 And a back that bends
It's not much, but maybe it's something on which
 Someone else can depend

I tried my best; it wasn't much
I tried to act with a velvet touch,
 But I have a tendency to be overwhelmingly blunt;
And I'm just like you,
 I'm on the hunt
So to hell with that bitch
 And her useless, loose, used-up cunt
I've got a love to find,
 I've got issues to bunt

Fuck these pathetic creatures
 And their empty lives
 I've got my demons to exorcise
You may be in control now,
But I promise you, I promise you,
 That you'll fall down from that house on the hill;
And there'll be no more gregarians
 Left for you to kill,
To drag down in your misery,

To swallow your pills—
No more cheap thrills

And I'm tired of running
 From the Men In Black
I'm through making excuses,
 And there's no turning back
It's time to show my cards,
 Time to mount my attack
It's time for me
 To start fucking you back
Fuck you and all you stand for
 I'm getting out now,
I'm closing the door

And don't give me that bullshit
 About you being rich
I'm sick and tired
 Of hearing you bitch
All this rage inside me
 Is bursting out like the seven year itch
 It's time to flick the switch
It's time you died,
 You pathetic and over-inflated bitch
 I'll see you in the ditch
Me with my conversation and hatred,
 You with your useless and outdated switch

Fuck you and your sports,
And your whores, and your junkies,
And your brute reptilian brains,
And your pseudo-Canada;
Fuck you and your drinking buddies,
And your incest, and your unemployment,
And your shoe size IQs,
And your bloody useless propaganda
 I'm gonna enjoy watching you go
 Go ahead and die, asshole

Eventually your spell will be broken

All the losers will move out,
 And there'll be nobody tokin'
You'll die a squirming, miserable death,
 You'll bow down and kneel;
And I'll be laughing my ass off
A million miles away
 In my house on the hill

Circa 2000

Hope against Hope: Some Initial Cautious Optimism Excursions
By Apollon Archelaos

"There is a crack in everything.
That's how the light gets in."
–Leonard Cohen, "Anthem"

"It frightens me, the awful truth of how sweet life can be"
–Bob Dylan, "Up to Me"

"Have you noticed that an angry man can only get so far
Until he reconciles the way he thinks things ought to be
With the way things are"
–Don Henley, "My Thanksgiving"

"Everything in moderation"
–The Delphic Oracle

L ike Mark, Apollon is an aged immigrant. He emigrated from a small Greek city to New York at twenty, full of hope and desire; nearing a long life's end, he is happy to report that most of what he wished to do has actually occurred. He considered himself an optimist when he entered the country, all bright-eyed and fresh, and is proud to say he is still genuinely able to call himself one. That said, he is no Pollyanna; his path to success has been littered with countless roadblocks, disappointments, failures, and regrets that show up in his thought. His optimism is thus always tinged with healthy doses of skepticism, rationality, and more than a hint of well-considered pessimism. Indeed, he has never had illusions about human nature and knows as well as any pessimist the barbaric atrocities of which he and his fellow humans are capable. Simply put, he believes in the possibility of continuing rational progress—but is also keenly aware of our self-destructive potential. Some may call him an "optimistic pessimist," but he prefers "pessimistic optimist"—or simply "realist." Though dark doubts and suspicions sometimes cloud his thought, they never engulf it; he keeps a sincere and genuine sense of hope through it all. Staking out a happy medium, he subscribes to neither original sin nor Rousseau's postulate that society corrupts. Like Clarke, another realistic optimist, he believes we are at our best when continually striving, seeking to better ourselves and forever reach for new, greater frontiers. In his view, humanity ceases the moment we cease to do this; for better or worse, we may be succeeded, but the creature, whatever it may be, will not be us. Apollon hopes this will never occur; he genuinely wants us to survive and prosper and truly believes in our capability. He thus comes down on humanity's side; he will place his bets on it with hope and trust—but always cautiously, and not without worry, as he is fully aware far greater minds have come down with even greater certainty on the other side. He claims no certain knowledge of our final outcome but is willing to wait and hope; unlike most, he looks forward to the eventual meeting between our progressive impulses and self-destructive inclinations with head held high and his thought coming down strongly on optimism's side.

The World I Know

Some people can create love
 From nothing at all,
Some can merely walk into a room
 And make shadows fall
Lots of people know where they've been,
 And a few can even tell you where they want to go —
 But uncertainty is the world I know

Some people have room for you
 In their hearts,
Some can ease your pain
 Before trouble even starts
A lot of people are no good —
 No, but some are
Some may say most of them,
 But I wouldn't go so far
Still, it's nice to believe
There's some help you can receive
 If you know the right place to go —
 And this is the world I know

You know, I never did quite understand you,
Why you do the crazy things you do
 I suppose you do it for love, or maybe money,
 Whatever your reason, it's pretty damn funny —
But don't worry; I won't let my true feelings show
 After all, you can't open your heart to others
In the world I know

I used to think the world was flat,
 Used to spit on the silver platter
I always had opinions
 But used to think they didn't matter
Most people don't act kind toward you —
No, but some do,
 And I hope I can find it in my heart
To be one of the select few —

And I still consider myself lucky
That I know one to be you,
And it only goes to show
That it's a great place, the world I know

It was a dark day, a bright day,
The sky was overcast with me and you
There was a choice between sin and salvation,
And the most trouble was being caused by those who
Could not choose between the two
There was good in the air,
Evil in the sky,
And a murderous look in the savior's eye
It doesn't make any sense — oh, no,
But it's the world I know

I sat hand-in-hand with my lover
In some hellfire pit,
And I remembered my friends who died from fame
And those who died from lack of it
It was a warm day in hell,
And then it began to snow —
Just another day in the world I know

A world of contradictions,
Smoke and mirrors
Filled with your highest hopes
And greatest terrors —
It's okay, my love; don't be scared
Of this, the final day
It's just that God's coming back to repair
All the mistakes He made
Come on — let's take a walk in the park
And make a brilliant stroll
Through this kingdom of the dark —
I'll lead, you can follow,
Let's explore the world I know

Some say there are paths so dark
That there love fears to go,

But you showed me even a heart as black as mine
 Can find solace in the world I know—
And that's why it hurt me so much
 The day you died
 I cried—oh, God, how I cried
  It was like a light had been
Switched off inside me,
  And shadows fell prey on me again
Oh, Lord, what did I do to deserve this?
  Oh, I know I sinned, I sinned,
But this is just too much,
  It feels like the end;
And I'll never forget the open casket
 And the last glimpse of you—
The flowers on your coffin
 Were red, white, and blue

   And this is the world I know

2001

Family Ties

Part I: Son

I never got on well with my father,
 He used to beat me when I was a kid,
 I try to forget all the things he did
Yeah, our bond was never close,
In fact, our relationship was quite morose
 "Like father, like son" — I certainly hoped not,
 I'd rather have been shot

But then the day came when everything changed —
 My father had cancer and was in the hospital on his deathbed
It felt it was my responsibility to visit him
 Before he was dead
My mother died long ago,
And I was their only child —
 It was a job I could not shed;
So I approached my father's room
 With a sense of impending dread

When I walked inside,
 I was shocked by the sight —
And I could not hold back my tears,
 Not with all my might —
He looked bad, worse than he ever had

 So I took his hand and tried to console him,
 I knew his chances were slim —
If, indeed, he had any at all —
 But I knew I should do all I could
Because I did not want to see him fall

 What proceeded was nothing less than a miracle,
 We patched up our differences in full
He apologized to me, and I to him,
 We made up for lost time

It's amazing how impending death
 Can bring people together —
I felt as if I'd found the father
I thought I'd lost forever

 Yes, we made up for lost time,
 And it was all sublime —
But I woke up the next morning
 And found out my father was dead
I felt as if an arrow
 Had been shot through my head

But, after my sorrow had passed,
I realized the two of us had bonded at last
 My father was dead, and I had cried,
But at least we'd make up our differences
 Before he died

Part II: Father
My son, I see you again at last,
I feel my life is going fast —
 But we can make up for lost time,
For what happened in our old lives
 Before I lose mine

I never knew how to treat you,
 I should apologize
I regret that I beat you,
 And I'm sorry for all the lies
I was a sad, confused man,
And you felt the wrath of my hand —
 But I hope I can make it up to you
Because I am a changed man

Thank God it went well,
 I am finally free
I can see so clearly now
 What I never before could see
Maybe if I'd seen before,
 Your childhood would not have been so tough,

But you are my son, and that is enough

I can rest peacefully now,
 Wherever I may go
 Because now I know
What I had always hoped,
And it has helped me cope;
 And now you know it, too
Because I heard you say,
Before I faded away,
 "I love you"

2000 or 2001

Equilibrium (Looking Back)

There were times in my life
 When I was going insane
I couldn't enjoy life
 Because of all the aches and pains—
And there were, oh, so many questions,
I wanted answers
 So many things I had to know,
 So many tears and fears,
 So many wasted years—
 Where did they all go?

I didn't understand why
All the kids at school picked on me,
I didn't understand why
All their rules never made sense to me,
I didn't understand why
My parents beat the shit out of me,
I didn't understand why
No girls ever hit on me,
I didn't understand why
No crowds ever formed around me,
I didn't understand why
The gods always frowned on me

But then, later in life, I seemed to find my niche,
 I was doing all right—
I had a job, money, a car,
 And a wife to sleep with at night
It seemed the Gods of Happiness
 Finally had me in their sights

And all those bullies,
 I guess they went to hell
And all those rules,
 They were broken in the end
And my parents,
 They went to jail

And all those girls,
  Why, they're for others with money to spend
And all those crowds,
  Well, they make an excellent group at the coffee shop
And all those gods,
  Well, it seems their days of prejudice have stopped

There were times in my life
  When I was going insane
I couldn't enjoy life
  Because of all the aches and pains —
And there were, oh, so many questions,
I wanted answers
  So many things I had to know,
  So many tears and fears,
  So many wasted years —
   Where did they all go?

All the questions, all the questions,
They're all behind me now,
  For, as my death draws near,
  It all becomes clear
  I've lost the pain and fear
That resentment brings —
I understand everything

2000 or 2001

Clearing out My Closet

*"Did I request thee, Maker, from my clay
To mould me man? Did I solicit thee
From darkness to promote me?"*
– *John Milton*, Paradise Lost

"Judge not, that ye be not judged."
–Matthew 7:1

*"Here's to the few who forgive what you do,
and the fewer who don't even care!"*
–Leonard Cohen, "The Night Comes On"

*"When the friend shows his inmost heart to his friend; the lover to his best-beloved;
when man does not vainly shrink from the eye of his Creator, loathsomely treasur-
ing up the secret of his sin; then deem me a monster, for the symbol beneath which I
have lived, and die! I look around me, and lo! on very visage a black veil!"*
–Nathaniel Hawthorne, "The Minister's Black Veil"

*"Ashes and diamond
Foe and friend
We were all equal in the end"*
–Roger Waters, Pink Floyd's "Two Suns in the Sunset"

Well, I'm clearing out my closet
Now that Armageddon's imminent
I'm dragging out all my skeletons,
Making their display permanent
God knows we all have enough regrets
Hidden away in this sorrowful life
We're all held down by disappointment,
Bitterness, anger, failure, and strife

I'm not keeping any dirty secrets now,
They're on display for the world to see
I have no fear of being judged,
I'll leave them up permanently –

After all, that won't be much longer,
 For the end is at hand,
And I highly doubt mine are much worse
 Than any other poor bastard's in this land

Yes, I'm clearing out my closet,
 Giving it a clean sweep
There won't be anything left to say,
 Not even a peep
Aborted plans, shattered plans, forgotten plans —
 They'll all be on display
Some may find them shocking, some passé,
 But there they will lay

I'll put my skeletons up against anyone's,
 No one's gonna beat 'em
You may be able to equal 'em, buddy,
 But you ain't gonna defeat 'em
We all hide away our ugly sins
 'Neath a black veil,
But the time has come to reveal them,
 They were getting stale

We shall all wear a scarlet letter,
 Though the letters may not be the same
We can kid ourselves that they're badges of honor,
 But they signify long-buried pain
It won't be easy to show the world
 What we've long been trying to hide,
But at least we might be able to breathe easier
 When they're finally outside

I won't judge you, buddy,
 If you won't judge me
I don't see how anyone has the right,
 I think it's time for some mercy
You may be shocked or appalled
 By what you see shining on someone else's breast,
But please don't try to kid anyone
 By claiming your shit smells best

No, we're all in this together,
 We bear the common human mark of shame
We've been dividing ourselves so long,
 But it's time to recognize the universal stain
Rise above your prejudice and xenophobia
 And accept the depravity of your fellow man
It may be hard, but at least you'll have the comfort
 Of finally knowing you're not the only sinner in the land

Of course it's easy to look for someone to blame,
 To search for a reason for our fallen state —
But, hell, man, what's done is done,
 At least now we can start with a clean slate
We'll be bearing marks
 As we trot off into The Land of Nod,
But at least we'll be there together
 Under the ever-watchful eyes of judgmental God

We once could hide our mistakes
 So very easily —
We could deny or shrug our shoulders and say,
 "Everything I've done is between God and me" —
But those days are long gone,
 For the end is drawing near
Soon, my friend, it won't be long,
 We'll all be in the clear

It's tempting to decry this development,
 To curse the times we live in —
But I think we can all agree it'll be a relief,
 'Cause it's hard carrying secret sin
We must find the courage to show ourselves,
 Must not back down or yield
If we can find this in our black hearts,
 All will be revealed…

Oh, Creator, what have you done to me,
Why have you exposed me so?
I was brought into this world without permission,

LIFE'S TRIUMPH by Bill R. Moore

You and my parents started this show
I had nothing to do with it,
Didn't put myself in this rat race —
Extenuating circumstance to be mentioned on Judgment Day:
We never asked to be born in the first place

2007

Book III:
The Best Medicine: Light Verse

by Bill R. Moore

Preface

Since I have long known at least as well as anyone that most of my poems, especially published ones, tend toward the dark, I thought it high time to carry out my long-held plan of publishing a light verse book. I do so not because I dread the arguably enviable Doom and Gloom title, though this book may go some way toward correcting any misconceptions and/or presumptions about me or my poetry, as these poems were written contemporaneously with already published ones. The essentially true old saw about how you don't get rich peddling gloom is also not my motive. I do it simply because I find the poems not unworthy of publication, at least in this self-consciously limited way. Several could have easily been in prior books; I excluded them not because of quality but for fear of bathos. *Reflections in Broken Glass* indeed originally had a light verse section, but I cut it for this reason and also because I was already looking forward to a collection like this, where I thought the poems might work better. I sincerely hope they stand on their own here. And what better way to start than with an ode to the sterling piece of modern technology on which all my books have unfortunately been written...

Ode to Microsoft Word

"…a business where if something works, it's obsolete."
–Arthur C. Clarke in regard to computer programming, 2010: Odyssey Two

Now I know how Sisyphus felt
When he vainly pushed his stone
Ah, how time never seems to melt
When a vast task you must work alone!

But no; it would be far easier to work alone
Than to rely on these cursed machines
Just as we settle into our comfort zones,
They fuck everything up behind the scenes

One step forward, two steps back—
That's what they make me do
I can't even stay on track
Or hope to move on to something new

Clarke said that, if his word processor broke down,
He'd go back to pen and paper
Hell, that sounds like the only game in town,
I think I'll take up the caper

Even the wretched typewriter, with all its faults,
Was nothing beside this
So many unasked for exits and halts,
So little completed bliss!

How many times can "saved" not be saved?
How many times can it fail to open?
Ah, if only its many failures could be shaved
We wouldn't have to be always mopin'

It costs more time than it saves us,
I long ago came to that conclusion
It makes us rave and cuss,
Broken by constant confusion

How many more errors must be unresolved?
Oh, Lord, how much more must we suffer?
If only these problems could be solved,
If only we could have some kind of buffer…

But no; just as someone goes to type the solution's plan,
It closes before they can save;
And even if it hadn't, I'm tellin' ya, man,
It wouldn't have opened before they fell in the grave

So we trudge on, having little choice,
Suffering from the ignored wreckage of Gates' vanity
We feel compelled to type out our inner voice,
But he clicked the "X" on our sanity

Sometimes I just want to uninstall this trash,
Flush it down the virtual drain
Its release was far too brash,
Its promotion far too vain

If only there were a "Help" feature for going insane,
A refund for all your wasted time,
A way to free yourself from the horrid chain,
A fruit dangling from the virtual vine—

But no; we push the stone nearly all the way uphill,
And it crashes down on us with renewed force
It toys and fucks with us still,
Makes us long for another course

But I think I finally found a solution,
A way to close the horrible door
The next time it curses you with its pollution,
Hit those magic keys — ALT-F4!

Yes, many have suffered throughout history,
Many have felt spat on and pissed;
But that we're hit hardest is no mystery,
Even the patience of Jobs couldn't compare to this

We've been living in a barren orchard,
But now it's time to leave
Yes, we suffered many a torture,
But no one's been this glad for an Apple since Eve

2009

Hello, Darkness
(A Rational Conversation with Myself)

Hello, darkness, my old friend,
 It's nice to see you once again
You know, you're the only one
 That's always been there for me in the end
Well, listen up—hear me out, poke out those ears,
 I've got another message to send
 I thought maybe you were wonderin'
  How I was getting along
Just thought you might like to know—
  Maybe I'm wrong
Just a little bit of news I'd like to share,
Thought you might care...

 Well, I just don't know what to do anymore,
  Don't know what there is to live for
Yeah, I thought I could make it, always thought I could shake it,
  But I just can't do it no more
 All life's virtues I've tended to ignore,
  Just don't know what's in store
Yeah, I once thought I could take the world by the balls—
  Lord, I think I've got 'em
You'll find out when you're on the top, yeah—
  Well, you're on the bottom
Just when you think you've got the very last problem solved,
 They throw another wolf at your door
You find out when you scale the ladders of life
 That one man's ceiling is just another man's floor

Yeah, what's good for one man
 May not be good for two
What's good for me, man,
 May not be good for you
I offer up my heart for salvation,
 You just break it in half
One man's theology
 Is just another man's belly laugh

LIFE'S TRIUMPH by Bill R. Moore

Out of all the crimes humanity has legislated out of nothing,
 Blasphemy is the most unbelievable
That you can kill a man today and repent tomorrow —
 That, my friends, is unforgettable
Go ahead and raise your expectations,
 Destiny is inflatable

Well, I talked to my ex-wife last night —
 "How are ya doin' — are ya feelin' all right?"
She said, "Well, I've seen better days,
 Just gettin' tired of the fight —
 But I know he'll come along and save me, some day: Mr. Right,
  He'll come along and rescue me from my limb"
And her husband just looked at her and said,
 "Man, you're in for some kind of plight
 I can't believe you're still lookin' for him"
Babe, nothin' satisfies you,
What the hell am I supposed to do?
Just don't know if I can make it through
 Oh, but you say I can make it —
Yeah, you can make it, too

I just don't understand your cautious optimism, babe,
 Kind of leaves me reelin' on the floor
 Oh, please, God, take that horrible rod away,
 I just can't take it anymore;
  But you say we've got to pay our way, not play our way,
We just can't go around tripping on our own feces —
Spare the rod, and you spoil the species
 Well, you can count your fingers, you can count your toes,
 Whatever you do, wherever you go —
 It doesn't matter which way the river flows
 Concupiscence is the source of our woes
 I don't know why the wind blows,
 Don't know why God never shows
 The only thing I know is I've got to go —
 Watch out for that painted rose

So I'm telling you right now before this goes any further —
I don't know a goddamn thing about your mother

I wasn't around when you were born,
The man in front of me would've sworn
What were the idiot's next-to-last words?
"Watch this" His last words? "Oops"
Well, I've been abused by dignity; it's really quite absurd
Have you heard?
God has spoken the Word
Save you from the lame duck
You were last in line?
Guess you're out of luck
Sorry you got fucked
Yes — how life sucks

But, with the wind at my heels at the break of day,
And with my back to the right with the sun to light the way —
I know how it feels to fight the way
Don't forget about me, baby,
I'll be back another day
I promise you this time I'll show you how to play chess,
I'll show you all the rest...
I'll even help you dress
Ah, but, if the arrow is sharp, and the point is slick —
Then, yes, babe — you can still suck my dick
God bless

2001 or 2002

The Day after the World Didn't End

Ever nearer the hour lurches —
The paranoid and unsure, non-perishables equipped,
 Cower in cellars, the fools in churches;
And the smart have their cards laid,
Their minds made —
 They're not going very far,
 They're staying right where they are

And, as the Y2K toasters fly off the shelves
That, days later, will cause their buyers to laugh at themselves,
 The hour looms nearer,
 And the truth becomes clearer
It's blindingly obvious as the suspense ends,
And the search for the source of the bullshit begins —
 Such an obvious case,
 Not that it wasn't in the first place

But there's one thing I don't understand
About all this paranoid bullshit in the land —
 For, even now, as the bug fades away,
And the New Year, not century or millennium,
 Shines brightly here in the present, clear as day,
Some still insist it happened or will next year —
Maybe one too many New Year's Eve beers?

Yeah, it's one thing to say this now,
 But I said it years ago —
And why people didn't believe me
Or others with far more credibility,
 I'll never know

I've had my fair share of failures in this land,
After all I'm only human —
But I've decided to bask in my triumph,
 Just this one time, kid
I mean, I don't want to say, "I told you so,"
 But I did

And, if you fell into their trap,
 Well, too bad, sucker
 I told you—I told you, motherfucker

2000

That's Just the Way It Goes

Well, I asked my girlfriend
 If I could start seein' other women again
She said, "What the hell are you askin' me for?
 You're a single man
 You're a single man"

That's just the way it goes, yeah
 Life stops, time flows
That's just the way it goes, yeah
 The wind blows

My wife said I never listen to her…
 At least that's what I think I heard her say
 I said, "That's not true; I hear you say you want a lay,
 At least once a day,
 At least once a day"

That's just the way it goes, yeah
 Life's real, time's just a pose
That's just the way it goes, yeah
 It shows

Well, I know your head, it aches,
And your heart, it breaks—
But there's only so much they're able to take,
 There's only so much, my friend,
They're able to take

That's just the way it goes, yeah
 Nobody knows
That's just the way it goes, yeah
 Too low for zero

 Julius and Ethel Rosenberg
With their son who wasn't even old enough to vote
Went out to meet Joan of Arc and other martyrs of note
They're all goin' to heaven in a little rowboat,

They're all goin' to heaven in a little rowboat

That's just the way it goes, yeah
 Time stops, life flows
That's just the way it goes, yeah
 I suppose

I told my lover I wanted her and no other —
 But, really, must she so often shove?
She just said back to me, unmercifully,
 "I'm gettin' tired of your Utopian view of love,
 I'm gettin' tired of your Utopian view of love"

That's just the way it goes, yeah
 Time freezes, life froze
That's just the way it goes, yeah
 In this episode

I swear on my black heart, boys,
 I've got just a little bit of soul
You sold yours at the crossroads, Mama,
 I'm keepin' a little bit of mine on hand to control,
 Keepin' a little bit of mine on hand to control

That's just the way it goes, yeah
 Life freezes, time froze
That's just the way it goes, yeah
 On this road

How are you doin', Mama?
 I heard times are hard down low
Well, I'm here sittin' on top of the world
 Fightin' back tears I can't control,
 Fightin' back tears I can't control

That's just the way it goes, yeah
 Time's movin', life just blows
That's just the way it goes, yeah
 Who the hell knows?

Well, there's forty-two broken hearts litterin' the streets
 And sixty-six souls gone corrupt
You just stand there lookin' at 'em, darlin',
 But it's my job to start shovelin' 'em up,
 Yes, it's my job to start shovelin' 'em up

That's just the way it goes, yeah
 Life's movin', time just blows
That's just the way it goes, yeah
 You better watch your toes

I still slay dragons with my pen,
 But the ink don't flow like it once did
You ask me if I'm serious,
 But I swear I'm just tryin' to kid
 Hell, I swear I'm just tryin' to kid

That's just the way it goes, yeah
 Time and life are so low
That's just the way that it goes, yeah
 Time to wrap up the show

So many people askin' me questions,
 They think I run the show
It's always been my nature to take chances,
 But I have to admit I don't know,
 Yes, I have to admit I don't know

That's just the way it goes, yeah
 Life and time are so low
That's just the way it goes, yeah
 Everybody knows

2001

Polygraph Graph

Well, I've lied before—
 Yes, it's true
I've lied about little things
 And big things, too
  I've lied to get by,
  I've lied so I didn't have to try,
  I've lied for the sake of a lie
  And a little white lie
Well, I've lied to appear false,
 And I've lied to be true;
But, please understand me,
 I've never lied to you

 I told you I lied to him
I lied to her, yes,
 And I lied to them
  I've lied my way out of tight places,
  Out of fenced-in corners and left no traces
  I've lied to many names and many faces
They think they hold the Joker, yeah,
 But I hold the aces;
But don't listen to them when they say
 I've been lyin' to you, too
 Listen, darlin'—I swear it isn't true
 Please believe me—I've never lied to you

These people don't believe me,
 But they're determined to try
They don't even act like they think it's true,
 Even after I've told them why
I know you don't want to believe them, darlin',
 Please just look me in the eye
I swear I'm not lying to you; just look at me—
 Could I ever tell you a lie?
There's so many other things
 I wish I hadn't decided to do,
 But I've never lied to you

Yes, it's true
I swore to you; we made a pact
I'd never lie to you, and that's a fact
  There's so many people who would try an' deceive me,
 But I couldn't lie to you — if only you knew
  You're just gonna hafta believe me

2001

Ice Cold Blues

I'm gonna walk into the bar, see if my friends are still there
Yes, I'm gonna walk into the bar, see if my friends are still there
I hope I see someone I know; I just can't stand this lonesome air

Yeah, but it's too loud in there; I'm gonna go outside where I can think
I said it's just too loud in there; I'm gonna go outside where I can think
I'm gonna put a bar in my car so I can drive myself to drink

I'm tired of all this bickering, tired of all this fighting
Yes, I'm tired of all this bickering; I'm tired of all this fighting
If the world is a stage, I want better lighting

All my friends at the old school, they're an illusion to me now
Said all my friends at the old school, they're an illusion to me now
We used to be close, but they've become unrecognizable somehow

I think I'm gonna go see a movie, learn a little about life
I think I'm gonna go see a movie, yeah, maybe learn a thing or two about
    life
But I won't be able to recognize any of it 'less it deals with strife

I'm walkin' through these streets alone; my feet are about to freeze
Yeah, I'm walkin' through these streets alone; my feet are about to freeze
It's so cold and lonely ice is formin' 'round my knees

Let's go for a ride, babe; I don't have to take you very far
Oh, let's go for a ride, babe; I don't have to take you very far
You shouldn't have told your Mother I don't have no car

I wanna get out of here; I've had enough of these
I said I wanna get out of here, 'cause I've had enough of these
But I ain't goin' nowhere; one of my girlfriends ran off with the keys

I've been good to you for a long time now, been good to you for years and
    years
I've been good to you for a long time now, been good to you for years and
    years

But you've been cold to me so long I'm cryin' icicles 'stead of tears

I've seen relationships; people rush into 'em way too fast
Yes, I've seen relationships; people rush into 'em way too fast
But you, you were my first love, and you will be my last

I've learned my lesson; I'm not screwin' up anymore
I said I've learned my lesson; yeah, I'm not screwin' up anymore
Before I get a chance to make another mistake, I'm gonna walk right out the
    door

2001

At Least I Got Laid

Well, it's rainin' outside,
 And there's bills to be paid
I feel like I've already died,
 But at least I got laid

Well, my dog just died today,
 And my best friend got flayed
Ain't got nothin' good to say,
 But at least I got laid

Well, I coulda been a star athlete, but I got hurt,
 An' it's been years since I played
My wife's stopped letting me go up her skirt,
 But at least I got laid

Well, I gambled away all my money,
 Lord, all the money I've ever made
I wasted my life savings, an' it ain't funny,
 But at least I got laid

Well, I'm fat, an' old, an' ugly, an' always sore,
 And the little hair I have left has grayed
My dick don't even work anymore,
 But at least I got laid

Well, my parents up an' left me,
 And my wife's an old maid
All my friends have bereft me,
 But at least I got laid

Well, I spent all my retirement on drugs,
 All my good investments have strayed
My daughter was just gang-raped by thugs,
 But at least I got laid

Well, I just got fired from my job,
 An' I get more depressed each time I'm weighed

LIFE'S TRIUMPH by Bill R. Moore

I'm a fat an' lazy old slob,
 But at least I got laid

Well, I scare off both young an' old,
 Even cannibals won't have me filleted
On top of everything else, I just caught a cold,
 But at least I got laid

Well, I left my home because everyone hated me,
 But I really wish I'd stayed
I can't even say the ugly girls dated me,
 But at least I got laid

Well, I ignored all the good advice I was given,
 Yes, I did not do as I was bade
It's a shitty life I've been livin',
 But at least I got laid

No one on earth will assist me,
 An' I can't even get heavenly aid
Everyone just seems to resist me,
 But at least I got laid

Well, my looks are already gone,
 And now my memory's starting to fade
I can't turn anyone on,
 But at least I got laid

Well, I ain't no diamond or pearl,
 I ain't even cheap, imitation jade
I'd get turned down by the world's ugliest girl,
 But at least I got laid

Well, I lost my winter house to a hurricane
 And my summer house to an air raid
Now I'm livin' in a homeless shelter that's small and plain,
 But at least I got laid

Well, I'm bein' hunted by a hitman,
 An' my family's been marked for death by Richard Slade

I can't find a job for shit, man,
 But at least I got laid

Well, my hand was shot off by a gun
 An' the other hacked off by a blade
Gettin' mutilated ain't no fun,
 But at least I got laid

I don't care who you are,
 If you'd switch places with me, I'd trade
Compared to me, anyone's a star,
 But at least I got laid

Well, my homeland's being destroyed,
 And now someone else is threatenin' to invade
No defensive forces have been deployed,
 But at least I got laid

I'm startin' to drown, and I can't swim —
 Hell, man, I can't even wade
There was only one life preserver, and they gave it to him,
 But at least I got laid

Well, even Jesus won't have me forgiven,
 And my wife hates me 'cause she says she calls a spade a spade
Yes, it's a worthless life I'm livin',
 But at least I got laid

There aren't no more words to rhyme,
 But that's all right; this song's already been okayed
The next time you think you've hit rock bottom, just say to yourself, "I'm
 Not as bad off as I seem; at least I got laid."

2007

An Open Letter to Cleopatra's New Lover

Let me tell you something, boy—
 You're in for one hell of a shock
I never really liked you much anyway;
 But I don't like to see anyone go off half-cocked
  That girl can ruin you like nobody else can,
She'll make you shrivel up in a shell and die
  And forget you were ever a man
She'll sweep you off your feet, all right,
  But then you won't know where to stand

I always thought you were pretty useless,
 I've seen few more pathetic specimens in my day;
And I'd almost like to see you suffer,
 But it saddens me to see any man being used in this way
I don't like to say, "I told you so,"
 But I did
You'll realize just how right I was
 The first time you see her flip her lid
When you start to squirm like a little worm,
Don't forget I warned you about the germ

Men to her are like punching bags,
She reduces them to a bloody pulp
 With her bitching hag
So many men have fallen prey to her way,
 It's been years since she was on the rag
Men are so weak—
Their legs are reduced to splinters
 Every time they hear her speak
Isn't it sad—isn't it sad?
It sure does make a long time man feel bad
She'll tell you you're the best she's ever had,
But you're really just another nad

 Well, you can cheat it, you can beat it,
 Do anything but defeat it
  You can slap on any name

You can romanticize it, you can fantasize it,
 Do anything but analyze it
Just look at all the poor dogs
 Being dragged down in the game
 I'm telling you, man, you just can't beat it
 I don't blame you for thinking you can seed it,
But don't come around when you die, askin' for an alibi
I'll just look you in the eye
 As you plead it

Her charms are many,
 Her vices few,
But it doesn't mean they're any less harmful
 Just because they can't be seen by you
I can't blame you for falling into her plan—
Hell, I did the same thing, man
I just don't want to see it happen again
A man's got to do what he can
For another man

She'd be abused if she weren't so used—
Lots of men brag about
 What they've sent up her sleeve;
But saying you've been with her
 Is about like saying you breathe
Don't offer her your innocence,
She lost hers long ago
 You think you can trust her,
 But you won't even have enough strength left to muster
  After she's done with your soul
  Trust me—I know
You'll swear to yourself you love her
 Before she even starts;
But before long you'll realize you're wrong,
 She'll make a piñata out of your heart

I know there's nothing I can say or do
 To stray you from your chosen path
I was just as blind as you
 Until she started wreaking her wrath

No one will believe bad news
Or unfortunate reviews
When they come from someone else
Sooner or later,
Every man's gotta find out for himself
You'll just have to learn, like we all do
If you only knew what you're getting into…

2001

Big Shot

Mouths come open in disbelief
 Every time, or so it seems,
 When you drive up in your limousines,
  And then you step out of the car
With your $625 boots
And your fancy suits—
 Who the hell do you think you are?

Woman around your arm
 That you hired for the day,
  And you wouldn't have it any other way,
Because they all think she's for real,
That you get to feel—
 But you wouldn't be doing it for the money,
 Now would you, honey?

 You're half the man you used to be,
A mere shadow of your former self—
 Can't you see?
Your life's one big joke—
 How can you live such a lie?
"I don't; the money does,"
 You say with a sigh,
 "I'm just a regular guy"

No, you're not,
You're a big shot,
 A slave to your ego,
 Who doesn't know when to let go,
Doesn't know when to quit
All you know for sure is that you're "it,"
 Always have been—
 You always win

Enough with this charade—
I can barely even see you through all that masquerade
 Deep down, you're really no different, despite her—

You're the same asshole you always were

2000 or prior

Red Light District

Just wait; it's great—
 You're bored? Well, no more
Just go into the dark alleyway
 And walk through the door,
 I guarantee you'll meet a whore
So come on, boys; let's go wallow in sin!
 Only fifty-five bucks a fuck
And even less if you let yourself in

Don't say you can't do it
 Because you know you can
No longer do you have
 To rely on your own hand
They get laid, they get paid,
 They don't care what you look like
Why, they'd fuck anyone, you know
If they had the dough—
 Even a little tyke

You get what you pay for
 And, if you're rich,
Well, you've got a wild night in store;
And even if not,
 Why, you can still get by
The less money, the less skin,
 But, either way you try,
The situation's win-win

And, after you've given head,
Why, we'll forget you were ever in her bed
Here, where love's just a job, and nothing is said
 Hot damn, boys!
I think the lights are turning red

2000 or 2001

It's Not about the Money

The athlete signs the contract
 And smiles at his newly gained honey
He looks at the camera and smiles
 And says, "It's not about the money"

And the thief in the police van
Reluctantly hands over the diamonds in his hand,
 The cops all are laughing, but he doesn't see what's so funny
 Why can't they understand when he tells 'em it's not about the money?

 The businessman in his mohair suit
Picks up his cell phone and learns
 He just sold some real estate in Beirut
He puts up his feet on the sand castle in front of him
 And relaxes on the beach, so sunny
He looks out from the tip of his cap and tells the disappointed
 Salvation Army pusher next to him it's not about the money

And the scholar turned drug dealer
 Lights up a joint and looks out at the great divide
"Life's lookin' pretty good to me,"
 He says to the hooker by his side
"I just sold another five pounds of weed
To this guy on Riverside"
She smiles at him, and he says,
 "I know I'm supposed to pay you, honey,
 But we both know this isn't about the money"

2000 or 2001

522

My Favorite Mistake

Ah, yes, I remember you well,
 You ended my libido's stoicism
I don't know why I kept coming back to you,
 I guess it was just a kind of schism
Even at the end, I still cowered up to you
 In an orgy of masochism —
  I guess I didn't know where else to go
You think I would've stopped after
 My heart began to break — but no
You're my favorite mistake

You promised me love, you promised me sex,
But then you tossed me aside like last month's check —
And now you're gone and I'm up to my neck
 In missed opportunities —
 Baby, you got me so blind I can't see
We were on top of the world,
 But now it's more like I'm drowning in the lake —
 And you're my favorite mistake

That first night I saw you,
 I acted so kind
I thought I could win you over
 But was foolish enough to stand in line
You said, "I've seen better looking things
Than you in a toilet bowl,
 You ain't no friend of mine"
So I took my broken heart to the other end of the table
And watched your breasts rise and fall
Underneath that little disguise you hide them behind —
 Shake, shake, shake
 You're my favorite mistake

They say a poor man is he who
 Has all his love in vain —
But me, I kind of liked
 Being addicted to that same old pain

I knew I should quit
 But just couldn't refrain—
And I'd still run like a puppy dog
 If you happened to call my name
"Good boy, stay, stay; give, but never take"
I guess you're still my favorite mistake

2001

Rainy Day Women

Well, I'm sad and I'm lonely,
 I think I'm in need of a fix
Gotta find a cure for the rattlesnake shake,
 Gotta find a way to get my kicks
Yeah, I could go to a brothel,
 But, you know, that's not my style
You know I'd much rather
 Crash at your place for a while
Hell, I want to get laid
 Before I go senile
I'm just across the street from my lover
 But might as well be a million miles
I think maybe it's time
 To bust out the rainy day women for a while

I could watch a movie, yeah,
 But, you know, that doesn't quite get it done
It's kind of a nice overture,
 But there are more exciting ways to have your fun
I just don't know what to do
When I'm around a beauty,
 I usually turn and run
My words just won't come out right
 Though I know every phrase under the sun
Maybe I'm a spineless bastard,
 But I know my limit,
And I think I'm gonna take out
 Those rainy day women I've been hiding in my pocket

Some people cry 'cause they lose one,
 But they're a dime a dozen
I don't see what the big deal is,
 It's all just for fun
They have a thousand different varieties
 At that shop on the street
 They've got 'em loud, obedient, and discreet—
 Every conceivable kind of meat;

And you don't even have to warm them up,
 The ice is already broken
 Just go in — don't have to worry about sin
There's no expectations or surprises,
 Just rainy day women in
 A million different shapes and sizes

I know you were just joking
 When you told me that was something I wasn't allowed to do;
But I have a guilty conscience,
 I won't come around no more if it bothers you —
 After all, there's always another avenue
 I'm sure there's a movie or two
 Or a keyhole to peek through
I'll be all right; don't worry about me
 I'm saving up for rainy day women
Numbers one, two, and three

2001

Stupid Girl

So, how are things up in Dreamland?
 Are you still lookin' for Mr. Right?
You know, maybe there's a reason he's stayin' away from you,
 It's not because your pussy's too tight
Well, I tried to love you,
 I really tried my best;
 And, for a time—yes,
 I thought you were better than all the rest
Ah, but, babe, you would put
 Even Job's patience to the test

Well, I hear you're smokin' some pretty big joints,
 Cruisin' around in your Mercedes Benz
You got a guy with his hands between your thighs,
 Peelin' off your cigarette, your bra strap, and your roll of tens
I can't see your eyes, babe,
 Take off those shades
Oh yeah, just get some birth control, Mama,
 And you got it made
You don't care anyway
 As long as you get laid

 Well, yes, it's true,
 I once was associated with you;
 And now I just don't know what I'm gonna do—
 I'd give anything to be through,
 To start something new
 God damn you, babe, you won't even let me start anew!
I'll be the first to admit it; I loved you once—
 At least I thought I did anyway;
And now I'm hearing the same thing from you,
 That's what you're starting to say
Ah, I shouldn't be surprised, I guess,
 It's nothing new
 Oh, man, do I feel sorry for you

Well, she makes you so sick of her

With her cocaine tongue a-flappin'
 And her bitch trap rappin';
And I'm gettin' so goddamn tired
 Of seein' that bitch thumping her Bible
She's hypocritical; she talks about us behind our backs
 But has sex with the preacher at the Revival
I'm tired of it
It's time to quit
I forfeit

 Oh, darling, can't you see?
 You've made a fool of me
I'm such a stupid, stupid man,
 I must have the easiest heart to break in the entire world
Oh, I'm such a stupid man, babe, but
 You're such a stupid girl
 Oh, babe, you're such a stupid girl
 You're such a stupid girl
It's time to burn
You've really got a lot to learn

2002

No-Pussy Blues

Lord, I got the no-pussy blues, an' can' find anyone to suck my cock
Said, I got the no-pussy blues, Lord, an' can' find anyone to suck my cock
If my woman don't come back soon, gonna hafta go back to the sweat sock

Well, I jus' can' get off, Lord, an' beatin' myself jus' won' do
Well, now, I jus' can' get off, Lord, an' beatin' on myself jus' won' do
I swear I'd take any two-bit whore, jus' as long as I had someone to screw

Well, my woman's been gone, Lord, and I've just about rubbed myself raw
Well, yes, my woman been gone, Lord, and I've just about rubbed myself
    raw
When's that woman gonna knock on my door, Lord, when's she gonna call?

Well, I'm real hard up, Lord, I can't get no pussy for shit
Yes, well, I'm real hard up, Lord, an' I can't get no pussy for shit
I need some real good woman to show me some ass or tits

I'm so damn desperate, Lord, I swear I'd go up the ass
Yes, well, I'm so goddamn desperate, Lord, I swear I'd even go up the ass
I swear I wouldn't even turn down my own mother if she happened to
    walk past

It gets so damn lonely, Lord, always pullin' on your own chain
Yes, well it's so goddamn lonely, Lord, always yankin' on your own chain
When's some woman gonna come along so I can end this swollen blue-
    balled pain?

Well, it's just about gotten to the point where I might even go for my dog
Well, it's just about gotten to the point where I might even go for my own
    dog
Hell, I'm thinkin' about gettin' up right now, goin' out and rapin' the hog

Well, that last whore I paid for, she wouldn't even let me kiss her
Can you believe that last whore I bought wouldn't even let me kiss her?
Christ, I'm beginnin' to think about hittin' up my own sister

Well, I've had the no-pussy blues since my woman walked out the door

Yes, I've had the no-pussy blues since my woman walked out the door
Can't even find no blow-up doll at the store

Well, I ordered a mail-order bride, but she got lost in the mail
Yes, I sent for a mail-order bride, but she got lost in the mail
Can't even find no schoolgirl an' settle for endin' up in jail

Well, the jailbait runs away from me, an' the prisoners won' let me drop the
     soap
Yes, the jailbait run away from me, an' the prisoners won' even let me drop
     the soap
All I can do is sit in my solitary cell and grope

Well, I got the no-pussy blues, an' it's about to drive me outta my head
Yes, now, I got the no-pussy blues, an' it's about to drive me outta my
     fuckin' head
My priest was about to fuck me, but then he saw what I said

2007

Portrait of an American Girl

Oh, there she is walkin' down the hall now,
 A Succubus in short shorts
She's haulin' so much valuable freight
 That she deserves a police escort
You better not get on her bad side, though,
 She always has a retort
The boys wouldn't do anything to her, though,
 They'd piss in their pants if she'd so much as snort

There's that boy carryin' her things for her again,
 She's got him wrapped around her finger
She could get him to lie down in bed
 Just like Christ laid down in a manger
It's that easy for her,
 She can do it without trying
With one significant batting of her eyelid,
 She can leave all the boys crying

They're following her around now,
 Hanging on to her every move
Her chest is so damn fine
 That it should be hanging in the Louvre
Well, she's got a date tonight,
 And it ain't you,
And you're so obsessed with her,
 You just don't know what you're gonna do
So you go out
 And you get one, too
It's the same old story,
 The obsession isn't new
You just keep on hangin' around
 Waiting for love to break through

Look at that shirt she's wearin',
 I believe her chest is hangin' out
Every day she causes half the boys
 To lower their sperm count

They'll bend to her every command and whim,
Desperately clinging to the thin chance
 That they'll get to pop her cherry stem
 They'll do anything she asks of them,
 Anything at all—
Anything that is, except turn their backs
 And walk back down the hall

 But she herself, she's so insecure—
 So worried, so unsure
She gets bored and restless,
 She needs a fix
She's got to find some boy
 To give her some kicks;
And she can get any one she wants,
 She just has to start turnin' her tricks
 The suave promise of one of her licks
 Gets the loyalty of their dicks

 But she sees black, she sees white—
 "Which shall I go out with tonight?
I have to make up my mind,
 Have to flex my might
The last thing I want to do
 Is give my desires any kind of slight—
But what if that other girl wants him?
 I guess there'll have to be a fight"

But sometimes she gets fed up with it,
 Has to find a place to hide
She's angry and sad and depressed,
 And she's cold inside
 She's bored to death of the same old routine,
It's not like there's a male body part
 She hasn't seen
Yes, but she always gets satisfaction
 From making them curdle their cream
She can always convince them
 That she's the girl of their dreams

Now, the boys claim to be strong,
 They claim to be where it's at—
But they just can't resist
 The appeal of the twat;
And you'd think they could do better,
 That they'd be able to rise above that,
But there's just no resisting the invitation,
 The chance to be another number in her hat
If she'd give 'em half a chance,
 They'd be camping on her doormat

And they're gullible as hell,
 They'll believe anything she says
It gives them a sense of security,
 Makes them think they know where it is
Yeah, they think they're important to her,
 But they don't mean a damn thing in her life
They're just a means to an end
 By which she relieves her strife

She uses them as she pleases,
 Relationships come and go,
And she'll temporarily toss them by the wayside
 When they cease to go with her flow
She swears she'll never talk to them again,
 Leave them alone to be a masturbator,
And she says it all with conviction
 Only to pick them up again later
Don't believe anything she tells ya,
 Don't be fooled into thinking she cares
She'll tell two guys two different things
 Just to simplify her affairs

She decides she's not going out tonight,
 So she stays by herself at home
Reading teen magazines
 And talking to other girls on the phone
"Oh, can you *believe* what she said?" and
 "Why can't the boys just *leave me alone*?"
Well, she knows it's really hopeless,

She knows her one real chance is gone
Too bad Mr. Right can't come
And make her his own

Well, all the boys at school
 Are just so icky,
And the teachers, they're all
 So stupid and persnickety
She'll have to wait until she gets older,
 There's just nothin' you can do right now to win —
But she goes and gets a date anyway
 'Cause she knows a girl's gotta do somethin'

Yeah, she plays around with them
 Like they're her little toy,
And she doesn't discriminate,
 She always had a thing for bad boys;
But she isn't lookin' to marry or have a kid —
 When push comes to shove,
 She's only lookin' for temporary love;
And her scheme works so perfectly,
 It fits her like a glove
All the boys are just too eager,
 They flock to her like doves

And maybe, later in life,
 She'll want something more,
But she'll never forget
 What she learned before —
That you can't get even
 Or settle the score
You just keep usin' and usin'
 Until you decide you don't want to anymore
 Eventually even she gets bored
Oh, all the things you have to worry about
 When you live as a whore!

2001

Cut Up Princess

I see you went and changed your mind again,
 It's really no surprise
There's no man in this land that can
 Take the sadness out of those eyes
You're a wandering spirit,
 You're a restless bitch
You say sometimes you just got to
 Scratch that polygamous itch
Well, you've got a story to tell
That could top any infidel
 I have no doubt of that
At this rate, if you hadn't taken time out to masturbate,
 Every man and his dog would've had your twat

Well, you say you're a Mormon —
 Baby, that ain't no excuse
Compared to you, even King Solomon's
 Marital practices seem obtuse
Yes, you're old enough now
 To change your name —
But, when so many love you,
 Is it the same?
We all know good and well
 That you wouldn't let any man stake his claim —
 Hence your name, hence your fame

Well, that last man that you were with,
 I heard that he came
I hope that don't mean trouble for you,
 We all know you've already had four of 'em slain
Don't pull an Eve
 Or you'll raise a Cain
 That man's got to be insane,
 That man has got to be insane
 Can you believe it's happening again?
 That man's done de-railed your train
 You'll do it again, you'll do it again,

You never will abstain
For you there's too much thrill
 In being profane
 It's just another stain, just another stain

Well, the dream is over,
 But the baby's still real
Didn't I tell you that's the price you pay
 For copping an illegitimate feel?
Well, he zeroed in on your fish
 With his reel,
 And now it's too late to close the deal,
 Too late to close the deal
Well, I hear you sayin', "Kill it!",
 And the fetus cryin', "Save me!" —
Do we kill the bitch
 Or keep the baby?
 Oh, me — oh, me...

What's a jack-knifed barber to do
 In a world gone wrong?
How many more times
 Must we sing this song?
We try our best to make you stay in your dress,
 But you just keep movin' right along,
 You just keep movin' right along...
 How long? how long? —
 Oh, how long must we sing this song?

2002 or 2003

The Last of the Big-Time Losers

Well, they tell me that, if it wasn't for bad luck,
 I wouldn't have no luck at all
People set up the dominoes,
 I get 'em to fall
People ask me about you, baby —
 I just start to stall,
I just pretend
 I never kissed you in the mall
I just tell 'em I was in another store
 'Cause I'm the last of the big time losers, baby,
And I don't have you anymore

All this talk about love
 Just drives me insane
I just can't relate,
 I always mention your name
It always seems to be
 The first thing to come out of my mouth;
And, when I finally see I've done it again,
 Things are already headin' south
I just make excuses
 And hand in my check
No, she won't let you kiss her,
 But what the hell did you expect?
But I'm the last of the big time losers,
 You don't have to worry about bein' next

Where the hell was God when I needed him last Saturday?
 I think I broke a nail
Pissed off some preacher,
 Now I'm goin' to hell
Don't worry; I'll bring you something
 From the fire sale
I'll be going soon,
 The Devil I shall meet
I won't have to stand in line,
 They're savin' me a seat

'Cause I'm the last of the big time losers, baby,
Just a rotten piece a-meat

Well, I'm going to hell now,
 My fate will be dire—
But don't worry; we'll always be together,
 I'm saving you a spot by the fire
You say you don't want no charity,
 You want work-for-hire;
But I'm bent out of shape
 From society's pliers,
 I can't even salute my sire
So don't ask me for no help,
 I can't even help myself
'Cause I'm the last of the big time losers, baby,
 Better go ask someone else

I think I'm going to live
 On Desolation Row
I've gotten too downtrodden,
 I need to cleanse my soul
I say, "The world's going
 To come to an end tonight, I tell ya"
And you say, "You're crazy,
 It's already tomorrow in Australia";
And I start to laugh—
 Maybe at you, or someone else—
But you just roll your eyes at me
 And cross yourself
'Cause I'm the last of the big time losers,
 You can just put me back on the shelf

Well, we had sex last night, baby,
 Tonight we're gonna have sex again
I motioned for you to come over here, and you did—
 And that was with just one finger; imagine what I can do with ten
Well, there's a party in your mouth tonight,
And everybody's comin'
 Save me a seat
 'Cause I hear you're so tight your lovin' squeaks—

But that's okay; you don't have to speak;
And hell, who knows, we might even
 See each other again in a week
'Cause I'm the last of the big time losers, baby,
 I'm chained, pussy-whipped, and meek

Well, I'm just like any other guy,
 I like "whisk he" on the rocks
I got my favorite spot in the men's room,
 I got *Playboy* in my malebox
You keep askin' what you can do for me —
 Why don't you just suck my cock?
It's okay; I've been spit on before,
 It won't bother me if you balk
'Cause I'm the last of the big time losers, baby,
 I might just have to give up and stalk

Well, my friend gets off at work
 Because he lives in a ho
I ask him if he knows where babies come from,
 And he says, "No";
But that's all right, that's all right, that's all right —
 I just let the little things flow
Well, I ask you about your virginity,
 Is it forsaken?
I grab your ass and say,
 "Is this seat taken?"
But you just sit back down
 And break all the bones in my hand
'Cause I'm the last of the big time losers, baby,
 I better go back to writing serious songs for the band

2001

Still in Love with You

Well, they raised my rent and my insurance
 When you moved in with me
I had to get a second job
 So we could afford a bigger TV
The little box I had just wasn't good enough
 For watching *The View*
Nothing that I had before
 Ever seems good enough for you—
And, hey, baby, don't worry
 When the bills come due
I won't ask ya to give up
 A jewel or two
You may call me crazy, babe,
 But I'm still in love with you

Well, you've been runnin' up my phone bill,
 Talkin' to your friends down the way—
And I had to buy a bigger kitchen table
 To accommodate them when they come to stay
You had me build two new guest bedrooms
 And a patio on the lawn—
Not to mention a swimming pool and a Jacuzzi
 Every night I work 'till the crack of dawn
I just bought you several hundred more dollars worth
 Of clothes and beauty products galore
 The next time you go to the salon,
  I'll be broke for sure—
But no, I didn't even raise an eyebrow when you said they didn't fit
 And, "When you go in to get my tampons, could you please return them, too?"
Believe it or not, babe,
 I'm still in love with you

Well, I spent all my last paycheck on your poodle,
 Now you're sayin' you need some pills
Before I can even get my check cashed,
 You're already rackin' up bills

Pedicure, manicure, hairstyling, makeover, makeup job—
 You look so damn good and tell me I look like a slob
Well, I haven't been able to buy myself
 A pair of clean underwear in a year
You spend all my money on groceries
 Before I can even get myself a six-pack of beer—
And yet you won't even cook for me,
 You always say you're too busy
Well, I guess if I walked through that many pairs of shoes in a week,
 I, too, would get dizzy
Oh, but it's true,
Babe, I'm still in love with you

I sent you to the doctor with a broken nail,
Bailed your ex-boyfriend out of jail
 Got a nanny and a babysitter for the children,
 Paid to get your Daddy outta the loony bin
  I'm payin' for your Mother to stay in a rest home,
  Talkin' to your depressed kid brother so he won't feel alone
I got you a breakfast room, a brand-new kitchen stove,
 A china cabinet, and a state-of-the-art den
Now you're wanting a limousine, an SUV,
 A sports car, and a Mercedes Benz
I'm workin' eight nights a week now,
 Gettin' paid overtime—
And it's all for you, honey baby,
 I don't get a dime
Oh, but what I tell you every night
 Before I leave to work the late shift is true—
You can't call me lazy, babe,
 And I'm still in love with you

I just got done installing your brand-new,
 Auto-massaging showerhead—
And I can't even get you
 To lay down with me in bed
I prepared a surprise candlelight dinner for you
 On my rare night home—
And you were out all night with your friends
 And left me sittin' there by the phone

LIFE'S TRIUMPH by Bill R. Moore

I was waitin' on that call that never comes
 Unlike it does for you
Even when I take you out to eat,
 You're talkin' on one of your cell phones to someone new
The guys tell me to hate you, babe—
 God, it's so hard
I'm gonna make things easy for you from now on, darlin',
 I'll just let you keep my credit card
I'm still savin' for that European Vacation,
 And I'm keepin' my promise about the yacht and the pleasure boat, too—
All just to show you, babe,
 That I'm still in love with you

2002 or 2003

Something for Nothing

"Why, I think it was about this time last year
 When I saw Elvis performing live—
I believe it was his duet with Hendrix, Morrison, and Jesus,
 It was down in Democratic Cuba—no jive"

 "Yeah, I saw an extraordinary thing happen today—
I was coming down to this coffee shop
 And guess what I saw on the way?"
 "Jesus sitting in the hay"
"What? No way! How'd you know?"
 "Why, I saw him, too"
"No, you didn't" "Yes, I did"
"Well, you know, now that I think about it,
 I'm a bit bemused
It might not've been Jesus I saw, after all—
Why, it might've been Elvis; I'm not sure
 They look so much alike I sometimes get confused"

I try to top your stories,
 And you try to top mine
"You mean you didn't see the UFO landing?
 Why, you must be blind
Yeah, I was watching the sky one day
 Over by the 7-11,
And a little green man and his circular ship
 Splattered down from heaven
I looked him in the eye and shook his hand,
And he handed me a $100 bill
And this gold wristband
 Seems they're pretty nice dudes—
Not like you stubborn non-believers
 With your bad attitudes"

"Here, take this money—sign of the times
Those polysyllables are really great for writing rhymes
 Just take this money and do what you do
You'll be rich with a big house, a nice car,

And a beautiful wife when you're through"

"I've worked everywhere in the country, son,
 And I was always the boss
Why, I worked at the FBI
 With Jesus Christ and Santa Claus
  So who are you to tell me what to do?
Uhhh… what do you mean you don't believe me?
You want me to leave? Well, just hand over
  The check, son, and I'll be through"

Yeah, I sit here bored and self-absorbed
Wondering how all those wonderful things
 Got somehow lost in the haze
'Cause there's nothing much to do anymore—
 I wish it was like the old days

"Oh wait, it is! Haven't you heard…"

2000 or 2001

Nobody's Baby Now

Do you know what they say
 About you and your Law?
They say you walk around with nails and a hammer
 Just in case you decide to crucify someone walkin' down the hall
 That can't be good for morale
How long has it been since
 You shot someone at the OK Corral?
 Better check; you may be overdue
I'm sure your friends at the morgue
 Never get tired of seein' you
 They say there's nothin' you won't do
For a price or if you ask real nice
I used to like you, baby —
 A lot, and more, and then some —
 But just look at what you've become
I don't know why, I don't know how,
But you're nobody's baby now

 Free as a bird, you walk the line
 His days are numbered; so are mine
 I guess anybody is who you may find
I wouldn't give anybody
 Who steps in your way ten seconds to live
You'd kill them within a single blink of the eye —
 Take or give
 They say you make Judas Iscariot seem forgiving —
It's people like you that make me
 Doubt life is worth living
 You're a sinner and a winner all rolled in one,
 Nobody else can exist with you under the sun
You gave us a recipe for Paradise
 But forgot to include fun
 Alas, alas — what's done is done,
 Now I'm going to turn and run
I once wanted you on a pedestal in my throne,
But now you're less desirable than the Devil's own
 I don't know why, I don't know how,

But you're nobody's baby now

You crush men like insects under your foot,
They say your heart is blacker than soot
I don't think I really believe it, though —
I was unaware you ever had one
If you did, it's long gone
It faded away into obscurity
Like the ghost of chance
Now the only head you think with
Is buried deep underneath your guns inside your pants
Now, I know you've never been one for romance,
But I hear you refused even the Lady in Black a dance —
I guess you think she's too easy
You need someone like Lady Luck — less breezy
Last night in the bar, I saw you sittin' all by yourself
When you came in, everyone decided to move
Not even your imaginary friend wants to talk to you
Your gloom could even block out the sun
Good God, girl, what have you done?
I don't know why, I don't know how,
But you're nobody's baby now

You've got one of those faces
Not even a mother could love
If it's true that God made Man in his own image,
It must've been His ass He was thinkin' of
When He decided to make you
An accidental by-product of your parents' so-called love
I heard you were rejected by the Self-help Program,
They said you were a hopeless case
They thought they knew how to make others hate you,
But, goddamn, if you didn't hold the ace
Any time any man gets down on himself,
He can raise his self-esteem by lookin' at your face
No one wants to hug you
So go give head to a guillotine,
I'm sure it'd love to give you a warm embrace
God can stop makin' sacred mutant cows,
There's no need when your milk is so cheap —

Too bad the price is so steep;
 And I just can't take the heat
I don't know why, I don't know how,
But you're nobody's baby now

2001

My Best Was Never Good Enough

Oh, please find it in your heart to forgive me, if you can, for thinking of you
I'm sorry, honey, but I just thought it was the right thing to do
Of course you were right all along, and I really should've knew
The only time I ever get it right is when I don't follow my instincts through
You know, I really try so hard — it's true
 But it's just so fuckin' tough
And now I'm blue
 'Cause, for you, my best was never good enough

If I'm right, you take the credit; if I'm wrong, I take the blame,
But that's just how it is — I know you've told me the same
I hope you don't misunderstand me, baby; I never want to cause you pain
I'd rather slit my own wrists or put a bullet through my brain
And that'd be just fine with me, baby — my loss is your gain
 How's that for playin' rough?
In clear skies or rain,
 For you, my best was never good enough

I know I can't refuse you; you put that under a ban,
And I know I'll be lost if I ever lose you; it's all part of God's plan
Right by your side, baby, is where I'll always stand
Even though you won't let me kiss you or even hold your hand
Well, today I saw you makin' love to another man,
 But I guess that's what I get for always bein' a cream puff
Anyway, it's all right, darlin'; you know I always understand
 That, for you, my best was never good enough

Yes, yes, I know — it's your turn to make all the decisions tonight
It was my turn last year or some other date out of sight
Yes, yes, I know I'm a hopeless case; I'm pathetic and just not bright
'Cause even in your arms I just can't get it right
You're a giant among pygmies, babe, and I'm just ever so slight
 Just give me fair warning before you start playin' rough
And putting that chain on tight
 'Cause you know as well as me that, for you, my best was never good
enough

I know you think you need a leash to be a lady,
And I hope I'm not oversteppin' my bounds by suggestin' that maybe
You could let me off the hook for just a little while, 'cause lately
The things you've been makin' me do have been drivin' me crazy—
But no, that's okay; I understand—you've been working hard all day, and
I've been lazy,
 And it's about time I started actin' like a man and bein' tough
Not everyone's lucky like me with a life that's nice and breezy
 But, for you, my best was never good enough

My two most favorite words are "Yes, dear"—
I say them often, say them loud, and say them clear,
But I always manage to be somewhere else when you need me here,
To be out of sight when you need me near
Maybe some day I'll learn, maybe even get rewarded with a beer,
 Or maybe even with sex—but, hey, don't worry, I won't let my demands
get too rough
I know when to steer clear
 You see, for you, my best was never good enough

I won't ever leave ya, baby, won't ever leave ya blue,
I'll stay right here beside you and see this thing through,
And I'll always know my place and leave everything up to you
'Cause I'm a good, little husband, and that's what good, little husbands do
I'll stop going out with the guys but let you go out with your female crew
 Don't worry—I can handle it; it's not too tough
I'll have everything cleaned up before you get back and even make you
stew—
But I know that, no matter how far I go, for you, it's true,
 My best was never good enough

2003 or 2004

Transit Mars

Mars may be a good planet,

But it's always cold as hell,
And some Martian citizen
Agreed that wasn't so swell
Yeah, so he hopped into his spaceship
And drove for all he was worth
He headed straight for his neighbor,
The infamous mother earth

Sure, he'd heard all the complaints about earth —
"Why, that's the planet of humanity's birth!"
He'd heard about the pollution, the death rates, the crime —
"So what if I'll have to wade through a lot of shit,"
The Martian said, "I'll get some quality sunning time!"
He knew he was taking a risk,
But it was an opportunity he couldn't afford to miss

He thought he knew what he had in store
But got more than he bargained for
Sure, he got some time in the sun,
But he had little other fun
Why, within a month of his arrival,
He got mugged, beat up, and received the clap
The Martian was so damn paranoid now
That he wouldn't even risk a quick nap

You were exiled from your home planet
And tried to find some faith in the human race
Yeah, you came here for some sanity,
But I guess you came to the wrong fuckin' place

He'd heard all the bad earth clichés
But took them all as naysays
The Martian had been to hell and back
Once subjected to earth's attack
He began to think Mars wasn't so bad,

How could he not after all the trouble he'd had?
He was tired of earth's bullshit,
And its membership he was about to forfeit

Yeah, then he learned about this thing called money
And something about paying rent
When he told his landlord he'd never heard of it,
The man didn't think it was very funny

Just when he thought it couldn't get any worse,
Some madman tried to put him in a hearse
His wife cheated on him, his best friend beat on him,
His car was stolen, and his house was robbed
Everyone he thought he could trust turned on him,
And he couldn't find a job

Well, now he was out on the street

And no longer had anything to eat,
So, the next time he saw one of those intergalactic cars,
He said, "Fuck this; I'm goin' back to Mars"

You were exiled from your home planet
And tried to find some faith in the human race
Yeah, you came here for some sanity,
But I guess you came to the wrong fuckin' place

You came to the wrong fuckin' place

2000 or prior

Money Blues

Well, I have $4, 477,619.45
I said, I have $4,477,619.45
But I can't even buy a ratty, old toothbrush; I can't cover the expense

I got four bags a-money left over from my last bankrobbin' run
Yes, I got four bags a-money left over from my last bankrobbin' run,
But I can't buy a damn thing with it; I'm gonna hafta liquidate my funds

Well, I paid $20 for my pillow, $500 for my bed
Yes, I paid $20 for my pillow, $500 for my bed
I can't even buy a mattress to go with it; I'm already sinkin' in the red

I can't pay no income tax; I can't even pay my rent
I can't pay no income tax, can't even pay my rent
Not even any pearls for my baby — all my money's done spent

Can't donate to charity, can't give no money to Uncle Sam
I can't donate to charity, can't give no money to Uncle Sam
I can't even give myself any; I'm savin' as much as I can

I'm beggin' on the street; nobody's fillin' my cup
Well, I'm beggin' on the street, but no one's fillin' my cup
But I just found a quarter on the ground; I'm movin' on up

I can't buy nothin' for you, babe; I'm broke — can't you see?
Why, I can't buy nothin' for you, babe; I'm broke — can't you see?
Well, if money talks, it must not be on speakin' terms with me

No, no, I ain't got no money
No, no I ain't got no money
Everybody out there's laughin' at me, but I don't think it's funny

I'm gonna get on welfare, maybe rob a bank or two
I said, I'm gonna get on welfare, maybe rob a bank or two
Make love to me one more time, baby, and I might even give a piece to you

I left my dreams to come here; I think I'm goin' back

Yes, I left my dreams to come here; I think I'm goin' back
Well, if money grew on trees, we'd all be in the black

2001

Buying My Way into Heaven

My righteousness has run its course,
I'm a free-running, sinful horse
The law is no recourse to me
'Cause I look at it negatively —
And if only I could look at life
 Like I look at you,
 Then maybe, just maybe,
 I could see things through

 But it doesn't work that way — oh, no —
 Happiness, it comes and goes
Why it picks on some and not others
 Nobody knows;
And, if I'm rampant and running free,
Well, then maybe that's how it's supposed to be —
 And it just goes to show

Yeah, but I'm buying my way into heaven —
 Maybe I'll write a book or two
Buying my way into heaven —
 Make up some bullshit and sell it to you
I'm buying my way into heaven —
 Maybe I'll preach from a pulpit or two,
 Reinterpret something and swear it to you
Buying my way into heaven —
When you're burning in hell, I'll be having fun

Glory, Hallelujah, Mercy be —
I saved you, and you saved me
The truth is there for all to see —
I am God; bow before me
 Would you give my soul for a goat
 If you could see the words He really wrote?
They say Genesis is fiction —
Well, maybe its just diction

But, ladies and gentlemen, please,

Put down your beers
And lend me your ears
I'll wipe away your tears
And erase your fears
Come on inside,
What is there to hide?
It's just your body —
 Well, and mine
 The truth is there for all to see,
  And we aren't blind
You can search for it
For years, and years, and years,
 But you'll find
 It's the same as it was all the time

Yeah, but I'm buying my way into heaven —
 Maybe I'll write a book or two
Buying my way into heaven —
 Make up some bullshit and sell it to you
I'm buying my way into heaven —
 Maybe I'll preach from a pulpit or two,
 Reinterpret something and swear it to you
Buying my way into heaven —
When you're burning in hell, I'll be having fun

Just a little bit higher, baby —
 Ah, yeah, that's it
Now you know that
 Once you've started, you can't quit?
You say you'll walk out on me 'cause I'm a sinner —
Well, that's just bullshit; I knew it was wrong the whole time,
 But I said I would
Consequences are a bitch,
 But it hurts so good

 Now the city's become a landfill,
 The whole world's gone to hell,
 And there's beer cans in the alley
 From the preachers up the hill
 The world's slipping into decadence —

Can't all you poor sinners see?
Well, the Devil's getting the last laugh —
Yeah, but me…

Yeah, but I'm buying my way into heaven —
 Maybe I'll write a book or two
Buying my way into heaven —
 Make up some bullshit and sell it to you
I'm buying my way into heaven —
 Maybe I'll preach from a pulpit or two,
 Reinterpret something and swear it to you
Buying my way into heaven —
When you're burning in hell, I'll be having fun

Ha-ha

2001

You Know Who I Am

Please allow me to introduce myself,
 I'm the Savior of the human race
You may think I'm someone else,
 But no man lives after seeing my face

Been watchin' over you since the Fall?
 Hell no — I consider that bullshit libel
You clearly just don't know Me at all
 I'm the little Jew who wrote the Bible

You know who I am

Sometimes I make you sick of me,
 Sometimes I just want you to suffer
Sometimes I kill your little baby,
 Sometimes I give cancer to Mother

Sometimes I like to start wars,
 Sometimes I like to end them
Sometimes I just torture whores,
 Sometimes I only befriend them

You know who I am

My friend Satan calls me unjust,
 I call him weak
He says it's justice or bust,
 I call him a freak

And don't be askin' me no questions, boy —
 Where were you when I laid the foundations of the world?
Who are you to question me and act so coy?
 You should know the kind of misery and torture I can hurl

You know who I am

Well, I really love my Baptists,

But they don't hold 'em under long enough
Hell, someone had to write this,
And I think it's time to start playin' rough

Catholic, Protestant — what's the difference?
Black is the color, none is the number
You're all serving out the same life sentence
Living beneath the spell I've put you under

You know who I am

Well, I say destroy another fetus now —
Them stem cells ain't good for nothin'
Hell, we don't like children anyhow,
And they might as well be used for somethin'

I admit I sometimes fib,
I have a weakness for having fun
I kill little babies in the crib
And say, "Only the good die young"

You know who I am

Some people say their boss is a Jewish carpenter —
I wonder if he made the cross he was crucified on
Well, if I had a pencil, I would sharpen her,
Write the third Testament, start another false dawn

I can't wait for the Last Trump —
It'll be even better than a white line
You better get in another paltry hump,
Be your last for a long goddamn time

You know who I am

Hitler, Hiroshima, 9/11,
I'm proud of you yet
If your life isn't undone,
Then don't you fret

Don't worry if you're doing well,
 You're gonna get yours
Yes, in the end, we all go to hell—
 Of that you can be sure

You know who I am

2002 or 2003, 2005

Man in the Long Black Coat

Well, they say him and his brother,
 They went off to hunt rabbits
You know, they always did have
 Such peculiar and indescribable habits
That man's too old to be a Catholic priest,
 Kid's too young to vote
Don't know where they're goin' or where they been,
 But they went with the man in the long black coat

They say some old man with a red right hand
 Came and took the world by storm
Never could understand God's plan,
 Seemed like shape without form
They say creation took six days —
 Well, it all happened on an uneventful morn
Things coulda been different,
 I would've sworn
Ah, well — that's all she wrote
Blame it on the man in the long black coat

Who wrote The Bible —
 Was it Jesus or Pilate?
 I don't give a shit,
  I just want a clean slate
Who the hell gives a damn about washin' the dishes? —
 I just want my supper on a plate
How can you have gain without pain?
 Love without hate?
You trick 'em, and then you've got 'em
You'll reach the top, but you're on the bottom
 Let's hope you can swim; hope doesn't float
It's all because of the man in the long black coat

Well, he's a man, he's a god, he's a devil —
The game is the same,
 It's just up on another level
 Kindness is coolness, but I'm a rebel

Don't you dare bitch at me,
 I've got better things to do
Than sit around swappin' bullshit stories
 And talkin' to you
All the interesting people went away —
 No word of goodbye, not even a note
Heard it had somethin' to do with the man in the long black coat

Well, he wears soft boots that make no sound,
 His goddamn coat, man, it drags the ground
There's always an applause when he calls,
 Just can't keep the commotion down
Ever since I've known ya, you've been hangin' around this joint,
 Looks like you're still hangin' around
 Will common sense ever be found?
How about my tote?
That goddamn man in the long black coat

Listen to me — did you hear?
I've giving my full-fledged attention
 With my one good ear
I'd listen to The Man,
 But He just makes it all too concise and too clear
 It's everything you always never understood
 And everything you always said and wished you would
Quit lookin' for the answer
 It's too obvious — can't you see?
Quit readin' between the lines
 And just look right straight at me
All you ever do is either criticize or dote
I think I'm gonna buy myself a long black coat

Well, okay — I've written the song now,
 I've done the deed
I sold half a pint of blood
 To cop a pound of weed
Okay — so, is that your final answer?
 I know you've been thinking all along,
 "What is the meaning of this song?" —
It's probably eating away at you like cancer

LIFE'S TRIUMPH by Bill R. Moore

Is it God? Is it the Devil? Is it me? Is it you? Is it... her?
 I don't know; but it's not my job
To mate Mephistopheles with a female mountain goat
I'll leave it up to the man in the long black coat

2002 or 2003

My Bloody Valentine

There was this girl in med. class,
 She used to haunt my dreams
I used to stare at the back of her shirt every day,
 Hoping to see through the seams—
But she wouldn't give me
 The time of day—oh, no
She had to have all the popular boys,
 She had to be a ho

Long, lonely nights sitting in my room,
 I had to make her mine
Well, I knew the holiday was coming up,
 And I decided she was going to be my valentine
Yes, I would make her mine

So I saved up my lunch money
 And bought her a nice, expensive card
I wasn't gonna cut any corners,
 I was going the whole nine yards;
And I wrote of how much I loved her
And how I always dreamed of her
 In my finest and neatest hand,
And I closed it and sealed it tight
 With a beautiful, big, red ribbon-band;
And I left a kiss imprint on it with my mother's lipstick
 And signed my name in my own blood on the signature line—
"To Elizabeth, My Bloody Valentine"

And I'll never forget the look on her face
When I gave it to her all wrapped in lace
 She looked shocked and wadded up the card,
And said, "Leave me the hell alone,
 You perverted bastard, Picard"

And I tore away with tears in my eyes —
I hadn't hoped for the best,
But this was too much of a surprise
So I went to the bathroom
And cried, and cried, and cried
Until the local baddy
Came in and asked me why I lied

I said, "What do you mean?"
And he said, "You told me you
Weren't down with the scene,
You weren't after my girl"
And I said, "I'm not; I'm only after
One girl in this world"

And he said, "Yeah, Elizabeth — and she's *mine*"
And I said, "*What*? Are you blind?!
Can't you see I really love her true?
She's the one for me; there's someone else for you"

And that's when he'd had enough
So he shoved my head into the toilet bowl
And started getting rough —
But I was saved by the bell
And that temporary hell
Dissolved away when into
A pile of shit my face fell

Humiliated, I set out for home,
But that stupid bully
Wouldn't leave me alone
He followed me to my house with Liz on his arm
And proceeded to do me more bodily harm

And I decided that night over a beer
 That I was done fucking around —
So I got a knife out of the kitchen cabinet
 And headed back toward town

No remorse — I was going to kill them both
 Who was she to defy me? The stupid fucking whore!
And who was he to boast?
 They would feel my wrath for evermore!

 I saw them together at the skating rink
 And slithered up to them like water down a sink
He looked at me sternly and said, "Now, you be nice"
 And it was then that I brought out my knife

I said, "Behold, ye sinners,
I've come to take you away
Now, bow down before me
Or else waste away"
And he said, "Look, man…"
 As she started to scream
So I leveled my blade at his head
 And cut it off clean

She was screaming and crying,
But she would soon be dying
 As I whipped out my knife once more
And looked at her with a gleam in my eye and said,
 "Now it's your turn, you dirty little whore"

And then I chased her down as she skated away
 But caught up to her in the end —
And my knife did wield,
 And her body did bend

Her last words were, "You bastard!"
 And I said, "Yes, darling, I love you, too"
And then I took my knife
 And finished slicing her through;
And then I kissed her dead body,
And said, "Goodbye, my love,
 Death has done us part"
And then I took my knife
 And pierced it through her heart

 Everyone else had left by then—
 For some strange reason, they were under the impression
 I was committing some terrible sin
I shook my head and laughed at their ignorance
 As I wiped the blood from my hands
"Those fools," I told myself,
 "They'll never understand"

So I dragged both their bodies
 Into my backyard,
And got out my shovel
 The ground was cold and hard,
But I dug them both a grave and dug it deep
 And the wind howled and moaned
As they lay at my feet

The marker read like this—
 "Here lies Elizabeth, My Bloody Valentine,
And some stupid motherfucker
 Who thought he could keep her in line
Let them lie together in sin and misery
As punishment for all their wrongs toward me
 Until the end of time"

 I thought I'd done a pretty good job,
But this blue-jacketed fellow came up to me

And told me I was a disrespectable slob;
And I said, "But you don't even know me!
Just ask Elizabeth; she'll tell you what a great guy I am"
But, regardless, he cuffed me
And took me away in his little armored van

And now I sit here all by myself,
 Alone in this padded room
Life's just no fun anymore
 Without Elizabeth and her goon—
But, every year on Valentine's,
 I make her out a card
My custodians all think I'm crazy—
Ah, but I can forgive them
 Because they've got it hard
They're not in love like me,
 They think love is blind;
And I know they're jealous every year
 When I write to My Bloody Valentine

2001

You Speak My Language

Well, I haven't made love
 Since my girl went away
If my walls could talk,
 They still wouldn't have anything to say
  Everyone says it was my fault —
That I pulled a Casanova,
  I pulled a John Gault;
But you reassure me —
She wasn't the one,
She wasn't true to me
I get so tired of bein'
 Beaten down to a bloody pulp
Everyone thinks they have to be
 A member of the cult
Everyone has somethin' to tell me,
Yeah, they all got somethin' to sell me —
 Except you, you speak my language

Well, I went to church,
 But they called me a sinner
I knocked on wood,
 But all I got was a splinter
There came a point when
 I finally decided to give up for good —
But I couldn't even crucify myself; they said,
 "Come down off the cross; we could use the wood"
I tried everything to get them to understand,
 I did everything I could
Yes, everyone always claimed to listen,
 But they never understood
I had begun to think
 No answer existed
I tried Easy Street,
 But even she resisted
 It didn't work; nothing did —
Except you, you speak my language

Teachers and preachers, friends and gurus, too—
 They all stood their ground
They all claimed to dole out help
 But hid under their desks when I came around
It's like my footsteps
 Were a terrible, foreboding sound
If you can't live it up,
 You won't live it down
I asked everyone I knew
 Just to make sure,
But people who shouldn't known better
 Just stood around like furniture
No one would give me the straight dope,
They wanted to put me under their microscope,
Yeah, no one was willing to cope—
 Except you, you speak my language

I read between the lines,
 Looked behind the scenes,
 I even searched in pornographic magazines—
 But no one would come clean
 Everyone was mean
 Or, at best, unseen
I wasn't askin' for much,
 Just somewhere to lean—
 But I guess that was too obscene
I couldn't find a King,
 Couldn't find a Queen—
I couldn't find anyone
 Who gave a hill of beans
No one cared; everyone sweared
They couldn't change the way I fared
 Because I was the most hopeless case
 They'd ever have to face
 No one showed any interest, not a trace—
Except you, you speak my language

2001

Country Joe Saloon

I was walking down I-35,
There was a cold wind blowin' down on my face,
And there was dust in my eyes
I was tired of the world not giving me a crumb,
So I stopped by the side of the road and stuck out my thumb

Trucker stopped by
And gave me the eye
He said, "I can't give you no change,
But I can give you a home on the range"
Now a range to me kinda sounded like hell —
But I realized my situation was hopeless,
So I decided I might as well

After a quick detour at a truck stop
And maybe a bar or two,
We went into his house and into his room
He had a television, had a kitchen,
And he had a saloon
He said, "We don't need anything else here, sonny,
The cows'll keep us alive"
And I looked out at his pasture
And realized it wasn't no jive

Pretty soon he turned the TV on
And his wife came in to cook,
Then his kids came home from the rodeo
And said their winnings were zero,
He just looked at 'em like they were a crook

He put his remote control down, zipped up his fly,
Got his beer, and resumed
He said, "Oh yes, I almost, forgot about you, sonny —
Welcome to the Country Joe Saloon"

Pretty soon it was Suppertime —
Steak and potatoes

He said, "You can chop it up, all you want to, son,
 But it's not gonna change; that's the way it goes"

 A couple more beers,
 A couple more smears —
And I couldn't take it anymore,
 I was near tears
He asked me to milk his cow,
 And I figured that was my chance
I started running for the barnyard door
 Like there was a fire burnin' in my pants

I thought I was gonna make it,
 But he stopped me dead in my tracks
He said, "You can leave the Saloon
 Anytime you want, sonny, but you still gotta pay the tax"

2000 or 2001

Professional Couch Potato

It's a strange sight to behold,

 This graying, balding man in his armchair —
Why, he occasionally shows feelings
Of an almost human nature
 It's hard to detect, but they're there
I guess even the couch potato
 Has to occasionally come up for air

Beer in the right hand,
 Remote control in the left,
A potato chip bag on top of
 His stomach's considerable heft —
 "La-Z-Boy" in the truest sense of the word
Come on; I've heard of laziness,
 But this is absurd

 Armchair quarterback, armchair romantic,
 Armchair critic, armchair fantastic
Armchair rocket scientist, armchair schoolboy in heat —
 You really ought to try it sometime,
You can be anything in the world
 Without having to move or spend a dime

You say you'll get over this kick —
 It's just a passing phase,
 One of your bad days
Well, it seems to me your bad days
 Are happening just about all the time,
 But you always give us the same old line —
 "I'll get around to it, just one more show"
 Too bad you can't get a job
As a professional couch potato

God bless the TV!
 It rules our lives
 Without it we couldn't possibly survive

Hell, they even have refrigerators
In our precious armchairs now
 Television viewing is getting less and less corrupt—
If they'd just give us a built-in toilet,
 We wouldn't even have to get up

We can get pizza delivered right to our door,
 We got beer on call
We got porno on 24/7—
 Hell, we've got it all
I got me a 500+ channel television
 And an armchair that's up to date
Hell, they must've seen me comin',
 Ain't this life so fuckin' great

Hold on; hold on; hold on—wait a minute
What's this about divorce?
 I thought we were going steady
Just let me know when you're in the mood, baby,
 I'm always ready

"No, you're not, damn it; all you do is watch TV,
Don't you ever have time anymore for me?"
 "Sure I do, honey; I'm just watching my favorite show
 As soon as it's over, I'll let you know"
"That's not good enough; I want some quality
Time together; and, I'm telling you, it's now or never"
 "Okay, okay, just a minute…"
 "A minute's not good enough; I've had enough—I quit!"

And so she packed her bags
 And walked out my front door
 She couldn't stand my hobby anymore,
 She'd had enough—
 But I decided it wasn't so tough,
I didn't need that bitch anymore,
Now I'd have a chance to watch TV more
 Hell, it's what I've always dreamed of—
 So much for love

And, twenty years down the road,
They found me in front of the TV —
 Sitting there all alone,
 Dead as a stone,
But my spirit isn't gone
For I live on

The curator of the Smithsonian
 Said everything would be just fine
They'd put me in the museum
 As representative of the Baby Boomer's decline

It's true; just you wait and see
 It'll be broadcasted (where else?)
On national TV

2000 or prior

The Making of Steinians

Gertrude Stein wrote *The Making of Americans*,
 In it she likes to repeat
Some say it tastes sour,
 Others claim it is sweet

I am not among the latter group
 Who claims it is sweet
There are some who claim it, however,
 Though she likes to repeat

Gertrude Stein wrote *The Making of Americans*,
 In it she repeats a lot
Some think there is more to it,
 Others think it's all she's got

I am not among the latter group
 Who thinks it's all she's got
I do not exactly like it, however,
 Though she repeats a lot

She herself admits repetition can be boring
 But keeps on doing it anyway
Some say it sets them to snoring
 And that it's all she has to say

I am not among the latter group
 Who thinks it's all she has to say —
But it can be boring, though it does not set me to snoring,
 At any rate, she keeps doing it anyway

Gertrude Stein likes to repeat a lot,
 She wrote *The Making of Americans*
Some people find it absorbing,
 Others wonder how they can

Yes, as I said, some people find it absorbing,
 And others wonder how they can

LIFE'S TRIUMPH by Bill R. Moore

Because she likes to repeat a lot,
 As in *The Making of Americans*

The writings of Gertrude Stein are annoying to some,
 As she employs the principle of distraction
Some see a myriad features in her writings,
 Others think that's the only one

Some see that she employs the principle of distraction
 And think that's her only one
Others see a myriad features in her writings,
 Those who can see past the distraction

Gertrude Stein likes to repeat a lot,
 Because of this, some people her writings shun
In order to see the differences in what she's saying,
 One has to pay attention

To see the differences in what she's saying,
 One has to pay attention —
One must be observant and diligent,
 One must not shun

Gertrude Stein is not easy to read,
 Because she employs the principle of distraction
From the chains of her writing, some people want to be freed,
 Others, however, find reading her fun

Some people want to be freed from the chains of her writing,
 While others find reading her fun
The reason, you see, why some of them find glee
 Is because they can ignore the distraction

Some say she is incoherent,
 That her writings make no sense
Still others say she makes sense
 If one doesn't try to force coherence

Some say she is not incoherent
 If one doesn't try to force coherence

Others say she is not coherent,
 That she makes no sense

Some say reading Gertrude Stein is hard,
 That, rather than reading her, they would put their own lives at stake
Others claim she is a bard
 And that those impatient, ignorant neophytes should try *Finnegan's Wake*

Some say anyone who finds reading Gertrude Stein to be hard
 Is an impatient, ignorant neophyte who should read *Finnegan's Wake*
Others say she isn't hard — that, in fact, she is a bard,
 On this they put their reputations at stake

I am not among the latter group
 Who would do such an outrageous thing
It seems obvious to me — can't you see? —
 That one gets out of it what one brings

Gertrude Stein likes to repeat a lot,
 Some say it is an outrageous thing
I am not among the latter group
 Because one gets out of it what one brings

2004

End of the World Blues

I'm sittin' here talkin' to myself, sayin' we've seen better days
Yes, I'm sittin' here talkin' to myself, sayin' we've seen better days
We may not be dead yet, but we're beginnin' to get lost in the haze

Brother kills brother; we all kill each other
Yeah, brother kill brother; we all kill each other
Maybe some day we'll get out of the way and run for cover

My baby left me this mornin'; I'm feelin' alone and blue
Said my baby left me this mornin'; I'm feelin' alone and blue
I thought maybe I'd get up and have a cup of coffee, but then I decided
    there was nothin' I really wanted to do

I went to church incognito; I feel down on my knees
I went to church incognito, feel down on my knees
I don't know why I did it, really — maybe it was just a tease

That man keeps givin' me weird looks; I bet he thinks I'm tryin' to steal his
    girl
Said that man keeps on givin' me weird looks; yeah, I bet he thinks I'm
    tryin' to steal his girl,
But I wouldn't touch that chick for a million bucks; I've seen more well-
    behaved   cockroaches in this world

I wish they'd turn down the TV; it's startin' to hurt my ears
I wish they'd turn down that TV; it's startin' to hurt my ears
It's not like it really helps us anyway; all it does is feed our fears

That girl over there in the corner, she likes to play around and wallow
Yeah, that girl over there in the corner, she likes to play around and wallow
If you're poor, she'll spit you out; yeah, but, if you're rich, she might swal-
    low

I've had a hard bag in this world; the only people I trust are me, myself,
    and I
Said I've had a hard bag in this world, only people I trust are me, myself,
    and I,

But I don't know why I trust even them; sometimes they act just a little bit
   too sly

My house is on fire; my neighbor's gun is cocked
My house is one fire; yeah, and my neighbor's gun is cocked
I'll have to go to the White House; the fallout shelter's overstocked

I don't know what to do anymore; I'm at a loss
Well, I just don't know what to do anymore, guess I'm just at a loss
I keep on spending all this money; maybe it's about time I started counting
   the cost

My heart is torn to shreds; my soul has evaporated
My heart is torn to shreds, darling, and my soul has evaporated
I thought you'd be different, but you're just like every other girl I ever
   dated

These women just won't stop talkin'; I can't even hear myself think
These women just won't stop talkin'; I can't even hear myself think
I'm fed up with their mental masturbation, but she sure does look pretty in
   pink

Love's a hard game to play; I think we're gonna lose
Yeah, love's a hard game to play; I think we're gonna lose
For you this might be a revelation; for me it's old news

You can't buy me off; put that money back in your pocket
No, you can't buy me off; just put that money back in your pocket
Okay, well, maybe for that much—but could you please add just one more
   cent?

This is the latest story, boys; I just heard it on the news
Yes, this is the latest story, boys; I just heard it on the news
The U.N. just bombed the embassy, and I got the end of the world blues

September 2001

Life's Triumph:
About the Author

Bill Roebuck Moore always enjoyed writing and learned to type at a very young age. He started in earnest on his poetry during his high-school years. He won a poetry contest in the ninth grade.

He loved books and was never without a book. He was good at sports, especially bowling and playing pool. He also enjoyed playing video games with his brother, Anthony, and loved to read and write. His favorite musical artist was Bob Dylan, about whom Bill knew just about everything. He worked for years on a massive book that is a critical review of Dylan's works.

Bill started taking college classes his senior year of high school, attending high school in the morning and college later in the day. He was valedictorian of his class in 2003 and he received an honor's scholarship to attend Southern Oklahoma State University in Durant, Oklahoma.

Bill met Jade online and they were inseparable and absolutely in love with each other right from the start. He smiled every time he looked at her, and they couldn't bear to be apart. After Jade would visit him in Oklahoma and have to return to Colorado, Bill would be physically sick that she would have to go away. They were each other's helper, confidante, and best friend.

They married in Paris, Texas on September 30, 2004. Bill worked as a freelance editor and writer and graduated summa cum laude in 2006. He continued that work while Jade went to the university and graduated summa cum laude in 2010 from SOSU. They loved playing pool together; they had a pool table in their tiny apartment that covered their whole living -room area.

Jade received a two-year fellowship to Cornell University in Ithaca, New York, and they moved there. They were very excited about the move and so many plans and goals for the future they had together.

On October 5, 2010, Bill and Jade were in a motor-vehicle accident. Jade was pronounced dead at Cayuga Medical Center a short time later. Bill suffered massive head trauma; he was transported to Robert Packer Medical Center in Sayre, Pennsylvania, where he died the next day. She was 24; he was 25.

www.ingramcontent.com/pod-product-compliance
Lightning Source LLC
Chambersburg PA
CBHW062353090426
42740CB00010B/1263